VICTORIAN GARDENS

VICTORIAN GARDENS

Brent Elliott

Timber Press, Portland, Oregon

First published 1986

First published in the USA by
Timber Press
9999 S. W. Wilshire
Portland, OR 97225, USA

ISBN 0-88192-037-1

Printed & bound in Great Britain

Contents

1 Introduction 7

The revolution in aesthetics · The propagandists · The rise of the head gardener · Technical innovations

2 Landscape into garden 21

The eighteenth-century garden in decay · From the picturesque to transcendentalism · Wordsworth · Artificial climate · The recognition of art · The aesthetic of scatter · The organization of the garden · From rustic to rococo · The emergence of the rock garden · Picturesque colour · From public walk to people's park

3 The uses of the past 55

Theories of garden history · Preservation and restoration · The return to formality · The cottage garden · The conservatory in the landscape · Gardens for an English revival · Enter Nesfield · The triumph of the Italian garden

4 Art and nature 79

The transcendentalist landscape · A note about fountains · The gardener as hero · The liberation of colour · Virtuoso horticulture · Woodland embellishment · The natural rock garden · Congruity and contrast · Biddulph Grange

5 The High Victorian garden 107

The High Victorian conservatory · Landscape principles in the 1850s · The coniferous landscape · Topiary · The influence of Biddulph · Colour theory and the bedding system · Design in the flower garden · The revival of mixing · The flower garden in the park · Extending the system · The garden of embroidery · Unifying the arts at South Kensington · In the wake of Kensington

6 History and horticulture 148

The reaction in colour · The rise of foliage · Carpet bedding · Revivalist planting · The old-fashioned garden · The reaction in landscape · Landscape principles in conflict · Landscape in rock · Landscape with ruins · Colour in the landscape

7 **The re-creation of nature** 185

The landscape in the conservatory · The alpine rock garden · Spirits of nature · The wild garden · The landscape of the imaginative ideal · The Japanese garden

8 **Horticulture adrift from history** 203

In the wake of carpet bedding · The re-assertion of colour · Sculptural bedding · New directions in the public park · The attack on the gardener · The Edwardian flower garden

9 **In search of a vernacular** 221

From Italian to Dutch · The old English garden · The horticultural vernacular · Arts and crafts · The Italian garden re-interpreted · Towards a Neo-Georgian style

Acknowledgements 244

List of Illustrations 246

Notes 248

Bibliography 269

Index 274

I

Introduction

The Revolution in Aesthetics

The Victorian garden arose out of the rebellion against the eighteenth-century landscape park. For three generations, the magic word 'Nature' had been invoked as the ideal which the gardener was to follow; but by the beginning of the nineteenth century, the ideal was starting to sound a little hollow.

What, indeed, was Nature? To one born in the early eighteenth century, the word carried connotations quite different from those current at the century's close.[1] 'Capability' Brown had been born in 1716, a mere thirty years after Thomas Burnet had published his famous theory that the earth had originally been a perfect sphere, and had been deformed with mountain ranges as a result of the Flood. Similar distinctions between fallen and unfallen nature were meaningful to Brown's contemporaries; as late as the 1790s, George Mason could ask, defending the shaven lawns and elegant streams of Brown's practice,

> whether nature is a more pleasing object in a dwindled and shrivelled condition, than when her vigour 'is as great, her beauty as fresh, and her looks as charming, as if she newly came out of the forming hands of her Creator?'[2]

But by that time, the assumption that original nature was something different from the nature we see around us had been largely abandoned. Uvedale Price greeted Mason's remarks with incredulity: the banks of natural lakes and rivers 'must always be partially worn and broken', not pristine. If gardens were genuinely to be based on nature, they could not follow the Brownian model.[3]

Once this less theological view of nature was taken, it became apparent to some that the features that formed the basis of Brown's parks were derived not from unaided nature, but from the relics of agriculture and industry: from the enclosure of commons, from hedgerows and boundary trees, from the serpentine lakes created to power watermills. William Marshall admitted that England did not boast natural landscapes in the sense that the virgin forests of America did; every tree in England probably owed its position to human interference. But the degree to which the English countryside was recognized as an artificial creation varied considerably from person to person, and this knowledge played only a minor part in the overthrow of the landscape garden.[4]

In the long run, however, this technical objection was less important than a psychological one; it was not the qualities of the material world but the relation of that world to the mind that mattered. Eighteenth-century aesthetics, to a greater or lesser degree, depended on the notion of the passive mind – the mind, in John Locke's famous images, as a blank slate written upon by experience, or a mirror capable only of reflecting what is imposed upon it from without.[5] Aesthetic categories such as beauty were assumed to be part of the external world, independent of the human will. The practical consequences of this doctrine ranged from the most general advice to 'follow nature', to the assertion that particular garden features or arrangements of scenery must inevitably invoke particular responses.[6]

In the new philosophies of the nineteenth century, on the other hand, aesthetic categories were seen as creations of the human mind, imposed by us on the external world. In the 1790s Uvedale Price attempted a systematic analysis of an aesthetic category called the 'picturesque', but promptly became bogged down in literary quarrels over whether the picturesque was a mental category or an aspect of the external world.[7] When Mr Gall proposed unexpectedness as a category of garden scenery, Mr Milestone replied, 'by what name do you distinguish this character, when a person walks round the grounds for a second time?'[8] Qualities which had once been attributed to the external world were increasingly attributed to the human mind instead.

An alternative approach was suggested at the end of the eighteenth century by a Scottish clergyman, Archibald Alison. It was a matter of simple observation that people differed on questions of taste; there was no artistic question on which universal agreement could be found. Different people had differing prejudices, whether the result of learning or of inherent traits of character; aesthetic response was therefore dependent, not solely on the properties of the object perceived, but on the personality of the perceiver. Nor was the individual's response always uniform: it was possible to become bored by something that had previously delighted one, or to discover beauty in something one had previously ignored; mood and preoccupation could influence one's response. Aesthetic perception, far from being a passive reception of impressions from nature, was proving a volatile and ever-changing process, determined more from within than without.[9]

Alison accordingly sought an internal factor which would explain these differences in response. This he found in the mind's tendency to make random associations of ideas, which were reinforced by habit and custom. Such associations were arbitrary and individual, but entered into all our mental processes.[10] On looking at a given scene,

> we are conscious of a variety of images in our minds, very different from those which the objects themselves can present to the eye. Trains of pleasing or of solemn thought arise spontaneously within our minds; our hearts swell with emotions, of which the objects before us seem to afford no adequate cause; and we are never so much satiated with delight, as when, in recalling our attention, we are unable to trace either the progress or the connexion of those thoughts, which have passed with so much rapidity through our imagination.[11]

Alison's theories were generally ignored when his *Essays* were first published in 1790, but after the second edition in 1811 they attracted a wider notice. Francis Jeffrey reviewed this edition in the *Edinburgh Review*,

1 The ideal of the English landscape garden as it survived into the 1820s: from Richard Morris, *Essays on Landscape Gardening* (1825).

and in 1816 repeated the substance of his review in his article on 'Beauty' in the supplement to the *Encyclopaedia Britannica*.[12] Jeffrey made an important amendment to Alison's theory, by jettisoning his insistence on trains of thought, which he felt to be narrowing and implausible; it was a matter of common experience that people could make aesthetic judgments without engaging in time-consuming reflections first. 'We know that all our acquired perceptions are at first gained by long processes of association – that the eye does not of itself see form or figure', he reasoned; but once the ability to recognize form had been acquired, it did not need to be re-acquired with every subsequent visual experience. Similarly, once the associations that underlie our aesthetic experience had been established, this category of response could be triggered just as immediately as could visual perception.[13] With this modification, associationism stood complete; even Sir George Sitwell's later additions of subliminal associations and subconscious impulses was virtually implicit in Jeffrey's version.[14]

In 1842, Sir Thomas Dick Lauder edited a new edition of Sir Uvedale

Price's writings on the picturesque, and in his lengthy introduction tried to bring Price's practical recommendations into line with this refined theory of associationism, 'which is now held to be the true Theory' – thus ensuring that the details of the doctrine were in the hands of the gardening world.[15]

The practical consequences were soon felt. Accounts of garden visits in the magazines regularly emphasized the historical associations of the house, named the famous people who had planted commemorative trees, or depicted the visitor regarding the vista and yielding to a chain of reflections in the proper Alisonian manner. The deeper impact of the doctrine, however, lay in the sudden bewildering freedom it offered the gardener. Associations being arbitrary and individual, beauty could be said to exist only from the individual's point of view; all standards were arbitrary, and all tastes equally correct. There were 'as many varieties of beautiful compositions, as there are varieties of character'.[16] Jeffrey had made it explicit: 'it seems calculated to put an end to all these perplexing and vexatious questions about the standard of taste, which have given occasion to so much impertinent and so much elaborate discussion.'[17]

No sooner was the principle enunciated than its proposers sought for ways ways to restrain its application: moral standards, public consensus, and degrees of education were all proposed as limiting conditions to the free exercise of individual whim. But no formula could be found that would work for very long, or for more than a particular social group. It would be no exaggeration to say that since the beginning of the nineteenth century we have lived in an aesthetic anarchy, and that the apparent dominance of any standard of taste in any of the arts has been only temporary. In the world of gardening, for every Joshua Major or William Robinson who attempted to dictate aesthetic standards to the public, there was always a Donald Beaton or a D.T. Fish at hand to proclaim the arbitrariness of such standards and defend the right of the individual to gratify his personal taste.[18]

'Gardens are works of art rather than of nature,' trumpeted Repton as early as 1808.[20] No theme is more important, no sentiment so regularly expressed, in the Victorian literature on gardening, than this affirmation of the artistic and unnatural character of the garden. Whether confidently asserting the superiority of art over nature, or merely acknowledging their independence, the notion is echoed over and over across the decades: by garden designers from Loudon to Thomas Mawson, horticultural journalists from Charles M'Intosh to Walter P. Wright, architects from Charles Barry to Reginald Blomfield; by Wordsworth and Sir Walter Scott, Donald Beaton and Shirley Hibberd, J.D. Sedding and Thomas Huxley, Godfrey Blount and Sir George Sitwell; and added confirmation could be found, by those who wanted it, in philosophers from Hegel to Nietzsche.

The mind was no longer a mirror, a passive reflector of the external world; it was active, self-determining, powered from within. Gardening, similarly, was no longer to be subservient to the natural landscape, but to be independent, imaginative, and original. The old idol of Nature had been overthrown, and out of the bewildering wreckage rose instead the idol of Art.

2 The counter-ideal: proposals for the revival of Renaissance formality from Charles M'Intosh's *Flower Garden* (1837–8) – the French garden.

The Propagandists

We have examined briefly the ideology underlying Victorian gardening; now we must look at the channels whereby it was transmitted.

In 1804, John Wedgwood and Sir Joseph Banks founded the Horticultural Society of London, eventually to become the Royal Horticultural Society in 1861. While, until its democratization under Sir Trevor Lawrence in the 1880s, it remained notoriously a society for the aristocracy and landed gentry, it did at least offer a reduced-rate membership for practical gardeners. Although through most of the Victorian period it maintained an official distance from questions of garden design, its influence on the technical development of the art was immense; and, beginning in the 1820s, the Society was to sponsor plant-collecting expeditions by David Douglas, Theodor Hartweg, Robert Fortune and others, and distributed their new introductions to its members.[20]

By that time there existed a number of colour-plate magazines to illustrate the new plants,[21] and similar expeditions were being promoted by private collectors, botanic gardens, and commercial nurseries such as Loddiges's of Hackney. The first public botanic garden had been opened in Liverpool in 1802, and this example was followed over the succeeding decades by other large towns – a process culminating in the establishment of the Royal Botanic Gardens at Kew in 1840.[22]

While these various agencies helped to promote a taste for horticulture, the development of the new taste in gardening was due initially to a few individuals. Foremost among these was John Claudius Loudon, a Scottish landscape gardener and entrepreneur who devoted his formidable energies to the advancement of horticulture.[23] In 1822 he published his immense *Encyclopaedia of Gardening*, which ran through eight editions in twelve years and continued to be reprinted into the 1870s. Despite the competition of such excellent works as Charles M'Intosh's *Practical Gardener* (1828), which had a similar career of reprinting and revision, Loudon's remained the major gardening reference work of the age. He was to follow it with similar encyclopaedias of plants, trees, and agriculture.

More importantly, he followed it with a venture into journalism. The first number of his *Gardener's Magazine* appeared in 1826, eventually becoming a monthly, and continuing until his death in 1843. For the first time there was a forum in which gardeners could discuss their work, both technical and artistic; campaign for better wages and improved working conditions; and debate the political questions of the day, and the merits of cooperatives, allotments, and cottage gardens. A heavy proportion of the text was written by Loudon himself, largely in the form of tours, both in Britain and on the Continent, describing and criticizing the gardens he visited. Through these discussions, he was able to put forward in a concrete way his opinions on garden style.

It was not long, however, before other magazines appeared to rival Loudon's, the head gardeners themselves entering the fray: Joseph Paxton (Chatsworth), Joseph Harrison (Wortley Hall), and Robert Marnock (Sheffield Botanic Garden) all launched periodicals of varying life-spans.[24] A rival genre, the florist's magazine, giving in detail the results of floral competitions, was initiated by George Glenny, whose *Horticultural Journal* (1833–6) made a blatant appeal to an aristocratic audience, and whose *Gardeners' Gazette*, begun in 1837, was the first horticultural journal to assume newspaper format. Glenny's immoderate venom, however, earned him the hatred of prefessional gardeners, and his magazine was swallowed up after ten years by Marnock's *United Gardeners' and Land Stewards' Journal*. The demise of Glenny's periodicals prompted hopes that the atmosphere of horticultural journalism would become less malicious and more cooperative – which indeed it did, until the arrival of William Robinson in the 1870s.[25]

By mid-century, most of the gardening magazines had died off in a clear demonstration of the survival of the fittest. The greatest survivor, and the century's major gardening paper, was the *Gardeners' Chronicle*, founded in 1841 by Paxton and John Lindley; edited for over sixty years by two Horticultural Society figures in succession – Lindley, then Maxwell T. Masters – it served after Loudon's death as the major campaigning organ for the gardening community.

It had nonetheless a rival as Loudon's successor, in the *Cottage Gardener*, founded in 1848 by the barrister and garden historian George W. Johnson. The title should not deceive: E. S. Dixon quipped that it was 'more suitable for a double-coach-housed "cottage of gentility"' than for a labourer's cottage,[26] and in 1861 the name was changed to the *Journal of Horticulture*. On many issues this new magazine maintained an opposition line to

Lindley's, even though its co-editor, Robert Hogg, was eventually a successor of his as Secretary of the Royal Horticultural Society. Some of the younger contributors to Loudon's magazine became regular columnists in the new journal; most notable of these was Donald Beaton, doyen of the bedding system and the gardening world's most original stylist. Born into a Gaelic-speaking Highland family, not learning English until his twenties, Beaton looked for his models to the major Scottish writers of the 1830s, to 'Christopher North' of *Blackwood's Magazine* and to the goading, clowning style of Carlyle. When he started writing for the *Cottage Gardener*, Beaton was head gardener at Shrubland Park; such was his fame that when he retired from that position, an admirer provided him with a garden in Surbiton for his horticultural experiments – the annals of which formed one of the themes of his weekly column.

Beaton was only one, if perhaps the most famous, of the gardening journalists who flourished in the wake of Loudon. Robert Errington, Thomas Appleby, Robert Glendinning, John Robson, Robert Fish and his younger brother David Taylor Fish – all of them nurserymen or head gardeners – had become figures of eminence by the 1850s. As they died or retired, they were succeeded by such younger writers as Shirley Hibberd and William Robinson,[27] whose fame is greater today, but who inherited the world, both horticultural and journalistic, that their predecessors had created.

The Rise of the Head Gardener

The magazines spread the message of the new ideology of gardening, but it was the head gardeners who interpreted it. In the late twentieth century, landscape architecture is a discipline with considerable status and gardening is officially regarded as a 'semi-skilled occupation'; but this is very different from the situation a century ago, that short-lived period when gardening could be considered a respected profession – when it could be said of a country house like Heckfield that it boasted two national figures, the speaker of the House of Commons and his gardener.[28]

The names of but few head gardeners have come down to us from earlier centuries; nor is this surprising when one considers what the activities of a gardener would have been at, say, a house with a 'Capability' Brown park. As far as the ornamental garden was concerned, the gardener's principal duty was simple maintenance. Any scope he had for innovation and the attainment of prestige lay in the kitchen garden; and those who did earn fame did so largely for their advances in fruit cultivation, like John Rose, credited with growing the first English pineapple, and William Speechly of Welbeck Abbey, author of a major book on grape cultivation.

All this began to change in the nineteenth century, with the need to learn how to cope with the exotic plants gradually flooding the country, and even more with the arrival of the magazines, in which gardeners could publish their results and make known their names to wider circles. And as the bedding system – the practice of planting tender plants outdoors during suitable seasons – developed in the 1830s, it became possible for the gardener to alter the appearance of the garden every year, and eventually every season. The transforming power which had been associated with the hand of the landscape gardener was soon to become the annual prerogative of the head gardener.

As the gardener's qualifications rose, so did his status – and that not gradually, but within a generation, thanks in large part to the example of one brilliant career: that of Joseph Paxton.[29] A Bedfordshire farmer's son, born 1803, Paxton began life as a garden boy at Battlesden at the age of fifteen; at the age of 19 he was busy constructing a lake there. At the age of twenty, he entered the employment of the Horticultural Society, at their garden at Chiswick; all gardeners were required, as a demonstration of literacy, to write an account of themselves in a ledger, and young Paxton's shows him self-consciously adding three years to his age.[30] The Chiswick garden was leased from the Duke of Devonshire, who was a frequent visitor, and encountered Paxton there; in 1826, he appointed the young man his head gardener at Chatsworth.

It was not long before Paxton was making alterations to the glasshouses, designing new buildings, rearranging the waterworks, acting as estate forester, laying out an arboretum; from there it was only a short step to making designs for the Duke's other properties, and thence to designing gardens for other clients by contract. In the 1840s he began to lay out municipal parks and cemeteries, and to engage in experiments on village and town planning. By the end of that decade he had extended his works into pure architecture, with the design of his first country house. He had already made his name as a horticultural authority, the sponsor of a major plant-collecting expedition, the first to succeed in flowering the giant waterlily *Victoria amazonica*; he had become known as an editor, with the *Horticultural Register* in 1831, and *Paxton's Magazine of Botany* in 1834, and then as a writer, with a treatise on dahlia growing (1838), and a series of collaborations with the eminent botanist John Lindley: the *Pocket Botanical Dictionary* (1840) and *Paxton's Flower Garden* (1850), not to mention the *Gardeners' Chronicle*, which they founded together in 1841. In 1850–51 he erected the Great Exhibition building in Hyde Park, for which achievement he was knighted, and his last years produced a flurry of visionary schemes for glass buildings. From beginning his career as an under-gardener, he ended his days as Sir Joseph Paxton, MP and railway millionaire.

Few could emulate Paxton's career, but all could aspire, and while none ever scaled quite the heights that he did, some came reasonably close. Among Paxton's contemporaries, we may single out John Spencer, head gardener of Bowood, whose extramural activities included being director of a bank;[31] or Donald Beaton, who became a gardener because he failed to obtain a bursary with which to attend university. He recorded that this choice of career meant 'cancelling all the applications for making a gentleman of me'; but by his fifties he had become a national figure, praised by botanists for his achievements in hybridizing, his name regularly invoked as a standard for excellence in garden decoration.[32] By the middle of the nineteenth century, the gardener was expected to be able to demonstrate his proficiency as an artist as well as a botanist. Indeed, in the wake of Paxton, skills as a builder and engineer were added to his burden. 'The usual fate of gardeners in large places has overtaken Mr. Stevens',

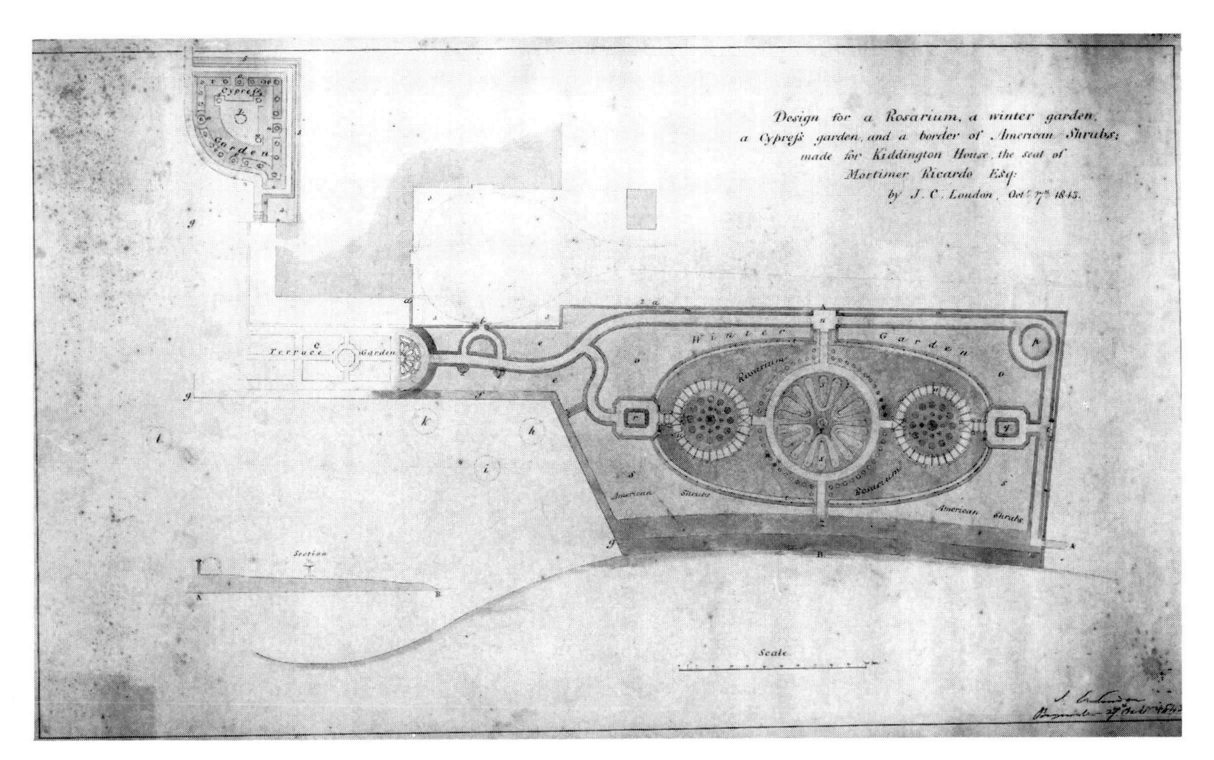

3 Kiddington Hall, J. C. Loudon's plan for a rosarium, *c.* 1843. In reaction against the cult of nature, Loudon recommended specimen shrubs, circular beds, rose arcades, and an arbour of trelliswork.

wrote D. T. Fish in 1872 of the head gardener at Trentham; 'I found him busy among bricks and mortar. To build new or repair or rebuild old houses is a sure and certain part of the duties of the modern gardener.'[33]

This rise to power was not achieved without a struggle, begun primarily by Loudon, for the improved education, wages, housing, and social standing of gardeners.[34] 'Why couple the knowledge and culture of professional men with the rewards of a livery servant?', asked the young D. T. Fish, who had studied everything from botany to draughtsmanship to prepare himself for his career, on receiving his first offer of a position at a salary of £30 per year.[35] Status, salary, and working conditions were to improve as the garden became more complex. Just as the new country houses of the period were planned for a detailed subdivision of tasks, so the garden increasingly became divided into departments – pleasure grounds, kitchen garden, glasshouses – each with its own staff and foreman, with the head gardener in overall control. Horticultural exhibitions and competitions also played an important part in the gardener's life, for they gave him his major opportunity of associating with other gardeners, of testing his abilities against theirs, and of gaining local – and eventually, perhaps, national – fame.[36]

By the later years of the century, the head gardener whose authority exceeded his master's had become a humorous stereotype. As an example from real life, take Thomas King, head gardener at Devizes Castle, who grew what flowers he preferred despite the family's wishes, frustrated his employer's desire to have birds in the garden by breeding cats and cutting down roosting trees, and, when the family finally sold the Castle, leased the grounds himself and ran them as a market garden.[37] The climax of the gardener's long quest for status can be seen in a lawsuit of 1869, when

James Barnes, 'Barnes of Bicton', brought a libel charge against his former employer Baroness Rolle for complaining that he had left the grounds in a disorderly condition on his retirement, and was awarded £200. It was, in a sense, the final recognition that the gardener had emerged from under his master's thumb.[38]

Technical Innovations

The full history of the technological progress of gardening in the nineteenth century has not been written, nor has anyone yet attempted to assess the contributions of professional gardeners to the development of botanical science. Here there is no space to give more than the briefest account of the immense changes that this period witnessed in the actual craft of gardening.

The first category of improvements was the invention of labour-saving devices, most notably the lawn mower. The first lawn mower was patented by Edwin Budding in 1830, and was based on his observation of cylindrical blades in the cloth mill where he worked; in 1833 he sold a licence to manufacture his machine to Messrs Ransome of Ipswich. It was soon discovered to be not only easier to use but less destructive to the ground than the scythe. The impact of the mower must not be exaggerated: lawns were, if anything, losing their popularity in the 1840s, being looked upon negatively as merely settings for decoration, and did not re-emerge as a positive design theme until the 1860s. The late 1850s even saw a wave of enthusiasm for lawn substitutes, like *Spergula pilifera*, that did not require mowing. But gradually the lawn mower was refined in construction and scope of operations; Shanks of Arbroath patented a five-roller horse-drawn mower in time for the Great Exhibition of 1851; steam and petrol powered mowers were on their way by the turn of the century.[39]

A formidable appetite for experiment resulted not only in remodellings of such standard equipment as plant labels and secateurs, but in a wide range of syringes, fumigators and dusting machines, transplanting machines, hygrometers, devices for measuring tree heights, fire extinguishers, sun-shades and hail protectors. How many important gardeners of the time did not leave their names affixed to some item of gardening technology, from boiler to glazing system? Charles M'Intosh and his verge cutter, Alexander Forsyth and his combination plumb-line and level, the Glenny watering-pot, the Paxton everything – let alone the fringe world of revolving frames (designed to expose plants uniformly to sunlight) and greenhouse railways (for moving tubbed trees into the open more easily).[40]

The greatest of all labour-saving innovations, however, was provided by the coming of the railways. On the local scale, it meant, for those wealthy enough to have private rail lines installed, a great increase in the speed and ease with which materials could be brought to the site; on a larger scale, it meant that types of building and decorative stone could now be brought from any part of the country, and the builder was no longer dependent on local quarries. The use of railways also revolutionized commercial horticulture, for the rapid transport of plants and horticultural produce meant that nurseries and market gardens were increasingly freed from the restrictions of locality; similarly, a head gardener in Scotland or the north could furnish plants for his employer's London house. The arrival of the motor car began to have a similar impact on local market gardening just before the turn of the century.[41]

The second great category of technical innovations was the introduction of new materials. The use of concrete for foundations was pioneered by Robert Smirke at Millbank Prison in 1817, and had entered the garden by the 1840s; by the 1870s we hear of gardeners engaging in pond-concreting competitions.[42] As a material for the facing of buildings, Roman cement was in use by the 1790s, but its brown colour meant that it had to be painted to make it resemble stone, and by the 1820s the search was on for cements that had a natural Portland stone colour; one outcome of this search was the development of James Pulham's artificial stone rockeries. Portland cement, once developed, became the standard mortar for the rest of the nineteenth century, valued because its hardness promised a long life – as we now realize, a longer life than many of the building units it was used to hold together.[43]

The late 1830s saw the introduction from France of asphalt, first used in England by George Claridge as a surfacing material for roads and cemetery catacombs; by mid-century there were many competing varieties, and their merits for making garden paths were a matter for earnest debate in the press. Some other 'new' materials were in fact revivals or rediscoveries of older techniques, most notably Minton's process for making encaustic tiles, promoted from the 1840s, and the revival of terracotta in the 1860s.[44]

Iron became of particular importance as a material for its use in glasshouses, after Loudon patented his wrought iron glazing bar in 1816. Cast and wrought iron competed against each other for horticultural purposes, until the commercial introduction of Bessemer's steel process in the 1880s began to compete against both. The great advantage of cast iron was the way it lent itself to prefabrication: by the 1870s, it was possible for a firm like Macfarlane's of Glasgow to issue a massive catalogue of castings, ranging from girders to decorative finials, with illustrations of the way in which complete glasshouses could be assembled from numbered parts.[45] It was a gardener who demonstrated the possibilities of prefabrication to the world most dramatically; Paxton emphasized the way in which the standardization of parts for the Crystal Palace reduced the possibilities of error, and the need for specialist skill, in its assembly.[46]

By far the most important of new materials from the gardener's point of view, however, was glass. The major improvement in its manufacture was James Hartley's sheet glass process, in 1847; this made possible for the first time the general use of large sheets of glass instead of the myriad small panes of the early years of the century, free of the bubbly texture of early plate glass that had acted as a series of burning-glasses to scorch the leaves of plants.[47] Hartley's patent came at the right time; the long-standing tax on glass had been abolished in 1845, the brick tax was to go in 1850, thus, with an easing of timber duty the next year, making it possible for the middle classes as well as the wealthy to erect glasshouses.[48] Within a few years, rival systems like Thomas Rivers's easy-to-construct orchard-houses and Charles Ewing's glass walls had sprung up to take advantage of the new market.[49] Glass panes also now had a greater likelihood of surviving in all weathers: the supersession of lead-based putties by the more pliable linseed oil putty meant that far fewer panes would break during the course of expansion and contraction, and the increasing popularity of wood over iron after mid-century was due partly to the same reason.

Countless greenhouses were altered in the 1850s, updating not only their glazing but their heating: the early flued walls had given way to steam heating, then to hot-water, and were eventually (later in the century) to give way to gas; Weeks's tubular boilers, introduced in the 1830s and 1840s, despite much experimental competition, remained a standard for efficient burning for two generations. There were, of course, less highly technological attempts to solve heating problems: Polmaise heating, a curious convection-based pipeless system, attracted much attention in the 1840s, and double glazing was being essayed by the 1850s. As the sophistication of greenhouse cultivation improved, so did the range of equipment for maintaining interior conditions, from thermometers and hygrometers to eaves drainage systems for collecting rainwater and automatic watering systems.[50]

Another refinement of glass construction was the closely-glazed case, most closely associated with the name of Nathaniel Ward. Though most commonly remembered today as a form of interior decoration, a device for growing plants indoors, its major use was as a means of transporting plants. Before the 1830s, most plant introductions were effected by bringing home seed wrapped in moist cloth; growing specimens, on sea voyages, had either to be kept below decks, in inadequate lighting, or on deck, where they were exposed to corrosive salt spray. The self-sustaining environment of the Wardian case – water that evaporated during the day remained within the case, and condensed again at night – meant that living plants could be brought to England with a minimal loss rate. George Loddiges soon exulted that whereas his nursery had been lucky to receive one specimen out of twenty intact before, to lose one out of twenty was now a misfortune. The number of exotic plants introduced into Britain skyrocketed.[51]

As gardeners began to cope systematically with the problems of growing hitherto unfamiliar plants, their horticultural expertise blossomed in a way unknown to previous generations. For Shirley Hibberd, looking back in 1883, the previous fifty years had 'seen horticulture developed from an empirical mystery to an art founded on the truths of nature and the achievements of science', and his aspersion of the garden-craft of previous centuries was widely echoed; Donald Beaton could declare that 'only four years before the first Reform Bill, some of the best gardeners in the country did not know or understand the principle of potting plants', and John Robson could remember a similar ignorance of propagation techniques in 1830.[52] Much of the credit for this achievement was awarded to John Lindley, whose *Theory of Horticulture* was published in 1840; Alexander Cramb credited that book with 'raising horticulture almost to an exact science . . . and so demolishing that huge monster – empiricism'.[53]

The development of horticultural science lay in great part in an immense programme of experimentation by early Victorian gardeners. The story of their achievement has never been systematically recounted, and can only be hinted at here. Experiments on hardiness – leading climbing plants through successively cooler sections of the glasshouse, trying greenhouse plants outdoors, growing tropical aquatics in heated tanks, heating the ground with hot-water pipes; experiments on wintering plants, or forcing them out of season; experiments on reviving open-air vineyards in England. 'Only think', wrote Beaton, 'of a cottage gardener having a plot of Pine apples growing at the end of his Rhubarb bed like so many globe Artichokes!'[54]

Experiments on trenching and drainage, soil sterilization by burning, the use of earth closets; the great Rothamsted series of experiments on fertilizers, begun in the 1840s; Darwin's investigations of earthworms and the formation of vegetable mould in the 1870s, and the later discoveries about soil bacteria.[55] Experiments on pest control, the use of tobacco for fumigation, the invention of lime-sulphur by a Margate gardener in 1847, the introduction of Bordeaux mixture in the 1880s.[56] Experiments on pruning, cordon training, and root-pruning for fruit trees.[57] Experiments on root control by buried concrete, and the blasting of tree stumps by dynamite.[58] Experiments on tree regeneration, from William Forsyth's notorious plaster for tree wounds in the 1790s to John Caie's method of filling tree cavities with cement to encourage new wood growth – the results of which are familiar to many an unwary chainsaw.[59] Experiments, above all, on plant breeding. Although the possibility of producing hybrids had been demonstrated by Thomas Fairchild in the early eighteenth century, no systematic programme of hybridizing was carried out until William Rollisson began breeding Cape heaths at his south London nursery in the 1790s, and real publicity had to wait for William Herbert's work with *Amaryllis* and *Gladiolus* in the 1820s. Thereafter the production of new hybrids became a competitive business, and by 1883 Hibberd could marvel that 'the hybridist who has thoroughly mastered the art may predetermine, with almost mathematical exactitude, what it is in his power to produce'.[60]

But of all technical improvements, the one that had the most obvious impact on garden design was the art of transplanting. Le Nôtre's achievements at Versailles had served as a model for intermittent practice in the eighteenth century, but in the 1820s the subject was reopened by Sir Henry Steuart, whose transplanting machine and technique of moving large trees bare-rooted served as the model for many experiments during the next decades.[61] Then, in the 1830s, an alternative technique was pioneered by William Barron: trees were moved with their roots still encased in a ball of earth, and instead of being dropped into a hole (which Barron felt damaged the roots), the rootball was rested on the ground and a new mound built up around it. Using this method, Barron achieved a minimal loss rate and was soon transplanting trees of immense size and age over long distances, to the amazement of his contemporaries: 'now the present occupant of a domain may complete and enjoy, in his lifetime, much more than our forefathers were able to achieve for their posterity even to the fourth generation'.[62] Under Barron's influence, skill in transplanting spread rapidly: other gardeners attempted refinements to the process, but as Beaton admitted, they were all picking up the crumbs

4 William Barron and his team in 1880, successfully transplanting the Buckfast Abbey yew, aged over 800 years.

from Barron's table.[63] Barron's most controversial exercise took place in 1880, when he removed the Buckfast Abbey yew, with a documented age of over 800 years, to the further end of the churchyard (a distance of sixty yards) so as to prevent its branches from damaging the structure of the building.[64] His sons continued the good work after his death, and carried on transplanting enormous trees into the interwar years.

These, then, were the forces that shaped the Victorian garden: rapidly changing technology, a new professional group to administer it, and an artistic ferment spread by the proliferating gardening magazines. The following chapters will chronicle the changes that resulted.

2

Landscape into garden

The Eighteenth-Century Garden in Decay

In the 1820s and 1830s, John Claudius Loudon made several tours of gardens, the results of which were reported in his *Gardener's Magazine* and his wife's abortive *Ladies' Magazine of Botany*.[1] Everywhere there were signs of decay and neglect, as the depression of the Napoleonic wars took its toll on the great landscape gardens. 'The noblest place in Britain, perhaps in Europe, Blenheim, is going rapidly to decay.' Among the evidences of neglect were trees growing out of the stonework of the gate piers, the dam of the cascade unable to retain water, and 'half the lake turned into a morass covered with rushes'.[2] The same fate was overtaking other celebrated gardens: at White Knights the 'conservatories are stripped of their most valuable tenants, and are now fast falling to decay'; the grotto at Marble Hill was dilapidated; Hall Barn neglected, Strawberry Hill going fast to decay; even such a recent garden as Repton's Southgate Lodge was ruinous. At White Knights, 'it envelopes the mind in a gloomy sensation to see summer-houses, fountains, and extensive covered walks, going to fast to ruin for want of that mainspring of all human works, money'.[3]

The world of which the great landscape parks had formed a part was changing rapidly, its favoured assumptions being eroded by a variety of forces, social, economic and intellectual. Ten years before Loudon began his *Gardener's Magazine*, England had been on the point of civil war; depression, agricultural riots, the execution of the first commoners for high treason, the first demands for universal suffrage – all these things had subsided by the mid-1820s, but they had left their traces behind. The great agricultural fortunes were giving way to industrial ones, whether of middle-class provenance, like the Wedgwoods, or aristocratic, like the coal-enriched Dukes of Sutherland. The political mobilization of the working classes was leading reformers to improve their lot, and restore the supposed harmony that had once existed between the orders of society. These changes were reflected in the basic structure of the garden.

The eighteenth-century landscape park could be summed up as the attempt to turn the setting of the house into an image of nature. Evidences of human industry and impact on the landscape were reduced; the kitchen garden was banished to distant portions of the grounds, where it would not impinge on the main views from the house. Gardeners' houses and tenants' cottages were concealed from the view; it was not unknown for entire villages to be moved by Act of Parliament because the landowners wanted to incorporate their sites into the landscape garden. The rationale for this destruction was visual consistency:

> The loveliest scenes ... are frequently disturbed by unaccording circumstances; – by the signs of cultivation – the regularity of enclosures – the traces of manufactures, and, what is worse than all, by the presumptuous embellishments of fantastic Taste. Amid this confusion of incidents, the general character of the scene is altogether lost; we scarcely know to what class of objects to give our attention ...[4]

The wholesale removal of villages and dispossession of tenants did not pass without arousing protests; Oliver Goldsmith's 'Deserted Village' was inspired by the removal of the village of Nuneham Courtenay to allow the expansion of the landscape garden.[5]

Loudon, among others, continued this vein of protest against the injustice of such removals, commending those owners who improved tenant cottages and equipped them with gardens, and eventually compiling an encyclopaedia of cottage architecture.[6] John Ruskin, who began his career writing for Loudon's *Architectural Magazine*, was to emphasize the discrepancy between the aesthete's delight in the picturesque hovel and the misery of its inhabitants. By the 1840s there was a widespread reaction against the elevation of aesthetics over convenience and efficiency in landscape planning. Thomas Dick Lauder criticized the neglect of road maintenance in favour of an air of picturesque neglect; Loudon campaigned against approach roads that wound their way around an estate instead of following the most convenient route to the house.[7] Uvedale Price had praised the careless cutting of wood as picturesque, and as late as 1874 Sir Thomas Dyke Acland was summoned before a magistrate for neglecting to have the hedges trimmed and trees lopped in parts of the Killerton estate, justifying his inaction on the grounds of picturesque effect.[8]

Efficiency emerged as an aesthetic value of its own, as the picturesque was gradually domesticated. The late eighteenth century had seen the creation of new model farms with architect-designed buildings and increased functional planning;[9] Loudon extended this existing taste to the kitchen garden, regularly commenting on the need for modernization, exulting in a good display of glass ranges, and helping to popularize orderly planning as an aesthetic merit independent of the remainder of the garden. With Loudon begins the long controversy over whether the kitchen garden should be 'made ornamental' by bringing the flower garden within its precincts, or whether the sight of uniform rows of cabbages and carrots was not ornamental enough by itself.[10]

The consequence of all this was that the component parts of the landscape began to be freed from subordination to an overall scheme. For some, this meant a painful process of realizing that aesthetic criteria had to take second place; for others, it resulted in a new aesthetic attitude, which accorded the elements of the garden an aesthetic autonomy – the flower garden, the cottage garden, the kitchen garden were to be regarded by their own criteria, independently of their impact on an overall view. The necessary precondition for this new aesthetic, however, was an end to the custom of making the values of the garden dependent on the values of landscape painting. This repudiation of painters' standards can be seen explicitly in this statement by the Leeds landscape gardener Joshua Major:

> a view to be represented on canvass is necessarily limited ... as paintings cannot afford correct examples, because the painter has not space in his limited picture for the introduction of groups and single trees, displaying their full beauty and true characters, are we to banish from the dress ground the majestic cedar ... the noble and elegant lime ... the deep-toned purple beech; the stately elm; the various pines, with their sombre shadows; or the pyramidal larch ...? ... We ask, also, what has the painter to do with the gay parterre, the delightful flower garden, – the soul's delight of the majority of mankind?[11]

From the Picturesque to Transcendentalism

The degree to which landscape painting ought to serve as a basis for landscape gardening had, of course, been the subject of the most famous debate in the recent history of gardening – the quarrel in the 1790s over the picturesque, the participants in which were Uvedale Price, Richard Payne Knight, and Humphry Repton.[12] Price and Knight stood for the primacy of visual values in the experience of landscape, offering landscape paintings as an appropriate model for the planning of the garden; the characteristics they found in such paintings they grouped under the label of the 'picturesque', a visual category distinct from the beautiful and more worthy of being introduced into landscape planning. Intricacy – 'that disposition of objects, which, by a partial and uncertain concealment, excites and nourishes curiosity' – became Price's criterion of excellence. For Repton, on the other hand, gardens were 'not to be laid out with a view to their appearance in a picture, but to their uses, and the enjoyment of them in real life'; he emphasized instead comfort, privacy, and the social uses of the garden.[13]

The most lasting contribution of the picturesque debate to gardening, however, lay in the common ground between the antagonists. Both Price and Repton agreed on the retention of terraces, on the propriety of formal and obviously artificial features in the immediate vicinity of the house, and on some degree of colour planning in the landscape. All the participants in the debate saw architecture in terms of styles, each of which had its own merits. Price and Knight saw both the wilderness and the architectural garden as governed by the same visual standard of intricacy; Repton could proclaim that 'Gardens are works of art, rather than of nature'.[14]

The union of Price and Repton, for the purposes of the gardening community, was largely the work of Loudon. He had begun his career as a disciple of Price, and had attacked Repton; but over the years, his respect for Repton had gradually increased, until, after he had edited Repton's works in 1840, he was thought of by the gardening community as Repton's interpreter. Many of his characteristic arguments – his emphasis on convenience, on functional appropriateness, on the primacy of artifice – aligned him more with Repton than with Price. In his *Suburban Gardener* (1838), he was to draw up a hierarchy of first to fourth-rate gardens, and even though this distinction related primarily to the size of the property, it had an obvious affinity with what has been called Repton's 'aesthetic of social illusionism', the way in which he planned the garden to illustrate the social position of the landowner.[15]

Already by the 1820s Loudon was criticizing the taste responsible for such celebrated gardens of the previous century as Strawberry Hill and Hagley.[16] The immediate stimulus for his mature position, however, was his exposure to the ideas of the French aesthetician Quatremère de Quincy, to whom he attempted to assimilate Repton.[17] Ironically, Quatremère's theory was a conservative one, offered as a defence of neoclassicism by setting limits to the proper field of the artist's behaviour, but Loudon and J. C. Kent, who translated his principal work, put his ideas to their own uses.

Quatremère had defined the purpose of art as imitation, understood in a certain rigid sense: 'To imitate in the fine arts, is to produce the resemblance of a thing, but in some other thing which becomes the image of it'. The landscape gardener, however, in professing to imitate nature, used the materials of nature itself. His work broke the rules; it was a deception rather than a true imitation, and therefore to be excluded from the circle of the fine arts.

> Wishing to deceive, and deceiving in order to please, he has thereby lost all right and all power of pleasing those who require of the arts the charm of imitation, and not the fraud of counterfeit. Let him then address himself to those who wish to be deceived, or who deserve to be so, that is, to the ignorant.[18]

The response of Loudon and Kent was that Quatremère had been led astray by the eighteenth-century rhetoric of nature. The merit of gardening did not lie in deceiving the spectator into believing that he was viewing the work of unassisted nature. It lay in self-conscious artistry, intended to be recognized as such: 'any creation, to be recognised as a work of art, must be such as can never be mistaken for a work of nature'.[19]

It should be noted that this theory provided no logical compulsion to look for a new style; the nature-worshipping gardens of the eighteenth century had been creations of art, and could be seen as such whether their original designers would have wished it or not. The very smoothness and regularity that Price and Knight complained of in 'Capability' Brown's landscapes marked them as artificial creations, and therefore exempted them from Quatremère's condemnation. Loudon noted this possibility explicitly:

> In this view of the subject, the modern style of landscape gardening is just as artificial as the ancient style, and this it ought undoubtedly to be, in order to bring it within the pale of the fine arts . . .[20]

He could, therefore, simply have urged the continuation of existing gardening styles, justifying them on the basis of his new aesthetic; and in his early writings he claimed to have purified the landscape style so that it could now satisfy Pricean requirements.[21] But the emphasis on architectural gardening in Price, as well as in Repton, carried the day; Loudon's continental tours between 1813 and 1819 revealed to him the great surviving geometrical gardens of France and Italy, and during the peak of his career they formed the model for correct style which he promoted.

Such was the message that Loudon was propounding during his later years; but he was not alone. Among his rivals was Charles M'Intosh, gardener successively to the King of the Belgians at Claremont and to the

Duke of Buccleuch at Dalkeith Palace, and the author of one of the more successful horticultural textbooks.[22] M'Intosh introduced a new strain, inspired by the French eclectic philosopher Victor Cousin, whose transcendentalist rhetoric went an important step beyond Quatremère's in substituting creation for imitation:

> Art is nature destroyed and re-constructed ... Taste is a faculty indolent and passive: genius is proud and free. The artist in destroying and improving matter advances toward the end of art, which is the triumph of human over physical nature ...[23]

While the rhetoric was more heated than Loudon's, the practical consequence – the elevation of artifice to a supreme position in the garden – was the same.

It was in an environment seasoned by views such as these that the collected writings of Repton appeared, edited by Loudon, in 1840, followed two years later by a collection of Price's writings, edited by Thomas Dick Lauder. Now gardeners could look back at the intellectual origins of their art; but they now looked back from a predominantly

5 A picturesque view of the seventeenth-century formal garden at Barncluith, published in 1842 as the frontispiece to Sir Thomas Dick Lauder's edition of *Price on the Picturesque*.

transcendentalist point of view.[24] The changes that Price and Repton had set in motion had already transformed the garden.

Wordsworth

An important channel of transition between the picturesque theorists of the 1790s and the transcendentalist attitudes of the later Loudon was provided by William Wordsworth.

Wordsworth's general proposals regarding garden design were consistent with Uvedale Price's. Exotic plants were appropriate near the house, which as an artificial creation deserved an artificial accompaniment, but there should be a gradual transition between this area and the wider landscape; this transition should be effected by introducing into the nearer portions of woodlands shrubs for spring and autumn colour.[25] Wordsworth's application of these principles was shown in three gardens which he planned, his own gardens at Dove Cottage (from 1799) and Rydal Mount (from 1813), and in his patron Sir George Beaumont's garden at Coleorton Hall, Leicestershire (1805–7).

All three gardens displayed a use of terracing and other formal features, but not carried out in an architectural manner. Both Dove Cottage and Rydal had stone-walled terraces with rustic summerhouses and rudely carved stone steps whose interstices were planted with flowers; ferns, moss, and climbing plants were encouraged to clothe the stonework. Loudon reported,

> There is a terrace walk, with some scraps of natural rockwork planted by art; and displaying at the same time the taste of the painter in the arrangement of the colours, and the science of the botanist in choosing the plants.

(An architectural effect grew gradually, and a level terrace with a gravelled walk was added at Rydal.) Similarly, at Coleorton, seats and steps were excavated into a rock-face to be covered with ivy and periwinkle.[26]

Both Rydal and Coleorton were characterized by a dominance of evergreen planting. Wordsworth's plan was for the creation of a winter garden at Coleorton, which would remain green and pleasant regardless of the seasons, using firs, holly, juniper and yew in 'green unfading bowers'; he planted such new conifers as *Cryptomeria* at Rydal, which one commentator compared to 'the ideal character of one of Martin's or Danby's imaginative landscapes'.[27] And a major role was allocated to historical, or at least poetic, precedent, at Coleorton; the grounds were to be divided by a green alley, and a bower, based on the pseudo-Chaucerian poem 'The Flower and the Leaf', was to be erected, paved with variously-coloured pebbles.

Wordsworth regarded Price as an important purifier of taste in gardening, but between them there was an important difference. Wordsworth regarded the beautiful and the picturesque neither as inherent qualities of objects nor as different faculties of mind. Instead, he used them to label categories of aesthetic response, to some extent dependent on education: 'the perception of what has acquired the name of picturesque and romantic scenery is so far from being intuitive, that it can be produced only by a slow and gradual process of culture'. The perception of beauty or sublimity consequently depended not on something intrinsic, whether in nature or in man, but on the individual's biases; Wordsworth's aesthetic was an active one, and consistently elevated the imagination, the projection of the mind, above the passive condition of taste, by which the mind accepted the impress of externally imposed dictates.[28]

It was, indeed, only because these responses were to some degree under the direction of the individual's will that one could attempt to improve people's taste. Thus, when he wished to condemn 'picturesque' interference with the landscape, he could explain differences in taste as a consequence of different stages of mental development:

> All gross transgressions of this kind originate, doubtless, in a feeling natural and honourable to the human mind, viz. the pleasure which it receives from distinct ideas, and from the perception of order, regularity, and contrivance. Now, unpractised minds receive these impressions only from objects that are divided from each other by strong lines of demarcation; hence the delight with which such minds are smitten by formality and harsh contrast.[29]

This deficiency could be corrected by a better understanding of nature – not the eighteenth century's external nature to which man ought to be subordinate, but a nature in which man was an active principle.

An interest in history and in the historical continuity of society spanned Wordsworth's career, although it became more obviously central as he grew older; and he showed himself very much aware of the way in which human activity had modified the supposedly natural landscape. This social dimension was something he sought to retain in the garden as well; he attacked the devastation of villages to make way for landscape gardens, and even in Price's garden at Foxley complained that the evidence of human society had been removed. His plans for the winter garden at Coleorton involved retaining two old cottages in the view.[30] For the eighteenth-century concept of nature, in general, he substituted that of the vernacular. Hence his hatred of whitewash, his insistence on chimneys which showed the colour of the local stone, his desire that cottages should 'appear to be received into the bosom of the living principle of things, as it acts and exists among the woods and fields'; hence also his condemnation of the great larch plantations that landowners of the late eighteenth century had introduced into the Lake District, subverting the mixed character of the existing woodland.[31] Hence also his preference for traditional flowers, even when not native, such as the hollyhock, which he feared was being ousted from cultivation by the dahlia.[32] Such vernacularism developed easily into historical revivalism, as instanced by the use of 'Chaucerian' precedent in designing the winter garden at Coleorton.

As Wordsworth's poetry became well-known in the 1820s, his influence lent weight to the growing campaign for art in the garden; while some of his poems mocked the pretensions of over-elaborate gardens, others celebrated the lawn and flower garden, asserting a place for 'gay parterres'.[33]

Wordsworth saw his vernacularism overtaken during his lifetime by an ideology of the supremacy of art, and condemned the taste of his neighbours who pushed the ostentation of art too far.[34] His direct influence on gardening lingered longest in the Lakes. A late instance can be seen at Wray Castle, built in the 1840s for a local surgeon. Stylistically, Wray

Castle was a late survival, related more to a Regency construction like Smirke's Eastnor Castle than to the painstakingly accurate castles that Salvin had pioneered in the 1830s: its castellated features were systematically exaggerated, and there was even an assemblage of mock ruins near the entrance. Wordsworth, however, praised it for adding 'a dignified feature to the interesting scenery in the midst of which it stands', and the grounds show unmistakable signs of his influence: an admixture of exotics behind the building, but a broad lawn with specimen trees sweeping down towards the main view of Windermere.[35]

Wordsworth died in 1850, three years after the completion of Wray Castle. Within ten years, an estate like Monk Coniston Hall was being planted on entirely different principles, as an arboretum with a wide range of exotic conifers, arranged partly in avenues. Once Wordsworth's direct influence was removed, the mid-century styles swept in, and gardening in the Lakes was brought into unison with the rest of the country.[36]

Artificial Climate

The growing importance of artifice in the garden was reinforced by the growing technical expertise of the gardeners, and the development of artificial conditions of cultivation. The simplest and most obvious form of this was to grow plants in pots or tubs instead of in the ground; Loudon pointed out that pot culture provided an unnatural condition which 'always checks and counteracts the natural habits of the plant'. The use of tubbed trees after the manner of Versailles was encouraged in the 1820s and 1830s by gardens such as Hendon Rectory, and by Elizabeth Kent, sister-in-law of Leigh Hunt and author of *Flora Domestica*, a manual on the use of potted plants.[37] The furthest extreme of artificial cultivation outdoors consisted of attempts to alter the local microclimate, as in the geothermal garden at Welton Place or James Main's proposal for heated ponds for exotic aquatics.[38]

The phrase 'artificial climate' had already appeared at the end of the eighteenth century to describe the conditions provided by the glasshouse, and Loudon predictably was seized by the implications of the phrase. A greenhouse 'is entirely a work of art: the plants inclosed are in the most artificial situation in which they can be placed'.[39]

The chief problem in cultivation under glass was ensuring adequate light for the plants. Amid much fevered attention devoted to the proper angle of glass for optimum lighting, Sir George Mackenzie in 1815 made a revolutionary proposal: 'make the surface of your green house roof parallel to the vaulted surface of the heavens, or to the plane of the sun's orbit'.[40] Attempts at domes for ornamental effect had been made before, and Samuel Ware's conservatory at Chiswick House boasted a central cupola from *c.* 1811;[41] but the thickness of wood required in the glazing bars to support the weight of glass militated against the admission of much light. Then in 1816, Loudon made Mackenzie's proposal practicable by inventing a curved glazing bar in wrought iron; now it was possible to build a dome or a completely curvilinear structure without most of the light being blocked by the width of the glazing bars required. The first

6 Hendon Rectory. This engraving from the *Gardener's Magazine* illustrates the use of potted trees to create movable garden scenery.

free-standing curvilinear house was erected by D. and E. Bailey of Holborn (who had acquired Loudon's patent) at Bretton Hall, Yorkshire, in 1827. Functional glasshouses were now a possibility from the gardener's point of view; and the key to this functionalism was iron construction.[42]

There was an important alternative to the curvilinear roof, however: long rows of panes arranged in alternating ridges to catch some degree of morning and afternoon sun. Loudon had in fact suggested such a ridge-and-furrow system before being carried away by the possibilities of curvilinear, but in the 1830s it was promoted by Joseph Paxton as an alternative to curvilinear, cheaper because it could be built in wood.[43]

Now that adequate lighting for protected cultivation had been ensured, the possibilities seemed endless. Loudon's early writings expanded into visionary schemes for climatic control, and the provision of diverse environments within one building. In 1817 he envisaged the day

> when such artificial climates will not only be stocked with appropriate birds, fishes and harmless animals, but with examples of the human species from the different countries imitated, habited in their particular costumes and who may serve as gardeners or curators of the different productions.[44]

The arrogance of this last proposal was never put into effect, but the idea of multiple environments was further promoted by Robert Marnock, whose original proposal for the Royal Botanic Society's conservatory was 'a succession of greenhouses stuck together' to form a sequence of differently lighted habitats for different plants.[45]

The practical reality was somewhat different from these happy expectations, and soon Loudon was recommending a greatly reduced plan for the ordinary gardener:

> within the last fifty years the accession to our stock of exotics has been so great, that gardeners are quite bewildered among them, and the nurserymen at present, in their recommendation of plants, act as if every purchaser were a botanist. This is the reason why we see so very few greenhouses that present

7 Chatsworth: Paxton's Great Stove. Built in 1830–40, it adopted Paxton's ridge and furrow principle to a curvilinear structure.

8 Woolverstone Park, view in the conservatory, 1874. The British school of conservatory planting: a collection of individual specimens rather than a composed landscape.

a gay assemblage of luxuriant verdure and blossoms: on the contrary, they are generally filled with sickly naked plants in peat soil, with hard names, which one-half of people of taste and fashion, and nine-tenths of mankind in general, care nothing about.

With disillusioned realism, Loudon concluded that 'oranges, lemons, camellias, myrtles, banksias, proteas, acacias, melaleucas, and a few other Cape and Botany Bay plants, are all that can with propriety be admitted in a small conservatory'.[46]

Loudon, under the influence of French experiments in interior landscaping, tried to restrict the word 'conservatory' to a glasshouse where plants were arranged in beds rather than in containers; the most famous early example of a conservatory arranged with beds was at The Grange, Northington, Hampshire.[47] During the 1840s the first English experiments were made in replicating exotic environments. In 1843, John Dillwyn Llewellyn designed a glasshouse for the cultivation of epiphytic orchids at his garden at Penllergare. A hot-water pipe, directed through a boiler, poured heated steam out at the top of a rockery, reflected into spray by a series of stone ledges, thus giving the effect of a tropical cataract. Orchid species mingled together 'in beautiful confusion', with 'a wild luxuriance

... unknown to the specimens cultivated in the ordinary manner'.[48] Similar experiments in 'picturesque' cultivation were carried out by N. B. Ward in his glasshouse at Clapham, and were promoted by Noel Humphreys as an improvement in interior arrangement.[49] This picturesque approach was to remain a minority interest for another twenty years, however; Loudon's definition of a conservatory was not widely adopted, and easily rearranged assortments of pots and tubs remained the basis of English conservatory display until after mid-century.

The Recognition of Art

By the 1830s, whether derived from Loudon or from others, the notion was in the ascendant that the garden should display the unmistakable signs of artifice. Loudon's theory of imitation, derived from Quatremère de Quincy, made little headway among his contemporaries as a philosophical idea, but the practical consequence he deduced from it – the principle of the recognition of art – was continually reinforced from a variety of sources.

Among methods of giving a garden an artistic character, there was the ideal of neatness and 'high polish', the maintenance of the garden in a condition which could not be mistaken for disorderly nature. The tours in the *Gardener's Magazine* repeatedly drew attention to those few gardens that could rival continental ones in this respect: at Tingrith House Loudon saw 'not a weed, not a decayed leaf'; at Whitmore Lodge 'the roses are gathered as they wither, and the leaves as they drop, every morning'. John Spencer first attracted attention for keeping sixty acres at Bowood in continual polish under the scythe. 'Clean as a drawing-room' became a standard to aim at; 'the marks of care and industry ought to appear constantly'.[50]

Grafting was one technique whereby gardeners could demonstrate their authority over the merely natural, and by the 1830s it had become standard practice for gardeners, from the grafting of mistletoe onto oaks to the grafting of deodars on to cedars of Lebanon. William Barron turned Elvaston Castle into a grafter's playground, with rows of grafted cedars in avenues, and specimens of weeping beech grafted onto mature trees to produce flagpole effects of dangling branches cascading at great heights.[51] The greatest triumph of nineteenth-century grafting was obtained accidentally in the 1820s when a Parisian gardener named Adam created a graft-hybrid of laburnum and broom, which produced flowers in three different colours on the same plant; the debate on the physiology of this creation dragged on through the century.[52]

Training shrubs into standards was another technique to become commonplace, although the deformation of natural habit aroused stronger opposition at first than the other innovations we have been considering. 'Mr. Appleby was just lucky enough to escape being transported for venturing to exhibit the first standards of Deutzia gracilis, and the last that were ever seen at Chiswick Shows.'[53] The popularity of standard roses in the 1840s finally made the technique generally acceptable.

All these techniques, however, were no more than flourishes applied to the basic structure of the garden. The revival of formal and architectural styles was the most obvious way of making the garden as a whole into a work of art; more difficult was the artistic transformation of the landscape garden, that legacy of an incorrect aesthetic. A finished statement on this problem was to be found in Loudon's 1838 manual, *The Suburban Gardener and Villa Companion*:

> *The Rules which, in Landscape-Gardening, may be derived from the Principle of the Recognition of Art* are numerous. With respect to ground, it must either be reduced to levels, or slopes of regular curvatures, as in the ancient style; or, in the modern style, to polished curvatures and undulations, which shall be, either from the beauty of their form, or from their clothing of herbage, distinguishable at first sight from the natural surface of the ground by which the work of art, that is, the lawn, park, or pleasure-ground, is surrounded. Wood, if the common trees of the locality are employed, must be either planted in lines, or massed in geometrical figures; or, if foreign trees and shrubs only are used, they may be planted in irregular masses or groups, and as single trees. If indigenous trees and shrubs are at any time introduced in the modern style of landscape-gardening, the greatest care must be taken not to crowd, or even group, them together in such a manner as that a stranger might conclude they had grown up there naturally. ... For example, in a country abounding with the common English oak, no artist, who understands his art, would employ that tree in his artificial plantations, unless at their boundaries, so as to harmonise them with the natural woods of the country; or unless in an avenue, or in some other way in which they could at once be recognised as having been planted.[54]

Such devices characterized Loudon's ideal of the imitation of nature using non-natural materials, i.e. exotic planting. The roots of the technique, if not the rhetoric accompanying it, may be found in Uvedale Price. Exotic planting became one of the major determinants of Victorian gardening; the most celebrated exotic collections, like Dropmore, demonstrated to their visitors that 'Nature must acknowledge the supremacy of Art'.[55]

The idea of exotics was in some ways problematic; how did one class trees that had once been exotics, like larches and horse chestnuts, but were now naturalized and commonplace? Associationism provided an answer: plants that lacked 'associations of culture and keeping' should be treated as indigenous, whether a botanist would count them as native or not.[56] Similarly, trees of unusual habit became immediate signals of art when planted so as to attract attention: most of the well-known weeping cultivars (of elm, beech, etc.) were introduced in the first quarter of the nineteenth century,[57] and the popularity of the Italian style brought with it a demand for fastigiate trees to produce the effect of Mediterranean cypresses. The first volume of the *Gardener's Magazine* contained a debate on the landscape use of the Lombardy popular.[58]

In 1832 Loudon introduced a new term to characterize the non-indigenous landscape; reviewing the work of the picturesque theorist William Sawrey Gilpin, he emphasized that 'it is necessary to understand that there is such a character of art as the gardenesque, as well as the picturesque', and hoped that this new coinage would 'soon find a place in the language of rural art'.[59] This wish was quickly fulfilled, and within a few years contributors to the *Gardener's Magazine* could be heard speaking of 'the present state of the gardenesque', using the term for the general ideal of the artificial garden. In these early uses of the word nothing more specific than non-indigenous planting seems to be implied. The 1838 edition of the *Encyclopaedia Britannica* adopted Loudon's coinage, but used it solely for the flower garden.[60]

In his *Suburban Gardener* (1838), Loudon expressed the distinction between picturesque and gardenesque in terms of his theory of imitation: the picturesque was 'the imitation of nature in a wild state, such as the painter delights to copy', while the gardenesque was 'the imitation of nature, subjected to a certain degree of cultivation or improvement, suitable to the wants and wishes of man'. Both categories, however, were required to use exotic vegetation in order to qualify as art. The initial terms of the distinction were effaced; but 'gardenesque' was now developing a new and more specific meaning as a principle of organization.[61]

The Aesthetic of Scatter

By the late 1830s Loudon, having introduced the concept of the gardenesque, was attempting to narrow its meaning to a specific mode of planting. Gardenesque was originally contrasted with picturesque, but by 1843 Loudon added the geometric to make a third 'style or system of art', and named as the key element in the gardenesque the 'distinctness in the separate parts when closely examined', although it was subject to the 'same principles of composition' as the picturesque when viewed as a whole.[62] The distinction between the original terms was no longer based on the use of exotic plants, but on the isolation of trees and flowers as individual specimens:

> All the trees, shrubs and plants in the gardenesque style are planted and managed in such a way as that each may arrive at perfection and display its beauties to as great advantage as if it were cultivated for that purpose alone; while at the same time, the plants relatively to one another and to the whole scene . . . are either grouped or connected on the same principles of composition as in the picturesque style, or placed regularly and symmetrically as in the geometric style. Hence there are two distinct varieties . . . the geometric gardenesque and the pictorial gardenesque . . .[63]

Loudon did not succeed in restricting the use of the word by other gardeners to this planting style, but the style itself was a major feature of English gardens in the 1820s and 1830s. Indeed, the tendency to isolate trees as specimens existed before Loudon's advocacy: Prince Pückler-Muskau, visiting England in 1826, grumbled about the 'ugly fashion now prevalent in England, of planting the "pleasure-ground" with single trees or shrubs', and referred to the practice of separating shrubs in beds 'so that you see more of black earth than of green foliage'.[64] After Loudon and M'Intosh, there would be less ground for complaint; Claremont was praised for obtaining a 'gardenesque effect' in the shrubbery by the close planting of undergrowth, and allowing specimen trees to rise clear of the general mass of foliage.[65]

The gardenesque involved not merely separation, but allowing each plant to 'arrive at perfection'. To see better what this means, we may take Loudon's planting style in his major park, the Derby Arboretum. Trees,

9 Redleaf, the 'English garden'. A gardenesque arrangement of trees and shrubs, planted so as to be observed as individual specimens.

he complained, were often planted so that their main surface roots were concealed; this was an error

> as contrary to truth and nature, and also to the health of the tree, as the shaft of a column without a base or a capital would, if employed in a building, be to architectural taste . . . I have directed all the trees to be planted on little hills, the width of the base being three times the height of the hill, so that the junction of the main roots with the base of the trunk will appear above ground.[66]

Loudon had recommended such a planting style for Kensington Gardens in 1837, and at Bicton, where he advised on the arboretum, the araucaria avenue was planted on mounds. William Barron's transplanting experiments at Elvaston Castle may have reinforced the idea.[67] Robert Marnock used his own variant in laying out The Plantation at Leighton Buzzard in 1844–45, creating circular platforms for specimen trees, a foot higher than the surrounding surface and with a slight rim to hold in rain.[68] The mound principle quickly caught on to become a major feature of mid-century planting.

We have noted that the use of isolated trees predated the concept of the 'gardenesque'. Loudon in fact should be seen, not as the originator of specimen planting, but as the man who introduced a concept of artistic grouping into the existing practice. He protested against the tasteless scattering of single trees in establishments like Regent's Park, and the *Gardener's Magazine* fulminated repeatedly against 'meaningless dotting'.[69] Most of the writers associated with Loudon's campaign for the gardenesque were concerned as much with a principle of organization for specimen trees as with their independence from their immediate neighbours. Robert Marnock proposed planting in groups of specified numbers; the Academician R. R. Reinagle argued that every beautiful object had a geometric outline, and that a scattering of trees became more beautiful the more closely it approximated to some recognizable figure. Grouping into glades was the recommendation of picturesque theorists like W. S. Gilpin.[70] Loudon's own eventual solution was the axis of symmetry:

> The axis of symmetry is founded on this principle: that all the most beautiful objects or scenes in nature are symmetrical; that every symmetrical object forms a whole; and that every whole consists of at least three parts, a beginning, a middle and an end; or, in other words, a centre and two sides. Now, in this centre, whether visible or supplied by the imagination is the axis of symmetry. In the simplest kind of symmetry, the two sides are equal and alike, and the axis is, of course, easily discovered; but in cultivated and refined symmetry, the sides are unequal, and so combined and varied with the centre, that it requires the eye of a philosophical artist to detect the axis.[71]

This proposal was combined with one for circular beds, whose beauty of form was independent of purely arbitrary associations.

Loudon's major allies in promoting his refined concept of the gardensque were two eminent head gardeners, Robert Errington and Robert Glendinning, and a nurseryman, George Loddiges. Errington, head gardener at Oulton Park, Cheshire, became a supporter of Loudon ('the "recognition of art" is a real principle, having its foundation in the human mind') and a prolific writer on landscape design.[72] From his writings we can extract a reasoned defence of the gardenesque principle in the flowerbed:

> The first point of distinctness I would urge is the propriety of keeping every individual flower distinct – no two allowed to touch. . . . I feel persuaded that, where beds of flowers are well conceived, the plants individually healthy, and blossoming freely, the relief afforded by intervening portions of cleanly raked soil is just the sort of relief that suits the human eye in the majority of cases.[73]

Errington attributed this principle to Loudon; it governed most early Victorian flower spacing.

Glendinning began his journalistic career writing in the *Gardener's Magazine* on specimen trees;[74] during the 1830s he was head gardener at Bicton, where he collaborated with Loudon on planting an arboretum (his successor James Barnes added the famous monkey-puzzle avenue).[75] Loddiges exerted a more immediate influence on planting style with his planting of Abney Park Cemetery as an arboretum, and the arboretum at his famous Hackney nursery in the form of a walk lined with irregularly spaced groups of trees.[76] Loudon adapted Loddiges's principle for an arboretum scheme in his *Illustrations of Landscape Gardening*, and it was to provide the model for Paxton's arboretum at Chatsworth in the 1830s.[77]

10 Bicton, the monkey-puzzle avenue. James Barnes planted this avenue with James Veitch in 1842, and widened it in a transplanting operation seven years later.

The Organization of the Garden

The problem of an organizing principle to connect otherwise scattered features made itself felt in the overall design of the garden as well as in its planting. The notion that particular garden features must evoke particular emotions in the spectator (by virtue of the passiveness of the mind) resulted in many late eighteenth-century gardens becoming collections of wide ranges of disparate buildings and objects; a glance at illustrations of Carmontelle's Parc Monceau will demonstrate the clutter of discordant images that such a garden could comprise.[78] The most famous example of such a garden in England in the early nineteenth century was Alton Towers, Staffordshire.

The fifteenth Earl of Shrewbury began his works on the garden at Alton before the end of the Napoleonic wars.

> The result . . . was one of the most singular anomalies to be met with among the country residences of England. An immense pile of building in the way of house, with a magnificent conservatory and chapel, but with scarcely a habitable room; a lofty prospect tower, not built on the highest part of the grounds; a bridge and an embankment over a valley, without water underneath; ponds and lakes on the tops of hills; a quadrangular pile of stabling in the midst of the pleasure ground; and, what may be said to have eclipsed, and still to eclipse, every thing else, a valley, naturally in a high degree romantic

> with wood, water, and rocks, filled with works of the highest degree of art in architecture and gardening ... such a labyrinth of terraces, curious architectural walls, trellis-work arbours, vases, statues, stairs, pavements, gravel and grass walks, ornamental buildings, bridges, porticoes, temples, pagodas, gates, iron railings, parterres, jets, ponds, streams, seats, fountains, caves, flower baskets, waterfalls, rocks, cottages, trees, shrubs, beds of flowers, ivied walls, rock-work, shell-work, root-work, moss houses, old trunks of trees, entire dead trees, &c., that it is utterly impossible for words to give any idea of the effect ...[79]

How could such a concatenation of diverse effects be given any feeling of unity? This was the problem that faced the sixteenth Earl, when he took possession of Alton in 1827. His first additions, such as a Choragic Monument to the previous Earl, and a series of conservatories by Robert Abraham, continued the classical style of his predecessor; but under the influence of Pugin, whom he commissioned to redesign the house, his taste swung radically to Gothic, and he began to impose a mediaevalizing vision on portions of the gardens. Nesfield, who was building a reputation as a designer of gardens appropriate to manors of the olden time, created a box-and-gravel bed in the pattern of the initial S, and tried to impose a greater harmony on some of the diverse architectural accompaniments. In the gardens generally, some of the profusion of features was simplified, but for some the result was an unhappy compromise:

> The present earl ... has obliterated a number of the walks, stairs, and shell-works; which we almost regret, because no trifling alteration can ever improve what is so far out of the reach of reason.

'The gardens have lost one character without gaining another', Loudon agreed. However, the head gardener, Alexander Forsyth, was by the 1840s carrying out a large-scale programme of planting rhododendrons and other flowering shrubs, developing the rock garden, experimenting with a heather garden, and filling the landscape with trees to remove the rawness of the contrasts between the disparate features; and in this work he was successful, for most commentators in the later nineteenth century found that the increased vegetation had a harmonizing influence on the garden.[80]

If such problems could occur on a great estate, the difficulties attending the designer of a suburban garden were magnified by the constricted scale of the site. Loudon and his associates warned repeatedly against attempting too much in a small space and producing incongruous results; Thomas Rutger, in particular, became a prolific source of model plans for the magazines.[81] One man's incongruity and confusion, however, could be another's successful unity of expression, as is shown by a villa garden that Loudon commended.

Samuel Barber, a neighbour of Wordsworth's at Grasmere, discovered Loudon ('a garden Encyclopedia is his only study') and became obsessed with the transformation of his grounds. To the Wordsworth circle he became a comic figure: 'His works at the cottage begin to be too ridiculous for anything', wrote Mary Wordsworth:

> Then he has his arched stone bridge, his waterfall, & is to have his Swiss bridge over the rocks to the alcove, that is to be, in the neighbourhood of the Fairy

11 Alton Towers, view of the valley garden. A generation of planting by Alexander Forsyth and others softened the disparities between the Earl of Shrewsbury's multifarious garden features.

> Chapel, & ten thousand other things – all found in the mass of wisdom contained in this said new book.[82]

Loudon, however, visiting his cottage and garden in 1831, pronounced them

> decidedly the most perfect things of the kind we have ever seen: notwithstanding the greatest temptation to indulge in extravagant fancies, nothing of the kind is to be found; and one wonders how it happens that the whole has escaped the common fate of even the finest places, viz. that of having some part incongruous with the rest.[83]

Barber's works certainly failed to observe the Wordsworthian requirement of respect for vernacular precedent, and were discordant with the gardening traditions of the Lakes; but from Loudon's point of view they illustrated the principle of thematic consistency, which in his eyes obviated the confused impressions of an Alton Towers.

Garden buildings were one difficulty; but since Repton – who boasted that he had incorporated no fewer than fifteen separate gardens at Ashridge – specialist gardens had grown to pose another problem for the designer. Woburn Abbey, another Repton composition, was celebrated for its heather garden, grass garden, and willow collection; and the American garden, or garden with peaty soil for growing rhododendrons and other flowering shrubs, became by the 1830s a virtual necessity for an estate of any pretension.[84]

The problems of garden organization were illustrated in 1840 by the competition for the Royal Botanic Society's garden in the inner circle of Regent's Park. Henry Laxton's original proposal was criticized for trying to cram too many features into the space, and the subsequent competitors veered between discordant inclusiveness and excessive reliance on some particular conceit to provide thematic unity – witness the plan of a Mr Essex, based on a map of the world, with a gardener's cottage at the north pole, lecture rooms in the Atlantic ocean, and the Sahara desert as a nursery.[85] The eventual design by Robert Marnock greatly simplified Laxton's, reducing the number of walks to a minimum, leaving the central mass of the garden an open lawn and screening the specialist gardens behind shrubberies and an elevated rockwork; the garden was bisected by a straight walk leading to the great conservatory, thus imposing an axis of symmetry.[86]

Marnock did not try the method of separating specialist gardens that he saw at Cassiobury, Hertfordshire, which he described in the same year as 'subdivided into many little compartments': 'These divisions or fences consist of laurel, box, yew, holly, spruce, &c. all of which are clipped into a great variety of forms'.[87] The lingering heritage of the eighteenth-century prospect, and the picturesque emphasis on distance, ensured that gardeners still thought in terms of a landscape spreading toward the distant view, and that architectural subdivision remained a decidedly minority practice until after mid-century.

From Rustic to Rococo

In condemning eighteenth-century naturalism, Loudon was also led to condemn an aesthetic mode which made statements about the primitive nature of man. The cult of ruins, in its extreme form, had led to the imitation of 'primitive' monuments such as Stonehenge; Adam Mickle had been involved in the creation of a 'Druids' Temple' at Swinton Park, Yorkshire, in the 1790s.[88] Far more gardens, however, based features not on the primitive past, but on the debased present: 'rustic' buildings, whose decoration suggested the crudest forms of construction, were admired for their picturesque quality, and could be safely introduced into landscape scenery as the most 'natural' of human structures. The main characteristic of the rustic style was the use of unbarked wood as a material, and the preservation or imitation of knotholes, stumps, and branches as part of the wooden structure. It was used not only for the façades and roofs of buildings, where it was often augmented by thatch, but for fences, bridges, seats, and flower baskets; the rustic basket in particular remained a popular

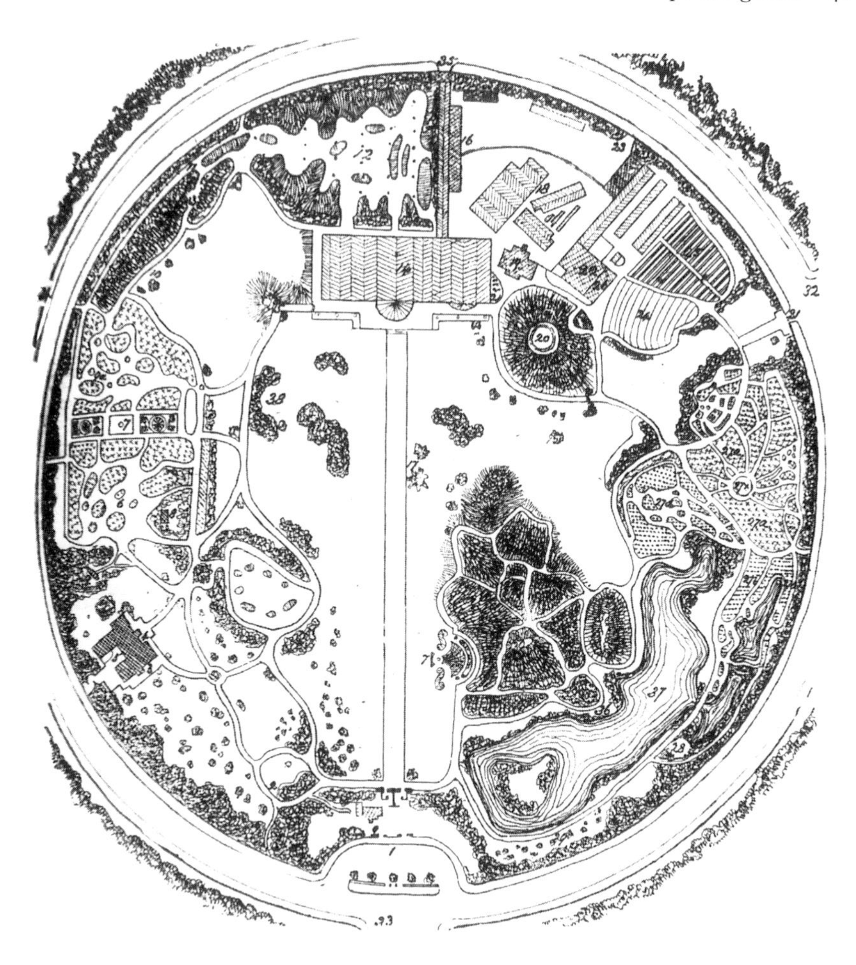

subject in gardens until after mid-century.[89]

Loudon included the rustic in the same general condemnation as the supposedly natural: in either case, 'the object is to deceive the spectator, and make him believe that the scene produced is of a fortuitous origin; or produced by the humble exertion of a country labourer.' The mind could take no pleasure in rustic buildings as works of art, 'unless we were told that they were artificial creations'.[90] Other critics, however, did not follow Loudon's extreme condemnation, and confined themselves to demanding the segregation of the rustic from the presence of other styles which would conflict with it; and the popularity of the style continued into the 1850s with little diminution. Books of designs for rustic garden furniture were produced during the 1840s by T.J. Ricauti, and H. Howlett, head gardener at St Osyth's Priory, Essex, won the *Cottage Gardener* prize for the best design of rustic baskets in 1851, producing a manual the following year.[91]

Attempts were also made to bring the rustic within the domain of art. Summerhouses thatched with moss were popular, and both Loudons

12 Regent's Park, plan of the Royal Botanic Society's garden. Robert Marnock's 1840 plan as carried out and modified by 1872.

13 A design from T. J. Ricauti's *Sketches for Rustic Work*, 1842.

recommended artistic mosshouses in which different colours of moss would be arranged in geometric patterns.[92] In 1850 Noel Humphreys suggested using rustic decorations for formal terraces, but Loudon would probably have rejected this idea as incongruous, as he would the juxtaposition of rustic bridge and vase of pelargoniums set in the lake at Bowes' Manor. He missed seeing Thomas Fish's famous Knowle Cottage, Sidmouth, so we do not have his comments on its juxtaposition of rustic beds, fishbowls, circular flowerstands, and rows of conch shells as edgings.[93]

Loudon promoted instead a manner of gardening which never received a stylistic label from contemporary critics, but which we may call the rococo revival, by analogy with a related decorative style of the time. Interior decoration based on the later years of Louis XIV and Louis XV began to appear in the 1820s, particularly in the work of Benjamin Dean Wyatt and his family; after the refurbishment of some rooms at Belvoir Castle for the Duchess of Rutland, its popularity spread rapidly, many aristocratic London houses being redecorated in this manner. By mid-century it was in sheer volume of works produced the most popular style of ornament, although by that time it had lost its critical esteem; its dominance at the Great Exhibition of 1851 led to widespread complaints about the standard of taste in the British arts.[94]

The gardens of Alexander Pope's day, before the arrival of the fully-fledged 'natural' style, won the praise of Loudon where they survived. Stowe, he thought, was perfect: 'nature has done little or nothing; man a great deal, and time has improved his labours'. (Contrast this with William Marshall's view, a quarter-century earlier, that 'Art has evidently done too much at Stowe'.)[95] And, whether by cultural convergence or by direct imitation, design elements based on the early eighteenth century began to reappear in the 1820s. The result was the creation of a semi-formal effect, identifiable as artificial while still retaining some of the familiar characteristics of the informal styles. The elements of this rococo revival can be detected on three different levels, from the large-scale organization of the garden down to the pattern of flowerbeds.

The symmetrical distribution of non-matching parts appears as a motif in Repton's flower-garden at Beaudesert, whose two parallel sections were laid out in different patterns. A similar plan was carried out at Ross Priory, by 1821, with two adjacent flower-gardens in symmetrical and free-style layouts.[96] The landscape gardener Philip Masey, who was promoted by Loudon, can stand as the representative exponent of the rococo mode in overall organization. The central features of his landscapes showed a symmetrical or axial organization, but the units would not match internally (geometric gardens of different pattern, for example), and elaborately irregular layouts like those of an early eighteenth-century 'wilderness' would be used as sections of the garden. Masey and his coevals probably derived much of their inspiration from Batty Langley, the most accessible of rococo designers, whose influence can be seen in Henry Laxton's plan for the Royal Botanic Society's garden.[97]

Formality without rectilinearity: the attempt to create recognizably formal features while still making obeisance to eighteenth-century ideas of the beauty of curves could be found in many contexts in the 1820s and 1830s. Robert Errington published a plan for a flower-garden composed of symmetrically arranged curves. Alfred Fox's maze at Glendurgan, Cornwall (1833), was laid out asymmetrically, using curving hedges.[98] Erasmus Darwin's attempt to derive our notions of beauty from the curves of the female form was developed by Sir Henry Steuart in the 1820s into a demand for laying out plantations of trees in ovals and circles. (Loudon in this instance supported the picturesque theorists in favouring irregular masses for plantations.)[99] The circle was especially favoured, as the form most independent of arbitrary associations. Loudon, following an idea of Repton's, was advocating circles as early as 1831, and at the end of his life was planning an arrangement of circular beds for 'standards of curious shrubs' like *Cotoneaster* and *Calophaca* at Kiddington Hall.[100] Loudon's circles became a major point of debate in the 1840s. Dickens put a circular lake and island in Mr Wemmick's cockney garden, but the real thing existed at Lord Ongley's Swiss garden at Old Warden, Bedfordshire.[101]

The characteristic motifs of rococo ornament in interior decoration were the acanthus, the volute, and C- and S-shaped curves. These rococo

14 Glendurgan, the maze. Alfred Fox planted this asymmetrical maze of cherry laurel in 1833.

curves also found their way into the flower garden as shapes for flowerbeds; Loudon began publishing bedding plans in rococo styles as early as 1828, when he featured William Baillie's plan of the flower garden at Dropmore; and thereafter the *Gardener's Magazine* reproduced several plans involving volutes, braces, half-moons, S-scrolls, and shell patterns.[102] Architects' flower gardens tended to rely heavily on such patterns; Charles Fowler produced a plan for half-moon beds in the parterre in front of his new conservatory at Syon Park.

Loudon encouraged plans which were at least broadly symmetrical. However, many older flower gardens on the naturalistic model had made use of serpentine beds drawn on the ground in more or less random assemblages: so many examples of Hogarth's curve of beauty. Examples may be seen in Maria Jackson's *Florist's Manual* of 1822. Before long, rococo beds, distinguished from the serpentine ones only by formality of curvature or a pointed coupling, began to join in such scrambles, and in consequence they began to share in the same condemnation.[103] Loudon's grumbles about newt-shaped beds led in due course to Shirley Hibberd's complaint about beds that twisted 'like eels in misery', but by the later date (Hibberd was writing in the 1850s) the rococo mode – still being practised by designers like Joshua Major – was included in the diatribe.[104]

15 Old Warden, the circular lake. Formality without rectilinearity in Lord Ongley's Swiss garden of the 1820s.

As the rococo revival lost its brief status as a favoured mode, gardeners turned their attention increasingly to the gardens of the seventeenth century. Charles M'Intosh, in particular, put the case for the superiority of rectilinear styles, citing Victor Cousin on the natural taste for regularity. He depicted the novice gardener reading the available literature and becoming corrupted by the emphasis on irregularity and curved lines:

> His square tulip beds, and his dahlias, planted at equal distances, must be given up for curvature and irregularity; and his
> 'Garden trim, with daisies pied,'
> must be made as nearly as possible to resemble a wild wilderness of thickets and patches, as unnatural and fantastic as the arabesques of the Mahometans . . .

As cases in point, he singled out for disapproval William Rollisson's 'finically grotesque figures' in the garden of Bethlem Hospital, and Loudon's Birmingham Botanic Garden, 'the plan of the borders' of which had been 'apparently borrowed from the old-fashioned tamboured muslin or printed calicoes'.[105] Naturalism and rococo, on the scale of the flower garden at least, were lumped together as indistinguishable, and equally to be condemned. Despite such advocacy of the virtues of straight lines, however, the popularity of the rococo style continued, unpublicized save

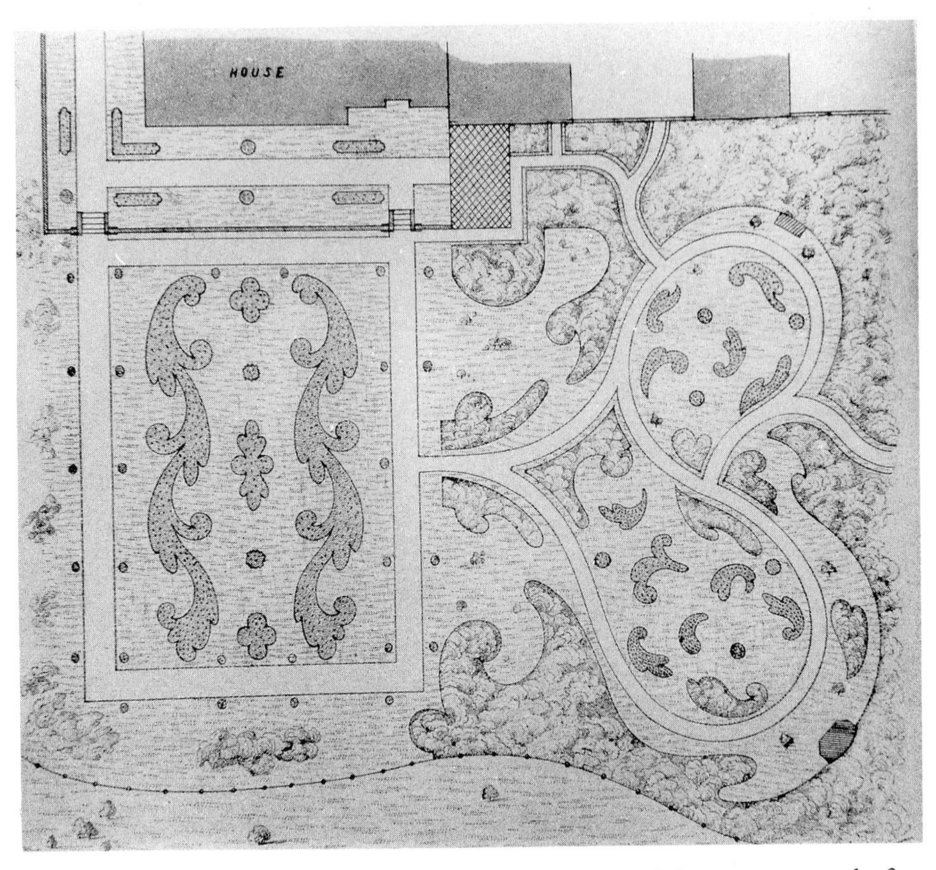

16 Joshua Major and Son, plan for rococo revival flower beds, from *The Ladies' Assistant in the Formation of their Flower Gardens* (1861).

by the polemics against it, into the latter part of the century; and after the 1850s, when several rococo features were incorporated into Shirley Hibberd's *Rustic Adornments for Homes of Taste*, it was absorbed under the general heading of rustic.[106]

The Emergence of the Rock Garden

Loudon acknowledged difficulties with the application of his principle of imitation to rocky scenery. The introduction of non-local rocks, although becoming a possibility with the spread of the railways, would obliterate 'the associations connected with solid natural rocks'; and so he concluded that a natural rocky outcrop could be turned into a work of art by exotic planting.[107]

Two traditions of rockwork construction were available to the gardeners of Loudon's generation. On the one hand, the naturalistic landscape of the eighteenth century had encouraged the study of rock formations for their accurate reproduction, intended to simulate the work of nature; the sketches for rocks in Le Rouge's *Cahiers* are the most famous example of this tendency, In England Humphry Repton had created a realistic rocky embankment at Sezincote, and at Welbeck Abbey he introduced a rockwork by plundering the nearby Creswell Crags for stone. Other gardens were created in disused quarries, while Uvedale Price linked rockworks to the tradition of the sublime.[108]

The alternative tradition descended from the use of irregular rockwork as a fanciful motif in baroque and rococo gardens, most notably in grottoes such as Pope's and later specimens decorated with shellwork. The rockery as a display of fossils and geological curiosities emerged as a notable and frequent garden feature with the Chelsea Physic Garden rockery in the 1780s; such rockeries continued to display shellwork and semi-architectural features like rocky arches; fanciful grottoes continued at least until mid-century.[109] Benjamin Andrews created a rockwork in Peckham from bricks, flints, and spar, studded with inset shells, incorporating a fountain, and yet could describe it as 'inartificial'. Another Peckham rockery, 'of itself a perfect parterre of many colours', became notorious in the 1840s for the use of red coral, 'the bright vermilion of which eclipses the hue of all the Phloxes and Mesembryanthemums that can be made to grow' on its surface. Price, who had thought that even the most whimsical rockeries could be redeemed by trailing plants, did not live to encounter this development.[110]

During the 1820s, a modified version of this rococo conceit emerged: one that was more 'natural', in that it used natural stone, and generally one type of stone only, instead of fanciful combinations, but whose construction obeyed rules of picturesque composition rather than specific rules of geological accuracy. The Academician Reinagle made it the first requirement of a rockery that it have a definite shape – a pointed shape being preferred. During the 1840s James Lothian and Freeman Roe helped to popularize tumbled masses of boulders instead of concretions of disparate objects, but continued to incorporate fountains and pools.[111]

The plants now grouped together as 'alpines' had, from the eighteenth century, a reputation as difficult subjects for cultivation, and were typically grown as pot plants; however, interest in their culture was growing. From Cassiobury's alpine valley in the 1820s to the lists of Mangles in 1839 and Lothian in 1845, one can see a steady increase in the number of alpine species recommended, with Hoole House boasting the most extensive collection of all.[112] The cultivation of alpine plants, not familiar in England, on a rockery was indeed one way in which it could be recognized as a work of art, and by 1834, Loudon could specify the culture of alpines as the purpose of proper rockeries, while distinguishing three approaches to the shaping of the rocks.

The first approach was the Reptonian naturalistic one, best exemplified by the 'rocky scars on the face of a steep bank' at Blenheim.[113] The second approach was that of the scale model, and Loudon's recommended example was Hoole House, Cheshire, where during the 1820s Lady Broughton erected a rockery as the termination to her flower garden. Spiky conical masses of rock towered three to four times the height of a man.

> The design of the rockwork was taken from a small model representing the mountains of Savoy, with the valley of Chamouni ... the part of the model that represents 'la Mer de Glace' is worked with grey limestone, quartz, and spar. It has no cells for plants: the spaces are filled up with broken fragments of white marble, to look like snow; and the spar is intended for the glacier.

The rocks were erected at the end of an expanse of lawn which had been filled with S-shaped beds when Loudon visited in 1831, but by his second visit these had been replaced, on his recommendation, with rows of circular beds.[114] The scale-model approach was seldom attempted elsewhere, however (an exception being the Surrey Zoological Garden),[115] and was not to be taken further for half a century.

Loudon praised 'the contrast between the smooth flat surface of the lawn, with the uniformity of the circular beds, and the great irregularity of the surrounding rockwork' at Hoole, and this contrast became the basis of the third approach. Both Loudon and M'Intosh singled out Richard Forrest's rockery at Syon Park as a supreme example of the style:

> The imitation is, indeed, so complete, that when the back of the visitor is turned to the superb conservatory, he might almost fancy himself at the entrance of a Highland glen. The turf on the edge of this rock-work is in parts studded with moss, while little knolls, which nobody would doubt being real ant-hills, are covered with wild thyme and hare-bells.

(A later generation, to whom the abrupt contrast of parterre and rockwork had become offensive, dismantled Forrest's rocks and scattered them further from the house.)[116] William Wells, patron of the arts at Redleaf, Kent, further developed the penetration of the pleasure ground by rocky scenery; finding abundant rock beneath the surface of the ground, he had portions of it excavated to leave a series of ridges and valleys in the lawns descending from the house. The effect was augmented by the creation of a rough stone pathway 'like the lava pavements in Portici'. Flowering shrubs and half-hardy flowers were planted in the rocky beds and gullies thus provided; the gardener, John Cox, became an early authority on alpines.[117] With Redleaf, we can finally see the arrival of the rock garden as distinguished from the rockwork.

Picturesque Colour

Little attention was paid to colour in gardening literature before the Victorian period. This cannot have been because there was a monotony of colour in the landscape garden; we know that gardens like Painshill boasted collections of exotics that must have displayed a fair variety of colours, and that trees like the purple beech were being offered by nurserymen by the 1770s. But the literature of the time gives no indication of how such a degree of colour was to be dealt with: no instructions for grouping, no advice on colour combinations to be encouraged or avoided. William Chambers announced that subtle gradations of colour were characteristic of the Chinese garden, but apart from James Meader, no English writer of the eighteenth century even gives a plant list arranged by colour.[118]

This strange omission can be accounted for only as the result of a basic prejudice of eighteenth-century philosophy. Locke had announced a distinction between primary and secondary qualities. Form was primary, inherent in the object, the essential element in perception; colour was an unstable side-effect. The artistic consequence was that colour was relegated to a subordinate status. Eighteenth-century painting tended to make line its organizing feature, on which colour was kept dependent by general rules: the use of areas of uniform colour for broad effect, the subordination

Rockwork, Lawn, and Camellia-house, at Hoole House from the North-East.

17 Hoole House, view of the rock garden and lawn. Figures give the scale of Lady Broughton's rock garden, modelled on the Alps at Chamonix. The original S-shaped beds on the lawn had been replaced by 1837 by circular beds on Loudon's recommendation.

of individual colours to a prevailing tone, the separation of warm from cold colours, the darkening of the foreground and lightening of the distance to give greater definition to the principal objects. The eighteenth-century landscape garden was essentially a garden of form, in which colour was considered as an accident – a stimulus to the emotions perhaps, capable of provoking agreeable or disagreeable sensations, but an unstable and temporary effect that was of insufficient power to enter into the basic organization of the garden.

This attitude toward form and colour did not go unchallenged. Berkeley had argued that we see 'only diversity of colours', that form was a matter of mental inference; scientific and speculative thinking in the early nineteenth century swung around to a conception of colour as primary, and form as derived.[119] When one compares Richard Morris in 1825, taking it for granted that 'form is the grand characteristic of matter', with Joseph F. Johnson a half-century later remarking equally blandly 'how vastly dependent form is on colour', one can appreciate the revolution in thought that had taken place.[120]

At the beginning of the nineteenth century, there was no body of advice on which the gardener could draw for the handling of colour. Repton was the first gardening writer to introduce a technical discussion of colour theory into his works, but this was unavailable to the great mass of gardeners until 1840, and not excessively helpful in any case.[121]

Picturesque theory helped to erode some colour prejudices, for instance, by emphasizing broken colour. But a fundamental principle of the picturesque was its assertion that garden design should be based on the study of paintings, and that meant on the whole the continuation of eighteenth-century colour principles. Price thought the 'too distinct and splendid' colour of spring blossom destructive of unity; Walter Nicol argued that green was 'the eye's own colour', and that flowerbeds on the lawn would tire the eye; the planting of foregrounds with dark green foliage, with progressively lighter colours shading off into the 'blue distance', was recommended by theorists from W. S. Gilpin to C. H. J. Smith.[123] In order, therefore, to come to terms with the new perception of colour, it was necessary for gardeners to assert their independence from painting, and this they did, beginning with Repton: 'I am at a loss', declared Henry Bailey, head gardener at Nuneham, 'to trace the analogy between a landscape painting and a flower garden'.[124]

However, the word 'picturesque' carried with it an ambiguity that Price had never intended; for if it was based on the study of paintings, then as the conventions of painting changed, sooner or later the 'picturesque' would have to follow suit. From Constable onward, prevailing tones gave way to the direct observation of the local colour of objects, and as painting ceased to imply Reynolds and Gainsborough, and came to embrace successively Turner, Dyce, Mulready, and the Pre-Raphaelite Brotherhood, so to a degree the gardener's 'picturesque' evolved with it.[125]

Colour experiments in the garden had two materials with which to work: trees and flowers. Price had drawn attention to the beauty of autumn tints in foliage, but this was in part because he regarded the colours of spring and summer flowering as destructive of the unity required for landscape painting; and perhaps for this very reason gardening practice tended instead to follow Repton, who had defended the proscribed seasons.[126] Joshua Major experimented with grouping shrubs by colour in the 1820s, and gardens such as Claremont, Montreal Park, and Highclere had become famous for their flowering shrubs by the 1830s. At Highclere the islands were planted with rhododendrons and other American shrubs, whose reflections in the summer reminded some spectators 'of some of Claude Loraine's glowing sunsets'.[127]

About 1840, the time Price's works were reissued, the idea of planting for autumn colour began to reawaken interest; once again Highclere was the garden cited as an example; the *Gardeners' Chronicle* in its first year put out a request for readers to take note of suitable shrubs, and writers began noting more regularly the effect of wild cherries, oaks, and rhus.[128] Permanent coloration of leaves also tended to find few enthusiasts during the first quarter of the century, but after that the taste gradually grew. James Mangles recommended grouping robinias, hollies, and bronze beech for colour effect at the end of the 1830s; and a few years later Admiral Grey defended the purple beech at Howick Grange to his wife: 'The contrast of its dark leaves with the vivid green of the oaks & the white May which literally covers the thorns is more beautiful than I can describe'.[129]

Most experiment in colour, however, took place within the flower garden rather than the wider landscape. Botanical exploration of South Africa and North America was yielding increasing numbers of brightly coloured flowers which first, as tender plants, made their way into the greenhouse; but in 1826 one of the first articles in Loudon's *Gardener's Magazine* could describe an experiment at Phoenix Park, Dublin, in

18 A fountain in a garden in Peckham, 1838. Composed of a variety of stones and ornamented with shells, this exemplifies the survival of the rococo manner in rockwork.

planting such flowers out in beds during the summer.[130] The preferred mode of grouping flowers in the first quarter-century was in highly variegated mixtures, probably as a result of the picturesque emphasis on broken and intricate colour. By the 1820s, however, voices like Leigh Hunt's could be heard, declaring that 'we are not fond enough of *colours*' and calling for a greater use of primary colours in large masses: 'the largest bed will look well, if of one beautiful colour; while the most beautiful varieties may be inharmoniously mixed up'.[131] Loudon advanced the same argument more systematically:

> Variety, however, is not produced by mixture, but by a succession of different things. Every part of a mass, formed on the principle of mixture, is the same in appearance, and the general effect monotonous; but every part of a varied whole differs from every other part, and the general effect is harmonious. In a mixture the most opposite things may adjoin each other; but in a variety things only adjoin which have a particular relation to one another, and to the effect to be produced.[132]

These arguments bore fruit; by 1830 Loudon could point to experiments at massing at the Royal Lodge at Windsor, at Robert Mangles's garden at Whitmore Lodge, Surrey, and above all at Dropmore, where the gardener, Philip Frost, seemed to him to have best demonstrated 'the advantage of placing beauty in masses'.[133]

From Public Walk to People's Park

At the beginning of this chapter we looked at the relation between the landscape garden and the tenant communities that were sometimes moved to make way for it. But what of the public at large? How much did they see of the great gardens of the day? The attitude which could contemplate the removal of a village in order to improve the landowner's view was not conducive to allowing public access to the garden, whether in the form of footpath rights or of allowing visitors. Prince Pückler-Muskau noted that:

> Whenever the high road lies through an English park, a part of the wall is replaced by a ha-ha, or a transparent iron fence, that the passer-by may throw a modest and curious glance into the forbidden paradise: but this effort exhausts the stock of liberality usually possessed by an English landowner.[134]

Loudon always noted whether an owner allowed the public to visit his garden, and praised those who provided this public service.

The question of public access was exacerbated by the problem of vandalism. In 1825 it was proposed to exclude the public from the grounds of Waldershare Park, Kent, because of obscene graffiti in the summerhouses and depredations in the Wilderness – 'it is treated more like the grounds of an alehouse than a nobleman's plantation'. Nearly half a century later, Joseph Hooker reported that 'mischievous and vulgar-minded persons' were carving graffiti on King William's Temple at Kew, and proposed fencing it off. On the other hand, there were those who claimed that it was not the working but the middle classes who were responsible for most vandalism.[135]

Outside London, there were few towns in the country which could boast extensive public walks. 'Till lately', wrote Loudon, 'Hyde Park, at London, and a spot called *The Meadows*, near Edinburgh were the only equestrian gardens in Britain; and neither were well arranged'. During the years that followed the Napoleonic wars, recovery from recession resulted in a building boom that encroached steadily on the existing open spaces.[136] Where speculative building schemes made some provision of parkland, this was seldom accessible except to the scheme's residents: Regent's Park was not fully open to the public until 1841. Such enclaves of publicly accessible garden as did exist were commercially managed: first, the gardens of inns and tea houses, and 'pleasure gardens' such as Cremorne and Vauxhall in London and Belle Vue Gardens in Manchester;[137] second, cemeteries established by joint-stock companies (for local authorities seldom attempted cemetery management until the Burials Acts of 1850 and 1852);[138] and third, the gardens of the botanical and horticultural societies that began to replace the older florists' societies in the 1820s, and which served as a venue for flower shows.[139]

In 1833, a Select Committee on Public Walks reported that with the expansion of building, 'the means of occasional exercise and recreation in the fresh air are every day lessened', and recommended the greater provision of open spaces for leisure pursuits. The early attempts to provide such facilities, however, rested with private benefactors, as in the cases of the Derby Arboretum (designed by Loudon for Joseph Strutt, 1840) and Prince's Park, Liverpool (designed by Paxton for Richard Vaughan Yates, 1842); and these, at least initially, limited their times of opening and charged admission fees in the same manner as existing gardens. Even a municipally established park like the Nottingham Arboretum (designed by Samuel Curtis, 1850–52) charged admission, and when five years

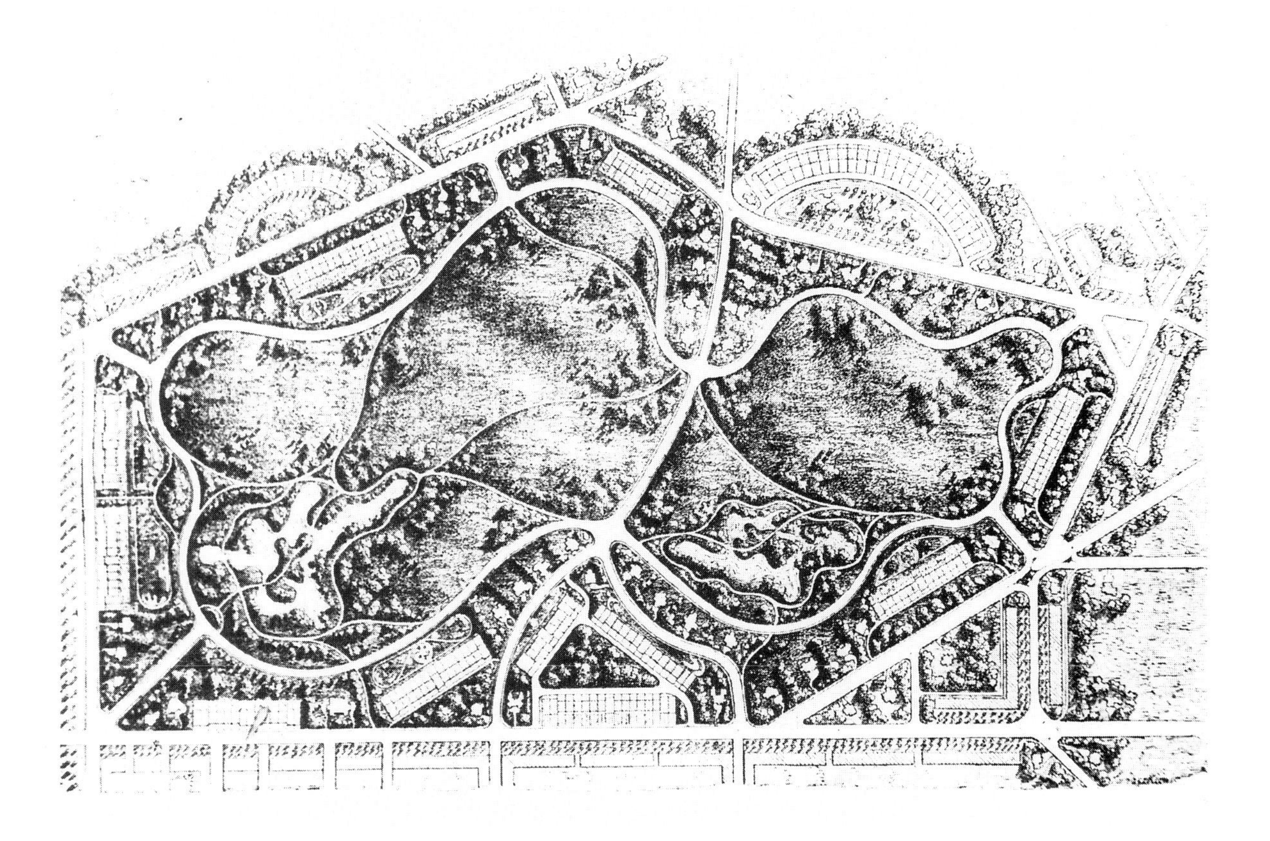

19 Birkenhead Park, plan of the park in the 1870s. Paxton's adaptation of the landscape tradition to an urban site, with rockworks and shrubberies to screen and channel views, creating an implied axis of symmetry.

later this practice was ruled illegal, the council retrenched heavily on its maintenance.[140]

Loudon was one of the most insistent advocates of the provision of public parks. His 1830 design for the Birmingham Botanic Garden was not carried out as he had hoped, but in 1836 he laid out a park in Gravesend, and three years later received the commission for the Derby Arboretum. The basis of the Gravesend park was an elaborately serpentine path, and a somewhat similar, though chastened, walkway led the visitor to the Derby Arboretum through the sequence of botanical orders (a device borrowed from the arboretum at Loddiges's nursery); but at Derby, as in the Birmingham plan, a series of straight paths crossing at the centre provided a more emphatic axis of symmetry.[141]

The first expressly designed municipal park, whose ground was dedicated to the free recreation of the local residents, was Birkenhead Park, designed by Joseph Paxton in 1843 and laid out by his protégé Edward Kemp; it promptly became known as 'the people's park', and as the American landscape gardener Olmsted recorded, 'the baker of Birkenhead has the pride of an OWNER in it'. Each half of the park contained a lake of irregular outline, with an island in the middle to prevent the extent of the lake from being taken in from any one view. The excavation of the lakes threw up masses of rocks, which were formed into mounds at the junctions of paths to conceal their courses. The park narrowed toward its centre, where it was bisected by a road; mounds and shrubberies were arranged at intervals to constrict the lawns into channels, thus creating an implied axis of symmetry of which Loudon would have approved.[142] The use of mounds was a development of his gardenesque planting principle, and in the wake of Birkenhead it was adopted by other parks, such as William Pontey's Ipswich Arboretum.[143]

In the year that works began on Birkenhead, an abortive proposal was made to extend a railway line to Kendal, thus obtruding on the scenery of the Lakes. Wordsworth, attacking the project, discounted the idea that the absence of a rail link would be inconvenient to tourists, and denied that the poor were interested in picturesque scenery, which required a greater education of sensibility than they possessed.[144] The success of Birkenhead, however, demonstrated that they were not insensible to the merits of gardenesque scenery, and the establishment of municipal parks began to increase. James Pennethorne, a protégé of John Nash, was responsible for the creation of a series of major London parks – Victoria, Battersea, and the abortive Albert Park in north London. Victoria Park had been begun in 1841, but in the wake of Birkenhead a lake was added to the original design, and a Paxton protégé, John Gibson, was called in to revise the planting scheme; he and Pennethorne collaborated again on Battersea. In 1846 three parks, all designed by Joshua Major, were opened in Manchester and Salford, and like Birkenhead these made provision for athletics and popular games.[145] By the middle of the century, the early designs of Loudon and Paxton were bearing fruit all over the country, and the style of Birkenhead in particular was being imported into town after town. Garden design was no longer an affair for the wealthy alone; its impact was now extending down to the lowest classes, and was becoming a matter of public policy.

3

The uses of the past

Theories of Garden History

In gardening, as in all other aspects of life, the nineteenth century witnessed the ascendancy of history as a governing value. Whether in the deliberate revival of the styles and customs of previous ages, or simply in the conviction that history conferred meaning, and that the significance of a thing could only be grasped by understanding its process of development, the importance of history as a mental framework grew rapidly through the early decades of the century.

The history of gardening had tended to be the history of how the correct taste triumphed over the false.[1] With the coming of the nineteenth century, however, there was an important change. The gardening traditions of different countries and of different periods began to be looked at as expressions of their particular cultures, to be judged on their own terms rather than by a supposed universal standard. The general effect was a relativity of styles, with the further consequence that each style might be appropriate to particular circumstances. Loudon thought that historical knowledge would teach the gardener 'how to effect the same object according to different systems', so that he could 'adopt the style or school best calculated for the situation, climate, and circumstances in which he is placed'.[2]

The new attitude toward history meant that for the first time people were put in the position of having to choose the style of their gardens from a range of equally commendable options. The confident assumption of their predecessors – still held in the 1820s by a Richard Morris – that the orders of classical architecture were eternal verities was fast being eroded, not only by Gothic but by non-European styles; Repton, for example, proposed the adoption of Indian architecture, as something independent of all established associations.[3]

Garden history thus became a matter of some urgency for gardeners, and the early years of the century saw the study reach a level of achievement from which it afterwards declined. The historical section of Loudon's 1822 *Encyclopaedia of Gardening* surpassed in scope and insight anything produced before, and most things since; even he, however, looked up to William Forsyth the younger (son of the royal gardener), who was preparing the definitive history of the subject. Forsyth's unpublished manuscript was sold on his death in 1835 and subsequently lost; but it had served as the basis for George Johnson's *History of English Gardening* in 1826, and Johnson was to become the principal authority on the history of horticulture for the next generation.[4] His magazine the *Cottage Gardener*, like virtually every magazine of the 1830s and 1840s, ran features on garden history,[5] and Donald Beaton set an example by researching the history of the garden where he was stationed.[6]

Loudon put forward a general theory of garden history, based on an opposition of formal and informal styles, each appropriate to a certain stage of civilization.

> Both these styles are, in different stages of society, equally congenial to the human mind. The Geometric Style was most striking and pleasing, and most obviously displayed wealth and taste, in an early state of society, and in countries where the general scenery was wild, irregular, and natural, and man, comparatively, uncultivated and unrefined; while, on the other hand, in modern times, and in countries subjected to cultivation, and covered with enclosures, rows of trees, and roads, all in regular lines, or forms, and where society is in a higher state of cultivation, the natural, or irregular style, from its rarity in such a country, and from the sacrifice of profitable lands requisite to make room for it, becomes equally a sign of wealth and taste.[7]

This theory was repeated by David Gorrie, Noel Humphreys, and Robert Marnock, among others, and became one of the most commonly accepted assumptions of the period.[8]

A refinement of this theory was the division of gardening into a series of national styles, which were reflected in the history of English gardens. Any traveller in Europe would be able to notice certain broad distinctions between the gardens of France, Italy, and the Netherlands, and these provided the designer's main alternatives to the so-called English style. Charles M'Intosh, in his *Flower Garden* of 1837–8, spelled out the differences in terms of stylistic attributes:

> ITALIAN: characterized by one or more terraces, sometimes supported by parapet walls, on the coping of which vases of different forms are occasionally placed, either as ornaments, or for the purpose of containing plants. Where the ground slopes much, and commands a supply of water from above, *jets-d'eau* and fountains are introduced with good effect.
>
> FRENCH: The French partially adopt the Italian style close to their chateaux and houses; and, beyond the terraces, lay out parterres, sometimes in very complicated figures.
>
> DUTCH: The leading character of the Dutch style is rectangular formality, and what may sometimes be termed clumsy artifice, such as yew trees cut out in the form of statues, though they require a label to inform the observer what they mean to represent.
>
> ENGLISH: It is generally understood, that the style termed English in gardening consists in an artful imitation of nature, and is consequently much dependent on aspect and accessaries. In the true English style, accordingly, we have neither the Italian terrace, the French parterre, nor the Dutch clipt evergreens. ... The pretended adherence to nature ... is wholly a style of conventional artifice, not so stiff and formal, indeed, as the Italian terraces, the French parterres, or the Dutch clipt evergreens, but still strictly artificial.[9]

From Repton was derived the notion that English gardening had been governed by each of these national styles in turn: in the sixteenth century, English gardening had begun as an imitation of the Italian, to be followed by the French after the restoration, and by the Dutch after the glorious revolution, before a novel English style emerged with William Kent.

Repton further suggested that the French and Dutch styles were merely variants of the Italian, and could be subsumed under the same label. To use any of these styles (or variants of the Italian style), therefore, was in effect to explore the national past of England.[10]

Preservation and Restoration

Loudon had expressed a special interest in old formal gardens that had survived to some degree intact. Busbridge, Knole, and Bilston won his approval for remaining in their original taste; Wroxton was particularly interesting, because the geometrical style had been kept up in every subsequent improvement. The Elizabethan mansion at Holme Lacy was preserved 'as a national curiosity', and Loudon plainly wished that the garden should receive similar treatment.[11] He was not alone in this fascination: Price and Knight both declaimed against 'Capability' Brown as the destroyer of terraces, and wished for their preservation; Price bitterly regretted having destroyed his own terraces at Foxley in his heedless youth.[12] The opening years of the nineteenth century, accordingly, saw the first efforts in garden conservation and restoration.

Avenues became the first conservationist issue. As early as 1790 Henry Holland was advising that a system of avenues be preserved, and Uvedale Price advocated their retention even when badly placed. Thereafter it became a consistent theme among picturesque theorists that venerable avenues ought not to be destroyed, even when the writers opposed the planting of new ones. Repton, who had made the compromise suggestion that an avenue could be partially retained but broken through in places to make it look less obtrusive from the side, was denounced as a vandal. By 1843, the *Gardeners' Chronicle* could offer the confident advice that it was barbarous to fell an avenue, and good taste to restore one where the line was incomplete.[13]

The second great issue was the treatment of ruins. For the eighteenth century, a ruin was a stimulus for meditation on time's reversals rather than archaeological evidence of a particular past, but for the gardeners of Loudon's generation, this attitude stood in the way of a genuine appreciation of history.[14] Repton opposed the tradition of making artificial ruins, followed by Loudon, Lauder, and Lindley, who argued that they subverted proper associations:

> The mere broken battlements – the mere ruined walls – the uncasemented windows contain no beauty in themselves. It is the history bound up with the ruin of that building that yields the charm. . . . It seems clear then that a mere ruin – and above all an artificial ruin of a building – with no connected ASSOCIATION OF IDEAS – has in itself *no beauty at all*.[15]

The 1820s and 1830s saw some scattered examples of a transitional stage: the creation of artificial ruins using real materials. The last major complex of ruins to be assembled before the prohibition sank in was at Virginia Water, where in 1826 a series of columns and other remains from Leptis Magna was erected to suggest a ruined temple, some pieces left prostrate. But unlike Mediterranean countries, Britain was not rich in classical remains, and pseudo-classical ruins were the first to go out of fashion.

Lord Wenlock, on the other hand, acquired the screen of York Minster, damaged in the famous fire, and turned it into a rockwork in his garden at Escrick Park.[16]

Once artificial ruins were out of the way, the treatment of genuine ruins remained as a problem. The first reaction against the sentimental cult of ruins was often simply to deny their nostalgic associations, and treat them purely as elements in a visual scheme. As late as 1845, the remains of a Roman wall in Chapel Field, Norwich, could be referred to as 'several hundred yards of rock-work-wall, admirably adapted for Alpine plants'.[17] Several ruins, such as those of Bayham Abbey, Battle Abbey, and Farnham Castle, were laid out as flower gardens in the early nineteenth century; in 1831, the remains of the abbey at Bury St Edmunds were taken over as the site of a botanic garden, while those of the Leicester Abbey were turned into a commercial nursery. At Canterbury, William Masters created the Dane John park, incorporating part of the old city walls; at York, Henry Baines turned the grounds of St Mary's Abbey into an ornamental garden with serpentine walks to serve as the setting for the new York Museum.[18]

Loudon's attitude towards ventures like these was ambiguous, but when planting encroached on the ruins themselves he protested. Signs of newly dug ground, he complained at Dryburgh Abbey, always created an idea of yesterday that checked feelings of veneration. His favoured models were Berry Pomeroy Castle and Melrose Abbey, where art was limited to exhibiting the remains of antiquity: no planting, no training of ivy. At Lochleven, he warned that trees planted near the ruin would eventually obscure it, and recommended their removal.[19] This respectful attitude took a long time to become standard; however, the impulse to augment the associations of age by clothing stone in vegetation was strong, and in the 1850s Donald Beaton was still urging ivy enthusiasts 'to forget that there is any thing like naturally-grown Ivy in the world, and getting rid of the idea of covered ruins, and all poetic fancies about Ivy'.[20]

The same conflict between respectful preservation and free manipulation affected attitudes toward surviving old gardens. Loudon preferred retention intact, as evidence of the taste of previous generations; in 1831 he visited Levens Hall, Westmorland, and voiced his disapproval of 'introducing georginas [dahlias] and other modern plants in this genuine specimen of garden antiquities'.[21] David Gorrie echoed this attitude in his plea that modern plants should be avoided in the restoration of Barncluith.[22]

Levens itself, whether or not Loudon knew it, was a restoration. The topiary garden had been created about 1700, but during the eighteenth century its maintenance had lapsed, and visitors late in the century made no mention of topiary.[23] In 1810 Alexander Forbes became head gardener, a position he was to occupy until 1862, and began to restore the garden, replanting some nine miles of box edging and recutting the topiary. It is difficult to say how much of the conception of the garden is Forbes's, for I know of no documentation that would show whether he recut the topiary to a known original pattern or innovated his designs. He certainly added new figures of his own, including all those in golden yew; the crowned lion, family crest of the Howards, was his, and it is possible that

20 Levens Hall, topiary figures. The letter B stood for the Bagot family, and was probably one of the figures added by Alexander Forbes.

the Tudor-centred symbolism (figures of Queen Elizabeth, judge's wig, etc.) was Forbes' work, carved out of the overgrown bushes left by his predecessor.[24] Another old topiary scheme was similarly restored at Chastleton in 1828.[25]

Genuine restorations slid easily into imitations of period styles. At Walmer Castle, Kent, William Pitt planted a walled garden in a supposedly monastic style.[26] In 1804, while Wordsworth was invoking a 'Chaucerian' precedent for an arbour at Coleorton, Repton was designing an old English garden, complete with maze and topiary, to accompany his son's Tudor-style lodge at Woburn; by 1813, working on his new terrace garden at Beaudesert, he was pleased to report that 'we are restoring the place to what they remember it in the beginning of the last century'.[27] Loudon, at the time of his death, was about to embark on restoring the garden of Castle Kennedy to a Le Nôtre condition, a project eventually carried out rather differently by Archibald Fowler.[28]

The Return to Formality

The 1820s were still largely the era of John Nash, of Papworth, of Henry Phillips's *Sylva Florifera* – of flowing landscapes in a 'free and easy' style

21 Virginia Water. Fragments from the ruins of Leptis Magna, assembled in 1826 to suggest a ruined temple.

poised somewhere between 'nature' and 'art', dominated by the flowering shrubbery. Flower gardens of increasing formality could be found in the work of Papworth and Lewis Kennedy, but these still tended to accompany subordinate buildings like conservatories and aviaries instead of forming a primary element in the garden.[29]

To provide a formal setting for the house could therefore be seen as revivalist in itself, regardless of its period style. Uvedale Price and Thomas Hope both defended symmetry in the garden as an absolute value, independent of historic character: Hope invoked the geometric design of snowflakes and the bilateral symmetry of the face to show that regularity was not in itself unnatural; Price demanded a transition zone between the formal character of the house and the informal landscape beyond.

> Nothing, as I think, can be more natural, or more pleasing, than to discover that intense design has been at work in the immediate environs of a house. . . . Any sudden transition from that manifest design which must necessarily be displayed by the architecture itself, to that absolute wildness which is to be found in untamed nature, must always be harsh and unpleasing. Straight

> terraces, terrace walks, statues, fountains, flights of steps, balustrades, vases, architectural seats, and formal parterres, knots, and flower-beds, are therefore most naturally the more immediate accompaniments of a mansion. They are employed, for the purpose of softening off art into nature, and thus removing the harsh effect of sudden transition, in the same way that an artist softens off hardness of outline in his picture.[30]

One widespread consequence of this reasoning was the reaction against the ha-ha. The sunk fence had created an impression of uninterrupted continuity between foreground and distance, while cunningly preventing cattle from encroaching on the house itself; but once it became desirable to admit artificial design within the curtilage of the house, there was no longer any need to maintain the deception. Repton and the younger Gilpin argued against the ha-ha on the basis of association: 'If it be contrary to good sense to admit the cattle on the dressed lawn, it is, I conceive, equally contrary to let it appear they are admitted.' But while Repton and such followers of his as Bridgewater Page were often content to use iron railings as 'invisible fences', Gilpin argued for the use of walls as an emphatic visual separation between garden and landscape.[31] By the 1850s the reaction had proceeded so far that some writers complained that excessive ornamental planting was being used to draw attention to the line of the ha-ha.[32]

A second consequence was the return of the flower garden to the precincts of the house. It was for this that Repton was primarily remembered; he had first stated the principle of the autonomy of the flower garden, 'independent of its accompaniment of distant scenery'.[33] It is possible to distinguish a series of logical stages in the development of the flower garden, even though these stages were not chronologically successive. First: flower beds near the house, even if in shape they adopted the 'naturalistic' conventions of the line of beauty – assemblages of such beds in random serpentine patterns can be seen in Maria Jackson's *Florist's Manual* of 1822. Second: flower beds arranged symmetrically; many of Repton's designs fall into this category. Third: flower beds with formal edgings; Charles James Fox's garden at St Anne's Hill had rose beds with low ivy hedges early in the century, and Lewis Kennedy helped to popularize box edgings in the 1820s.[34] At last came the discrimination of patterns by period style; and by the 1830s, the *Gardener's Magazine* and its rivals were bristling with patterns variously labelled classical, Gothic, Elizabethan, Dutch and French, although in few cases were the distinctions between the styles readily discernible.[35] 'Most persons professing to possess good taste' disapproved of these styles, reported Robert Marnock in 1838, yet 'Whether in bad taste or otherwise, French and Italian gardens, when neatly executed and highly kept, are objects that seldom fail to please.'[36]

The extension of formal design from the immediate confines of the house into the wider landscape was a more difficult step to take. The gradual rise of terraces from the initial advocacy of Price and Knight to general acceptance can be nicely traced in the development of the Newcastle architect John Dobson, from the informal landscape of Cheesburn Grange in 1813, to the terrace walks of Meldon Park in 1832.[37] The eighteenth-century removal of terraces was now thought to be aesthetically destructive; for W. S. Gilpin, 'the want of an architectural

22 Clumber Park, the terrace. William Sawrey Gilpin's terrace, terminated at the lakeside in a balustraded wall.

separation from the park' damaged the effect of an old house.[38] The most famous of his own terraces was at Clumber Park, Nottinghamshire, where he had found the house sited on sloping ground with only an iron fence to mark its separation from the park:

> that space is now occupied by a double terrace, the lower one laid out in a parterre garden, and ornamented with vases, fountains, &c.; the whole surrounded by a balustrade wall, with a flight of steps down to the lake. The result fully justifies the undertaking.[39]

By the 1840s, Thomas Dick Lauder could rejoice that the 'old system of having nothing but shaven grass, and bare gravel around the house' was 'fast giving way to the introduction of walled or balustraded terraces, and all the rich decorations of the old gardens'.[40]

The most elaborate feat of terrace construction took place at Drummond Castle, Perthshire, where Lewis Kennedy and his son George reconstructed the garden in the 1820s and 1830s. The terrace garden was given its final form by George Kennedy in 1838–42. A garden was known to have existed there in the seventeenth century, and to be historically appropriate, the new garden was cast in the form of a St Andrew's cross, centred on a sixteenth-century sundial; throughout the century gardening writers described it as a mingling of the Italian, Dutch and French styles. It was planted with patterned beds of rhododendrons and heathers, and a report on the garden in 1837 describes its effect seen from above as 'like an immense Carpet of brilliant Colours', but what mainly seized the writer's imagination was the effect of the terracing and the flights of steps (which eventually had to be replaced and simplified, Scotland's climate being more erosive than Italy's).[41]

So extensive was the change by the 1830s that the residual advocates of the informal landscape park began to see themselves as revivalists of a now abandoned system. In 1835, John Dennis attacked 'the modern devastator of a good grass-plot' in much the same terms as Price had attacked the devastators of terraces.[42] And while Loudon and his associates were arguing that houses ought to be fitted with gardens in the appropriate period style, others, such as Joshua Major, were insisting that garden design had no fixed principles that could compel an association with particular architectural styles:

> The fact of our finding Italian, Dutch, and Flemish gardens, indiscriminately associated with the old English, Elizabethan or Gothic, Grecian and Italian, styles of architecture, is sufficient to prove to any unprejudiced mind ... that the adaptation of Landscape Gardening to these different styles was always a matter of mere fancy and fashion, rather than of any fixed principles whatever.[43]

The Cottage Garden

In 1829, Robert Southey published *Sir Thomas More*, a set of dialogues criticizing the decay of society and the dissolution of old social bonds. At one point his characters compare a series of manufacturers' cottages, bleak and gardenless, with some old cottages built of local stone, with rose bushes around the door, and hollyhocks, beehives, and fruit trees in the garden; the latter 'indicate in the owners some portion of ease and leisure' by comparison. Southey's polemic met with a brisk rejoinder from Macaulay: 'Does Mr. Southey think that the body of the English peasantry ... ever lived, in substantial or ornamented cottages, with box hedges, flower gardens ... and orchards? If not, what is his parallel worth?'[44]

This exchange encapsulates the problem of the cottage garden: to what extent was it a genuine feature of the ancestral English past, and to what extent a nineteenth-century invention? A Tory like Southey saw cottage gardening as a traditional custom, subverted by the enclosure movement and the industrial revolution; a radical like Loudon gave no indication of a long tradition, and the examples he discussed in the *Gardener's Magazine* were all recent innovations by paternalistic benefactors.

The multiple meaning of the term accounts for some of the confusion. In the early nineteenth century, 'cottage' was a fashionable term for a type of villa. When horticultural revivalists later spoke of the cottage garden as a survival, praised it for its preservation of old gardening ways, and told stories of recovering near-vanished plants from it, their primary model was not the labourer's dwelling but the small farmhouse and even the small manor house.[45] To Loudon and other early nineteenth-century reformers, a cottage garden meant the garden of a labourer's cottage; and cottage garden competitions later in the century specified that a 'cottager' must be a 'person of the working class, and must not receive any professional assistance or paid labour in the cultivation of his garden or produce'.[46] In this last sense of the word, there is little evidence for the existence of cottage gardens before the end of the eighteenth century, when Thomas Bernard wrote an account of a successful example near Tadcaster and recommended its example on a national scale.[47]

Loudon regularly praised landowners who set up cottage gardens, and in 1836 published his *Encyclopaedia of Cottage, Farm, and Villa Architecture* as a practical manual. By mid-century, the provision of gardens was an important factor in pioneering industrial communities like Saltaire.[48] This meant abandoning the picturesque preference for rustic and aged-looking materials, and encouraging an aesthetic of neatness, cleanliness and efficiency instead. Ruskin was famous for his denunciation of the way picturesque taste condemned cottagers to poverty, but he was not alone. For Tom Taylor, the 'moss and weather-stain', guelder-roses and jessamine, of the traditional cottage concealed plagues, 'foul miasma' and fevers:

> And then I wish the picturesqueness less,
> And welcome the utilitarian hand
> That from such foulness plucks its masquing dress,
> And bids the well-aired, well-drained cottage stand,
> All bare of weather-stain, right-angled true,
> By sketchers shunned, but shunned by fevers too.[49]

The primary function of a cottage garden, to the reformers, was food production; Alexander Forsyth was to criticize estate owners who insisted on having their cottagers grow roses, and most manuals on cottage gardening omitted flowers altogether in their insistence on fruit and vegetables.[50] Allied to this was the campaign for the provision of allotments, promoted during the 1830s and 1840s by the Young England movement as a revival of ancestral practice.[51] Generally speaking, it was on rural estate villages, where the cottages served as an indication of the landowner's taste, that the cottage garden became identified with a style of flower garden. At Harlaxton, Gregory Gregory created a village which Loudon held up as a model; the gardens were planted by his head gardener, 'no two gardens . . . planted with the same climbers'.[52]

Loudon's designs for cottages gave great emphasis to the Italian style, but attempts at old English revival came to dominate the field. John Adey Repton's gamekeeper's lodge at Woburn (1804) was in an Elizabethan style, and in 1826 a cottage design in the 'ancient English style' was exhibited at the Royal Academy. During the 1820s P. F. Robinson popularized the Swiss style, a form of cottage-sized architecture with seventeenth-century baroque decorations; the estate village of Old Warden was built entirely in this style. At Edensor, planned by Paxton for the Duke of Devonshire, there was a mixture of Swiss, Tudor, and Gothic buildings, with sizeable gardens. A similar revivalism affected the design of the garden as well as the cottage; Loudon introduced yew hedges into his cottages at Great Tew.[53]

In order to conserve expense, the proponents of cottage gardens usually recommended the use of perennial plants which did not need protected cultivation. In 1851, Robert Adamson's list of recommendations included perennials, bulbs, and florists' flowers – though finding a place for calceolarias, verbenas, and pelargoniums as well; J. S. Barty was complaining that cottage gardens were becoming fashion-conscious.[54] They were certainly on the increase. 'In a circle of no more than two miles in diameter, round my house', wrote Donald Beaton in 1852, 'there are as many cottage gardens, if not more, of the best class, than are to be met with in the same space in any other part of the country, and they were all made and planted within the last twenty years.'[55]

The Conservatory in the Landscape

We have seen that the curvilinear iron glasshouse was in the ascendant by the 1840s, justified on the grounds of its functionalism. A different sort of functionalism was being promoted among the architectural profession, however, principally by Pugin, the rising star of the Gothic revival. Arguing that stylistic features whose functions were obsolete should not be revived, he used the fashion for conservatories as a stick with which to beat the builders of mock castles:

> What can be more absurd than houses built in what is termed the castellated style? What absurdities, what anomalies, what utter contradictions do not the builders of modern castles perpetrate! . . . On one side of the house machicolated parapets, embrasures, bastions, and all the show of strong defence, and round the corner of the building a conservatory leading to the principal rooms, through which a whole company of horsemen might penetrate at one smash into the very heart of the mansion! For who would hammer against railed portals when he could kick his way through the greenhouse?[56]

Architects were beginning by the late 1830s to give more serious attention to the impact of the conservatory on the landscape. Did the curvilinear glass shell harmonize with the house it stood adjacent to? From the revivalist's point of view, it was seriously inconsistent with the associations the style of the house was intended to promote. The major step toward resolving this discrepancy was taken by William Burn, whose innovations in the practical planning of houses made him much in demand. By 1840 he had completed a conservatory at Dalkeith Palace, free-standing, at a distance from the house, designed on a circular plan; unfortunately, the smoke produced by the central chimney blocked the sunlight so effectively that it soon had to be abandoned for horticultural purposes. (The great stove at Chatsworth and the Palm House at Kew set a precedent for placing chimneys at a distance, connected with the boilers by a tunnel.) What was significant stylistically was the decorative detail of the conservatory: the stone piers and bases were incised with a pattern based on Jacobean strapwork. About the same time Burn replaced Anthony Salvin as the architect of Harlaxton, Lincolnshire, the most splendid Jacobean-revival house of its time; here the conservatory was built as an extension of the house, and the strapwork motif served to unify it with the rest of the building.[57]

The consequence of this attention to stylistic harmony between the house and conservatory was that the old masonry structures, which once looked as though they were going to be abolished in the name of horticultural efficiency, never died out. By mid-century it was standard to speak of the 'architect's conservatory' as one in which plants became sickly or died.[58] Gardeners tended to put the interests of plants first, and thus remained wedded to curvilinear. Robert Marnock abjured architectural style to the point of wanting not a building but simply a glass covering for an area of ground, and gave as his requirement 'a shell of glass of the lightest and slightest description consistent with due regard to strength'.[59] Iron therefore remained the favoured material for construction. Paxton's ridge-and-furrow experiments were causing some stir, but even his first great conservatory, the stove at Chatsworth (1836–40), although using wooden glazing bars, combined the ridge-and-furrow system with an overall curvilinear effect.[60] Possibly the most stylistically austere of curvilinear houses was built for the Horticultural Society at Chiswick by Loudon's old associates, D. and E. Bailey, in 1839–40; Loudon compared its shape to the hull of a ship with its keel in the air, and George Gordon later dismissed it as 'classic'.[61]

But by far the most important glasshouse of the period was the Palm House at Kew, built in the years 1844–48. The story of its building is now well known: how Richard Turner, the Dublin ironfounder, submitted proposals to Kew for the structure, which were then revised in consultation with Decimus Burton. Turner, as an engineer, was attracted to the possibilities of Gothic form, since the idea that Gothic had originated as a result of functional requirements was being promoted by both Pugin and Viollet-le-Duc. Burton, most of whose early work had been in the Greek revival, and who had recently worked with Paxton, took a more purist line, complaining of 'The Ecclesiastical or Gothic style' of Turner's elevations, and the 'numerous ornamental details in fretwork, crockets, perforated parapets, etc.'. His own recommendation instead was 'A conventional style suitable for horticultural purposes', avoiding 'all extraneous ornaments', both 'classic and ecclesiastical'. Turner's technical innovations and Burton's insistence on de-stylizing the building resulted in the culminating expression of the curvilinear style.[62] And because the Palm House was placed on a formal terrace with parterres on either side (despite Edward Kemp's complaint that the absence of nearby trees destroyed its landscape effect),[63] it gave a new authority to the position that the 'styleless' curvilinear glasshouse was not incongruous in a setting of revivalist gardens.

Gardens for an English Revival

The return to historical styles of gardens proceeded hand in hand with similar revivals in architecture. The recovery of the English past entailed the abandonment of classical styles – foreign in origin, and never quite naturalized – and the exploration of styles which could be regarded as native. As early as 1798, James Wyatt considered 'the designs of Inigo Jones before he went to Italy' as appropriate for a monument to Sir Edward Coke. From a slow trickle, the reaction became a flood in the 1820s, when public buildings began to appear in Tudor, Gothic, and Italian styles simultaneously – many architects, like Cockerell, experimenting in more than one style.[64]

Various responses to the breakdown of classicism had different implications for the garden. Many advocates of the picturesque favoured the building of castles, a trend begun by Richard Payne Knight with his Downton Castle in the 1770s; and although by the 1830s Anthony Salvin was improving standards of historical accuracy, castles became, in the eyes of most Victorian architects, an archetypal instance of falsehood – a building type revived for purely visual reasons, regardless of its function. Mediaeval castles had been built for defence, and not equipped with gardens; and nineteenth-century castles like the Regency Eastnor or the early Victorian Bayons Manor were set amid informal landscape parks, exactly what garden revivalists did not want to encourage.[65]

23 Lews Castle, Stornoway. The castle was built in the 1840s and the curvilinear conservatory added soon after. 'Who the mischief ever saw a conservatory hanging on to a baronial castle, like a Chinese pagoda?' asked one critic.

Sir Walter Scott's Abbotsford (1816–23) initiated a related revival, the Scottish baronial. The garden was filled with architectural ornaments, and visible from the courtyard through a pierced Gothic screen; rosaries and a trellised walk extended up a slope towards 'a sweeping amphitheatre of wood'. Loudon considered Scott's tastes antiquarian rather than artistic, but his balance of architectural features and picturesque woodland was influential on Scottish gardens through the 1830s. In the 1850s, however, the balance was altered by Scott's heirs, who turned the courtyard garden into a parterre with geometric topiary.[66] Similarly, at Drumlanrig Castle, Scott's plantations were eventually subordinated to the restoration of the lost formal gardens, with Edward Blore producing plans in 1838 and Charles Barry in 1840. Neither scheme was carried out; grass slopes rather than balustraded walls defined the terraces; but two of the old compartments were restored to new patterns, and became greatly influential in Scotland for their use of heathers instead of bedding plants in the parterres.[67]

Many architects turned to Gothic, at first thought of in sixteenth-century terms. Repton designed a fanciful Gothic garden for Ashridge, with a fountain modelled on a market cross, and proposed that round-headed trees should be planted near Gothic buildings, while the horizontal lines of classical buildings demanded conical or pointed trees for contrast.[68] The 1830s saw much confusion over the degree to which the Tudor style ought to be assimilated to Gothic or to Italian. Payne Knight had used a Tudor building to illustrate a picturesque house in an informal landscape; Lauder invoked both Francis Bacon and Drummond Castle as models. Suggestions for appropriate garden ornament ranged from sundials, to vases and fountains, to Saul's mannerist flower-holders in the shape of Swiss guardsmen, based on the painted figures of Elizabethan church monuments.[69] The elevation of thirteenth-century as the norm for Gothic, beginning in the late 1830s, eventually segregated Tudor from true Gothic, depriving Gothic buildings of any authentic models for gardens; a Pugin sketch for Scarisbrick Hall shows a quartered parterre without any specific period allegiance. Thomas Hudson Turner collated the available information on mediaeval gardens, but with little effect on practical garden-making.[70]

By the 1840s, enough information on Tudor buildings had become available to allow the perception of Elizabethan and Jacobean as distinct styles. C.J. Richardson in particular stressed the formality of the Tudor garden, listing parterres, bowers, canals, fishponds, bowling greens, wildernesses and labyrinths as its main features.

> The most important and interesting feature of the gardens were the terraces, imitated from the Italian, and (when the ground favoured the design) ranged successively one above the other, and connected by flights of stone steps and balustrades. These were adorned with vases and statues, and displayed both taste and grandeur in their forms; those at Haddon Hall, in Derbyshire, are universally admired for their elegance and good effect.[71]

Richardson invoked Claverton Manor also as a model, and Roos's terrace garden at Falkland was based on it.[72] Similar decorated terraces formed the setting for Harlaxton Manor, the most important of Jacobean-revival houses, in the late 1830s, and although the gardens merged into picturesque woodland, the straight approach road, crossed in parallel lines by multiple sets of gates, carried the feeling of formal design across the landscape. Even elements of the planting, such as the use of savin, were based on an understood Jacobean precedent.[73] Richardson himself, when he came to design Vinters in 1850, created a 'Jacobethan' terrace with a baroque double staircase descending into the garden.[74]

By the 1840s, attempts at the recreation of Elizabethan or Jacobean gardens were becoming widespread. At Gawthorpe Hall, Lancashire, Charles Barry made an Elizabethan garden around a central stone-edged bed.[75] At Montacute, Somerset, Ellen Phelips and her gardener, Pridham, removed a genuine Tudor mount to reconstruct the terrace garden around a sunken fountain in the Tudor style.[76] At Hatfield House, the second Marquess of Salisbury had terrace gardens constructed on either side of his restored Elizabethan house, and added a maze which by the end of the century was being mistaken for a genuine piece of seventeenth-century work.[77] At Knebworth, in 1847, Sir Edward Bulwer-Lytton laid out the gardens 'in the style favoured in the reign of James I., with the stone balustrades, straight walks, statues, and elaborate parterres'; the garden was of his own design, and laid out askew during his absence while he was sending instructions by post.[78]

All these instances adopted a form of garden consonant to some degree with picturesque effect, and certainly providing viewing platforms for extended prospect. But there was an awareness of the alternative form of English Renaissance garden, based on enclosed units without wide vistas. 'Christopher North' dreamt of an 'old English garden – such as Bacon, or Evelyn, or Cowley would have loved', with enclosing holly hedges and yew arbours, in the 1830s; Joseph Nash's *Mansions of England in the Olden Time* illustrated topiary at Levens Hall and a herbaceous border at

24 Gawthorpe Hall. Sir Charles Barry's 1849 recreation of an Elizabethan formal garden with a central stone-edged bed.

Hatfield; and Robert Southey's popular work *The Doctor* held up the ideal of the seventeenth-century herb garden, based on Gerard, Parkinson, and Culpeper, enclosed and deliberately anti-picturesque in feeling. The first major garden to put this ideal into effect was Arley Hall, Cheshire, where in the 1840s R. E. Egerton-Warburton created a garden of hedged alleys, topiary, and herbaceous borders.[79]

Such a repudiation of the picturesque, however, roused strong opposition, and in 1848 John Lindley mounted an attack on the Elizabethan revival. 'It is not absolutely self-evident', he said in a paper given to the Horticultural Society, that an architectural revival required a matching style of garden, and argued instead that the garden should harmonize with the landscape, not the building. He attributed enthusiasm for the Elizabethan style to the ignorance of its advocates, and surveyed the writings of Bacon, Lawson, and 'Didymus Mountaine', finding in their notions of garden-making 'a most Lilliputian grasp of mind and imagination', a taste fit for making a tea-garden: 'beyond having pretty flowers in certain seasons, there seems nothing to redeem the offensive ugliness of the whole design'. Even Bacon was extravagant, though in some respects a prophet of better things to come. 'There is no wide expanse of surface; no undulation is spoken of; no changing views created artificially yet natural in effect . . . .'[80]

25 Drumlanrig Castle, proposals for the gardens, 1840. This plan shows the attempt to restore something of the seventeenth-century formal garden, with compartments near the castle returned to parterre use.

It is not surprising, therefore, that early attempts at a non-picturesque form of Elizabethan revival remained largely abortive. By the 1840s, instead, two new styles were emerging as the basic forms of revivalist garden: one based on the seventeenth-century parterre, and one on the surviving gardens of the Italian Renaissance.

Enter Nesfield

Through the work of Anthony Salvin, William Burn, and Edward Blore, the different forms of the Elizabethan and Jacobean revivals were becoming the dominant fashion for country houses during the 1830s; and a common style of garden design attached itself to their buildings, through the work of William Andrews Nesfield, who worked with all three. Born in 1793, he reached the rank of Lieutenant while serving in Canada, and during the 1820s became well known as a painter in water colours.[81] The architect Anthony Salvin was his brother-in-law, and his first venture into garden design was probably his unexecuted plan for North Runcton Hall, produced in 1834 to accompany Salvin's works.[82]

His name was first made public in a gardening context by Loudon, who featured his north London villa in the *Gardener's Magazine* in 1840. Salvin had designed a little Italianate villa for him at Fortis Green, and Nesfield had landscaped the grounds. The main view looked out over a rococo pattern of box-edged flowerbeds, a scroll-shaped dwarf terrace with a rose hedge on top, and a highly emphatic fence dividing the garden from the middle distance. There was little as yet stylistically distinctive about the garden, although it was copied by other designers; but by the time the article appeared, Nesfield's advice was 'now sought for by gentlemen of taste in every part of the country'.[83]

Nesfield did not advertise his services, finding his clients through his social connections – although in some cases, as at Scotney Castle, his proposals were rejected by owners fixated on picturesque informality. With Burn (Salvin's successor at Harlaxton), he worked at Stoke Rochford, Lincolnshire;[84] but it was Worsley Hall, Cheshire (1846), a Jacobean house by Blore, that brought his special talents into public notice, and showed how far he had advanced from the rococo pattern of Fortis Green. Here he laid out a scroll-flower pattern in box at either end of the upper terrace, and a French-style parterre on the second; the design for the latter was taken from Dézallier d'Argenville's *Theory and Practice of Gardening* (1712) – then often attributed to its translator John James. Robert Errington drew attention to the 'chaste and unique' parterres in 1846, and from them on Nesfield's career as a parterre designer gathered momentum.[85]

The *parterre de broderie*, using box and gravel alone, had been a major device of the late seventeenth century, and its revival was already underway by the time Nesfield appeared; Loudon had published the pattern used for Worsley Hall as early as 1812, and similar designs had been used at Syon Park and Oxburgh Hall by mid-century.[86] In 1837, C.F. Ferris had published a little book on *The Parterre*, offering several designs, but this work was little noticed.[87] Many gardeners on encountering Nesfield's work were uncertain whether to think of the box patterns as a form of ground cover, as an edging that had usurped the main body of the bed, or as a substitute for flowers altogether. Donald Beaton wrote in 1852 that 'This style is all but quite new in this country', although he had heard that box embroideries and patterns of coloured gravels were common on the Continent; 'but here, with our moist climate, and our superabundance of half-hardy and fine-leaved plants, we need not resort to such extremes'.

26 Buckingham Palace, undated sketch by Edward Blore for formal garden. Note the architectural form given to the proposed mounts.

Many gardeners could not quite see the point of a flowerbed that offered so little scope for the gardener to show his handiwork. Thomas Appleby, seeing 'the celebrated Mr. Nesfield' at work at Eaton Hall, Cheshire, reported with asperity that his patterns were useless as flowerbeds: 'The scrolls run out to a great length, and are, in many places, not six inches wide!! nay, even less than that. This struck us as rather bordering upon the ridiculous'. A commentator in 1850 hoped that Nesfield would abandon his 'bygone custom' and use modern planting.[88]

Nesfield's repertoire was not limited to the box parterre, however, for he also designed mazes, bowling greens, and arboreta. The perceived lack of harmony between parterre and landscape was an issue in picturesque theory; Nesfield's response, when he could not use terracing to provide an open prospect, was to make the transition between parterre and pleasure ground with devices such as a geometric lawn studded symmetrically with trees, as at Somerleyton.[89] From 1843, he was engaged on his major landscaping commission: the Royal Botanic Gardens at Kew, where he was working in association with Decimus Burton. Here he laid out the Broad Walk, supervised the planting of the arboretum (a department in which he claimed particular expertise), and created a terrace as the platform for the Palm House. In front of the terrace he altered the outline of the pond, making one end an architectural basin and leaving the other informal, to make the transition between the terrace and the wider landscape; on the other side he opened up a *patte-d'oie* or goosefoot pattern of three radiating vistas. On the terrace itself he planned a parterre which, had it been carried out to his original plans, would have featured the first public display of topiary for over a century:

> with regard to the Verge plants, they ought to be clipped into various artificial shapes – i.e. to be orthodox – therefore any natural forms which are most quaint and formal of course will answer best – such as upright comn. juniper – Irish yew – red Cedar – large box – small leaved Phillyrea – portugal Laurel

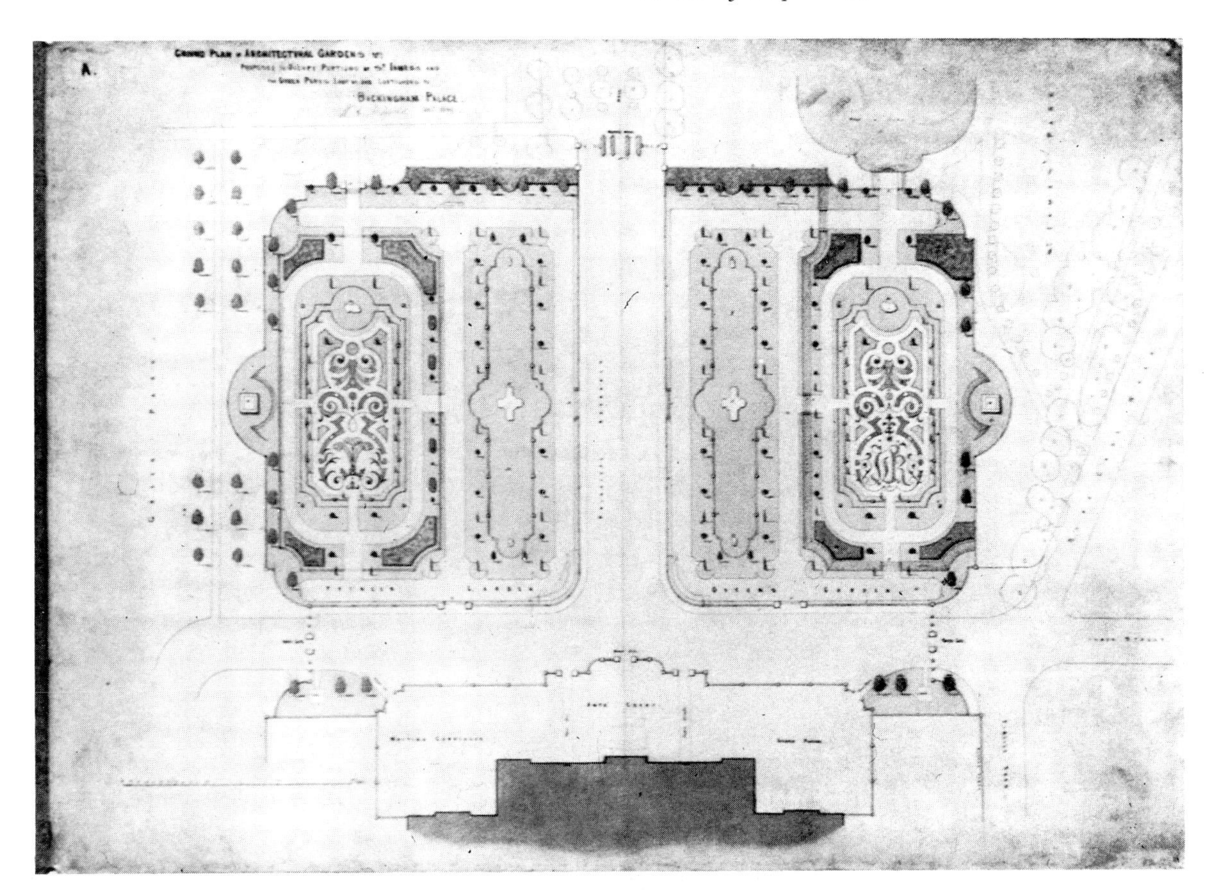

as standards – the Phillyrea does capitally clipped as a round ball or standard ... at any rate the more you ring the changes on the *spiral*, the *round*, or the *pyramid like Versailles*, the better –[90]

27 Buckingham Palace, proposed parterres. Nesfield's plan of 1849 for a system of canals and box embroideries to rival the gardens at Versailles.

Kew was Nesfield's most publicly accessible commission, but his association with Edward Blore nearly brought him a project that would have given him an even greater place in the limelight. Blore produced his revised plans for Buckingham Palace in 1846; surviving sketches show him envisaging a great fountain-centred parterre with geometric mounts. In 1849 Nesfield submitted his plans for a formal garden to make a worthy entrance display for the Palace. The forecourt would be laid out as a pair of parterres, with fountains 'on the largest scale admissible' as their central units, bounded by box-edged panels. The fountains would be 35 feet high; the sculptural groups would represent the army (south parterre) and navy (north), together with portrayals of the nation's sovereigns –

in order to avoid the adoption of Ancient Classical Sculpture – which (besides being common-place) would not be in strict accordance with the National character and sentiment of the design ...

The parterres would contain a monogram bed, with the Queen's initials worked in box and coloured with gravels (pounded red brick and white Derbyshire spar).

Queen Victoria, however, preferred the mock-rural view of St James's Park to a baroque parterre, and the plan was abandoned in 1850. Nesfield

28 Worsley Hall, the terrace garden. Edward Blore's terraces and early parterre planting by W. A. Nesfield are shown in this 1856 view by E. Adveno Brooke.

was nonetheless involved in some aspects of planning the surroundings, and with Pennethorne removed the Marble Arch from the Palace precincts to a new location at the northeast corner of Hyde Park in 1851.[91] It was not until after her death that Buckingham Palace was given a more formal approach, and by then fashions in landscape architecture had changed; England was not to have its Versailles.

The Triumph of the Italian Garden

The Italianate villa, through the work of John Nash and Loudon, became a dominant style for the suburban villa; after the 1820s, it found a sympathetic audience among the neoclassically-minded who could not make the transition to the 'debased' forms of Elizabethan. Thereafter, its evolution paralleled that of the Tudor styles; as Elizabethan gave way to the more ornate and sumptuous Jacobean, so the more restrained Italian of Charles Barry's early club houses gave way to the enriched 'Anglo-Italian' of his country houses.[92]

The most important early model for the Italian house was the Deepdene, Surrey, which Thomas Hope rebuilt in 1818–23 with asymmetrical ground plan and elevations; in keeping with the ideas of his essay 'On the Art of Gardening', he gave it a setting of terrace and steps, with sculptural embellishments, tubbed orange trees, and a flower garden with masses of blue salvias.[93] Wilton House emerged shortly after as another model. James Wyatt began altering the house in 1801, and re-erected a fountain

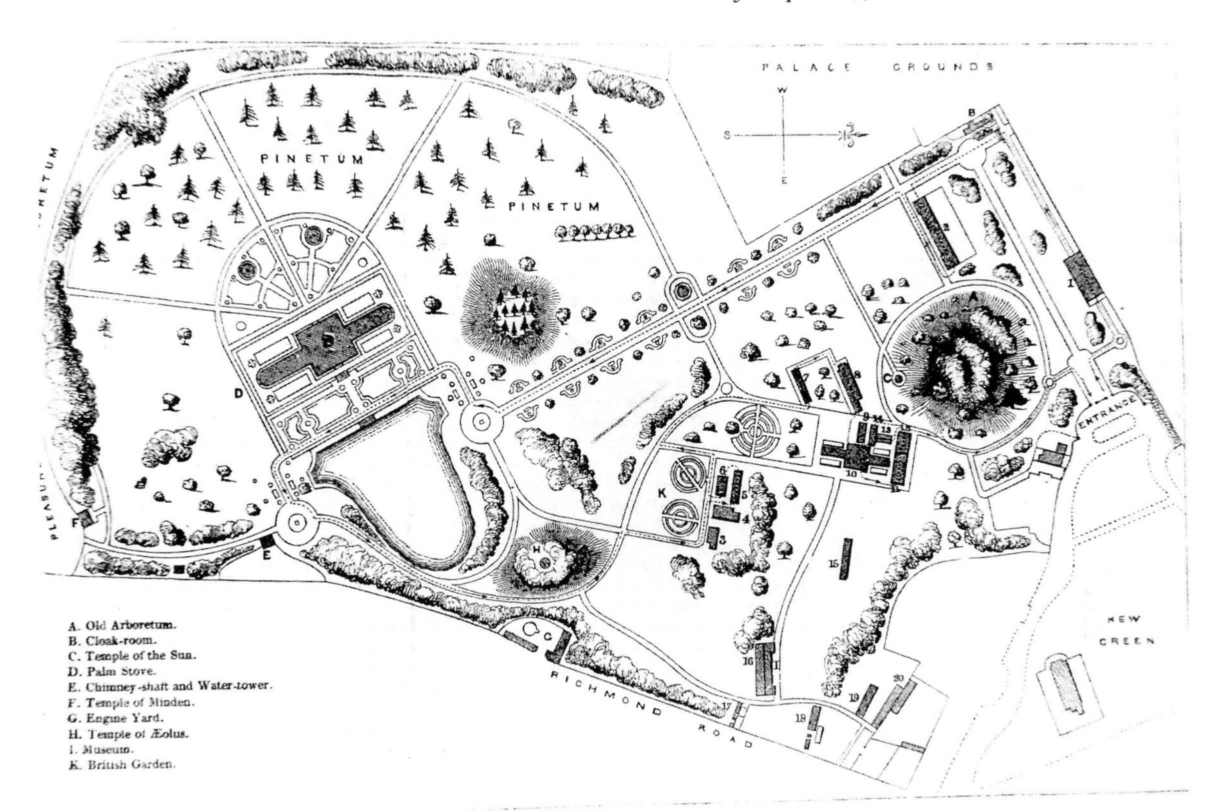

29 Kew, plan of the Royal Botanic Gardens in the 1850s. Nesfield's alterations included the broad walk, the revised shape of the pond, and the parterres and vistas around the Palm House.

and an ornate porch on the west side as part of a new terrace garden. In the 1820s Lady Pembroke, with the assistance of Richard Westmacott, remodelled the terrace into an Italian garden with cypresses, parterres quartered into panels, and much addition of statuary.[94]

The early discussions of the Italian garden emphasized as its characteristic features terracing, the use of gravel instead of grass, statuary (which often seems to have been the main feature distinguishing 'Italian' from 'French'), and the importance accorded to evergreen trees. The inability to grow orange trees outdoors was often felt to be an insurmountable barrier to the success of the Italian style in England; but the use of Portugal laurels trimmed into shape as substitutes at Chatsworth and Trentham solved that problem. Similarly, cypresses and other fastigiate conifers that could replace poplars became rapidly popular for Italian terraces.[95]

Trentham proved the turning point in the fortunes of the Italian garden. Charles Barry had travelled extensively throughout Europe after the Napoleonic wars, and had observed the Renaissance gardens of Italy;[96] Trentham was to be the first of a series of gardens based on the precedents he had studied. He began remodelling the house in an Italianate style in 1833, and in 1840 works began on the garden. The site was virtually flat, and Loudon had long since written off the possibility of a great garden there; so his praise for Barry's solution attracted much attention to Trentham. Barry excavated the ground between the house and the lake into two great shallow terraces, with elevations of only four to six steps. The upper terrace was centred on a circular fountain, the lower on a pair of rectangular panels, between which passed a broad gravel walk leading to

30 Wilton House, the Italian garden. A view by E. Adveno Brooke, 1856, showing the terrace garden designed by Sir Richard Westmacott in 1820–21.

the lakeside balustrading and a cast of Cellini's *Perseus*. (Barry's son later speculated that Nesfield had helped Barry in the layout, and on the basis of this statement a myth later arose of a regular partnership between them.)[97]

Barry's plans for Trentham, however, remained incomplete. He had envisaged the extension of the terracing much further into the landscape, turning the lake into an architectural basin, and creating a miniature Isola Bella on the island in the lake, but was not allowed to carry his scheme this far – though the Italianate quality of the lake was enhanced in the short term by the provision of a gondolier. Barry's son later acknowledged that 'he was accused sometimes, not quite unjustly, of desiring to extend the domain of Art, even at the risk of encroaching upon Nature herself'; his vision of an English Isola Bella, however, was shared by Charles M'Intosh and James Mangles, who made a similar proposal for St James's Park:

> Could not an 'Isola Bella' be made of the little Island facing the palace in St. James's Park, by fronting the *Western end* with eight receding rows of porcelain cased oblong boxes, disposed in octagons, about two feet deep, filled with flowers, with a gravel walk between each row, the boxes diminishing upwards

> to an *apex*. Each tier to rest on an iron frame two or three feet high. Porcelain vases at the *corners of each octagon*, would add greatly to the effect.[98]

The example of Trentham boosted the popularity of the asymmetrical Italianate mansion with a terraced garden. Nesfield designed a celebrated Italianate garden at Grimston, Yorkshire, whose main features were an Emperors' Walk, flanked with busts of the Caesars, and a flower garden whose stone edgings and absence of tracery for once pleased Thomas Appleby.[99] The high point of the fashion came when Prince Albert and the builder Thomas Cubitt remodelled Osborne, on the Isle of Wight, in that style.[100]

In the wake of Trentham, the concept of the Italian garden began to amplify itself. George Fleming's bedding schemes attracted great attention, ensuring that gardeners became enthusiastic about the Italian style as one which allowed them to display their art. And, because the term 'Italian', in the Reptonian theory of garden history, could encompass French, Dutch, and English Renaissance, the word gradually became an umbrella label for the revivalist styles. George Kennedy, his style chastened since Drummond Castle, redesigned the terrace garden at Bowood, Wiltshire, in 1851, in a manner at first called French but later Italian.[101] Paxton's major country house, Mentmore, was designed in an Elizabethan manner based on Wollaton Hall, but the proposed range of terraces was in Barry's style, and the eventual parterre was referred to as an Italian garden.[102] By the 1850s Nesfield's gardens were beginning to be absorbed under the Italian rubric; Matthew Digby Wyatt affirmed that the Villa d'Este had been the model for the Elizabethan garden.[103] Features radically distinct to an architect, such as a balustraded wall and a grass slope, were for many gardeners encompassed within the general category of 'terrace'; the Italian garden at Powerscourt, near Dublin, planned in the 1840s and carried out in the 1860s, was based on a series of semicircular grass steps.[104]

Meanwhile Barry had gone on to follow Trentham with a series of great houses and gardens. From 1844 he was at work at Harewood, Yorkshire, creating a balustraded terrace which was planted with the aid of John Fleming. A plan survives for a bed in the shape of the initial H, but this was not carried out; instead there was laid out a series of stone-edged beds, with scrolls of yew, heather, and dwarfed oak.[105] At Cliveden, where John Fleming once again served as head gardener, Barry simplified the parterre into two borders of triangular beds leading to an enormous circular bed.[106]

After Trentham, however, the most celebrated of Barry's gardens was Shrubland Park, which he began to remodel shortly before Donald Beaton retired as head gardener. Virtually all of Beaton's work in the gardens was effaced in the process: 'Beautiful in themselves, they seemed to agree too little with the house, which had now assumed some architectural pretensions'. Beaton, however, was enthusiastic about the alterations, and played a major role in publicizing them.[107]

The hill on which the house stood was carved into a series of terraces. The main terrace was a long green drive, extending for nearly a mile through a variety of gardens, incorporating a Swiss cottage, a 'French' garden within a laurel wall, and a circular fountain garden with another great display of massed bedding. This terrace was reached by an immense

31 Shrubland Park, view from the upper terrace. Barry's great staircases shown in an 1856 view by E. Adveno Brooke.

staircase descending the hillside in four flights, while further steps led down into the park. The treatment of the great staircase was the garden's most innovative feature; vases of scarlet pelargoniums ornamented the landings, and on either side of the staircase the slope was turned into a wilderness:

> a curious effect is produced by allowing some Arbor-vitaes, &c., to tower up here and there among the Box; and against each rest the Box is carried through at a high level, as high as the top of the balustrading at the point, until it joins the untrained trees and shrubs that constitute the hanging hill on either side. Near the base of the steps a unique and pleasing effect is produced by a curious bed, formed of lines of Yew, about 18 inches high, and as much through, interwreathed in a singular manner, and enclosing scrolls of turf, silver-sand, and flowers. But the most striking feature consists of a large double-headed serpent, laying lazily across the back of each bed, formed of variegated Box, twisted over, among, in, and through the Yew.[108]

Shrubland Park became the High Victorian period's most important model of the complete architectural garden. The wilderness planting of the terrace slope was quickly echoed in gardens like Rhianva, Sir John Hay Williams's terrace garden in Wales, where the vegetation was allowed to grow unchecked once planted, and Linton Park, Kent, where the slopes of William Masters's Italian garden were covered with laurel 'cut to the exact shape of the ground, with Cedars and other symmetrical-growing trees rising up amongst them at regular intervals'.[109] The bedding schemes of the successive head gardeners were widely publicized; but most importantly, the series of well-defined descending stages between the architectural platform and the parkland became the ideal of graded transition between art and nature.

4

Art and nature

The Transcendentalist Landscape

By the 1840s the doctrine of the creative imagination was taking root in the gardening world. The informing spirit of the garden was increasingly seen as emanating from man's mind rather than from nature; the 'genius of the place' was giving way to the 'inventive genius of man'.[1] This new rhetoric appeared most often in discussions of three gardens, Chatsworth, Elvaston Castle, and Trentham; their head gardeners, respectively Paxton, Barron, and Fleming, were regarded with awestruck hero-worship by some of their contemporaries. With their technical brilliance and speed, their ability to create masterpieces from unpropitious circumstances, and their command over, and disdain for, mere nature, they defined between them what might be called the heroic age of gardening.

Let us begin with Chatsworth. This was already a garden of great fame and magnificence when, in 1826, Joseph Paxton arrived as head gardener, twenty-three years of age, but with immense vigour and the experience of work in the Horticultural Society's garden at Chiswick. Within two years he was taking a hand in alterations to the grounds. A broad outline of his career has already been given in the introductory chapter; here we shall concentrate on his reconstruction of the gardens at Chatsworth.[2] The criticisms made by Loudon on the state of the gardens in 1831 may serve as a useful point of departure. His main argument was that the composite nature of the grounds – a Brown landscape, in which various seventeenth-century features had been allowed to survive – resulted in an unsystematic scattering of potential effect; he suggested a massive reorganization of the grounds, so as to give a larger and better proportioned platform to the house, to concentrate the 'avowed art', above all the waterworks, on the west front, and to restore the rest of the grounds 'not to nature, but to a more natural style than that which they now assume'.[3] Paxton replied by ridiculing Loudon's 'visionary schemes' and defending, with reservations, the existing disposition of features; and, after this rebuke, Loudon was to become one of Paxton's supporters.[4] But, far from following Loudon's advice on concentrating and separating the artistic and the natural, Paxton was to bring art and nature into deliberately startling juxtapostion.

The example of the weeping willow makes this clear. Originally made in 1693, this was a relic of a taste that had fallen into disrepute by the nineteenth century, the taste for joke fountains that drenched the unsuspecting visitor. The original fountain having fallen into disrepair, a

32 Chatsworth, the weeping willow fountain, a restoration of a seventeenth-century water joke.

new one was modelled under Paxton's direction, made of some eight thousand pieces of copper and brass assembled in the shape of a decayed weeping willow, discharging eight hundred jets of water from its branches. It would be difficult to conceive of a more ostentatiously artificial feature, but it was erected in a partially concealed glen in the middle of Paxton's new naturalistic rockworks.[5]

The restoration of the weeping willow can be seen as part of the Duke of Devonshire's programme for recovering the baroque atmosphere of the estate. When Paxton arrived, Jeffrey Wyatville was building a new wing in keeping with the original building, and many of Paxton's alterations augmented the effect of the surviving seventeenth- and early eighteenth-century works. During the 1830s he went three times on tour with the Duke of Devonshire: in 1834 to Paris, where they visited Versailles and St Cloud; the next year on a round of the major English gardens; and in 1838–39 to Italy. By 1839, the immediate vicinity of the house had been graced with a mixture of trees in natural form – araucarias and deodars – and Portugal laurels trained into ball-headed standards, in imitation of the orange trees at Versailles and the Tuileries.[6] Small-scale formal gardens were created near the house and the old orangery; classical columns were introduced into one of these as supports for climbers.[7] Most important of all, between 1833 and 1844 he rearranged the waterworks and created the Emperor Fountain, then the world's tallest, in honour of an abortive visit by the Emperor of Russia.[8]

The cascade, dating from the 1690s, was surmounted by a viewing temple by Thomas Archer. From this the spectator could look down a long series of ramps, resembling a staircase, over which water flowed until it disappeared into culverts. This arrangement was criticized in the early nineteenth century for its abrupt transition between 'supposedly natural and avowedly artificial', but Paxton's extensions in the late 1830s not only did not remove this abruptness, but added further startling juxtapositions. More than half the cascade was re-laid, as it was discovered to be at a slight angle to the house. New waterfalls and reservoirs were created in order to provide a sufficient height of fall for the water to power the gravity-driven fountains. High above the waterworks, an immense aqueduct was constructed, its series of arches made of undressed blocks of stone, terminating in a waterfall of nearly eighty feet; below this naturalistic falls helped to convey the stream to the cascade pond. On the slopes by the upper end of the cascade was sited a square pond, for powering the willow tree; years before in the debate with Loudon, Paxton had maintained that standing bodies of water ought to be on the lowest ground,[9] but this rule of naturalism was cheerfully broken in this instance.

An unsympathetic critic can often alert us to implications that would otherwise be missed, and Joshua Major's account of the cascade helps us to appreciate what Paxton was doing. The cascade itself presented 'a singular and (if the mind could be diverted from a sense of inharmonious composition) a not unpleasing effect'; but the continual interruptions to the visible course of the cascade, its disappearance under the lawn, and the alternation of naturalistic and architectural features offended him.

> Now, to my taste, many of these features are objectionable, not because the effect is not in some cases pleasing, but because the associations are not in unison. The arched wall, for example, is too visibly intended for effect, and too devoid of architectural character, to class with the [temple] and steps below, and of every thing in harmony with the natural commencement of the fall. Were we to allow the formal steps, they are never sufficiently covered with water to be effective. The abrupt disappearance also of the water under fine kept lawns, the combination of forest trees, wild undergrowths, and brilliant flowers, – art and nature thus bringing together gaiety and sombreness, order and wildness, – all this is, in my opinion, opposed to the dictates of good taste.[10]

This manipulation of associations, this playing-off against each other of qualities often felt to be inharmonious, characterized most of Paxton's works at Chatsworth. The great conservatory was placed in the utilitarian kitchen garden. The Emperor Fountain emerged from a mass of rockwork, from which the cast-iron pipe rose nakedly exposed. In 1842, he began to assemble a series of rockworks on a massive scale, in imitation of the Strid at Bolton Abbey; yet among the piles of stones, in the middle of this depiction of natural scenery, a sixty-foot hollow was laid out as a straight walk, with a formal staircase at either end. 'Here Nature and Art revel in luxuriance', remarked one commentator, but the revel was characterized by a high degree of deliberate incongruity.[11] No visitor to Chatsworth was ever allowed to imagine himself among the works of Nature; at every stage, the personality of Paxton was stamped unmistakably on the gardens, and the visitor was left in no doubt that he had witnessed the shaping hand of one man's genius.

A Note about Fountains

When fountains were debated in the early part of the century, the discussion centred on the question of whether the artificiality of a *jet-d'eau* was to be preferred to more natural water features like waterfalls, and later over the most appropriate sculptural style. Renaissance models were the most popular, although from time to time some distinctly Mannerist models like Godwin's musical dial fountain were proposed.[12] But from the first excited reports of the Emperor Fountain at Chatsworth, the effects to be obtained from the manipulation of water itself became an important theme.

Once again, Joshua Major serves to pinpoint the nature of Paxton's achievement by singling it out for criticism. The Emperor Fountain, from his point of view, was a failure because it pushed at the boundaries of acceptable art:

> With regard to the grand jet, it is more calculated to surprise than to excite permanent interest. To many it may appear a wonderful example of the height to which water may be thrown; but even in producing this effect, the column is forced too high for its substance. It consequently becomes incapable of retaining its solidity, and is dispersed by the wind, deluging to a considerable distance the dress ground about it, thereby destroying much of its interest, and becoming in reality a nuisance. . . . no jet ought ever to rise higher than it has power to remain solid, otherwise, instead of falling in drops or bubbles, it is spread into mist or spray, and is liable to be forced out of perpendicular with the least wind, thereby destroying the effectiveness of the fountain, the form and regularity of which constitute its main beauty . . . [13]

But it was exactly this ambiguous play with water, partly suggesting and partly denying a solid form, that was of interest to Paxton and his like-minded contemporaries. Even before the Emperor Fountain had been constructed, the 'formal architectural effect' of the Chatsworth fountains had earned praise for precisely the way in which water was 'dissolved into the most exquisite spray when projected to the height of 60, 70, or even 90 feet', as opposed to the 'heavy and lumpish masses' formed by lower jets.[14]

A spectacular attempt to emulate the water effects at Chatsworth was at Enville Hall, Staffordshire, where two contrasting displays could be turned on for visitors: a sculptural fountain, the river-horse, ornamented by a series of jets at different heights and angles, and one massive jet, a pump-driven counterpart to the gravity-powered Emperor. Robert Fish recorded his impressions of the sight in 1864:

> The boatman by rowing to the jet puts on ever so many devices; but to us one lofty jet was *the grand* one . . . One great charm was that we were privileged with the sight of numerous beautiful rainbows, two or three in the dashing spray at one time. We had never seen any but the slightest appearance of them

> in similar circumstances before, but here they were massive, and no sooner was one gone than another and another appeared.

33 People's Park, Halifax. Paxton's fountain, constructed by Simpson of Pimlico, consisting solely of jets. This fountain was later replaced by a sculptural group brought from Somerleyton Hall.

The play of the rainbows seems to have been a regular and predictable feature, for Brooke on his visit referred to the fountain 'falling around in absolute clouds of the most brilliant and variegated colour'.[15]

(This was not the only effect of transitory colour cultivated at Enville, which was also celebrated for its illuminations during fêtes, 'as many as 160,000 variegated lamps being sometimes used'. George McEwen was also noted during the 1850s for his experiments in illumination in the Arundel Castle gardens.)[16]

With the Emperor, Paxton stripped the fountain's structure down towards its bare essential, the simple jet; then he built up again, deploying groups of jets arranged in figures. As demonstrated in the gardens of the Crystal Palace, and his later parks such as People's Park, Halifax, 'the new Paxtonian system of water-works, without the accessories of architecture and sculpture', could create works of great scale and complexity, devoid of extraneous associations, working with patterns of moving water alone.[17]

The Gardener as Hero

Publicity came earlier to Paxton than to William Barron, his principal rival for the role of heroic gardener. Barron was apprenticed at the Edinburgh Botanic Garden, and in 1830, having helped to plant the new conservatory at Syon House, he was appointed head gardener at Elvaston Castle, near Derby, with a commission to lay out new gardens.[18] These had to be created almost entirely from scratch, and on an unpropitious site; the first four years were spent almost entirely in trenching the ground and laying drains.[19] Planting proper began in 1835.

As the Earl was not a member of the Horticultural Society, he could not take advantage of their new introductions, and was dependent on nurserymen for trees already in commerce. Barron studied propagation techniques in order to increase his stock of plants economically, and then turned to transplanting for immediate effect, developing his own system which was described in the first chapter. Before long Barron was successfully carrying trees over thirty miles – immense cedars and yews, often hundreds of years old; a topiary arbour with clipped birds, 19 feet high and 13 in circumference; even a 33-foot yew with a decayed and hollow stem – all made the journey to Elvaston and proceeded to thrive in their new homes. Loudon described them after transplanting, 'held fast in their situations by guy ropes, like the mast of a ship'.

> Numbers of large plants . . . had to pass in their journey to it through the town of Derby, and so large were they that the windows on both sides of the street were much broken by them.[20]

Not surprisingly, Barron gained the reputation of an effortless mastery over nature – not only in transplanting but in the pruning and grafting of conifers as well.

More than any other feature, it was for its avenues, complex constructions several rows deep, that Elvaston became famous. Here, to convey the overpowering experience that Barron's avenues constituted for his contemporaries, is Robert Glendinning's description of the great east wing avenue:

> On each side are arranged circular beds, leaving in the centre 150 feet of turf quite clear. These beds are edged with common Yew, trimmed about 2 feet high; the centre of each bed is planted with Hollyhocks, and around the edges next the Yew are dwarf Dahlias. Thus they represent immense green baskets full of flowers . . . The first line of plants behind these takes a wavy direction agreeably with the circles, and is composed exclusively of Irish Yews from 8 to 10 feet high. The first straight line of plants in the rear of them consists of Araucaria imbricata, alternated with Picea nobilis and Cryptomeria japonica; consequently there is twice the number of Araucarias as of each of the others. The second row is planted with Cedars of Lebanon and Deodars alternately. The third line with Pinus insignis, Douglas Firs, Picea Webbiana, Abies Pinsapo, and Hemlock Spruce. These latter alternating with the Pinus insignis, which constitutes the principal feature of this line, being all large plants. Both sides are, as above, planted for the extent of half a mile, the plants being all selected specimens.

Similarly, the great east front avenue was arranged in ranks of Irish juniper, red cedars and variegated cypress, the former trimmed into columns, Chinese junipers, and yews, each row higher than the one in front, and the whole fronted by a small yew hedge. The pinetum was divided into two great sections, one devoted to pines and the other to spruces and firs, each bisected by an identical avenue; this time the rows were arranged as follows: Irish yews, golden yews, araucarias, and deodars grafted on cedars of Lebanon. 'If any artificial assemblage of trees can reach the sublime in gardening', wrote Glendinning, 'this, we imagine, is no mean example of one.'[21]

34 Elvaston Castle, Mon Plaisir. William Barron's reconstruction of a seventeenth-century plan by Daniel Marot, shown in a view by E. Adveno Brooke in 1856.

These avenues were but a preparation: closer to the Castle lay a series of formal gardens equally coniferous – some eleven miles of evergreen hedges, 'shorn as smooth as an Axminster carpet' – and little less overwhelming. Barron designed these gardens to a symbolic programme. The Earl of Harrington had scandalized society by living openly with his mistress; when he became Earl they married and retired to seclusion at Elvaston, keeping society at bay. The gardens became a shrine to the worship of love, considered as a chivalrous quest, and the crusading knight and his lady formed the theme of the decorations.[22]

The theme was set explicitly in the Alhambra garden, whose 'Moorish' pavilion housed an image of the Earl kneeling before his wife. The planting was made to parallel the architecture: columns and entablatures imitated in yew, so smoothly shorn as to be 'as perfect as if they were hewn out of stone or marble'. This was followed by the garden of Fairstar, with a Gothick wing by James Wyatt, inaccurate enough to be made to stand for Moorish, as the hall: the interior decorations featured such devices as hearts, lovers' knots, birds of paradise. Once again, the topiary mimicked

35 Elvaston Castle, the Alhambra garden. Brooke's view of Barron's topiary imitating architectural effects.

the architecture, shaped into minarets and columns, the latter sometimes capped with crowns of grafted yew; a crescent-shaped bower of roses continued the Moorish theme, and marble statues were placed in compartments with scroll bedding.[23] In the garden of the Earl's three sisters, a geometric design was planted with masses of scented plants, honeysuckles and roses being specifically named.[24]

The most publicized of these gardens was the one known as 'Mon Plaisir'. This reproduced a seventeenth-century design by Daniel Marot, probably the closest equivalent to a mediaeval plan available to Barron and the Earl. The garden was enclosed by walls of yew, 'the tops cut off as square as if they were pieces of masonry'; within these wound a covered walk forming a long tunnel of arbor vitae, with small viewing windows cut into its walls. Loudon, who did not know the provenance of the design, praised it for its 'ancient character'. Symmetrically positioned on the lawn inside were yews carved to form niches for statues; yews trimmed into columns, with crowns of yew grafted on their tops; and, as the central feature, the one major departure from Marot's design. Surrounded by a star-shaped formation of yew and holly beds, embellished with scrolls of bedding plants, stood a monkey-puzzle, the tallest specimen at Elvaston; as this was planted when araucarias were still not commercially available – probably the most expensive single plant in the garden – it could reasonably stand as a symbol of the crusader's quest in foreign lands.[25]

Apart from the achievement of creating such an elaborate and mature garden from scratch in little more than a decade, the startling quality of Elvaston was its complete artificiality. Although a lake and rockwork were created at some distance from the house, and attracted much admiration, the dominant effect was still the triumph of formality, the repudiation of the claims of the natural. For Robert Glendinning, Barron had dispensed entirely with the picturesque. The gardens were substantially complete by the early 1840s, but because of the Earl's reclusive habits they remained a closed book to the public. Only a few select personages from the gardening world gained admission, among them Loudon, Thomas Appleby, and the American nurseryman Robert Buist. Each in his way was overawed, Appleby rolling on the ground in ecstasy, Buist continuing to explore the garden by moonlight. In 1849 and 1850, Glendinning took the gardening world by surprise with a detailed account in the *Gardeners' Chronicle*; his unsurprising verdict was that Elvaston was 'the greatest work of gardening skill, both in extent and design, which perhaps any man ever accomplished in one life-time before'.[26]

In 1851 the Earl of Harrington died, and the gardens were at last thrown open to the public. It was, however, the end of Elvaston's height of glory; the Earl had overspent himself, and his successor was forced to reduce the gardening establishment from ninety to eight. By the 1870s the effects of reduced maintenance and failure to thin out were evident, and Thomas Baines predicted that the struggle for life among the trees would soon turn into 'a war of extermination'.[27] Barron opened a nursery at nearby Borrowash in the 1850s and began to offer his transplanting skills commercially, eventually emerging, in a changed climate and with a new style, as an influential landscape gardener.

The Liberation of Colour

At neither Chatsworth nor Elvaston was ornamental bedding a principal feature. But throughout the 1830s and 1840s the interest in filling the flower garden with nasses of colour was steadily increasing, and the new flowers being introduced from hotter climates yielded much brighter and more emphatic colours than the herbaceous plants traditionally available.

As the debate grew over the comparative merits of massing and mixing colours, one of the most potent arguments offered for massing was 'that masses of flowers of one sort in a garden are in direct imitation of nature herself, who in a wild state scatters profusely en masse'. Looking back later on the origins of the bedding system, Andrew Murray attributed the initial impulse to an attempt to imitate 'the vast flowering prairies of Mexico ... It was the Nemophilas, the Coreopsides, the Eschscholtzias of these plains that first formed the glowing beds' of English gardens.[28]

The analogy with nature no doubt helped to maintain an interest in massing, but it was to be replaced as a leading argument by the insistence that the flower garden was to be a work of art, not of nature. This new emphasis was primarily due to John Caie, head gardener to the Duke of Bedford at Bedford Lodge, Kensington, who by the end of the 1830s had decisively seized the intellectual leadership from the earliest proponents of massing such as Philip Frost of Dropmore. In 1838, his account of Bedford Lodge was published in the *Gardener's Magazine*,[29] and from the late 1830s to the early 1850s he published sporadic articles on colour schemes. Personal contact played a larger role in spreading his ideas, though; Caie helped to set up one of the most important of gardeners' societies, the West London Gardeners' Association, through which he came in contact with Robert Fish, whom he described as 'his interpreter'. D. T. Fish, Robert's younger brother, later reminisced about the impact Caie had had in the 1830s:

> Take, for example, the bedding-out system, of which in its best form he was undoubtedly the originator. He was literally possessed with, lost in it, for years. He would talk for hours of the proper proportion of green to grey, of light and shade, the contrasts and harmonies of colour, the relative breadths of flower-beds and shrubberies to open spaces, of gravel to grass, of life and repose in landscape, of cold colours and warm, of the proportion of tall trees to dwarf bushes and flowers, &c., until the Dowager Duchess of Bedford's garden ... became a lesson-book of decorative landscape art for all England.[30]

Caie's principles may be itemized as follows. First, colours should be 'clean, simple, and intelligible', and presented in solid masses, not mixed together; Caie repeatedly condemned the 'small artist' who aimed for variety at the expense of expressiveness. Second, colours should be arranged primarily for contrast: it destroyed effect to have adjoining beds

> in which the colour of one mass is at all traceable in that of the other; for example, orange and reds, blue and lilacs, must never appear together, but orange and purple, yellow and blue, blue and white, red and blue always contrast well, and set off one another.

Third, the size of the beds, as well as their positioning, should be borne in mind in planting; beds of equal size demanded colours of equal brightness, while a small bed of bright colour balanced a large one of subdued colour. The heights of the plants used ought also to be proportional to the size of the beds. Fourth, simple forms for beds should be preferred to complex ones; circles were best of all. Last, 'order is the source of peace', and this could only be achieved by balance and proportion (not the same thing as symmetry, which Caie did not insist on). Solid masses allowed the eye to rest, instead of continually agitating it by small juxtapositions; the eye's first impression ought to be one of dignity and 'greatness of expression'.[31]

These principles of massing were increasingly adopted by the gardening community throughout the 1840s, and by mid-century it was widely considered an error not to contrast colours;[32] D. R. Hay argued that only colours widely separated on the rainbow could harmonize together.[33] In 1845 the Royal Botanic Society offered prizes for the best examples of colour arrangement on a small scale.[34]

Over this period, the choice of plants suitable for summer bedding consolidated itself. Some bedding lists of the 1830s, such as Robert

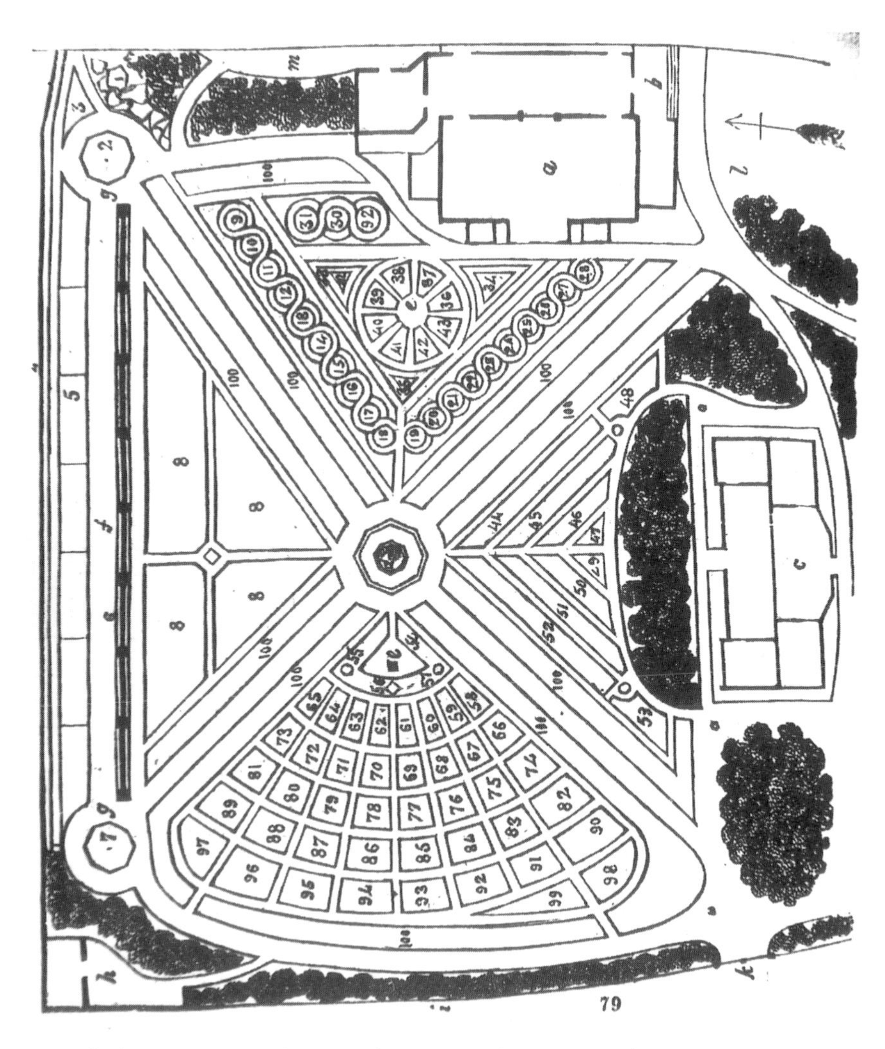

36 Bedford Lodge, John Caie's plan of the garden. Its diversity is shown by the planting of the lower fan in early summer: *Gilia*, 58, 60, 95; stocks, 66, 68, 73; *Cheiranthus*, 67, 72; verbenas, 74, 79; petunias, 77, 84, 87; pelargoniums, 75, 78; calceolarias, 76, 85–86, 88; lupins, 81, 89–90, 97. Other genera included *Lasthenia*, 59; *Crucianella*, 61; *Nemophila*, 62–63; *Eutoca*, 64; *Collomia*, 65; *Alyssum*, 69; *Polemonium*, 70; *Iberis*, 71; *Clarkia*, 80; *Lysimachia*, 82; delphiniums, 83; *Oenothera*, 91; *Geum*, 92; *Antirrhinum*, 93; *Mimulus*, 94; *Chelone*, 98; *Asclepias*, 99. Some of these would be replaced later in the season by additional verbenas, phlox, *Nierembergia*, *Erigeron*, *Eschscholtzia*, *Malope*, etc.

Mangles's, recommended Californian and Mexican flowers – *Nemophila*, *Collinsia*, *Gilia*, *Collomia*, *Platystemon*, and *Eschscholtzia* – all of which were represented in the schemes at Bedford Lodge in 1838.[35] However, another group of plants used by Caie eventually came to dominate all of these as bedding plants. Various species of South African and South American plants rapidly gained favour for their brilliant hues: *Pelargonium* (originally called *Geranium*, to much subsequent confusion), *Lobelia*, *Petunia*, *Verbena*, *Calceolaria*, *Salvia splendens*; these came to be the primary bedding plants, because the vast ranges of hybrid forms produced from them alone virtually covered the spectrum. During the 1830s and 1840s they were intensively hybridized, and by 1850 the bedding range covered six colour groups: yellow, purple, scarlet, blue, pink, and white.[36]

Caie left London to become head gardener at Inverary Castle in 1856, leaving Donald Beaton, formerly head gardener at Shrubland Park, as the main publicist of the bedding system. But by that time the bedding system was so well established as to seem indestructible, with a future of perpetual experiment and improvement in store for it – if only the refinements of colour theory could be sorted out.

> We have a new school, which can hardly be said to have had existence in 1825, and its merits were not discussed in print before 1831 or 1832 . . . and here we are now practising and studying in this new school without a vocabulary, a grammar, or a dictionary (and the old books only make our darkness more visible) the best plans according to the old style of planting.[37]

Virtuoso Horticulture

We have already seen the impact of Trentham on the development of the Italian garden. Despite the importance of Barry's design, however, the garden's fame during the 1840s and '50s was largely based on the horticultural achievements of its head gardener, George Fleming, who made Trentham a byword for innovation on a heroic scale, the testing ground for ideas that were to filter into advanced practice a decade later.[38]

Fleming arrived at Trentham in 1841 to carry out Barry's plans for the gardens, and his exploit in turning the barren site into a rich and fertile estate – laying a network of drains six feet deep and intermixing the soil to that depth with ashes and manures – rivalled Barry's in terracing a virtually flat site. As part of these works Fleming designed for himself a Gothic cottage which so impressed Barry that he made only minor alterations to his plan.[39] He next improved the glass ranges and caught public attention with his experiments in heating. In 1848, Robert Glendinning summarized his achievements to date in a series of articles in the *Gardeners' Chronicle*, and by the 1850s Trentham had developed a high reputation as an experimental and as a teaching garden.[40]

Fleming played an immense role in popularizing the bedding system, making Trentham the best-known and most influential garden for this purpose until the opening of the Crystal Palace Park. Fleming and Donald Beaton competed with each other in their bedding experiments, and Trentham served in effect as a demonstration ground for many of the principles Beaton expounded in his writings. Here one could study 'harmony of colour; the true definition of contrast; the graceful blending of the trailing with the erect species'; the importance of heights and proportions of growth as well as colour in parallelism and contrast. Each season brought innovation to the gardens: 'every year they are diversified, every year more expressive; and the thousands of plants required in its decoration brings the arrangement to a gigantic scale'.[41]

Two innovations, which emerged simultaneously at Trentham and Shrubland Park, deserve particular notice. The ribbon border was a long narrow bed arranged in rows:

> Each border is occupied with three continuous lines of colour extending their whole length. The first on each side of the walk is blue; the second yellow; and the third, on one side, is scarlet, and on the other, white. The following are the plants employed on one side: – Nemophila insignis, for blue; Calceolaria rugosa, for yellow; and the Frogmore geranium, for scarlet.[42]

Shading, 'the highest style in the art of flower-gardening' (attributed by Beaton to the invention of Lady Middleton at Shrubland), was based on Berlin wool work: rows or groups of plants with extremely similar colour were planted adjacently, to 'blend so perfectly that you cannot tell where

37 Trentham, the lake. Although Barry's plan for a miniature Isola Bella in the lake was not carried out, an Italian element was added by the provision of a gondolier. View by E. A. Brooke, 1856.

the one ends or the other begins', thus creating an apparently seamless sequence of colours over some distance.[43]

Both of these devices were used to extend the flower gardens further into the landscape. In the 'rainbow walk', his last major addition to the flower gardens in the 1850s, Fleming pushed shading to its highest development:

> Two beds, divided by a gravel walk, in a direct line 200 yards long, slope gently towards the river; each, about 9 feet wide, is planted with flowers to represent the colours of the rainbow. The left side also contains a succession of circular raised beds, with festoons of roses; and a background of hollyhocks tower up in front of a well-trimmed, thick hedge of evergreens, shaded in turn by forest trees and others.

Elsewhere, within sight of the Italian garden, a serpentine bed of forget-me-nots, known as 'the rivulet', wound down towards the lake in imitation of a meandering stream.[44]

Beyond the confines of the flower garden, Fleming drained a twelve-acre area of fen and turned it into an arboretum. This was planted in irregular masses, exhibiting the same juxtaposition of 'natural' and artificial as at Chatsworth. Deciduous and coniferous trees, natives and exotics, were placed in contrasting groups. The outlines of the shrub beds followed the best picturesque rules for natural contours, with deep recesses and extensions, but the entire area on which these beds were placed was carpeted by the smoothest turf possible. Unexpected combinations abounded: hollies grouped with ferns; Mexican trees with American rhododendrons, heath borders, and a wild honeysuckle; arbutus and yew forming a background to a collection of hawthorn varieties. Glendinning praised the effect of 'wild bushes which appear as if they were dropped by nature on the lawn'. Heaths were used extensively as ground covers to edge, fill spaces, and form independent beds as foregrounds to the main groups. Some of the groupings were based on geographical distribution: besides the Mexican/American group just noted, there was an Italian cluster, and an Irish plantation composed of arbutus, Irish yews, furze, and ivy.[45]

Another ambitious experiment was undertaken by the banks of the lake. The major masses consisted of heaths and *Berberis*, with white and yellow brooms and a variety of herbaceous plants on their margins; but this marginal planting also consisted of plants with ornamental foliage, positioned for viewing from the opposite shore – rhubarb, cardoons, giant *Heracleum*. After Fleming's example, other gardeners, like John Caie, quickly began experimenting with foliage groupings.[46]

By the early 1850s Fleming was extending his sights, and carrying his experiments in colour grouping into the broader landscape. This time it was Thomas Appleby who carried the news of Fleming's enterprise to the world:

> Mr. Fleming has carried out the planting masses of shrubs of one colour with good effect, especially with the Rhododendron . . . in particular situations may be seen a large mass of the white varieties – in another, a mass of purple, another of rose, another of scarlet. These, at the part where they come in contact, are judiciously intermixed, so as to soften and blend the two colours together. This attention to planting trees and shrubs, so as to give masses of breadth and colour, is a mark of the onward march of a higher taste in laying out and planting pleasure grounds; and such men as Mr. Fleming, placed in a position to be able to carry such novel views into effect, may be considered as the benefactors of landscape gardening.

Robert Errington, similarly, regarded Fleming as having created by his colour groupings 'a sort of middle distance, – what I must call transition ground' between the gardens and the surrounding woods, and thus having given a new sort of visual unity to the entire landscape.[47]

By the 1850s, the lake was silting up as a result of effluent from the river Trent, and Fleming's last structural alterations involved the transplanting of several trees to accommodate the new course of the stream, and the use of ground covers to carpet the newly exposed ground and make it look old. 'Mr. Fleming bent the course of the river, cleansed it in a singularly off-hand way of its impurities, and gave new life to the locality', wrote Appleby, who saw the works soon after completion. Within a few years, the new riverbanks were thriving with bullrushes and irises, and the area had been planted in characteristic Fleming style: 'we wind amongst masses of the white Rhododendron and orange Azalea, which are particularly striking, in contrast to the purple colours formerly so much used. We were also struck with the liberal use of the woodbine, foxglove, and Scotch thistle in these grounds . . .'[48]

In 1860, Fleming was appointed steward for the Sutherland estate, and henceforth his mind was put to work on agricultural and administrative matters. His successors simplified many of his additions to the gardens.[49] But for twenty years Fleming's reputation for effortlessly contriving miracles, like Paxton's and Barron's, had helped to cast the figure of the gardener in a heroic mould.

Woodland Embellishment

The extension of artificial character at Trentham from the garden proper into the landscape was the culmination of a trend which included arboreta of exotic trees, winter gardens, planting for autumn colour, and the colour grouping of American shrubs at gardens like Highclere and Claremont. By 1830, at gardens like Bagshot Park and Caen Wood, the exotic collections were being introduced into the ordinary woods and plantations that surrounded the pleasure-grounds. 'It seems to be part of the plan of management at Bagshot', reported Loudon, 'to distribute exotic trees over the margins of the native woods, and so, gradually, to give them a highly enriched and botanical character.'[50]

Probably the most significant and widespread example of this practice was the use of rhododendrons as underwood, to replace the laurels so frequently used for that purpose. The self-seeding of rhododendrons had been observed at Caen Wood, Bagshot, and Fonthill by 1830,[51] but was still being proclaimed as a novel discovery in 1841, when Sir George Mackenzie and others excitedly announced the fact to the *Gardeners' Chronicle*. Philip Frost had already grasped its implications, and was busy transforming the Dropmore landscape:

> In the woods here we have, by a little attention, thousands of self-sown seedling *Rhododendron ponticum*, growing on any kind of soil except stiff clay . . . When in bloom, nothing can surpass the beauty of Rhododendrons in woods; last year the woods here were quite enchanting with them. It is very easy to fill woods with them, by sowing the seed broad-cast, where it is desirable to have them.[52]

As the 1840s advanced, the mixing of exotics with native woodland trees became steadily more common. This new taste was nowhere more strikingly exemplified than in the proposals announced in 1853 for turning Hampstead Heath into a municipal park. Learning that part of the Belsize estate was to be sold for building, C. R. Cockerell urged that a portion of the land be seized for public use and a grand boulevard constructed from Primrose Hill to the Heath, which could be partially terraced and planted as an arboretum. The proposals were greeted with enthusiasm by the *Gardeners' Chronicle*:

> In our existing parks that charming diversity of trees, from which so many picturesque effects are derivable, is impossible. Elms, Limes, Planes, and Sycamores must always form the principal features of places lying on the heavy cold soil of the north, or in the smoke-begrimed plains of the west of London: but in the soil of Hampstead Heath all the finer forms of vegetation may be

> expected to thrive; masses of American plants may blend with groves of Deodars and all our glorious new conifers, while the trees of the United States, with their autumnal drapery of crimson and green and gold, would create an 'Indian summer' at the gates of London.[53]

The plan was not carried out, of course, and the only planting was that of speculative housing on the Belsize estate.

Chatsworth and Trentham showed how to juxtapose garden flowers with forest trees and wild undergrowth, but they were not alone. At Dropmore, Philip Frost was introducing 'masses of common Brake, Blackberry bushes, and Sweet Briar . . . in striking contrast with the dressed ground', and conversely, naturalizing fuchsias under the beech trees in the woods – a 'mutual blending of Nature with Art'.[54] At Watcombe Park, Brunel's Torquay estate, Alexander Forsyth planted the banks of a sweeping valley with pines and tulip trees, mixed with such Trentham-like groupings as masses of *Escallonia* and *Berberis* towered over by giant *Heracleum*.[55]

The planting of bulbs and wildflowers in lawns, apparently a Scottish practice from early in the century, was commended by Lauder, and by 1850 some English gardens were experimenting with naturalizing bulbs in meadows, despite problems in reconciling floral swards with summer scything.[56] It remained a minority practice, however, until the 1860s, when John Fleming, who had already pioneered the use of spring bulbs in the parterre, employed masses of naturalized bulbs, primroses, and violets in landscaping a valley at Cliveden.[57] After his example, naturalized bulbs became a speedily popular fashion; spring flowers colonized the waste places at gardens like Elvaston Castle; indeed, the oldest great snowdrop fields probably date from this time.[58] The seed firm of Barr and Sugden, opened at Covent Garden in 1861, became the country's pre-eminent bulb establishment under the direction of Peter Barr; one of its special offers from its first year was its packets of mixed annual seed, for the purpose of scattering in woodlands and vacant places, to create a rich floriferous effect.[59] Finally, in 1870, William Robinson gave the tradition of woodland embellishment its textbook. *The Wild Garden* was based to a great extent on the practice of gardeners like John Fleming, whose valley at Cliveden Robinson thought the best example of recent landscaping near London, and its stated principle of 'naturalizing or making wild innumerable beautiful natives of many regions of the earth in our woods, wild and semi-wild places, rougher parts of pleasure grounds, etc.' summed up forty years of gradual experiment by head gardeners in all parts of the country.[60]

The Natural Rock Garden

The practice of rockwork-making in the 1840s was made stormy by conflicting ideologies. On the one hand, the advocates of the geological agglomerate, of coral and flints, and of upward-pointing spikes were still active; indeed, Joshua Major was offering instruction on the making of conical rockeries in 1852, and Robert Thompson was still recommending a studied variety in the position of the stones as late as 1859.[61] On the other hand, the advocates of the imitation of nature were gaining ground; most of the gardening magazines recommended this position; and the necessity of 'a bold natural appearance in its general form and outline' was the dominant wisdom of the day.[62] Three rock gardens in particular were singled out in the gardening press as exemplary.

At Pencarrow, Cornwall, Sir William Molesworth and his gardener Corbett constructed a rockery in 1831–34 at the fringe of the Italian garden. It was composed of rocks, some weighing up to three tons, brought in carts by local farmers; the rocks, instead of being quarried, were chosen from specimens found lying at least partially exposed, and placed in position already clothed with lichen and moss. Edward Luckhurst described it in the 1870s:

> bold in character, broken and picturesque – a high ridge with projections and detached masses advancing so far in front of it as to form all sorts of nooks and recesses containing Ferns, Heaths, dwarf flowering shrubs such as Fuchsias, Berberis, Andromedas. The rocks are not deposited in regular strata, but are arranged as a series of irregular peaks in imitation of the Dartmoor tors . . .

Luckhurst was the only writer to mention the Dartmoor effect, which probably formed no part of the original intention.[63]

William Barron began constructing a rock garden at Elvaston Castle in 1838, in effect transplanting rocks as methodically as he had transplanted trees. Most of the rockwork skirted the new lake, towering in places to heights of more than forty feet. 'Enormous columnar rocks of great height', 'scattered boulders of rocks, which rise in majestic grandeur out of the turf': the rocks were planted with masses of conifers and hollies, carpeted with *Cotoneaster* and *Berberis*, while a collection of shrubs and alpines was liberally scattered about. Robert Glendinning, predictably, was awestruck by the 'inconceivable' scale of the creation:

> When we contemplate, for a moment, that this is entirely a work of art, and consider the tens of thousands of tons of rocks all brought from a great distance, employed in its formation, we are left to conclude that it has not only no rival as a work of art, but there is nothing at all approaching it, in any garden in this country.

The Duke of Wellington pronounced it the most natural-looking rockery he had seen; but Barron had not been totally subservient to nature in his design, and from time to time the boulders were arranged in circles or arches – instantly dispelling, as John Robson remarked, the notion that the mass was a natural one.[64]

Paxton began the great rockery at Chatsworth in 1842, and two years later it was reported that 'huge masses of rock are collecting and forming into a rockwork, the like of which has never before been seen. Some of these masses weigh upwards of 370 tons.' A portion of the rockwork was arranged as an imitation of the Strid at Bolton Abbey: 'it appears as if Sir Joseph Paxton had, by some supernatural means, cut out a slice of one of the Derbyshire hills and transferred it to the spot'. Pure naturalism, however, was never Paxton's aim, and a straight walk and formal staircases were led through part of the rockery. Masses of rock were cemented together to compose larger wholes; one monolithic construction, known as the Wellington rock, towered some forty feet high, with a waterfall

38 Chatsworth, the rock garden. An imitation of the Strid at Bolton, constructed by Joseph Paxton beginning in 1842.

cascading down its facade.[65]

These three rock gardens were regarded as setting new standards in naturalistic construction; yet within a generation all were to be condemned or dismissed as failures or bad examples. Both Chatsworth and Elvaston had rocks grouped to form arches or viewing windows; such arches, argued Major, 'are never seen in nature, and ought never to have been introduced'. By the 1870s it was being asserted that the Chatsworth rockery could deceive nobody.[66] It can hardly be assumed that Paxton and Barron were ignorant of geological formation, but this was the only explanation Peter Mackenzie could offer for failure in rockwork construction:

> If a poor fellow be sent to the hulks for violating an unreasonable human law, surely the uninstructed pretender that seeks to invert any of Nature's plans, and pass them for what they are not, should be sentenced to seven years' solitary confinement among the wildest of the coal-formations. Are there not some who pretend to imitate the wild, romantic masses of rocks and trees in the creation of Salvator Rosa, who know as little about the arrangement of the stratified and unstratified rocks of our country as about the fossil megatherium?

A visit to a Highland glen was his recommended form of education.[67]

This passage indicates the transition in concepts of the natural. For the generation of the 1830s the standards of naturalism were: consistency of material (a reaction against the rococo shellwork-and-coral rockery); natural scale (a reaction against the scale-model alps at Hoole House); and massiveness of stones. But by the end of the 1840s new criteria gave rise to more vigorous debate.

The two new criteria were congruity of position and stratification. Rockwork should not be attempted in the vicinity of the house, where obvious art should reign, but only where rocky outcrops would be likely to occur in nature, and it could not be regarded as natural-looking unless it presented an identifiable pattern of stratification. The arrangement of rocks should not defy the laws of geology: heavier rocks should not lie upon lighter, nor should they be inclined at different angles from each other; stones should lie upon their natural bed, and outcrops of sedimentary rocks should lie in parallels.[68]

These rules would outlaw Joshua Major's conical rockeries, but they would also, for some, outlaw the rockeries at Pencarrow (too near the house) and Elvaston (unstratified, rising in parts directly out of turf). For this reason, Robert Glendinning protested against the rule of congruity of position as a prejudice which the creative genius was privileged to disregard.[69] And one great exception to the rule of congruity was allowed: Sir Charles Isham's rockery at Lamport Hall, Northamptonshire, begun in 1848, which received uniformly favourable treatment in the horticultural press despite its commanding position in front of the house. It presented a surface full of 'deep recesses, bold protrusions, mounds as if fallen from ruins', and was planted with a wide range of climbing and carpeting plants, but above all it included dwarfed trees – for instance, a miniature willow three inches high – often the result of root-pruning. By this expedient, the planting was to some degree kept in scale with the rockwork: the aesthetic of scale modelling was developed to such a degree that its sheer consistency of approach seems to have overawed potential objectors.[70]

The interest in stratification was to have the consequence of encouraging the use of artificial stone. Paxton and others had created rockworks by cementing stones together; by the 1840s, as the demand for naturalism increased, the idea emerged of using cement as a uniform surface, to conceal the random assemblage of materials being used. In 1843, a contributor to the *Gardeners' Chronicle* recommended painting rockworks with Roman cement to obviate a disjointed appearance. Roman cement, widely used for architectural and decorative purposes since the 1790s, was dark brown in colour, requiring painting in order to resemble the Portland or Bath stone for which it was used as a substitute. By the 1820s, therefore, the race was on to develop alternative cements with a Portland stone colour.[71] One pioneer of Portland cements was James Pulham, originally a decorative modeller in cement and plaster; he died in 1838, to be succeeded by his son, also named James.[72] In that year the first rock garden in 'Pulhamite stone' was begun at Hoddesdon Hall; as the younger Pulham was 18 at the time, the initial idea was probably his father's, even if he was responsible for most of the execution.

> This rockery, to all appearance, consists of huge pieces of granite; but in reality it is composed of large blocks of artificial stone, formed of brick rubbish,

cement, &c. Though completed only a few months, the stone had the appearance of having braved the storms of a thousand winters . . .[73]

From 1848 the younger Pulham was operating from Broxbourne, Hertfordshire, and gradually abandoning the manufacture of cement in favour of its use in the construction of rockeries. His earliest works seem to have mixed natural and artificial stone; the most important of these was at Highnam Court, Gloucester, begun in 1849 for Thomas Gambier Parry, employing Pulhamite stone for a series of rocky outcrops. Masses of clinker would be assembled, the Portland cement mixture poured over them, and the resulting concretions mounded into the semblance of boulders; sandstone was most often simulated, both because of its colour and because its sedimentary formations could be efficiently copied, often tilted in imitation of faults. Praise for his successful replications of geological detail accompanied Pulham throughout his career.[74]

Congruity and Contrast

The same years in the 1840s and early 1850s which saw the heroic works of Barron and Fleming burst into public consciousness also saw a vigorous call for a return to congruity, a re-assertion of the value of the genius of the place rather than of the gardener. The seeds of this reaction were sown with the republication in 1842 of Price's *Essays on the Picturesque*. While much of the detailed argument in the *Essays* was no longer relevant to horticultural interests, much else remained, and in the late 1840s, after the death of Loudon, a number of voices were raised to re-affirm the Pricean tradition of picturesque unity as opposed to the Reptonian tradition of diversity.

First, in 1847–48, a long series of articles on the theory and history of landscape gardening was published in the *Gardeners' Chronicle* by its editor John Lindley.[75] Then, in 1850, Edward Kemp, Paxton's foreman at Birkenhead Park, now its superintendent, brought out the first edition of his *How to Lay Out a Small Garden*. In 1852, two veteran landscape gardeners published treatises retrospectively based on their practice: *The Theory and Practice of Landscape Gardening* by Joshua Major of Leeds, and *Parks and Pleasure Grounds* by the Scottish gardener Charles H.J. Smith.[76] The Scottish picturesque received additional support two years later in the young David Gorrie's 'Features in Scottish Scenery', published in the *Scottish Gardener*.[77] Despite their various differences among themselves – Major, in particular, was treated with extreme disrespect by Lindley and others,[78] and they disagreed in their estimates of Paxton and 'Capability' Brown – their works shared enough similarities to justify presenting their ideas as a single argument.

The most important question was the use of contrast in garden organization. Major examined at length Paxton's yoking together of art and nature at Chatsworth – the coupling, for instance, of wild undergrowth with fine lawns, or of formal staircases with 'rude natural-like rockwork'. His objection was 'not because the effect is not in some cases pleasing, but because the associations are not in unison'; and this fault he saw not as a deliberate play with associations, but as a failure to attend to the principles

39 Pencarrow, the rock garden. A pioneer of naturalism when constructed in 1831–34, although later rock gardens placed greater emphasis on laying stones on their natural bed.

of the picturesque. In the 1820s, he recalled, he himself had been led into employing the 'free, cheerful, and flowing' style in inappropriate circumstances:

> I remember having, upwards of twenty years ago, an extensive quarry to operate upon in the grounds connected with a gentleman's house. I laid this out with graceful winding walks and smooth lawn, planted the whole with corresponding flowers and cultivated shrubs, and erected suitable rustic seats. The whole presented a scene highly interesting and pleasing, and is considered such to the present time. Yet, I must confess, I was then in error; – congruity was overlooked, 'smooth shaven lawn', and graceful winding walks, and cultivated shrubs, had no business in such a locality.[79]

Smith and Kemp similarly censured the 'mixture of the formal and the free, the decorated and the simple, the picturesque and the polished'. There should be a clear demarcation between the precincts of the house and the surrounding park, where nature, or its effective imitation, should reign.[80] Congruity of setting was paralleled by congruity of ornament within the garden proper. Lindley attacked inappropriate forms of sculptural decoration, condemning the use of the pyramid and the obelisk ('you can never clothe it with that Association of Ideas which alone can give it interest'), and argued that the intrinsic associations of subject matter were more important than historical precedent.[81] Smith criticized the use of sculpture in Britain altogether, where it could never carry the associations of antiquity it did in Italy.[82]

Congruity of association in the wider landscape tended to focus on questions of scale and appropriate position. Smith, Major, and others insisted that stationary water ought always to be placed on the lowest ground, although Lindley, defending 'Capability' Brown, argued that lakes did not always occupy the lowest ground in reality.[83] The question of terraces was more engrossing, as it meant coming to terms with the ideology of historical revival. David Gorrie urged that national styles in gardening were related to the geological conformation of their native landscapes, so that formal styles were out of harmony with the picturesque scenery of Scotland.

> The terraced gardens of Italy cannot change places with the formal gardens of Holland; and, if the strictly geometrical style, with its clipped hedges, and its vegetable sculpture, has found a place for a time even in countries naturally picturesque, the reign of that style in such countries has been but temporary, and taste, in its progress towards perfection, has discovered that contrasts may be too violent, that novelty cannot be of long duration, and that harmony, while it admits of both novelty and contrast, keeps them within due limits.[84]

Major and Lindley both wished to limit the exercise of art near the house, condemning historical revivalism (at least in its Elizabethan form), though only Major would have proscribed terraces altogether.[85]

The question of scale is of particular interest, for it was on this issue that Major himself was found wanting by his contemporaries. Queen's Park was one of his three Manchester parks, opened in 1846. The following year, a correspondent in the *Gardeners' Chronicle* itemized a series of faults he found in it: an absence of curving walks; a profusion of straight paths with acute angles; grass borders as uniform as ribbons flanking the paths;

diminutive lakes averaging five yards by three; brooks two feet wide, with waterfalls of three feet, crossed by disproportionately large bridges. Major defended the straight walks as appropriate to areas set aside for games, and argued that the diminutive lakes were merely undulating swells in the rivulets, adding that:

> There is certainly one sheet of water deserving the name of lake, which is five times the dimensions of the one described to you as being the largest, and only 12 yards by 8; the margin of which is naturally varied with graceful curves, and well furnished with trees and shrubs, producing a most happy effect; and a more pleasing sheet of water, for its size, we venture to say, it would be difficult to find. It is on a small scale we admit, but it is as large as the abrupt nature of the ground would allow.

Major's argument was, in effect, that he had striven to maintain congruity of character throughout the landscape, but that discrepancies in scale were unavoidable; that of his opponents was that discrepancy of scale nullified any other form of congruity. Lindley in particular turned his ammunition on Major:

> Seriously, however, we do not see that any material portion of the charges is denied. The multiplicity of angles still remains. The Grass margins, like ribbon strips, are confessed. The bridge of 16 yards over the two feet wide brook is not disowned. The dear little Strawberry-hill playthings – the Gothic parapets of wood – are hushed over by poetic license. There is a '*swelling*' rivulet as well as '*swelling*' walks; and these chronic or periodical swellings were *not* designed to be lakes. Out correspondent was a stupid person for calling them so. But there is one piece of water worthy of that name. It is not 12 yards by 8, but at least 60 yards by 40. O Windermere and Ulleswater hide your diminished heads! Manchester art beats your natural beauty and magnificence hollow. For the artists themselves say of their own work 'a more pleasing sheet of water it would be difficult to find.'
>
> And this is LANDSCAPE GARDENING in the 19th century.

Robert Glendinning added his weight to the condemnation, faulting the park for an absence of 'unity of expression'. Major was finally forced to abandon his aesthetic arguments and to claim that the park could not have been made more artistic without sacrificing the sports facilities.[86]

Unity of expression was a double-edged concept. Glendinning found it at Elvaston and Trentham, in the imposition of the artist's style on the landscape, but Smith argued that simple unity could never be obtained; a park being too large to be viewed as one picture, 'absence of discordance' was all that could be hoped for.[87] On the other hand, it could also be used to imply the accommodation of the garden to the existing character of its surroundings. Thus, David Gorrie: 'however beautiful an ornate park may be in itself, it is lacking in harmony and in fitness if its beauties have no connection with those of the country around it'.[88]

The question of the propriety of associations was central to the Pricean revival; but most of these writers reverted to a narrow and literalist view of associations. David Gorrie, for instance, declared that 'the first principles of landscape gardening are founded on mental ideas and poetical associations'. For this reason he claimed that Loudon's gardenesque style had corrupted gardening by shifting the emphasis from poetry to botany; it evidently never occurred to him that taxonomy or geographical distribution could be regarded as themselves a source of associations.[89] And certainly the idea of gaining an effect by frustrating customary associations did not endear itself to Joshua Major, who detected this insidious tendency in Paxton's work. The columns in the geometric garden at Chatsworth were not ruins, not even arranged to suggest the outline of a previous building; they therefore appeared to him 'void of association, – modern pillars introduced for no other purpose than to support climbers'.[90] Kemp alone, no doubt because of his training under Paxton, was prepared to aim at a pure response to form independent of the narrower types of association.[91]

The influence of this reaction should not be over-estimated. Of all these writers, only Edward Kemp had a decisive influence on gardening style, and his views had been significantly modified by the time of his third edition in 1864. Chatsworth, Elvaston, and Trentham were excitingly new and powerful; Loudon's influence was still greater than that of any of his rivals, and there were major figures like Robert Glendinning to uphold the example of Elvaston against imposed rules of propriety:

> It is by accomplishing such feats, in defiance of natural obstacles, and in opposition to existing prejudices likewise, which have been set down as defined principles, that these rules and theoretical injunctions have been exposed.[92]

But the idea of congruity was in the air; it haunted the minds of the gardeners of the 1850s, who had to follow where Paxton and Fleming had led; and as a result the practical influence of the great gardens of the 1830s and 1840s was cautiously channelled, as gardeners looked for ways of reconciling the conflicting ideals.

Biddulph Grange

The garden that was publicized as providing the solution to the quandary was Biddulph Grange, Staffordshire. James Bateman, its owner, had an immense horticultural reputation, based primarily on his work with orchids,[93] but also on the rockworks at his father's garden, Knypersley Hall. 'Noble rock work and giant proportions' was the verdict of his later collaborator, Cooke, while Robert Errington thought that 'The mantle of Price seems to have fallen on his shoulders... When he copies, it is from the highest school of all – Nature'.[94] In 1842, Bateman moved to the nearby Biddulph Grange; the main works began with the arrival of Cooke in 1849.

E. W. Cooke achieved his greatest fame as a marine painter, but his artistic development led him equally into the gardening world: he was the son-in-law of George Loddiges, and the protégé of William Wells of Redleaf, where he was sketching the rocks in 1836, by which time he was also associating with Robert Glendinning.[95] Cooke's first visit to Biddulph was made in September 1849; the garden was substantially complete by the mid-1850s, although Cooke's works continued sporadically into the 1860s. In the meantime, Bateman had begun opening his garden to the public, and Edward Kemp had publicized it in two series of articles in the

Gardeners' Chronicle, in 1856 and again in 1862. Kemp was by this time the acclaimed author of *How to Lay Out a Small Garden*, and his words had weight; it is his words that will be quoted in what follows.[96]

The Grange was an Italian-style house, given an architectural setting by an Italianate terrace with yew hedges trimmed into piers. One of the features framed by these hedges was an embroidery parterre, using beds of China roses and a mosaic pattern of box and coloured sands. Away from the house, the garden was subdivided into sections for different categories of plants, including a herbaceous border, American garden, rose garden and dahlia walk.

The most important of such divisions, the pinetum and arboretum, attested to the influence of Chatsworth and Elvaston respectively. The pinetum was arranged on either side of a long curving walk, in a manner loosely modelled on the arboretum at Chatsworth, and readily accepted by Kemp as 'doubtless the only true' idea of a pinetum. The trees were elevated on mounds, after the manner of the Derby Arboretum and Birkenhead Park, 'bringing the beautiful forms of many of the sorts between the spectator and the sky, without any intervening background'. The influence of Elvaston was shown in a multi-layered avenue added after 1856: wellingtonias and deodars; banks behind them clothed with briar roses; then red-flowering chestnuts, then Austrian pines. Bateman's practice differed from Barron's in his inclusion of deciduous subjects, and the arboretum, to which the avenue led, expanded this into an experiment in colour grouping to rival Fleming's at Trentham: maples, thorns, furze, heaths, *Liquidambar*, and *Rubus leucodermis*, 'of which there is a large jungle, and which is remarkable for its singular white stems'.

If colour formed an organizing principle in the arboretum, in the heart of the garden the emphasis changed to plant form – the more exaggerated the better. The rootery had been emphasized in the literature on Chinese gardens from Chambers onward, and was represented at Biddulph by an area studded with the stems of old trees inserted, roots upward, in the ground, to be draped with ivy and other trailing plants.[98] The stumpery again made use of old roots and stumps, jutting forward from the banks and forming rustic arches, but yielding place to rocks as the path descended into 'China'. This was an area devoted to Chinese trees and shrubs, and particularly to spiral, weeping and fastigiate forms.

These diverse regions of the garden were connected, and segregated from each other, by an astonishing array of devices, enumerated by Kemp:

> Ornamental walls, or walls covered with Ivy or other climbers, Yew, Holly, and Beech hedges, covered ways or corridors of wood or stone, irregular or more formal archways, tunnels or cavern-like passages, mounds of earth, rockeries, masses of roots and trunks of trees, with larger or smaller groups of shrubs, are some of the means by which these changes are brought about.

It was this range of linking devices that excited Kemp's most enthusiastic response – and not merely because all the stones were set on their natural bed. In many ways the garden risked violating the standards of decorum he had insisted on in his writings, and in his first account of the garden, he made his reservations clear: 'the excessive multiplication of parts, which breaks up the whole area into small portions, interferes with unity and

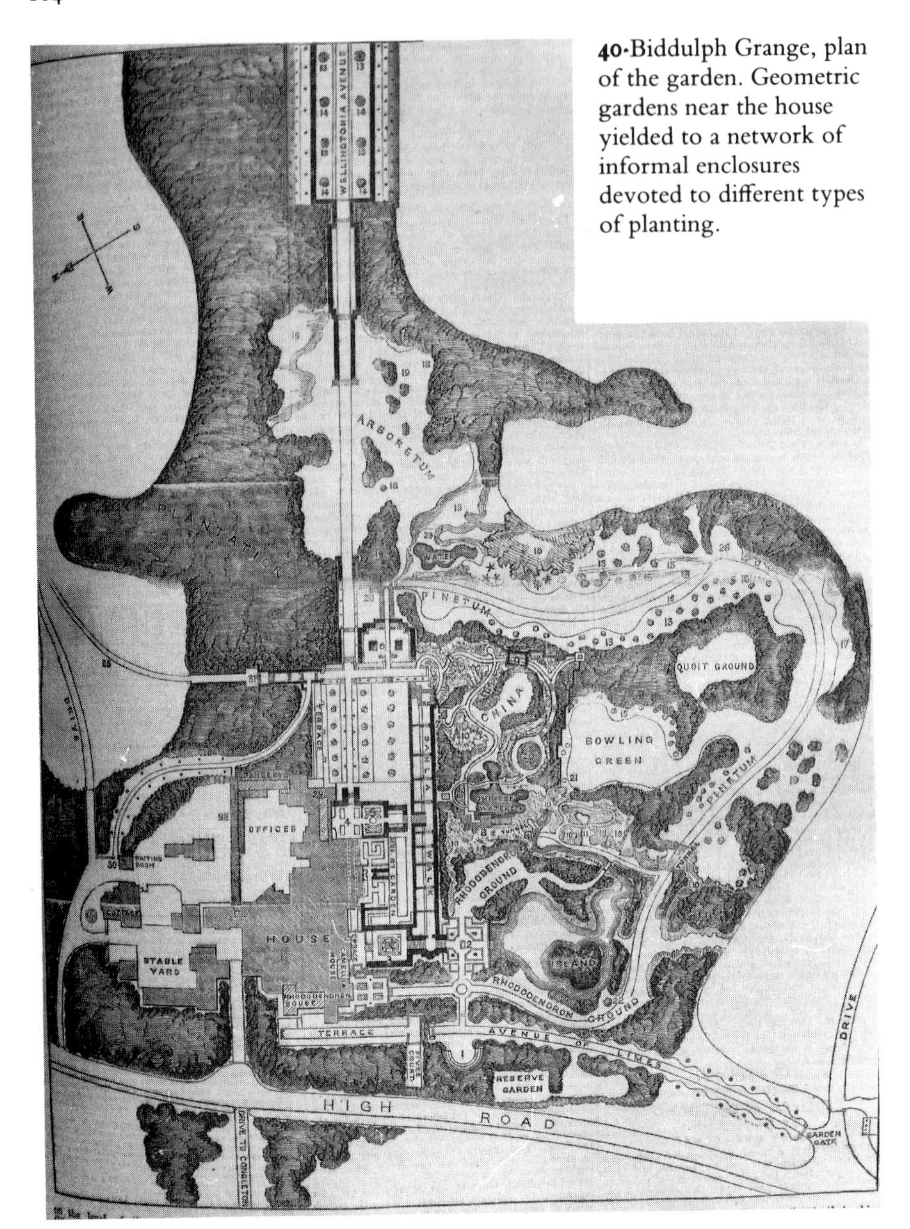

40·Biddulph Grange, plan of the garden. Geometric gardens near the house yielded to a network of informal enclosures devoted to different types of planting.

connection, and produces, in some degree, a want of breadth and repose.' But the hesitant note was overshadowed by Kemp's enthusiasm for the way Bateman and Cooke had surmounted all the occasions for incongruity that their multifaceted garden had offered.

The treatment of the terrace, with its parterre and stone dressings, satisfied his requirements for architectural harmony; the rockworks were distant, unseen from the windows, and the extensive planting which subdivided the sections nearer to the house formed 'an irregular wavy sea of shrubs and trees in which there is nothing incongruous, and which form no unpleasing foreground to the country and hills beyond'. In the further reaches of the garden, the variety of screening techniques avoided the sharp visual contrasts which affected Paxton's work at Chatsworth.

It was not the avoidance of incongruity by itself, however, that made Kemp regard Biddulph as 'a very high achievement of art'; it was the presence of a unifying principle that made the risks of incongruity worthwhile, that justified what would otherwise have been 'trifling' irregularities. The 'great and true secret' of the design, Kemp wrote, was:

> the preparation of a suitable home for nearly all the hardy members of the great plant family, which the curiosity or taste of man has discovered or cultivated . . .
>
> The principal consequences have almost necessarily arisen out of the adoption of the rule of action just mentioned; and these are the creation of a great deal of picturesqueness, and variety of outline, and the production of an unusual number of separate and independent areas, each of which has a character of its own.

There was another theme running through the garden, however – that of history. Kemp's confident analysis might account for the Chinese garden, planted predominantly with Chinese plants, but could not explain the Egyptian Court, an architectural exercise in yew and stone: yew hedges, pyramids of yew on slightly raised mounds with an edging of dwarfed golden yew (an echo of Elvaston), and sphinxes flanking a stone entrance which led to an Egyptian idol. And China was characterized not only by its characteristic vegetation but by a sequence of garden buildings designed by Cooke, including a Chinese bridge, pagoda, and temple; a rockwork to represent the Great Wall of China, complete with lookout tower; a dragon parterre; a stone frog; and models of a Chinese bull and dragons prepared by Waterhouse Hawkins. Kemp's 1856 account balanced admiration for the skill of the imitation with superior European contempt for the originals:

> The chief design of this singular piece of landscape, beyond the primary one of collecting together the numerous Chinese and Japanese hardy plants with which our gardens abound, appears to have been the representation of one of those eccentric and somewhat grotesque efforts of gardening art in which the Chinese are said to indulge, and some crude idea of which has no doubt been familiar to every one from childhood, in the old Willow-pattern dinner plate. Into a marvellously small area, the Chinaman delights to crowd his miniature models of mountains and lakes, bridges, and other architectural embellishments, and to furnish the whole with his stunted and crippled trees, or with those exaggerated strainings after picturesqueness exhibited in the use of little decrepit and half dead trees, or other deformed and monstrous vegetable objects. With his puny fort or prospect-tower crowning one of his tiny hills, and his quaint covered bridge and cosy pleasure house to decorate the pool on which a full-rigged junk rides securely at anchor, he probably dreams that he has created a prodigy of art, and adds large dragon-shaped flower beds, and other equally harmonious details, to complete the scene.
>
> Most of these curious features have been aptly imitated and embodied by Mr. Bateman in his Chinese garden . . .

(By 1862, however, Kemp had come around to acknowledging that Hawkins's bull would have been even better if it had been more grotesque.)

In 1840, George Wightwick's curious treatise *The Palace of Architecture* had envisaged a complex of gardens, including a Chinese garden with artificial rockwork and an Egyptian garden with sphinxes and obelisks.[98]

This work may have influenced Bateman's design; the Crystal Palace, with its courts devoted to different nations and periods of art, has been suggested as an analogy. The inspiration for the historical organization, however, was a religious one. In the 1840s, the imminence and accurate dating of the last judgment still excited the concern of educated men, provoking upheavals at the universities; and, in a pamphlet on the second coming published the year before Cooke began his works at Biddulph Grange, Bateman quoted with approval a recent evangelical tract which identified geology and archaeology as portents of the end of history:

> We live in an age of fossil geology. In all directions the buried remains of past ages are dug up and brought to light with persevering zeal. The records of China, and the ruins of Copan and Uxmal; the sculptured triumphs of Sesostris, the mounds of Babylon . . . all of them are brought out from their hiding-places, and rise like spectres from their tombs. A thoughtful mind will perhaps discern, in this rage for the discovery of antiquities, this rehearsal of all past history, a sign of some great change that is approaching, the consummation of the whole course of Providence for six thousand years. . . . The past, in ten thousand forms, is made to converge on the present, that we may thus be prepared for a future which shall cast them both into the shade.[99]

As a preliminary to the second coming, the world was once again bringing all its past history into light; and the garden at Biddulph Grange, by evoking vanished and alien civilizations, served as an affirmation that the millennium was coming. Bateman's works at Biddulph also extended to fossil geology, which had been mentioned as another harbinger of the millennium; by 1862 he had created a geological museum in his house, arranged in sequence according to the six 'days' of creation – understood by then to be geological epochs rather than literal days; the wall of the museum porch was inset with Roman remains, thus adding another civilization to those represented in the scheme.[100]

Bateman may well have overstretched his resources in his works at Biddulph, for in 1871 he sold up and moved; eventually he was to create another rock garden near Worthing.[101] But by the time of Bateman's departure, the impact of Biddulph on the development of Victorian gardens had already been decisive.

5

The High Victorian garden

The High Victorian Conservatory

Great as the impact of Burton and Turner's Palm House at Kew had been, it was soon to yield place to an even more influential model, one which would eventually reverse the trend the Palm House had represented.

The story of the Great Exhibition building of 1851 has often been told, and need not be rehearsed in detail here.[1] Paxton was a latecomer to the scheme which earned him his knighthood; his proposal was sneaked in at the last minute after a design had already been selected.

Basing his plans on a glasshouse he had built at Chatsworth in 1849–50 to house the giant waterlily *Victoria amazonica*, Paxton designed a rectilinear building, with cast-iron columns that drained the roof, wooden glazing bars in a ridge-and-furrow pattern, and wrought iron crossbars for strengthening. The original plan envisaged a tiered structure with flat roofs; eventually a central transept was added to accommodate existing trees on site, thus achieving Nesfield's wish that the building should be 'broken in the centre'.[2] In sheer size, the building surpassed anything previously attempted in glass; it covered an area of 19 acres, and stood 64 feet high on average, rising to over 100 feet in the central transept. Its building was completed in record time, thanks to Paxton's use of prefabricated parts.

It had been planned to dismantle the structure, now called the Crystal Palace, after the exhibition, but there was much agitation for its retention, and Paxton organized a limited company to reassemble the building in another location.[3] The remodelled Palace was opened as the centrepiece of a new park on Sydenham Hill in south London in 1854. Seldom can a building have been erected under circumstances so propitious for its success as a popular model. The taxes on glass and bricks had been abolished only a few years previously; it therefore immediately established itself as a model of economy at the moment when glass building became feasible for the middle classes for the first time.[4]

The impact of the Crystal Palace was also felt on planting. The proposal to erect such an immense structure in Hyde Park had roused much apprehension: would the elms already existing on site survive being thus enclosed? Far from dying under Paxton's transept,

> it appears that while the dirty, half-starved Elms, growing as if wild in the open park, made shoots at the most a foot long on the average, the well-fed, well-cleaned, well-lodged trees under the transept, made shoots from 6 to 7 feet long.[5]

This incident can be said to mark the swing away from the predominantly tropical collections of the 1840s to the more temperate ones of the next decades. The cessation of duties may have made construction cheaper, but fuel was still expensive, and the domestic conservatory had to practise some economies; the *Gardeners' Chronicle* exulted that, after the Crystal Palace, heating had become needless.[6] It is no accident that the most publicized conservatory of the decade following the Crystal Palace was the Temperate House at Kew; and at Enville, the third of the great glasshouses of the 1850s, the planting range was restricted to camellias, azaleas, oranges, and fuchsias.[7]

The dominantly wooden construction of the Palace, furthermore, was important at a time when the merits of iron and wood as materials were being debated intensely, with gardeners tending to follow Paxton in advocating wood. Iron expanded and contracted faster than wood, causing the breaking of panes on winter nights on a larger scale; it needed specialist attention and maintenance, and required professional ironworkers to repair it. Wood was cheaper, and had none of these disadvantages; furthermore, the success of the ridge-and-furrow system showed that curvilinear form was not required to ensure satisfactory lighting for plants, and the functional necessity for iron disappeared.[8]

And so we find that the major glasshouses of the 1850s returned to a predominantly wooden construction. The new Crystal Palace at Sydenham had a more complex structure with crossing transepts, and required an increased proportion of ironwork for the additional curved sections, but still relied largely on wooden glazing bars. Gray and Ormson's great conservatory at Enville, Staffordshire, built in 1853–55, followed the Crystal Palace's proportions, with wooden sashwork and wrought iron ribs and girders. And Decimus Burton's commission for a Temperate House at Kew in 1855 stipulated a maximized use of wood, so that the Kew staff could carry out repairs without calling in outside professionals.[9]

The use of iron did not cease, of course. Architects had awakened to the use of iron in the 1840s, and continued its use after gardeners had returned to wood; indeed, Paxton's use of prefabricated sections had set a precedent for firms such as Macfarlane's of Glasgow, who began to issue huge catalogues of cast-iron parts for ready assemblage. Curvilinear forms were still valued for ornament after they had lost their functional justification, and iron could yield more delicate detail than wood. And so, by the 1870s, the principles underlying glasshouse construction had reversed themselves since the days of Loudon and Mackenzie: functional houses were made of wood, and iron was used when required for its decorative qualities. And in 1874 Lascelles's process for bending wood by steam pressure made it possible to erect a curvilinear conservatory made from wood alone, with 'as easy lines as the fine iron curvilinear houses built by Mr. Turner', thus removing the last structural argument for iron.[10]

As decoration became more important in the conservatory, Gothic attracted increasing attention as the most appropriate style. Burton had rejected the Gothic details in Turner's original proposals for the Palm House; but Paxton's unexecuted post-Palace scheme for a Crystal Sanitarium[11] revived elements of Gothic planning, and in the conservatory at Enville, with domes in a 'Gothic-cum-Moorish' style, a full-blown version

emerged. By the 1870s the functional arguments for Gothic, promoted by Pugin forty years earlier, had made it the favourite architectural style for glasshouses:

> Gothic affords the true foundation for taste in the construction of plant houses. The sloping roof need not be concealed; the necessary uprights lend themselves readily to the form, and the curves that are admissible are admirably suitable. The idea of Egyptian, Grecian, and in part of Byzantine, is the *exclusion* of light; the idea of Gothic is the admission of light, every line of the construction leading to doors, windows, and pitched roofs, such opaque walls as occur being rather as accidents, or, at best, accessories.[12]

Perhaps the most imaginative example of Gothic planning was the abortive scheme, promoted by the nurseryman John Wills in 1877, to protect the Albert Memorial from air pollution by surrounding it with a great glasshouse, designed to be in architectural harmony with its details.[13]

One final and long-reaching consequence of the Crystal Palace was the popularity of glazed buildings for exhibition purposes. Public winter gardens began to appear in many towns and cities in the 1860s, and the process continued into the 1890s.[14] Many of the later winter gardens, however, had ground storeys enclosed in masonry, only lightening into glass on higher levels. The precedent was set by the Alexandra Palace in North London, which burned down soon after its opening in 1873 and

41 John Wills's proposal for a conservatory to house the Albert Memorial (dimly seen under the central dome). The wings were intended to contain geographically arranged exhibits of the plant life of the world.

was rebuilt in a more 'fireproof' manner. (A wing of the Crystal Palace had been similarly destroyed in 1867.)[15]

Landscape Principles in the 1850s

'The modern taste in gardening in England', announced the *Gardeners' Chronicle* at the beginning of the 1850s, 'is gradually leading to a something of higher aim and wider scope than the mere landscape pleasure-ground of the last century'.[16] Nowhere was this transformation of the landscape ideal more evident than in the park that Paxton, and his protégé Edward Milner, created for the re-erected Crystal Palace on Sydenham Hill.

Twenty years before, the formal element of such a design would have been limited to the immediate vicinity of the glasshouse, not extending beyond the terrace on which it stood; Paxton's scheme, on the contrary, extended the system of terracing as a central axis down the hillside, around which all the other features were focussed. Cascades and flights of granite steps created 'one great geometrical line' spanning almost the entire garden; the terraces, a central walk, and symmetrically placed features such as two conical hills surmounted by arcades for climbing plants, extended perpendicular lines to govern the upper half of the park. Two separate systems of fountains were employed: a permanent system of jets and fountains on the upper terraces, and a second system, turned on only at certain times, of 'water temples' and jets grouped around the great basin in the centre of the park. 'English landscape' occupied its outer and lower fringes; at the bottom, concealed by tree cover from the main vista, lay an irregular lake with islands, peopled by models of prehistoric animals.[17]

The Crystal Palace represented a great step beyond Chatsworth in terms of formal organization; if Chatsworth may be compared to a Renaissance garden, with separate focuses of unity in different areas, then Crystal Palace Park could be compared to a baroque garden with one overriding axis of unity. Undoubtedly much of the inspiration for the park came from Paxton's visit to Versailles and other Le Nôtre gardens while on tour with the Duke of Devonshire in 1834; and Freeman Roe had already urged the example of Versailles's fountains on his contemporaries.[18] Thomas Rutger saw in the Park's symmetry a decisive superiority to Kew, and the Paxton-Milner team went on to produce an equally axial smaller-scale landscape in People's Park, Halifax.[19]

Crystal Palace Park represented a triumph of art rather than the contrasting interplay of art and nature so characteristic of Chatsworth; Rockhills, Paxton's own villa garden overlooking the Palace, continued the tradition of forceful juxtaposition. From his verandah on one side of the house extended a bank of flowers nearly forty yards long and twenty feet wide, planted in great masses and lines of pelargoniums and calceolarias; on the other side, the terrace with its rows of araucarias and standard rhododendrons looked out onto a rocky foreground:

> The whole face is massed with double Gorse, among which bunches of *Ribes sanguinea* rise here and there, and masses of white Broom in other parts – that is to say, a wild-like upper moorland covered with scrubby brushwood, as by chance, and looking as the outer edges of a wilderness ...[20]

The debate over contrast had left its mark, however, and the 1850s were to see far more attention lavished on ways of bringing the flower garden into harmony with the wider landscape.

In the wake of Chatsworth, Elvaston, and the gardens of Charles Barry, the priority of a formal setting for the house had become accepted practice, most commonly understood in terms of terraces to provide an elevated viewing platform. The archetypal eighteenth-century house lay in a depression or at least at the bottom of a visible descent, in order to express the idea of openness to nature; in the middle of the nineteenth century, the house was expected to dominate the landscape and express the power of the directing mind. In the mid-1840s Robert Glendinning had designed a sunken parterre at Poles Park, Hertfordshire, so that park scenery dominated the main view; a decade later Robert Fish found this behaviour incomprehensible.[21]

Even though the older advocates of the picturesque complained about terraces introduced without due cause, 'architectural gardening' was on the increase throughout the decade.[22] One of the most celebrated examples of the imposition of a formal structure on an unpromising site was Rhianva on the Isle of Anglesey, where in 1850–51 Sir John Hay Williams had a steep hillside terraced to accompany his French Renaissance chateau. In an attempt to maintain a harmony with the surrounding countryside, walls were covered with fuchsia hedges and hydrangeas; plants, once introduced, were often allowed to grow unchecked, and William Robinson was later to use Rhianva as a model for the 'wild garden'.[23] When W. H. Baxter, the curator of the Oxford Botanic Garden, laid out the garden at Headington Hill Hall in 1856–57, he had to resort to extensive excavation in order to create a slope for the house and throw the ground into descending terraces.[24]

Much argument was devoted to the question of stylistic harmony between house and garden. The very presence of a house was generally thought to compel a geometric plan for its immediate curtilage, although most writers agreed on the importance of avoiding excessive angularity in the forms of the garden. At the beginning of the 1850s, when Noel Humphreys launched his campaign for terracing, Drummond Castle, Elvaston, and Alton Towers were the gardens most often recommended as examples; Humphreys even tried to adapt the rustic style to the requirements of formal terracing. A gardener like William Paul, on the other hand, was prepared to allow the 'English or informal' style around the house on occasion, and expressed a preference for Gothic buildings because their lack of a well-defined tradition of garden ornament allowed the designer some scope for individuality.[25] By the end of the decade, the most potent model for the organization of the garden was Shrubland Park, with its architecturally segregated degrees of transition from the purely geometric to the wild:

> it is now universally admitted that the garden surrounding the house, whether an architectural terrace or bedded lawn, must of necessity possess uniformity; that the shrubbery immediately adjoining must partake of the same character, somewhat modified; while the more distant portions and the park are willingly abandoned to the landscape gardener.

The young gardeners who rose to prominence as writers in the late 1850s, like D. T. Fish and Shirley Hibberd, took this graded transition as the self-evident basis for garden layout.[26]

Planting choice was another way in which the garden could be harmonized with the house. Paxton and his fellow gardeners differed from the architects in wanting to clothe stone surfaces with vegetation; Beaton praised the way in which the terrace walls at the Crystal Palace were planted with *Berberis*, trimmed into curtains and festoons.[27] Different tree selections accompanied different styles, but no longer on Repton's basis of overall form (conical for Grecian, round-headed for Gothic). Edward Kemp recommended associations by virtue of leaf patterns; thin- and feathery-leaved trees contrasted well with the massiveness of classical buildings, while 'light and playful' Gothic buildings required broader and deeper leaves. Trees could be planted nearer to Gothic buildings than to Grecian.[28]

Linking the garden with the wider landscape, especially where the ground was not high enough to accommodate successions of terraces, led to several problems. Loudon's campaign against serpentine and circuitous roads had been successful by mid-century, and functional convenience had become so much the landscape gardener's dominant consideration that complaints were raised about approach roads blasted through irregular terrain as though in preparation for a railway. 'The main thing to avoid', wrote John Arthur Hughes in the mid-1860s, 'is the formality of a railroad; but as a road is manifestly an artificial work, why should it not be as perfect as skill can make it?'[29] The view from the house was generally taken as more important than the view of the house from the grounds, and where terracing was not an issue, most theorists urged the provision of some central object in order to give a breadth of composition to the landscape; any sequences of objects were to be composed of odd numbers rather than pairs so as to ensure that something was centrally placed – a central void would cut the landscape in two.[30] Some degree of colour planning was also necessary to effect a smooth transition into the distance: picturesque theorists demanded the planting of lighter colours on the boundaries of the vista, to merge with the 'blue distance'.[31]

Further difficulties arose over the treatment of water. Humphreys urged the adoption of geometrical fishponds and water-lily tanks in the vicinity of the house; naturalistic lakes ought to be placed only in the parkland some distance away. Paxton's pupils in the 1850s adopted a mixed style. Hartsholme Hall, Lincoln, was one of Edward Milner's first independent commissions after the completion of Crystal Palace Park; here the town's reservoir lay within the grounds, and Milner arranged it as an informal lake that narrowed into a long formal canal. Edward Kemp arranged a similar mixture of natural lake and regular canal at Garswood.[32] In the 1860s, Nesfield was to use a similar device at Coombe Abbey, where a geometric, moat-like canal was ushered into a wider lake in the middle distance with a weir marking the point of transition.

Once in the further reaches of the garden, away from the precincts of the house, a considerable variety of options was open to the gardener. At Welton Place, Northamptonshire, the garden of the noted hybridist Trevor Clarke, a wilderness was created in one corner of the grounds,

42 Welton Place, the wilderness. A Swiss cottage, miniature lake and rockworks in a distant part of Trevor Clarke's garden.

complete with Swiss cottage, miniature lake and rockwork.[33] Shirley Hibberd's ideal garden was marked by uncontrolled profusion of incident once the formal terraces were past:

> At every opening point in the shrubberies you will place some object to arrest the eye – a statue, a pile of rock, a fine acacia, an orange or azalea in a tub, a trained pyrus or weeping ash, to form a distinct object on the sward or on a border beyond the path; in some places where you would have a shady passage leading to view of the open country, you will plant an avenue, perhaps a quincunx, and the path here will be of mossy sward *closely shaven*, instead of gravel.[34]

In the attempt to find a stylistic label for this transition zone from the architectural to the parkland, the existing vocabulary of garden aesthetics was modified.

The meaning of the picturesque was changing during the 1850s. For Uvedale Price, the picturesque had been a generalized concept, applicable to both the formal terrace and the informal landscape. With the dominance of architectural gardening, however, the vocabulary was realigned. Price's

43 Poles Park, the parterre. Designed by Robert Glendinning in the 1840s, and sunken so that park scenery could dominate the view.

'intricacy' meant 'slight and insensible changes' in the landscape, but a box parterre was obviously intricate in a way that shadows and changing tints were not. Thus the concept of the picturesque was narrowed as many of its original values were restricted to the architectural garden, and the word came to be used as a synonym for informal and naturalistic. The standard books of the 1850s define the picturesque as irregular, 'an imitation of nature', and distinguish it from the formal.[35] Increasingly, it was restricted to small-scale contexts such as the rock garden or the fernery; Hibberd cautioned that he 'would have no puerile conceits anywhere; no attempts at *the picturesque* should be made'.[36]

The meaning of the gardenesque was also modified during the decade after Loudon's death. Kemp distinguished it from formal and picturesque as a third term, and referred to 'the mixed, middle, or irregular style, which Mr. Loudon called the gardenesque'. He completely ignored its earlier popular meaning, the display of plants as individuals, finding its characteristics instead in 'serpentine or wavy lines', 'a blending of Art with Nature': 'Its object is beauty of lines'. This usage of gardenesque to mean a mixed style was followed by Charles M'Intosh and Shirley Hibberd; Robert Thompson made a creditable attempt to replace it with the more precise label of 'free symmetrical', but unfortunately his coinage was not widely adopted.

> The design therefore is not purely geometrical; it is more free, but yet it constitutes a symmetrical whole, and accordingly its style may be designated

44 Hardwicke House, the rosary. Most rosaries, like this one designed by D. T. Fish in the 1850s, were isolated so as not to interfere with the main views from the house.

the free symmetrical. This we think a more definite term than the *mixed*, the *middle*, the *irregular*, or the *gardenesque*, as this style is also called.[37]

The gardens of the 1850s and 1860s were broadly governed in their organization by these basic principles: an architectural setting for the house, a graduated transition to the surrounding parkland, a central axis or organizing feature, and a dominant role accorded to the view outward from the house. By 1860 Donald Beaton could claim that the gardeners of the day were Repton's equals in design, and his superiors in planting.[38] It is to the planting of the landscape that we must now turn.

The Coniferous Landscape

Within a few years of the revelations from Elvaston Castle, the popularity of the pinetum was reaching its peak. Thomas Appleby, touring the north in 1852, reported that many of the prominent industrialists' estates were being planted with conifers; at Stourhead, apart from purple beeches, all the tree planting in the 1840s and 1850s was coniferous.[39] In 1852, Barron published his little book *The British Winter Garden*, in which the claims of coniferous planting were advanced earnestly:

> what is so common as to see, even at the present day, *close to our mansions*, such common-place things as elms, ashes, sycamores, poplars, or any other rubbish

45 Headington Hill Hall, the terraces. W. H. Baxter, curator of the Oxford Botanic Garden, transformed a steep slope into this terraced garden, depicted in a watercolour of 1858 by J. S. Austin.

that the nearest provincial nursery may happen to be over-stocked with; all stuck in to produce either immediate or lasting effect!

His complaints were echoed shortly after by William Paul, who found it astonishing that gardens should be '*suffered to remain* crowded with the lumpish and unmeaning trees and shrubs planted half a century ago'.[40]

The introduction of exotic conifers had peaked in the 1820s with the work of David Douglas; foremost among his introductions was the Douglas fir. The deodar arrived from the Himalayas in the 1830s, followed by the Atlantic cedar from North Africa; about 1840 William Lobb was finally able to send seed of the monkey-puzzle, for so long an expensive rarity, to the Veitch nurseries. In the 1840s came Hartweg's Californian conifers and a variety of South American and oriental species from Veitch, most notably *Cryptomeria japonica*, which Robert Glendinning hoped would become as common as the cedar of Lebanon.[41] But all of these were cast into the shade by the discovery in the early 1850s of the redwoods and wellingtonias of California. The wellingtonia was greeted by the rhetoric of the sublime; Appleby hoped that his descendants would see 'entire woods of it, and avenues planted to a great extent'.[42]

The signal merits of evergreens for landscape planting formed a theme that extended to the end of the century. Gardeners like Glendinning and Errington praised the 'new tone' that conifers were adding to British scenery, their all-season colour, their variety of shapes and forms.[43] Barron, in the early 1850s the most conspicuous enthusiast for evergreens, pushed the taste to its extreme: he envisaged the replacement of deciduous hedgerows on a national scale by holly hedges, thus transforming the entire countryside into a winter garden. Nor was Barron a lone eccentric: his proposals were greeted with enthusiasm by the *Florist*, which foresaw that 'the face of our English landscape must be entirely changed'.[44]

46 Crystal Palace, Sydenham Hill. Lithograph of 1854 showing the new park with its baroque system of canals and fountains along a central axis.

Many conflicting views were advanced about the best way in which to arrange evergreens in the landscape. The older advocates of the picturesque, while appreciating the new look of conifers, did not alter their basic principles to accommodate them. C. H. J. Smith advocated a continuous mixture of trees on the lawn, with a few exotics of peculiar form or colour isolated as specimens – 'staring trees' – near the house; he recommended the treatment of Lebanon cedars in John Martin's engravings for *Paradise Lost* as models of correct placing. Thomas Appleby, on the other hand, objected to the use of single trees, and recommended the planting of groups of one species each.[45]

Throughout the 1850s and 1860s, avenues enjoyed a great popularity as a method of arranging conifers in the landscape. As recently as the early 1840s, revivalists had still had to defend avenues as an historical feature worthy of respect, and to condemn their destruction as in barbarous taste; after Elvaston, however, any remaining inhibitions about their use were swept away. 'Wherever there is an opportunity, plant avenues', said Appleby, recommending gardeners to visit Elvaston, Chatsworth, and Bayfordbury for models. By the middle 1860s avenues had become such a standard feature that J. A. Hughes could blandly state, 'Of course there is no objection to an avenue of any kind'.[46]

Appleby's main caution was that avenues should comprise one species only; a decade later, Kemp gave the added warning that curved or irregular avenues were inartistic – straight lines only were suitable. Hughes noted a growing fashion for avenues, not of single trees, but of regularly spaced clumps.[47] At Sennowe Hall, Norfolk, one of his first landscapes after Elvaston, William Barron created an entrance drive with rows of cedars and Douglas firs; otherwise, avenues of multiple rows were not often attempted.[48] One of the most elaborate of avenue systems was planted at

Madresfield Court in the later 1860s by William Cox: avenues of fir and Atlantic cedar intersected at right angles, and formed a triangle with a further elm avenue (avenues of oak and golden yew appeared elsewhere in the grounds).[49]

In many cases, however, avenues proliferated without formal organization. At Welbeck Abbey and later at Kew, avenues of different species were planted in various parts of the grounds, taking their position from local features of ground and water without being aligned on one focus or in a mutually symmetrical pattern.[50] By the 1870s, this method of arrangement was frequently criticized as haphazard and unsystematic; thereafter, avenues once again began to withdraw to their context of formal approach.

The landscape treatment of systematic collections, which included too many species to be amenable to the avenue system, remained a problem in the 1850s. Chatsworth provided the model of trees arranged in sequence along an informal walkway, a plan which Nesfield tried unsuccessfully to formalize at Kew. C. H. J. Smith recommended arranging an arboretum in the shape of a star, in order to convey the arrangement of families in Lindley's system of classification. In 1850, John Spencer planted a much-publicized pinetum at Bowood, in which the trees were grouped according to their country of origin, and this geographical arrangement was greeted with some enthusiasm.[51]

All these schemes emphasized systematic arrangement over mere visual effect; when Nesfield proposed grading trees by height in the vistas at Kew, and abandoning rigorous botanical order, Glendinning accused him of sacrificing the object of an arboretum for the sake of appearance.[52] In the 1860s, however, William Coleman was to provide an alternative model by planting the arboretum at Eastnor Castle for picturesque effect;[53] the rejection of systematic and geographical groupings at Eastnor – and a group of associated gardens like Westonbirt – was noted with approval in the horticultural press, and became characteristic of arboretum planting in the last third of the century.[54]

Topiary

Another result of the influence of Elvaston Castle was the sudden burgeoning of interest in topiary. Already in 1835 W. S. Gilpin had felt it necessary to remonstrate against the clipping of trees;[55] despite Loudon and some revivalists, however, the reintroduction of topiary was an uphill struggle. Apart from The Whim, a Scottish garden where a fancifully cut hedge was created in the 1830s,[56] examples of newly-made topiary seldom received publicity before 1850. Even in gardens based on Elizabethan or seventeenth-century models, the effect of topiary was generally sought by using naturally fastigiate trees – poplars and some of the new coniferous introductions – instead of clipping. Even the training of bushes as standards could be regarded as a species of topiary, as Donald Beaton made clear:

> Standard bushes were made with great industry by our ancestors, and the thing is as old as the hills, but in those days they pruned and clipped them into all kinds of fantastic shapes, which is altogether foreign to our present taste.[57]

47 Wellington College, seen from the lakes. A landscape of cedars, wellingtonias, araucarias and rhododendrons, planted *c.* 1858–62 under the direction of E. W. (later Archbishop) Benson, with, reportedly, assistance from Prince Albert.

The legend persisted that topiary had been a Dutch introduction in the late seventeenth century, although the style that Addison and Pope had mocked was really a survival of Tudor fashions.[58]

The favourable publicity directed to Elvaston, however, encouraged the admirers of topiary to come out in the open. The year after Glendinning first drew attention to Barron's achievements, Noel Humphreys published a defence of topiary in the *Gardener's Magazine of Botany*, and his discussion shows the limits within which a topiarian enthusiasm tended to operate at mid-century. His model for topiary was Italian rather than Dutch: 'an Italian landscape without Cypresses, or an English one entirely without Poplars, might be compared to the view of a city without steeples' as an example of monotony. Figurative patterns, anything sculptural, he dismissed: 'architectural and other simple and severe forms in foliage' were all that was acceptable – like topiary amphitheatres, or the hedges and columns of Elvaston. (The taste which led Barron to transplant an arbour clipped into the shape of a peacock had to wait another generation to become more widespread.)[59]

Such architectural forms dominated the topiary revival during the 1850s. A series of yew hedges, trimmed to suggest fortifications, was laid out at Sudeley Castle, Gloucestershire, as part of a restoration programme reaching its final stages under Gilbert Scott's direction in 1854. Similar fortifications at Castle Combe were publicized a few years later.[60] This became a favourite model for topiary for the next quarter-century. 'We

48 Sudeley Castle, topiary hedges accompanying Sir George Gilbert Scott's restoration in the 1850s.

are so far from objecting to the terraces being bordered with mathematically-cut evergreen hedges', wrote a commentator of the 1870s, 'that we prefer them in many instances to stone balustrades'.[61]

If the wall had its vegetable counterpart in the hedge, obelisks and finials had their counterparts as well. Edward Kemp approved of 'globular, or pyramidal, or conical, or square' shapes, as counterparts to standards,[62] and the use of such chaste geometric forms for vertical emphasis increased during the 1850s. Some schemes of this sort were quickly able to pass as works of great antiquity (in part because of a prevailing false impression that yew was slow-growing). At Owlpen Manor, Gloucestershire, a new house was built about 1840, and the yews of an overgrown early eighteenth-century parterre were trimmed into pylons at some point after; by the early twentieth century the topiary was passing for an eighteenth-century creation.[63] Even more successful in this regard was Packwood House, where there was a surviving eighteenth-century mount and a line of yews; in the middle 1850s the orchard on the slope below was replanted in part with specimen yews. Already by the 1890s Reginald Blomfield was deceived about their age, and helped to circulate the story that they dated from Cromwellian times, and represented collectively the Sermon on the Mount and the Multitude below. (This version of the meaning of the topiary need not be a retrospective interpretation; the yews at Heslington Hall, York, were already known as the Twelve Apostles by the

1a (top left) Colour scheme by John Caie, published in the *Florist's Journal* (1841).
1b (top right) Undated colour scheme, *c.* 1850, for the Yellow Sand Garden at Drumlanrig Castle.
1c (bottom left) Proposals for colour combinations from Gardner Wilkinson's 1858 work *On Colour.*
1d (bottom right) John Fleming's colour scheme for spring bedding in the great parterre at Cliveden (1862).

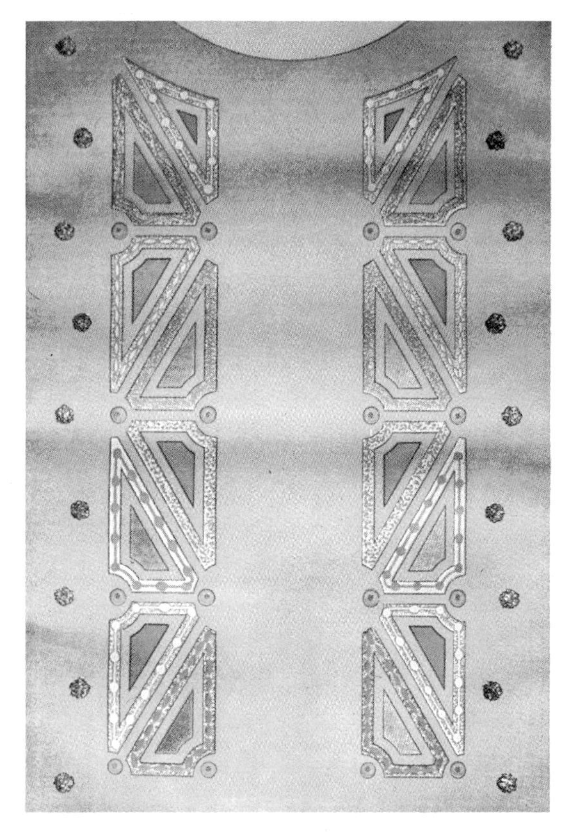

2 Baron Hill, the terrace garden. The herbaceous planting of the beds is Edwardian, but the topiary was already complete by the 1870s.

3 Belvoir Castle. This Edwardian view by Charles E. Flower depicts the spring bedding begun by William Ingram and continued by his successor W.H. Divers.

4 Bowood, the terrace garden. A view by E. Adveno Brooke, 1856, showing the terraces as redeveloped by George Kennedy in the early 1850s.

5 'In the Pleasaunce'. Atkinson Grimshaw painted this view of his garden at Knostrop Hall, Leeds, in 1875.

6 Drummond Castle, the terrace garden. Lewis and George Kennedy worked successively on the restoration of this garden in the 1820s and 1830s, with George creating the elaborate parterre based on a St Andrew's cross, shown in this undated watercolour by Jacob Thompson.

7 Enville Hall, the great fountain. A view by E. Adveno Brooke (1856) of the great jet, showing the rainbow effect for which it was celebrated.

8 Chatsworth, the rock garden. The Wellington Rock, assembled from smaller masses of rock by Joseph Paxton.

9 Cannon Hill Park, Birmingham. This postcard view, dated 1908, shows a floral crown composed of carpet bedding plants arranged on a galvanized wire frame.

10 Trentham, the Italian garden. Charles Barry's Italianate architecture was complemented by George Fleming's experiments in summer bedding.

11 Shrubland Park, the fountain garden. A view by E. Adveno Brooke (1856) of one of the secondary gardens along the nearly mile-long terrace. The fountain garden was nearly circular, with roses and half-hardy plants arranged in six colours.

12 The Willows, Ashton-on-Ribble. A formally enclosed garden designed by Thomas Mawson, *c.* 1899, and completed in 1912.

1830s, and may have served as the model for the Packwood arrangement.)[74]

The known popularity of mazes in former times, and the surviving example at Hampton Court, made them the favourite device where more elaborate forms of architectural topiary were attempted. A Dutch garden and multicursal yew maze were created in the Bridge End Gardens, Saffron Walden, about 1840, probably designed by William Chater;[65] a maze was the last work of Donald Beaton's at Shrubland Park before his retirement, and the only part of his work that survives today.[66] In 1841, the *Gardeners' Chronicle* recommended a plan from John James as a model for historical accuracy, and the maze at Hatfield House, laid out in the 1840s in a purely rectilinear pattern, passed successfully for 'seventeenth-century' by Reginald Blomfield's time.[67] Nesfield was to be particularly associated with mazes as a result of his designs at Somerleyton Hall and the Royal Horticultural Society's garden in Kensington.[68]

The Influence of Biddulph

Traces of the influence of Biddulph Grange can be detected in a variety of ways in the 1850s, beginning with the imitation of specific features. It was probably due to E. W. Cooke's influence that a rootery was incorporated into the grounds of the Crystal Palace; Cooke went on to add one to his own garden at Glen Andred. Kemp, however, played his part in promoting the concept in the third edition of his *How to Lay Out a Garden*, published after his series of articles on Biddulph had been completed:

> In localities where stone is not easily procured, or where it abounds so much that the use of another material would be preferable, for the sake of variety, the *rugged stumps* or *roots* of old trees may be substituted, and will yield quite as much picturesqueness.

He also added advice on the harmonious arrangement of rockworks, and the turning of shrubberies into arboretum walks, that showed the lessons derived from the individual features of Biddulph.[69]

The more general principle of variety, nebulous as it may sound in the abstract, took on a new feeling in the 1850s. The immediate stimulus was the Crystal Palace Park in Sydenham, which differed from previous public parks in its inclusion of a wide range of educational features: a realistic depiction of a Derbyshire open-pit mine; an aquarium; and above all, a display of the earth's geological past in the form of a series of models of prehistoric animals grouped about the lake. Each successive epoch was arranged with a separate island as its focus, forming a graded sequence from the amphibian life of the carboniferous period to the most recent mammals. The models were designed in cement by Waterhouse Hawkins, at almost the same time that he was making the Chinese bull and dragons for Biddulph.[70] E. W. Cooke was at this time engaged in planning the interior courts of the Palace; it seems probable that he was also involved in some decisions about the planning of the park.

The influence of the Crystal Palace on the provision of educational features in public parks was immense: in every city in the kingdom, from the 1860s on, aviaries, zoos, and conservatories for the display of exotic vegetation multiplied, making the aim of botanical education underlying such early parks as the Derby Arboretum only one strand in a broader programme of public instruction.

Whether the religious inspiration underlying Biddulph Grange was ever grasped by the outside world is highly uncertain, but there is one tantalizing parallel dating largely from the 1850s. At Hough Hole House, a villa near Macclesfield, the Swedenborgian James Mellor created a garden which was an allegorical representation of the route of Christian in *The Pilgrim's Progress* – from a marshy lawn to represent the Slough of Despond, to a steep flight of steps for the Hill Difficulty. '"Hough Hall," we fear, notwithstanding all Mr. Mellor's pains, will scarcely commend itself to the landscape gardener', reported some visitors in the 1880s, and it was not a garden that would have met Kemp's criteria of propriety – paths had to be retraced in following the scheme, the nature of the allegorical devices was not always obvious, and the sequence was confused by elements from *Uncle Tom's Cabin* being intermixed. A central mill-stream running underneath the house, however, did provide a visually unifying feature, and the visitors noted that the garden was 'stocked with curious plants, some of them very uncommon'.[71]

For Kemp, however, the great merit of Biddulph Grange lay not in individual features but in the way in which the transcendentalist effects of Chatsworth, the arboriculture and avenue planting of Elvaston Castle, and the horticultural virtuosity of Trentham were reconciled with the new propriety of which he was a major spokesman. Unlike its three great predecessors, Biddulph avoided the ostentatious contrast of art and nature; Kemp, who had at first seen the environmental grouping of plants as the garden's organizing principle, came to attribute almost equal importance to the garden buildings, as determining whether the appearance of art or of nature should have the upper hand: 'there is nowhere that confusion of the rude with the cultivated, or the purely picturesque with the formal, which constitutes the deformity of so many gardens'.[72] The result can be seen in the third edition of Kemp's *How to Lay Out a Garden*, which contained a new emphasis on architectural gardening, as well as a long section on 'Compact combination of parts', in which the lessons of Biddulph were elaborated for a variety of situations.

Kemp's own practice changed considerably after he had fully digested the experience of Biddulph. In the middle 1850s, the maintenance of a simple visual congruity was his major goal, and a pre-Biddulph garden like Daylesford Hall showed a straightforward terrace and tree grouping.[73] Within a few years his plans had become radically more complex, with Leighton Hall, near Welshpool, perhaps the turning point: here in 1858, he erected a viaduct from which different parts of the garden (ranging from a winter garden to a lake) could be seen, a mount with a viewing seat for the winter garden, and a walk which descended from the mount 'into a narrow natural valley ... the banks being covered with rocks and roots'. The effect was later augmented with stone cascades. At Stanley Park, Liverpool (1866–70), he manipulated terraces and hills to create a series of independent enclosures, with Gothic buildings by E.R. Robson.

At Underscar, near Keswick, where a natural dingle at the foot of Skiddaw furnished the opportunity for a shrubbery walk, Kemp led it through a pinetum, a wooded bank, rockery and rootery, rhododendron plantation, and a series of rustic bridges – his '*beau idéal* of what a walk of that description should be'.[74]

The idea of enclosure and of the creation of independent scenes gradually spread, to rival the open prospect and central vista of the Italian garden as practised by Barry and his followers. A well-publicized example created during the 1860s was Alfred Smee's garden at The Grange, Wallington, Surrey, which contained a croquet ground, pear walk, mossery and alpinery, fern glade, and separate sections devoted to genera such as *Saxifraga* and *Sedum*; Smee gave as his ideal the creation of a multiplicity of pictures, and tried to create 'little spots of cultivated wilderness, or of special cultivation . . . where they are least expected'.[75] And when Cooke came to lay out his own garden at Glen Andred, Sussex, in the same years, he predictably used elaborate rockworks to segregate a variety of scenes of an encyclopaedic nature: evocations of British history (Scotland, Glencoe, a Druid's dell); of British worthies, largely horticultural (the Newton apple tree, Ward's rock and mount, Loddigesia); and imitations of vegetation complexes (holly combe, heather bank, arboretum and stumpery).[76]

Colour Theory and the Bedding System

By the 1850s the proper use of colour had established itself as the leading artistic question of the day. The arrival of the Pre-Raphaelites put the seal on the revolution in British painting; the stained glass revival had long been under way. Ruskin had proclaimed that all the great epochs of architecture had used highly colourful decoration for their buildings. The fact that the ancient Greeks had used bright colours on their buildings and sculptures was now accepted and beginning to have consequences among English artists: the great neoclassical sculptor John Gibson had caused a furore by exhibiting a 'Tinted Venus', and by the end of the decade Marocchetti and others would be creating polychrome sculptures. An important literature on colour was becoming available, with translations of Goethe and Chevreul, and reprints or new works by theorists like George Field and D. R. Hay.[77]

After the departure of Caie, from whom he acknowledged having learned the art, Donald Beaton was the principal spokesman on bedding for his generation; but he owed this position of authority not to a dogmatic stance, but precisely to his ready expression of uncertainty, puzzlement, and surprise at the quality of other people's results. He regarded the rules of colour as still undecided, and determinable only by continued experiment; in his recommendations, therefore, he left as much latitude as possible for individual taste and trial, and restricted himself to the broadest and most general principles. His ideas were propounded in the pages of the *Cottage Gardener*, but were taken up by other writers as well, Shirley Hibberd in his younger days helping to promote his views.[78] He was already in demand for devising bedding schemes by 1845, when he

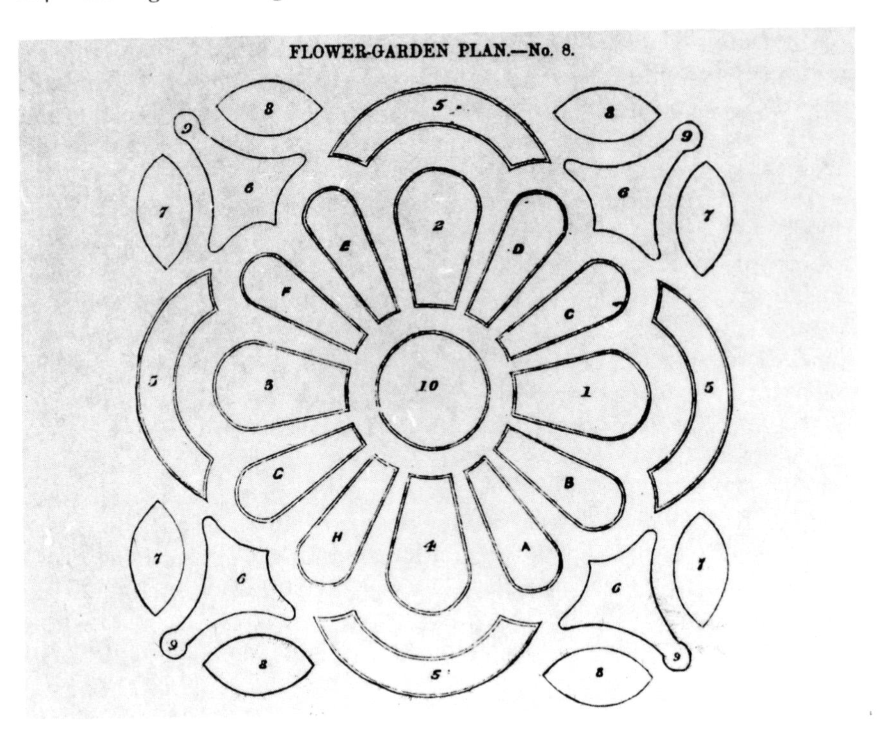

49 Plan for a flower garden, from the *Cottage Gardener* (1853). This design by Donald Beaton was used at Bainton Rectory, and later attributed to Paxton. 1–5, pelargoniums; 6, crimson China roses; 7, calceolarias; 8, lobelias; 9, petunias; 10, mixed fuchsias and heliotropes; A–H, verbenas.

was invited to arrange the flowerbeds at Falkland; and for a few years he ran a service in the *Cottage Gardener* of commenting on flower-garden plans sent in by readers; but while he mingled praise and correction, he made it clear that he could offer only the most superficial comments on a scheme he had not seen in person.[79] One of these plans, the only one he commended as exemplifying his principles, and which was transparently his own, was copied at Bainton Rectory, Yorkshire (and subsequently attributed to Paxton).[80]

There were so many styles to try, and so many complications to be considered. A colour scheme was only an abstraction unless it took into account such variables as setting, prospect, degree of shade, atmospheric effects. The Purkinje effect, for example, whereby red is seen as an advancing colour in broad daylight but in declining light it is the blue end of the spectrum that advances, was known to Beaton and Caie, who specified varieties that were seen to best effect at sunset. Beaton advised the gardener to observe his proposed bedding scheme at different times of day and in different weather conditions before being satisfied.[81]

Beaton did recognize some genuine theoretical advances, however, and eventually laid claim to two particular achievements.

> I think I have dispelled the vulgar notion of placing scarlet or glaring colours in the midst of a group of beds. I also think that I have shaken the public faith in the opinion of great painters, as to the right grouping of flowers without reference to the natural ground colour on which the groups are disposed.[82]

Let us now examine these two principles.

Note that Beaton did not condemn the use of scarlet, merely its position in a group. In 1850 he reported favourably on that season's arrangement of flowers in the main parterre at Kew, where bright colours filled the peripheral beds, and the central ones were occupied by subdued colours; this arrangement directed attention outwards and increased the apparent size of the display. Caie approved: 'having a subdued colour for a central mass ... is an idea in the onward direction'; and over the next couple of years Beaton pushed the idea of central neutrality.[83]

The question of ground colour is more complicated, and involves the notion of complementary colours. Erasmus Darwin, in the late eighteenth century, had observed that, if one looked sufficiently long at a particular colour, say blue, and then looked away toward a neutral background, one saw an after-image in a different colour – in this case yellow. He had remarked that the Newtonian system of colour did not explain this; and Goethe, in Germany, conducting a systematic investigation of the phenomena of after-images, used these pairs of 'complementary' colours as the basis of an alternative theory of colour which he opposed to Newton's. In effect, Newton had been studying the transmission of light and Goethe the mechanisms of perception, but it took some time before this distinction was appreciated. Goethe's *Theory of Colours* was translated into English in 1840 by Charles Eastlake, and certainly became known to the gardening community; within a few years W. P. Ayres was citing it to the effect that 'Every decided colour does certain violence to the eye, and forces the organ to opposition' – so that if one looked at scarlet flowers, one had to look at green foliage for relief.[84]

Meanwhile, in France, the chemist Michel-Eugène Chevreul had been commissioned to improve the use of dyes by the Gobelin tapestry works, and as a result of his investigations published in 1839 his work *De la loi du contraste simultané des couleurs*. Two years after its publication, John Lindley drew attention to it in the *Gardeners' Chronicle*, followed by W. P. Ayres. Its basic principle was that complementary colours always suited each other:

> Now the complementary colour of red is green; of orange, sky-blue; of yellow, violet; of indigo, orange-yellow; and consequently blue and orange-coloured flowers, yellows and violets, may be placed together, while red and rose-coloured flowers harmonise with their own green leaves ... In all cases, however, where colours do not agree, the placing white between them restores the effect.[85]

In 1849 Lindley returned to the theme, spurred on by a revised edition of Chevreul's book, and this time he presented detailed instructions for monthly colour schemes.[86] The time was now riper for definite rules of grouping, and the notion of arrangement by complementary colours permeated the literature within a very short time. Colour charts were drawn up, lecturers and correspondents reiterated the principles, and in 1854 Chevreul's book was translated into English.[87]

These assertions were challenged by Beaton, who regarded Chevreul's recommendations as based on abstract speculation rather than real experience of flowers. His principal argument was that proposals for the arrangement of complementary colours ignored the ground on which the flowers were placed.

> The principle is, that *every colour we use is placed in the centre of two other colours*, whether we can see them or not ... The natural system is, that the deepest

> and most intense colours, as well as the weakest colours, of all our bedding plants, is in the centre of a green of equal or unequal intensity, – the inequality not depending on the strength of the colour; and both the green and the colour *on it*, are covered over equally with a third natural colour, a light grey, which is the best term for the light of our sun, over and around a bed of flowers . . .
>
> Complementary colours, as they call them, can, therefore, never be obtained from flowers growing on plants, because all flowers are then on one complementary colour, green, of various intensity . . . If the Chevreulites allow us a peep of the grass, their scale is 'done for.'[88]

(This was not altogether fair to a follower of Chevreul such as W. P. Ayres, and Lindley had urged that the plants must hide the ground from view.)[89]

Beaton's view that green cancelled the effect of complementary colours was contested,[90] and the rivalry entered into full swing: on the one side Lindley, with the Horticultural Society's garden at Chiswick as a testing ground and James Donald at Hampton Court as a convert; on the other, Beaton in his new role as adviser on flower-bedding at Kew, with allies at the Crystal Palace and various private estates. It was Beaton who emerged triumphant. After two seasons, Donald abandoned the attempt to arrange the beds at Hampton Court on a complementary basis, and eventually even Chiswick succumbed. 'The chromatic scales spoiled Dr. Lindley's Crocuses', jested Beaton. In 1857, the *Gardeners' Chronicle* published its first sceptical leader on Chevreul, acknowledging the importance of ground colours, whether grass or gravel; and by 1859 it had swung around to the attack, repeating all of Beaton's allegations:

> even if CHEVREUIL's [*sic*] maxims were true they cannot be applied in gardens. The truth is that plants do not furnish the means of carrying out his views; either the requisite colours to form CHEVREUIL's harmonious combinations do not co-exist, or the plants in which they occur are so different in their manner of growth as to render it impossible to use them for purposes of contrast; their flowers are not on the same plane, or they are so mixed with green as to lose the quality belonging to the coloured parts . . .[91]

Beaton was not mentioned; indeed, the new anti-Chevreul stance went further in the direction of dismissing rules of composition than Beaton liked. Nonetheless, 'the clouds have cleared up, the atmosphere is free, and the Doctor has recanted'; Chevreul had been 'thrown overboard with as little ceremony as if he had never been his right-hand man on colours'.[92]

Beaton would have considered himself vindicated had he lived to hear Ostwald's criticism that Chevreul's colour system had never been reproduced satisfactorily even in the Gobelin tapestries. For one thing, he had been misled by Goethe's insistence on yellow, red, and blue as the three primary colours into spacing them equidistantly on his colour circle, with the consequence that the opposing points of his circle were not true complementaries.[93]

Lindley was shortly to find a new authority, for in 1858 the Egyptologist Sir Gardner Wilkinson published a book *On Colour*, which was directed primarily at architects and decorators, but which included a section on colour for the geometrical garden. Wilkinson, while handsomely acknowledging his predecessors, including Chevreul, began by expressing a contempt for abstract theories and detailed rules, and particularly for the importance ascribed to complementary (or, as he termed them, accidental) colours. Just because two colours were related as after-images did not show that they were harmonious, he declared; some complementarities proved actual discords in practice. Much more important were the positions and distances at which colours were placed; he also re-emphasized the importance of ground colours, but would probably have been considered retrograde by Beaton for his disinclination to admit subdued colours into the garden.[94]

Beaton left no recorded comments on Wilkinson; the two theorists whom he approved were the flower arranger T. C. March, and Owen Jones, who had been responsible for the colour decoration of the Crystal Palace and who in 1856 was to publish his *Grammar of Ornament*, putting patterns and colour schemes into an historical sequence. Even more than Wilkinson, whom he greatly influenced, Jones was primarily concerned with the proper use of colour for buildings, but Beaton commended his Great Exhibition lecture on colour as applicable to the garden, and said, 'you might fancy Mr. Jones did little else, since he left college, but plant flower-gardens, according to the rules laid down in THE COTTAGE GARDENER'.[95] Colour was to be used to create the visual impression of form, and this was best achieved by 'the use of the primary colours on small surfaces and in small quantities, balanced and supported by the secondary and tertiary colours in the larger masses'. In place of complementarity, Jones based his colour groupings on the visual appearance of foreground and background: blue was a retiring colour, yellow advancing, and red intermediate, while white should be used as a separating agent. This proposal needed to be supplemented by an awareness of the altered effects of colours under different conditions of light, but Beaton could regard it as a step in the right direction, analogous to his own work.[96]

One example will suffice to show the ways in which Beaton's and Jones's work could differ. 'No composition can be perfect', Jones had declared, 'in which any one of the three primary colours is wanting',[97] but Beaton was prepared to justify the omission of primaries in certain environments. When the remodelled Crystal Palace was opened at Sydenham, one of the great features of the garden was the extensive use made of yellow calceolarias. Some objections were raised to the exclusive use of red and yellow in the bedding, and the absence of blue and white. Beaton replied that blue and white were already so predominantly present in the fountains, the stonework, the glass walls, and the sky itself, which on such a radically sloping site formed a major element in the view, that a proportionate balance of blue and white flowers would completely tame the effect of the beds: 'and then, also, if you understand the drift of my story, let me never hear such silly questions again, as – "Don't you think they have too much scarlet and yellow?"'[98]

And so the science of colours stumbled on, productive of much dust and heat but still leaving many gardeners to find their inspiration in the art galleries rather than the textbooks. Turner, 'the famous red and yellow Royal Academician', was invoked in the *Gardeners' Chronicle*.[99] In the early 1860s, one critic wrote of John Robson's bedding schemes at Linton Park, Kent:

> It cannot have escaped the notice of those who have seen Rubens' masterpieces that that great master of colour produced the main tone and effect of his paintings by the very course now taken by Mr. Robson – a judicious use of his deep blue and deep red.

The invocation of Rubens was not arbitrary; he was a figure of controversy among theorists of art for his 'brilliancy' and 'extreme splendour of light', resulting (according to the theory of the time) from his use of unmixed primary colours in juxtaposition to create an effect of flicker. His paintings therefore could be taken as offering a reasonably precise analogy to what at least one of the schools of bedding was trying to achieve, and would furthermore show that Robson's grouping arose 'from the purest taste, as well as being productive of the most artistic results'.[100]

Design in the Flower Garden

Although principles of colour grouping could be found in architects' manuals like Owen Jones's, this did not mean that the gardener and the architect were now aligned on questions of design. Between the architect who wanted to make the flower garden an historically appropriate decoration, and the gardener who wanted a proper colour scheme, a rift was opening. John Arthur Hughes asserted that no practical gardener could lay out a garden.[101] The practical gardeners' retort was that too many architects' plans for flower gardens were frivolously irrelevant. 'There are hundreds of flower-gardens', wrote Beaton,

> in which no mortal can make a satisfactory disposition of colours, because the design of the beds was made by some clever person, perhaps a great artist, who did not understand that such a design is merely a means to an end, not the end itself – a good picture. If the design is very pretty on paper, the chances are that it is a stupid piece of business.

Mixed beds were the only solution in such cases; if the gardener tried imposing a balanced colour scheme on a faulty plan 'the planter was a fool, to expose the plan so palpably, unless he meant to do so'.[102] That last phrase indicates a degree of tension between gardener and architect that rarely emerges so bluntly in the literature.

By the 1850s horticultural opinion decisively favoured simplified shapes of flowerbeds; elaborate or fanciful figures in flower gardens of this period are usually the work of the architect. Gothic architects were particularly liable to produce such plans, for Gothic country houses had no historical precedent; what sort of garden would a thirteenth-century country house have had? At Elvetham Park, for example, in the late 1850s, S. S. Teulon projected a parterre with crescent-shaped beds – probably evoking the crescent-shaped lake that had featured in the celebration of Queen Elizabeth's visit in the 1580s.[103]

Against such examples as this, Beaton and his colleagues could invoke the standard of the Crystal Palace, where under George Eyles's management there was 'no straining or hankering after the shape of the beds ... Stars and garters, heart and tongue, and kidney-shaped beds, and all fantastical forms and plans for beds are beneath their notice.'[104] Nonethe-

50 (opposite) Putteridge Bury, Robert Fish's floral avenue: a sequence of matching pairs of pincushion beds. Rose beds: edged with nasturtiums, 1, 9; with verbenas and *Cerastium*, 17. Standard fuchsias: surrounded by pelargoniums and other plants, 2, 14, 24; by calceolaries, 4, 11, 22. *Ricinus*: with verbenas etc., 7, 13; with *Canna* and heliotrope, 19. Pelargoniums mixed with other bedding plants: 3, 6, 12, 20, 21. Acacias and pelargoniums, with pinks, 5; with *Maurandya* and verbenas, 23. *Cassia corymbosa* with pelargoniums or calceolaries and other bedding plants, 8, 15, 18. *Datura* with lobelias and calceolarias, 10, 16.

less, beds had to have some shape, and from the late 1840s, when George Fleming's ribbon beds began to attract notice, the gardeners began a programme of eager experimentation with flowerbed design, in part to combat that of Nesfield and the historical revivalists.

The first development we must notice was an increased interest in symmetry, which had not been an important consideration in John Caie's bedding; but as Beaton stressed the use of subdued colours for the centre of a scheme, he began as well to advocate symmetrical colour groupings around this centre. From about 1853 he acted as adviser on bedding at

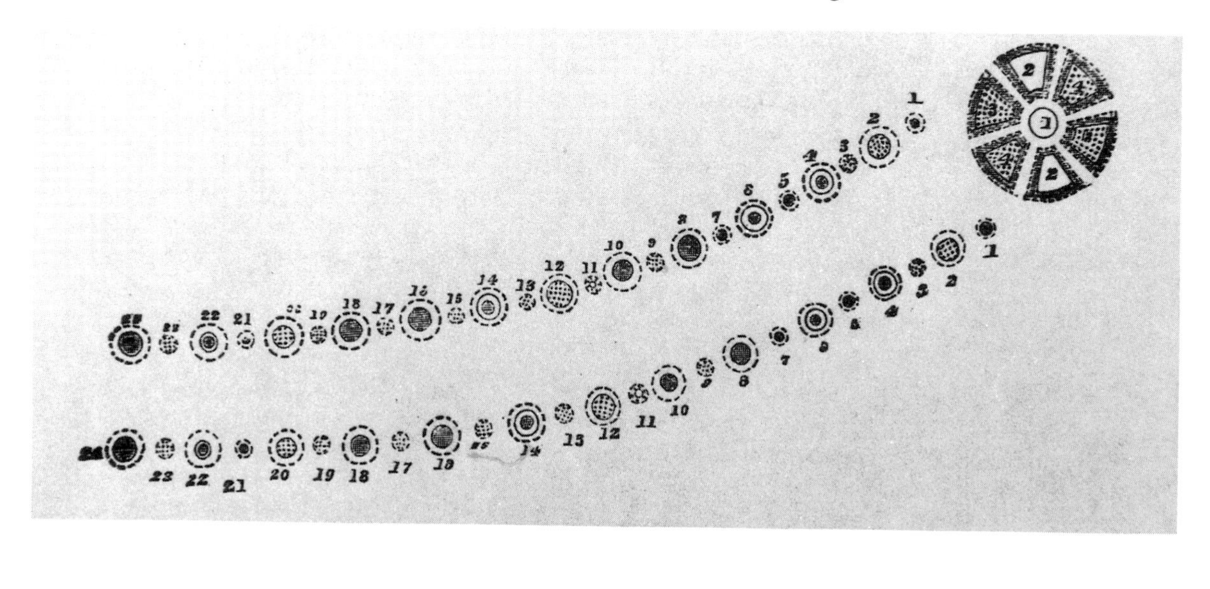

Kew, and repeatedly pointed to the symmetrical disposition of beds in the Palm House parterre as a model.[105]

Gardner Wilkinson urged that beds be arranged so as to suggest lines leading into the landscape, but this suggestion would have been considered redundant by most gardeners of the time, who had been busy planting literal lines for a decade. Ribbon borders were, if not invented, at least popularized by George Fleming at Trentham; other Midland gardens, like Enville and Dudmaston, became famous for ribbons; and an abundant literature on the subject sprang up during the 1850s. The original ribbons were serpentine, snaking through the landscape, but in the 1850s most ribbons were straight lines and served as the geometrical garden's substitute for the herbaceous border. Public gardens generally confined themselves to three rows per ribbon – red, white, and blue was a favourite pattern – but at gardens like Enville the ribbons could easily be seven strands wide. Gradation of heights, debates on contrast versus shading, the use of 'architectural planting' like hollies and variegated shrubs as alternatives to bedding, all emerged as issues to complicate matters and produce a fertile field for experiment.[106]

Once ribbons were established, their possibilities for landscape use were explored more systematically. Errington and Beaton helped to promote what they called the 'promenade style', in which borders were arranged parallel to walks, planted symmetrically on either side;[107] there soon followed the 'wheel style', as concentric promenade borders were arranged at successive heights around prominent mounds – a technique first demonstrated on the Crystal Palace's Rose Mount.[108] By the early 1860s more radically serpentine ribbons were returning.[109] The final elaboration came with the development of guilloche patterns, variously called scrolls or chains, developed independently by ribbon-borderers and by gardeners interested in architectural precedents (the often used name Florentine chain hinted at Italian mosaic pavements as a model). This was one design on which architects and gardeners agreed, and chain and scroll patterns enjoyed a continued popularity into the 1880s.[110]

Raised beds of different sorts began to make an appearance in the 1850s, as a response to complaints about monotonous flatness.[111] The first intimations came with the revival of interest in standard shrubs; George M'Ewen issued a plea for pyramidal pelargoniums, in which cause he was joined by Noel Humphreys, Shirley Hibberd, and of course Beaton, who blithely added, 'But why talk only of Geranium pyramids? There is hardly a plant going which my successor at Shrubland Park does not train to that form.'[112] Simple training was quickly supplemented by the creation of floral pyramids, in which a rubble cone would be thickly planted with the dwarfer bedding hybrids to give a prominent three-dimensional burst of colour; although experimented with as early as the 1830s, they did not become widely popular until the advocacy of Shirley Hibberd in the late 1850s.[113] Their simple geometric shape suggests that such cones were a floral counterpart to topiary, but they met with fervent opposition from some gardeners, most notably Alexander Forsyth, and by the 1860s there was a small-scale revival of Loudon's circular beds as a restrained alternative.[114] William Earley was noted in that decade for his complex variations on circular shapes for beds – interlocking circles, hoops and rings.[115]

51 A pelargonium pyramid, as recommended by Shirley Hibberd, in an engraving of 1866.

A further refinement of the pyramidal principle came with 'pincushion beds' (so called because one could stick anything into them). These were generally circular, composed of concentric ribbons increasing in height around a central standard, and were arranged symmetrically along the sides of walkways. The most famous display of pincushions was the floral avenue at Putteridge Bury, Hertfordshire, where Robert Fish had gone as head gardener after leaving London.[116]

These vertically modelled beds were followed by panels – rectangular beds, derived from ribbon borders but assuming more complex patterns, which could be arranged in a series without the need for an overall symmetrical colour relationship. Beaton, with his dislike of complicated internal subdivision of beds, stayed largely quiet on this matter; the early proponents were the Somerset nurseryman John Scott and David Thomson, head gardener at Archerfield, East Lothian, who made his debut onto the flower-bedding scene with panels that incorporated small raised beds as part of their internal pattern.[117]

As the 1850s progressed, a new ideal of massiveness began to pervade the architectural profession; solidity, weight, sublimity, and vigour became keywords of appreciation.[118] The same standards were invoked for the desired impact of the garden; R. H. Cheney urged that

> the garden should not be inferior in boldness and massiveness of design in order that it may form a fitting base on which the house may rest ... When a magnificent platform is to be filled with flower-beds, the patterns should be large, and the masses of flowers sufficiently important to aid with the richness of their colour the grandeur of the forms.[119]

And as the 1850s ended, a new style of bedding emerged that met this criterion of massiveness better than any of its predecessors. John Robson, head gardener at Linton Park, was responsible for the innovation. In 1858, he laid out a flower garden to be looked down upon from an upper terrace; the parterre was centred on one prominent bed, oval in shape but designed to look like a circle when seen from the terrace, and within this a simple figure was 'planted in three colours only – scarlet, blue, and white; the latter being used as the ground colour'. The blocks of colour were as uniform as Robson could make them (even flowers which cast internal shadows were excluded), and its sheer size – a single bed 70 by 90 feet across – gave it a strength and massiveness that awed its first viewers: here the flower garden had achieved that feeling of the sublime that the age was demanding in its architecture.[120]

The Revival of Mixing

As early as 1845, Robert Errington warned that the vogue for half-hardy plants would drive the older perennials out of the market, but despite later propaganda, there is no evidence that herbaceous plants were ever truly neglected as a result of the bedding system.[121] The impression conveyed by Donald Beaton's writings is that every sizeable garden had a herbaceous border as well as its display area of bedding. 'A garden without a border for mixed flowers is seldom to be met with', he wrote in 1859, at the height of the bedding system, and a few years later James Anderson pointed out that 'the much-vaunted herbaceous [flowers], which the partisans of parterre flower-gardening are accused of banishing from their gardens', were in fact 'only removed to less artificial borders, where they are more at home'.[122] In smaller gardens, which could not afford the expenses of bedding, perennials and the equally neglected annuals continued to furnish the flowerbeds, and these categories of plants were estimated to make up half the seed shops' volume of trade.[123]

Beaton felt that the varying heights of such plants made the application of colour principles to them more difficult: 'I never yet saw a mixed flower-bed, or a mixed flower-border, so planted as to give one an idea of any progress at all in the ancient art of mixed planting.'[124] Despite its difficulties, however, mixing had its partisans, and in the late 1840s Errington opened a campaign on its behalf, questioning whether beds ought to be considered only as part of an overall scheme, and recommending that they should be treated as self-sufficient, with edgings and internal contrast.[125] During the next few years, he nostalgically praised the mixed borders of his youth, and noted with delight that mixing seemed once again to be on the increase.[126]

Others were not so delighted, and a long-running controversy was initiated, one critic complaining that mixing and edging exchanged 'the massive and decided for the "little prettinesses" of persons of small intelligence'.[127] The arrival of the ribbon style and its derivatives tilted the balance in favour of edgings and subdivided beds, but the unsystematic distribution of colours remained a problem. The proponents of mixing offered diametrically opposed ideas about its placing in the garden: one writer proposed limiting massed beds to clumps on 'the other side of the water', and concentrating mixed beds in the foreground; Errington, on the other hand, recommended mixed beds as transition scenes between the bedding display and the wider landscape.[128] John Caie waxed poetic in advising against mixing:

> make choice of decided colours, and avoid streaky colours as you would star-shaped beds; the former will impress you like the beauty of the full moon, and the latter like the same moon reflected on the surface of some agitated lake.[129]

It was Beaton who found an acceptable formula for mixed colours. By 1850 he was proclaiming the principle he had seen adopted at Kew, of making the central bed in a parterre neutral in colour. He concluded that any bed of variegated plants would function as a neutral, and described a bed he had planted with *Verbena venosa* and variegated pelargoniums, which a visitor claimed resembled shot silk.[130] Beaton was taken with the name, and hastened to propagandize.

> Let all the nurserymen in the country be laid siege to for variegated scarlet geraniums, to make 'shot silk' beds with this next summer; for if we do not strike while the iron is hot, the half of us may forget the thing altogether before another season comes round.

He was later to note ruefully that the nurserymen had threatened to pull his head off if he ever swamped them again with clamouring customers without giving them sufficient warning to lay in better stocks.[131] The next few years witnessed many experiments, most of which Beaton thought failures, but even after the immediate craze died away, his shot-silk beds were periodically invoked in advice on bedding throughout the rest of the century.[132]

The mixing of colours, despite such experiments, was more normally confined to borders rather than beds. Many geometric parterres retained mixed borders around their walls or balustrades until the ribbon border showed a way of bringing organized colour even to such perimeter situations; thereafter, mixed borders were increasingly kept away from the main body of the flower garden so as not to interfere with the colour scheme. (For similar reasons, roses were largely ostracized from the parterre during the 1850s, as the colours then available were not bright enough for the desired effect; most rose gardens were made in isolated enclosures where they would not impose on the view when flowering was over.)[133] Kitchen gardens, secluded or hedged walks, beyond the neatly mown lawn 'as a break in the beginning of the true English landscape' – these were the accustomed homes of the mixed border. Edward Kemp suggested that symmetrical massing was appropriate for buildings in the Greek and Italian styles, while the irregularity of mixing made it more appropriate for English Gothic buildings, a position supported by advocates of the Elizabethan revival.[134]

The arrangement of plants in a mixed border remained a problem. Straight lines and uniform spacing were often resorted to for ease of maintenance. Shirley Hibberd recommended a repetition of plants or colour groups at intervals, and suggested that borders, unlike flowerbeds, would benefit from deviations from symmetry – 'an occasional breaking of the whole arrangement'. Beaton, on the other hand, tended to despair. 'Mixed borders we all have, or ought to have', he said, but 'I never yet saw even a good or tolerable disposition of such plants anywhere'. The proper treatment of the mixed border, he thought, was the ultimate problem of garden art: 'If we could but teach, or rather unteach, the system of planting herbaceous plants, we might hope to succeed in learning the true art of flower-gardening at last'.[135]

The Flower Garden in the Park

Floral display was coming to dominate the private garden, but its impact on the public parks was delayed. Some of the early parks – for example, Joshua Major's in Manchester – made an important use of flowerbeds, but the criticisms that were levelled at Major's work for its absence of unity of expression did little to advance the floral cause. The botanic gardens, on the other hand, and Kew above all, found bedding a useful way of displaying a portion of the plant kingdom, and were devoting more attention to massing during the course of the 1850s. Beaton's words will serve to explain the principle behind this emphasis:

> In these public gardens, where the great bulk of the visitors know little or nothing about the laws of colours, the best plan would seem to be that which is most likely to attract the attention of the crowd. Get the multitude first into a frame of eye, so to speak, to *see* flowers, by presenting them in brilliant masses of the strongest colours, – a blaze, in fact. Then will be the time to present them scientifically.[136]

It was the Crystal Palace at Sydenham that decisively changed attitudes toward floral display in public parks: the old complaint about impaired unity of expression could not be levelled against its design, and public enthusiasm was evident. Within a few years of its opening, the floral trend had made significant inroads into the royal parks.

In the late 1850s, Lord John Manners, Commissioner of the Board of Works, proposed to increase the public benefit from the parks by laying out flowerbeds within them. The proposals were greeted with horror by partisans of the English landscape; Sir Joseph Paxton, by then MP for Coventry, spoke against the proposals, for fear that the parks would come to rival the Crystal Palace.[137] Nevertheless, Manners proceeded with his plan. In the late summer of 1859, Samuel Broome remarked on the transformation of Hyde Park, where 'No fewer than from 30,000 to

40,000 bedding plants' had been planted, and reported a widespread approval of the change: now 'the working classes could see a display of summer flowers without going to Kew'. The social importance of staging a visual display for the poor was taken up strongly in the gardening press; to provide this innocent pleasure was the first step toward weaning them from their 'depravity', which was really the consequence of a lack of opportunities for better things.

> Flowers are wanted in the people's parks just because the people's houses have no gardens, and nine-tenths of those who frequent the parks have no opportunity of seeing growing flowers anywhere else.[138]

Manners's policy was continued by his successor W. F. Cowper (later Cowper-Temple), who served as Commissioner from 1860 to 1866, and called on Nesfield to advise on the alteration of Hyde and Regent's Parks. At the end of his term the *Gardeners' Chronicle* praised him for having increased the enjoyment of the parks 'by all classes, but especially by the poor', and for having turned the parks from 'large prairies, fairly wooded', into artistic landscape gardens. The perimeter of Hyde Park as far as the Marble Arch was now a 'feast of colour'; Markham Nesfield's Italian garden had made Regent's Park a rival to the attractions of the Royal Botanic Society's garden it encircled.[139]

By the mid-1860s, the municipal parks of London were hastening to follow the example of the royal parks. An additional advantage of bedding was now being discovered: in a polluted atmosphere, where conifers were usually failures, plants that were placed out for a season only were the most secure means of ensuring some degree of horticultural interest. 'Even Kennington Common, which now aspires to the name of Park, has its bordering of flowers, as bright as the smoke and vapour from an adjoining factory will let them be.'[140]

Extending the System

The 1850s were the years of the dominance of the flower garden. From being a segregated enclosure, screened from the landscape, it had become a centre of attention, the compulsory foreground for views from the house, and was gradually extending its sway beyond the immediate confines of the house into the rest of the garden. Debate broke out at each step of its outward progress. The status of flowers in the kitchen garden was controversial, for instance, but at Culford Hall, Peter Grieve, formerly Barron's foreman at Elvaston, showed his sense of a head gardener's dignity by designing a formal avenue of yew hedges and flowerbeds leading through the centre of the kitchen garden to the door of his own house.[141]

As the role accorded to formal bedding increased, complaints began to be heard about its short duration. The flowers of the half-hardy perennials like pelargoniums and calceolarias did indeed last for a longer season than those of most hardy herbaceous plants, but even so, summer bedding had a season of only four months; were the beds to lie bare during the other eight?[142] During the course of the 1850s, accordingly, various suggestions were made for extending the season, or providing ways of filling the beds at other times of the year. One ready suggestion, associated with Caie and Beaton, was a return to the use of annuals, which had become less popular with the advent of the half-hardy perennials; another, associated with Shirley Hibberd, was the plunging system, of inserting potted plants directly into the soil for immediate effect.[143]

In 1855, Samuel Broome, gardener at the Inner Temple, substituted chrysanthemums for the roses that had previously decorated the gardens; by this simple expedient, the bedding season was extended into October and November. The Temple chrysanthemums caused a sensation; Broome was quickly followed by Joseph Dale, his colleague at the Middle Temple, and from 1857 into the 1870s hardly a year went by without detailed reports of their rival displays in the press. Chrysanthemums were soon established as the normal autumnal extension of the bedding system.[144]

The use of evergreens to form winter gardens had been a well-known practice since Wordsworth's day, but these had generally been permanent features. Some gardens, however, used evergreens as temporary decoration by plunging them in pots into the flowerbeds; and by the mid-1850s this practice was being advocated under the name of 'winter bedding', with hollies, *Cotoneaster*, *Skimmia*, *Mahonia*, and *Gaultheria* as favourite plants.[145] James Duncan's admixture of shrubs for year-round effect at Basing Park attracted attention, the Derby Arboretum had circular beds of dwarf conifers,[146] and during the 1860s some gardeners experimented with ornamental kales and dark-leaved beets as bedding plants.[147] But it was William Wildsmith at Heckfield Place who was to develop winter bedding into its most complex form: his beds had 'neat designs worked out in them, in which golden Hollies, Aucubas, small Conifers, Euonymus, Heaths, and carpets of short Heath, fill in with other carpets of Sedums, Herniaria, &c.'.[148]

The season was thus being effectively extended into the autumn and winter by 1860; but attempts were also being made to push the season back in the other direction. Already in the late 1840s Henry Burgess was urging the planting of bulbs in order to give a display until May, when the summer bedders would be planted.[149] A major problem, however, was the arrangement of the often paler colours of spring bulbs; by 1850, Donald Beaton had announced his intention of giving 'my whole strength and power to this subject', and asked his readers for the results of their experiments: 'we could between us make spring flowers as clear as bedding Geraniums'.[150] The major advance in this field, however, was the work of John Fleming, head gardener at Cliveden, who began experimenting with spring flowers in the mid-1850s, and who published an account of his work, *Spring and Winter Gardening*, in 1864.[151]

Fleming challenged the idea that spring bulbs were more limited in colour range than summer bedding plants, and assembled an acceptable palette of scarlet, red, yellow, white, and blue by using a wide range of anemones, pansies, tulips, hyacinths and the like. With these he experimented with colour schemes in Barry's great parterre. In 1862 he attempted mixing colours, but found that the 'grand effect' of the parterre was diminished as a result, and thereafter kept his colours separate and distinct. Fleming's system transferred the bare season from spring to

52 Heckfield Place, the terrace garden. William Wildsmith's winter bedding, from an engraving of 1884.

autumn, when the bulbs were planted, but, thanks to his propaganda, spring bedding became increasingly popular during the 1860s.

Apart from Cliveden, the most famous garden for spring displays was Belvoir Castle, where William Ingram, head gardener from 1853, was sometimes credited by his partisans with being the true originator of the system. The real point at issue was Fleming's association with the geometric parterre, while Ingram's curvilinear beds in dells and on sloping banks were taken up by the proponents of a more 'natural' style. J. C. Niven praised his use of ground covers to conceal the soil in his flowerbeds – 'no stiff formal cut margins and 6 inches of mother earth, to show that art had got the whip-hand of nature, were to be seen'.[152]

Fleming, however, was also engaged during the 1860s in planting the open vistas and woodland walks at Cliveden with spring-flowering subjects, creating banks where the bluebells were said to rival the blades of grass in number, and filling the woods with primroses, oxalis, and wood anemones. Other gardens were following Cliveden's example by the end of the decade.[153] The end of the 1860s saw spring gardening burst on the public eye, in H. G. Quilter's short-lived Lower Grounds at Aston, Birmingham, where daisies and violas in different colours were arranged in borders, scrolls, and circles; thereafter it was widely adopted in the public parks.[154]

By the mid-1860s, then, several options were available to the gardener who wished to extend his summer display throughout the year. John Arthur Hughes recommended the whole gamut: winter walks with yew or holly hedges and conifers, ivy beds, spring bedding, chrysanthemums, and permanent beds of coloured gravels.[155] It is to this last feature that we must now turn.

The Garden of Embroidery

Gravel had been a key constituent of revivalist gardens from the beginning of the nineteenth century, admired for its pristine effect, easy management, and contrast with the colour of grass. A garden without gravel risked an accusation of melancholy; Loudon and Marnock regularly remarked on the merits of gravelled paths.[156] The effect of gravel as a ground colour for the flower garden was more controversial, however, and some gardens of considerable fame, such as Trentham and Alton Towers, abandoned or restricted their early use of it. C. H. J. Smith recommended that gravels 'of a warm shade, such as light sienna' were the best for garden use.[157]

Two different historical traditions underlay the revival of interest in gravels. It was known, on the one hand, that in Tudor times the patterns of knots had been continued through the winter months by the use of coloured earths; this memory lay behind suggestions for the use of gravels, ground glass, and pounded brick for winter gardens.[158] On the other hand, the *parterre de broderie*, using box and gravel alone, had been a major device of Louis XIV's time, and instructions for its layout could be found in John James, whom Nesfield had already used as a source of patterns. In practice the two traditions blended together. John Fleming called such designs 'polychromatics', but gardens of embroidery became, at least during the 1860s, the preferred term.[159]

The revival of ornamental gravels was beset with difficulties. Nesfield's correspondence with Sir Charles Tempest about the parterre at Broughton Hall is revealing in this respect. An alley of yellow spar ran around the parterre, while a pattern of crushed tile and spar in red, white and blue filled the interstices of the box. A letter of 1857 tells the story of a failed experiment at Stoke Edith, Herefordshire, where Nesfield had recently laid out a parterre:

> When last I had the pleasure of visiting Broughton, you mentioned knowing of some quarry in your neighbourhood affording an agreeable blue colour which I did not notice sufficiently at that time in consequence of having several specimens of blue & other colours of *artificial gravel* with me (which were shown to you & Miss Tempest as top dressings to the gravel alleys of the proposed parterres) – now it appears these materials contain *lead* which is *poisonous* to vegetation. A letter of this morning from Lady Emily Foley states that the *blue* sent by my order to her had killed the box which annoys me much.[160]

In Scotland, the architect Alexander Roos was making similar experiments: 'The best colours which I have used in the arrangement of gardening are: – brick dust, mineral coal, copper ore, various kinds of shells, chalk, coloured marbles . . . quartz, glass and particularly the remains of a glass casting.'[161]

Nesfield's greatest baroque parterres were created during the 1850s – Holkham, Eaton Hall, Crewe Hall, Broughton; the early 1860s even saw him creating a parterre at Downton Castle, formerly Payne Knight's picturesque haven. Increasingly, he incorporated monograms into his box arabesques: letters, heraldic devices, family crests. Such figures had appeared sporadically in the 1840s, but soon became a Nesfield trademark; interlaced letters formed the basis of his massive parterre at Crewe Hall, the effect of which was nicely captured by an opponent of the style:

> Nothing for instance, in its way, can be more beautiful than to look down from the long gallery at Crewe Hall upon the formal garden with its curves of variegated gravel and its thick box edging, its broad terraced walks and flights of steps, guarded by quaintly-carved balustrades and strange heraldic monsters. But it hardly strikes one as a garden; it is rather an appendage to the house itself, adding to its stateliness, and recalling, by its prevailing colours of buff and blue, the old traditions of the family.[162]

The interest in monograms points to a general shift of interest from the later to the earlier seventeenth century, from the authority of Dézallier to that of the Tudor creators of knots; the equation between the knot and the modern geometric garden was being made by the mid-1850s.[163]

The development of Nesfield's style was watched with anticipation and alarm in different quarters. Edward Kemp used the Ruskinian argument of authenticity to attack the use of gravelled figures, claiming that 'a *flower-garden*, like all other art-like creations, should invariably *be* what it *professes* to be; and not depend, for any part of its effect, on coloured sands or gravels'. Nothing could justify subordinating flowers to a mere pattern.[164] On the other hand, many gardeners regarded flowers and gravels as equally appropriate when segregated, but found their conjunction disruptive of unity. Monograms did not necessarily call for box and gravel, however; Beaton, on first seeing box embroideries in the early 1850s, had predicted the supersession of gravels by 'half-hardy and fine-leaved plants',[165] and as the fashion spread, head gardeners proved that they could handle the device in their own way. At Hardwick Hall, where the initials ES, for Bess of Hardwick, were built into the balustrading of the roofline, the same initials, in the shape of massive flowerbeds, formed the main feature of the parterre.[166]

Even Kemp, however, was prepared to tolerate the use of gravels for winter gardens, in accordance with Tudor precedent, and this was the line Nesfield followed in a press statement issued in 1862, in which he urged coloured alleys as an alternative to the monotony of evergreens.[167] Many people, of course, welcomed the 'chastity' of Nesfield's effects as a counteragent to the increasing dominance in the garden of formal bedding. The following passage appeared in the *Florist* for 1860:

> We understand that the first landscape gardener of the day is much averse to over-floral decoration, and that, taking advantage of the many suitable forms

53 Hardwick Hall, west front. The flowerbeds reflect the decoration of the building in using the letters ES, the initials of Bess of Hardwick.

> of evergreens for decorating geometrical gardens, he is employing them more largely on every occasion, as well as more simple figures. We therefore hope to see, at Kensington Gore, good examples in this style of art, by the gentleman we allude to – Mr. Nesfield.[168]

The garden referred to was the new garden of the Royal Horticultural Society, destined to be the most controversial of Nesfield's works, and the one most in the public eye.

Unifying the Arts at South Kensington

The Horticultural Society of London underwent a financial crisis in the late 1850s, which provoked its new president, Prince Albert, to institute a scheme to revitalize the Society's fortunes. In 1861 it received a new charter as the Royal Horticultural Society, and a new centrally located garden to compete against the Crystal Palace and Regent's Park. A site in Kensington had been requisitioned, and a development team assembled replete with eminent names of the day: Francis Fowke and Sydney Smirke, architects; Godfrey Sykes and Joseph Durham, sculptors; Nesfield, landscape gardener; and George Eyles, late superintendent of the Crystal Palace, foreman and eventual superintendent. The opening of the garden on 5 June 1861 was Prince Albert's last public appearance in London before his death from typhoid.[169]

54 Holkham Hall, the parterre. Nesfield's box embroidery of the 1850s.

The architectural structure of the garden was the culmination of the Italian style – but derived now from more richly polychromatic models than either Osborne or the works of Barry had been. The garden was partially enclosed by a series of arcades, each based on a different model: the Byzantine 'Lateran arcade' on the southern boundary, modelled in terracotta; the middle, or Milanese, arcades running up the east and west sides, based on fifteenth-century Milanese brickwork; and the north, or Albani, arcade extending on either side of the conservatory, based on details from the Villa Albani. The conservatory itself, an iron structure designed by Fowke, boasted a tessellated floor designed by Messrs Minton as a showpiece for the rediscovered art of mosaic: the patterns were variously based on Pompeian, early Italian, and Renaissance originals, including that of the altar slab at Santa Maria Trastevere in Rome.

Nesfield's plans for the garden were revised by committee before work started, and he was required to include a system of canals that he had not originally intended. The garden was designed to rise from its initial viewpoint at the entrance; the visitor first encountered an ante-garden divided into four plots, two forming miniature amphitheatres, one containing a holly and hornbeam maze, and one planted with limes, tulip trees and deodars. The terraces were organized around the canal system: a great cascade fed by an artesian well, two oblong canals recessed below ground level, and some small central basins with minor jets.[170]

By the Milanese arcades Nesfield designed a set of ribbon borders, or

55 The Royal Horticultural Society's garden at Kensington. A photograph of Nesfield's geometric garden from Andrew Murray's *Book of the Royal Horticultural Society*, 1863.

'friezes', in a Florentine scroll pattern based on Italian church floors; these were intended for bedding, but with an admixture of gravels for winter effect. In other, more centrally placed, panels, he laid out monogram beds purely of box and gravels: the chosen motifs were the four symbolic flowers of the United Kingdom, the rose, thistle, leek and shamrock. (The gravels used were as follows: white Derbyshire spar, purple fluorspar, Welsh slate, pounded brick, and coloured glass.) The *Gardeners' Chronicle* (whose editor, Lindley, was now the Society's secretary) published a joint press statement by Nesfield and Eyles on the subject of embroidered parterres. Beaton was enthusiastic, predicting that the box lines 'cannot fail to become the sampler patterns for imitations in this style of terrace gardens', although preferring the all-gravel parterres to those that attempted a mixture of gravel and flowers. 'I should hail the flowing lines of Mr. Nesfield, at Kensington Gore, as the best auxiliaries to what I have myself been aiming at in my doings and sayings for the last twenty years', he said in summary; 'I never yet saw flower gardening carried on in such high order.' His major recommendation was that the RHS should set up a committee of ladies to decide on colour schemes for the gravels.[171]

Beaton welcomed the garden as a model for future urban gardens; Robert Fish urged employers to let their gardeners visit it as an educational experience. Shirley Hibberd saw in it 'an example of garden architecture which has no match and no parallel for novelty and for unity of design', and acclaimed the precision of Eyles's workmanship. Opposed to these was Beresford Hope, who dismissed it as a more elaborate version of a commercial pleasure garden, 'a moral Cremorne', and predicted dolefully that little of horticultural interest would be successfully grown in the smoky climate of London.[172] The composite inspiration of Nesfield's late style, however, made it difficult to find an acceptable label. The *Athenaeum's* reporter floundered in his attempt to indicate the tradition in which

Nesfield was working:

> in these magnificent arcades we have something new to our country and our century – something exquisitely Italian ... in these successions of terraces, in these artificial canals, in these highly ornamental flower-works we have something of the taste and splendour of Louis Quatorze. It was of such a garden as this that Bacon must have dreamt.

Hibberd summed it up by describing the garden as 'a very complete amalgamation of the French, Italian, and English schools'.[173]

Prince Albert had envisaged the garden as the nucleus of a great cultural complex in South Kensington that would reunite all the arts that had been sundered since the Renaissance. The garden itself was not only to exhibit architecture and horticulture, but to serve as a public display gallery for sculpture. Accordingly, a search for sculptural embellishments was inaugurated, beginning with the controversial acquisition of a large polychrome French fountain, a move defended vigorously by Donald Beaton in his last writings before his death. A series of statues commissioned from contemporary sculptors eventually ornamented the garden.[174]

Within a year, complaints about its lack of shelter and floral character were beginning to become general; the Society was urged to pull down some of the arcades and erect a greater conservatory in their place.[175] The Kensington Garden Committee consulted Nesfield about alterations, and received a rebuke for having overruled some of his plans in the first place. 'As mature trees are indispensable adjuncts to scenery', he wrote, 'the levels of the architecture should have been adjusted as nearly as possible to the levels of such sites of existing tall trees, as were fit to be retained', instead of beginning by felling most of the trees on site. The canals had interfered with his plans for mass planting; the garden was too open for his current taste, and should have been more compartmentalized. His suggested remedies were: to reduce the architectural dominance by screening the walls with arbor vitae, revealing only the copings, and to narrow the open space by hornbeam hedges enclosing open groves.[176] The Committee proceeded cautiously, but by 1864 a modified version of his plans for enclosure was being carried out. Yew hedges and fences of poplar and laurel were forming avenues down the central portion of the garden; covered ways were being formed; rhododendron hedges were planted on the slopes. Complaints resounded immediately that the main features of the design were being obscured from view, and the landscape gardener Joseph Newton wondered whether Nesfield had been consulted: 'Surely he never can permit his beautiful Italian garden to be converted into a drill ground.'[177]

In the Wake of Kensington

The Royal Horticultural Society's garden represents the culmination of the Italian garden in England. Whether for praise or blame, it dominated the consciousness of the gardening world in the 1860s. Its influence was immediate and widespread; as early as the latter part of 1862, the *Gardeners' Chronicle* could find that:

> The flower gardens of our farmhouses are being laid out *à la Nesfield* ... Vases,

56 Witley Court. A geometric arrangement of clipped evergreens replaced the usual box embroidery in this late garden by Nesfield, *c.* 1864–5.

> statues, Minton pavements, and terra cotta columns are turning out of doors dead walls, dirty gravel walks, box edging, and hideous red flower pots. In effecting this Kensington is taking a great part; old Chiswick standing aghast at innovations which seem to be the very incarnation of horticultural Red Republicanism.[179]

The Kensington influence was apparent in such publications of the 1860s as Samuel Beeton's anthology, *The Book of Garden Management* (1862), which included advice on design from D. T. Fish; Andrew Murray's *Book of the Royal Horticultural Society* (1863); and John Arthur Hughes's *Landscape Gardening and Garden Architecture* (1866).

After Kensington, Nesfield, now in his seventies, increasingly relied on his sons for assistance with his work. William Eden Nesfield trained as an architect under Salvin, and during the 1860s went into partnership with the young Norman Shaw; in 1864 he built an extension at Coombe Abbey, Warwickshire, where his father laid out a box parterre and lake to accompany his designs.[180] Markham Nesfield, on the other hand, turned his skills to landscape design, and briefly enjoyed the largest reputation of any designer of his generation. We first hear of him assisting his father at Witley Court, Herefordshire, at the same time as the works on Coombe Abbey; here, in order to complement a large classical building by Whitfield Daukes with a heavy horizontal emphasis, the arabesques of box were dispensed with in favour of a symmetrical arrangement of evergreens clipped into balls and other simple geometrical forms, grouped around an immense fountain designed by Nesfield senior and representing Perseus. Witley was well publicized, and Nesfield was once again declared 'the master spirit of the age' for his work. It was a departure from his recent

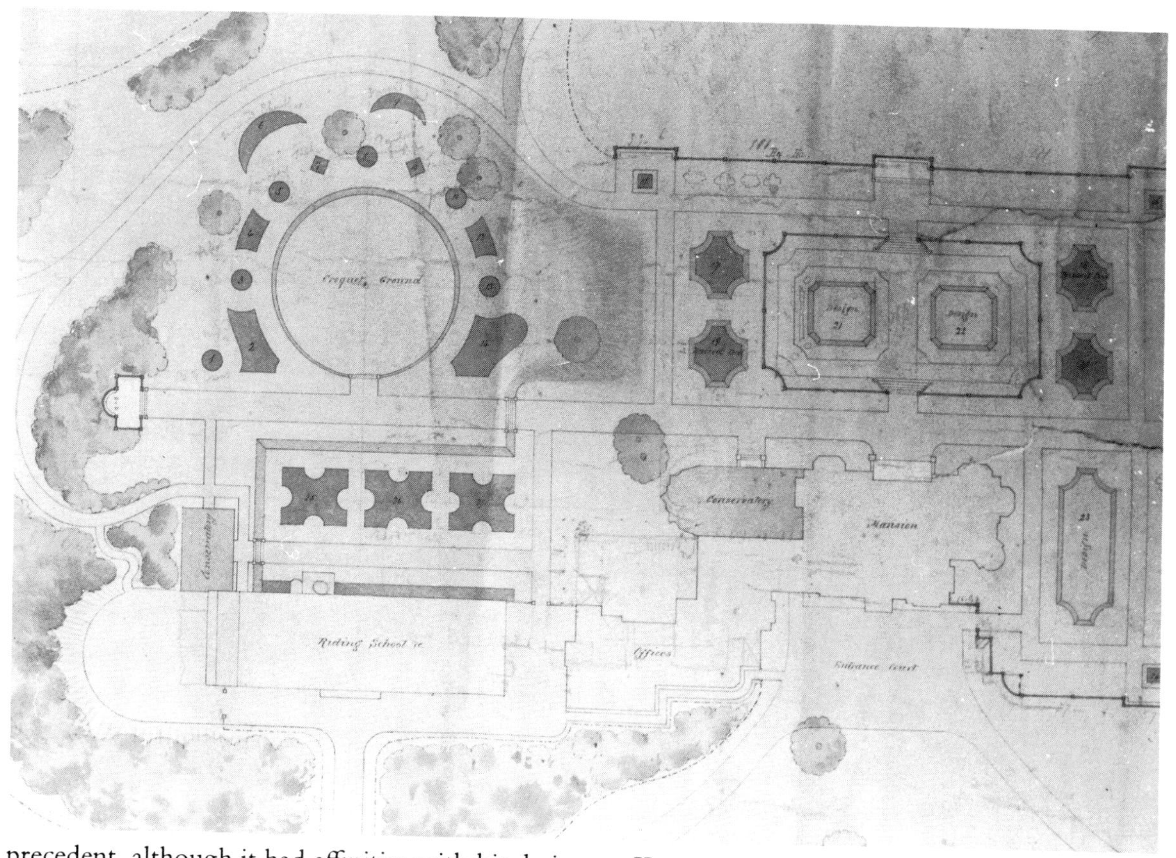

57 Crown Point, plan for the garden. A design of 1869 by Broderick Thomas showing terraces, raised beds, and a croquet ground with a circular hedge.

precedent, although it had affinities with his designs at Kew twenty years before; and its influence can be seen in some of the gardens accompanying Eden Nesfield's houses in the next few years, such as Kinmel Hall, where the topiary content of the parterre was greatly increased.[181]

In the 1860s Nesfield was consulted on the royal parks, and Markham was made responsible for alterations to Regent's Park. Here he created a new Italian garden in the southeast corner, continuing the line of the broad walk with a floral avenue based on a sequence of Italianate ornaments. The elaborately floral borders used a motif of repeated circles, but abandoned any attempt at parallelism between the two sides of the walk. (He showed a similar freedom of handling at Glanusk Park, where he broke the lines of the terraces in order to preserve existing trees.) The great chains of colour were greeted enthusiastically by the gardening press, including the young William Robinson, then employed in the Royal Botanic Society's garden a few yards away, who described the planting as altogether original and prophesied lasting fame for its young designer.[182] Unfortunately, Markham was not long to enjoy his reputation; he was killed in an accident in 1874 while riding out of Regent's Park, with only a decade's work behind him.[183]

Nesfield had made embroidered parterres popular, and they were made by a variety of hands throughout the 1860s at gardens like Balcarres, where Lady Lindsay was credited with the parterre design, and the royal estate at Balmoral.[184] By far the most elaborate of the embroidered parterres laid out in the wake of Nesfield was at Castle Ashby. Sir Digby

58 Castle Ashby, the parterre. These intricate flowerbeds were designed in the late 1860s, using the Northampton family's monogram as a motif.

Wyatt was carrying out alterations, including new terraces, in the 1860s, and the parterre designs were reportedly the work of the Marquis of Northampton himself. Two parterres, one brightly coloured in the traditional manner, the other a design in 'comparatively subdued tracery', were laid out so as to be seen from different rooms. The tracery represented the initials and heraldic devices of the Northampton family, with borders in stylized figures of rose, shamrock and thistle; the planting consisted of pelargoniums, lobelias, and purple verbenas, on a carpet of white verbena.[185] This reliance on chains of flowers to form complex figures made maintenance difficult by comparison with simple box: but within a few years a new form of planting was developed that solved this technical problem – carpet bedding.

Nesfield's parterres were regarded by some as the height of elaborate art, and by others as chaste and restrained in comparison with the fashionable bedding of the 1850s. From these two viewpoints we can trace the development of some of the influential young gardeners of the 1860s. In one camp were D. T. Fish and William Miller, head gardener at Coombe Abbey, both briefly associated with Nesfield, and who continued until the turn of the century to defend the stylistic principles of the 1860s.[186] In the other camp was Joseph Newton, who laid out box parterres in the 1860s and praised them as an alternative to 'colour-gardens', but was to follow the ideal of restraint beyond the box embroidery, and to emerge as an opponent of bedding and a champion of uncluttered park scenery.[187] A parallel transition can be seen in the work of William Broderick Thomas, some of whose work in the 1860s could serve to illustrate Hughes's principles of architectural gardening, but who was to reduce his architectural elements in the 1870s and create the lakes and rock garden of Sandringham.[188]

The ideal of the Italian garden had developed from the mannerist terraces of Barry to the baroque parterres of Nesfield; now, in these post-Kensington works – Witley, Castle Ashby, Regent's Park – that ideal was changing once again. The revised ideal was stated very clearly by John Arthur Hughes in his *Landscape Gardening and Garden Architecture*, when he invoked Tasso's description of the garden of Armida as 'an epitome of the whole art of landscape gardening'. As Hughes described it, this was a garden like Kensington, with its maze in the ante-garden and its canals and cascade beyond:

> At the entrance of the garden are the marvellous sculptured gates, showing that there must be wonders within, but not disclosing them; then the labyrinth; then the cheerful expanse of garden opening to the view, with its still, shady pools, its sparkling cascades and fountains, its flowers for colour, shrubs for texture, and herbs for odour . . .

But then the rest of Tasso's account was drawn in, with details not to be found at Kensington:

> . . . its sunny eminences and bosky dells, its miniature woods and '*spelonche*' – for which, in an English garden, we would substitute a 'fernery;' and, above all, the absence of effort.[189]

Hughes may have been imagining Armida's garden as a variant of the Royal Horticultural Society's, but included in his account were precisely the qualities which were to be valued by the anti-Nesfield reaction. Add the woods, dells, fernery, and effortlessness, and suddenly the garden looks very different from Kensington; and it was this sort of garden that became the goal of the 1870s.

6

History and horticulture

The Reaction in Colour

By the middle of the 1860s, the bedding system was moving steadily in the direction of massiveness of effect, and towards the reduction of the plant range involved. In part this simplification was the result of greater experience with the performance of bedding plants; Shirley Hibberd noted in 1864 that 'the odds and ends of the bedding list that, previous to the year 1860, made so many features of interest' were 'nearly all swept away', to be replaced by zonal pelargoniums, which 'are now so varied in habit and colour that with geraniums alone a skilful artist can produce almost any effect that may be required'. By the 1880s the scarcity of verbenas and calceolarias was much remarked on, and the new tuberous begonias were competing for pride of place with the zonals.[1]

But new attitudes towards colour were beginning to emerge at the same time, and the tradition of high contrast – 'primary colour with symmetrical flatness' – was coming under attack. Ironically, Owen Jones and his colleagues unintentionally furnished their opponents with the materials for their first onslaught. Carlyle, in *Sartor Resartus*, had argued that clothing had a psychological rather than a functional origin; even the naked savages of tropical countries decorated their bodies by tattooing. It was probably Carlyle's argument that inspired Jones and Henry Cole, when compiling the exhibits for the Crystal Palace, to include tattooed shrunken heads and decorated canoes as examples of Polynesian art; Jones later elaborated on savage decoration in his *Grammar of Ornament*. The raw materials were thus available for an argument based on a notion of primitive art,[2] and this argument was applied to gardening in 1862 by Andrew Murray, the Assistant Secretary of the Royal Horticultural Society.

As the author of the *Book of the Royal Horticultural Society*, Murray did not dare much criticism of the new Kensington garden, and confined himself to saying, 'There are a good many (some think too many) examples of coloured gravel and ribbon beds in the Garden.' However, he had already sent a pseudonymous letter, signed 'One of the Old School', to the *Gardeners' Chronicle*, denouncing the trend toward bright colour, and drawing on the Crystal Palace exhibits for ammunition:

> Does not the gaudy glitter of these beds address itself to the lower elements of our taste? It is the savage who is caught by the gayest colours, and a liking for them and personal ornament is a remnant of primitive barbarism which is

59 Some of the most popular subtropical plants: *Musa ensete*, as it was then known, outdoors in a Cornish garden (left) and a pampas grass shown in an engraving of 1857 (right).

> shared by us all, but possessed in smaller and smaller proportions as we ascend the scale of civilisation; we all pay homage to this original weakness, but the highest bred and most cultivated minds feel it least, and when they do yield to it are the first to discard it, and in the present case I am happy to see signs that they are beginning to do so.[3]

Murray did not deny a role in the garden for ribbon borders, but thought they should be confined to public parks. However, his argument about primitive tendencies was now in the public domain. Two years later Revd A. Headley, a popular gardening columnist under the pseudonym of 'Wiltshire Rector', availed himself of it: 'The uncivilised negro girl delights in a red cotton handkerchief; the English lady asks for something less gaudy and more refined for her head-covering.' Soon 'the glaring colours of savages, the daubs in the homes of the poor' were being adduced as an objective measure of taste, a reproof to tolerant mid-century associationism.[4]

'But why should the *greenist* decry the colourist?' demanded D. T. Fish, defending the love of colour from the charge of vulgarity. He quoted Ruskin's *Stones of Venice* on the 'connection of pure colour with profound and noble thought', observing that his authority 'ought to silence those who affirm that the love of colour is a relic of barbarism fit for the childhood of the race – a pleasure that we have outgrown as children do their love for dolls or toys'. Amongst his arguments for the profundity and even the divinity of colour, however, he adduced a dangerous notion:

colour blindness. 'There are men, some say nations, who are colour blind . . . they cannot take it in, and therefore they deprecate it as useless, vulgar, rude, or barbarous'.[5] The idea that a physiological defect could account for variations of taste in colour appreciation was quickly seized upon by the enemies of bright colour, and it became a standard gibe that only colour blindness could account for the striking contrasts of mid-century bedding.

Theories of colour were in flux. Upholders of Chevreul lingered on, and added Shirley Hibberd to their number as he gradually dropped his early discipleship of Beaton. Some speculated about chromatic theories in which colours could be arranged like musical notes. Rumours were heard of James Clerk Maxwell's demonstration that the primary colours were not red, blue and yellow, but red, green and violet.[7]

The most widespread change was a greater insistence on the idea of neutrality as a relief to the eye. The implications of Beaton's advice about using neutral colours for the centres of bedding schemes were developed; most mid-century bedding, it was now said, was deficient in neutral tints and greens, and in consequence suffered from 'glare'. The old-fashioned bedders might say that grass and leaves functioned as an adequate counterpoint to flowers, or even quote the painter Cattermole to the effect that in Nature there was no such colour as green, but these voices tended to get lost in the general roar. Positive colour was increasingly seen as a drawback, to be mitigated by ever greater amounts of foliage.[8] Scarlet and yellow began to be regarded as an index of an impure taste. Hibberd invoked Chevreul to criticize the yellow calceolarias at the Crystal Palace, on the grounds that yellow was out of harmony with the green of the surrounding grass, thus starting a campaign against yellow that flickered intermittently throughout the closing years of the century.[9]

For a change in colour preferences to be enforced, the painters most beloved of the bedding enthusiasts had to be toppled from their pedestals. Rubens had been invoked for his 'sparkle', and this very association with the bedding system earned him the condemnation of Forbes Watson, who found his colours 'showy' and florid: 'But is Rubens, with all his gorgeousness and prodigality, ever ranked with the very greatest colourists? Now, our gardeners very closely resemble him here.' The *Gardeners' Chronicle* might adduce the example of Raphael draping St Peter 'entirely in green and red, the colours of the Pelargonium', but the young gardeners were more likely to look to the delicate harmonies of Albert Moore as a colour standard. By 1880 the *Chronicle* was mocking 'garden Pre-Raphaelites' with 'just a touch of Whistlerism about them', who conceived of gardening solely in terms of 'nocturnes of green and gold or green and purple'.[10]

Many young gardeners of the 1860s and 1870s began to earn their praise for their avoidance of 'garishness'. One of George Fleming's successors at Trentham, Zadok Stevens, 'no red-hot colourist', was noted for toning down his eminent predecessor's schemes.[11] Part of the popularity of spring bedding lay in its more pastel shades. Amateur gardeners like Frances Jane Hope and Henry Arthur Bright recommended a radical diversity in the planting of flowerbeds, so that the beds would be regarded individually and not as part of an overall scheme. Shirley Hibberd, on the other hand, recommended subverting contrast by making one colour dominant in a scheme, varying its tones throughout the composition; such one-colour gardens became widely popular by the end of the century.[12]

Hibberd called this plan 'nature's method', and his example was a field of buttercups: the amount of green visible between the flowers was much greater at close range than at a distance, so that the tone varied with the angle of vision. This argument was typical of the period; as the bedding system came under attack, its defenders responded by reviving the old arguments about massing in nature. Hibberd, C. P. Peach, R. P. Brotherston of Tyninghame, and D. T. Fish were only the most eminent of the writers who pressed the analogy with natural scenery; here is an anonymous writer in the *Gardeners' Chronicle*:

> There was more of Nature and also of art in the massing and bedding out than in the mixing or dotting style. Nature masses always – dots, isolates, seldom or never; or if she dots at all it is mostly on an already furnished base, as Buttercups and Daisies on the verdant sward – the first example, and still the richest illustration, of pincushion flower-gardening. Does any one question that Nature masses her beauties on a large and magnificent scale, let him away to the brown heaths and shaggy woods, and see what grand breadths of light and shade, of grave and gay, she forms of brilliant flowered heaths, golden Brooms and Furze, contrasted with dark Pines, Weeping Willow, or Silver Birches.

Heath, furze, heather, bluebell woods: the range of examples cited was small but consistent. For Fish, at least, it was sufficient to prove the artificiality of mixing as a method of planting: 'those who follow Nature at her best, group, mass, bed out.' Gardens were more in danger from excess of neutrality than from glaring colours.[13]

Fish, whose elder brother Robert had been John Caie's 'interpreter', made it his business to defend the embattled principles of Caie and Beaton. As we have seen, he also invoked Ruskin, but this was a more dangerous ally, for the proponents of mixing could find ammunition in him as well. From Ruskin stemmed the attitude, introduced into the debate in the late 1860s, that a genuine love of plants must be directed toward them as individuals rather than as masses. Forbes Watson, a young Ruskinian doctor, gave the most coherent outline of this attitude in his *Flowers and Gardens*, published posthumously in 1872. In this work, he complained that modern gardening looked on plants 'as mere masses of colour, instead of as an assemblage of living beings', and that consequently 'the imaginative, or higher' element of flower beauty was made subject to 'the sensuous, or lower'.

> But why should we not receive the garden as a pure creation of the gardener, feel that it is beautiful, and be satisfied with that, without looking any further? ... Because in such a manner we shall never gain a strong interest in the individual flowers.

Bedding-out was inherently evil, for it exhibited plants at one stage of their life-cycle only, and thus frustrated a full knowledge of them as living beings; they should be allowed to die and rot *in situ* instead of being removed once their bloom had gone.[14] Watson went even further, to attack the florist's interest in hybridization; a wild rose was the work of

God, and to prefer a cultivated variety was an impiety. A preference for double flowers, in particular, was evidence of a vitiated taste.[15]

To the plantsmen of Beaton's generation, a delight in a plant naturally implied a delight in its massed effect: 'Who could sleep half the time without a long row of [eschscholtzia] after once seeing it that way?' To Watson and the like-minded, this sort of mass planting was 'an expensive substitute for a coat of paint'; true appreciation of plants, and true taste in gardening, could only express themselves as a love of individual specimens. After the vigorous propaganda of Robinson, Farrer, and the like, this attitude was to become a fixture of twentieth-century horticultural rhetoric: we can see in Watson the first systematic exposition of the modern doctrine of the plantsman.[16]

Watson's rhetoric was continued by William Robinson. While working in the herbaceous department at the Royal Botanic Society's garden in 1865, he had praised Markham Nesfield's bedding schemes, but within a few years had first announced his preference for a garden of botanical rarities, and then swung to a dogmatic opposition to bedding in general.[17] This final position was formalized in 1872, when he mounted an attack on C. P. Peach, a defender of the bedding system. Announcing his repudiation of the Victorian latitude in matters of taste, Robinson claimed that one day true taste would be shown to rest on laws as immutable as those of modern science; rejecting, therefore, any appeal to the popularity of bedding, he could 'deny *in toto* that any but the feeblest interest can be excited by it'.

It should not be thought, however, that all those who rejected the use of the bedding system and of colour planning carried their exclusion to such extremes. H. N. Ellacombe, for example, whose garden at Bitton was invoked as a model by William Robinson, distanced himself from his young admirer, and expressed a willingness to disagree cordially with Peach.[18] This tolerant attitude was probably typical of most of the gardening community in the 1870s, but the peaceful coexistence of disparate styles was to become increasingly fragile.

The Rise of Foliage

Most of the proposals for increasing the proportion of neutral colour in the garden focussed on the use of foliage plants.

The ornamental use of plants with prominent foliage can be traced back to George Fleming's work at Trentham in the late 1840s.[19] Ferns were then emerging as a subject of interest, both horticultural and botanical; books devoted solely to ferns had begun to appear in the late 1830s, leading to an explosion of botanical interest, professional and amateur. Fern collecting became a national pastime, recommended by Charles Kingsley as preferable to Berlin woolwork for young ladies; by the 1860s, several nurseries were specializing in ferns.[20] Their shade-tolerance made them ideal for growing indoors, in Wardian cases; by 1850 the magazines were offering instruction in growing ferns on rockwork, and the fernery, whether in the open or under glass, became one of the areas of the garden for which the terminology of the picturesque was retained. The popularity of ferns was described as the 'greatest triumph of flowerless plants over flowers ever recorded'.[21]

Other foliage plants began to spring to notice in the wake of ferns. Variegated-leaved plants were exhibited at the Horticultural Society in 1852; zonal pelargoniums with patterned leaves rose to favour in the following decade. Ivy, long popular as a climbing plant, was being used for bedding by the 1860s; mosses, used for years to cover moss-houses, were annexed to garden use in the late 1850s, and the nurseryman Augustus Mongredien received an enthusiastic press for his moss garden on an irrigated bank.[22]

As early as 1851 Thomas Moore was urging the bedding of common foliage plants like rhubarb, maize and kale; his proposals were revived in the early 1860s by John Robson and Frances Jane Hope.

> Take, for instance, an edging of Parsley; then a row of dwarf-topped good-coloured Red Beet; next a row of Altrincham or Orange Carrot; afterwards a row of the Variegated Kale (pink, white and purple), and back this with a line of Asparagus, and here we have a ribbon-border composed of things all useful as well as ornamental.

Hope planted kales, of every shade from purple to white, in patterned beds in her flower garden at Wardie Lodge, Edinburgh. These experiments were widely followed; another interesting, but less popular, innovation was the use of ornamental gourds, for instance trailing down a turf bank from a terrace.[23]

These were hardy foliage plants, already available, wild or in cultivation; but once foliage had become a desirable quality, more exotic plants were deliberately sought for. The earliest reports of the bedding of *Canna* and *Maranta* came from Germany in the early 1850s; as late as the 1880s, such assemblages of foliage could still be called 'German beds'.[24] Such foliage plants were being recommended by Beaton by 1860, and featured in Barr and Sugden's catalogues from 1862; E. J. Lowe, a prominent fern grower, and Shirley Hibberd published volumes on *Beautiful-leaved Plants* in the 1860s. Many of these plants were tender, only suitable for outdoor culture during the summer, but pampas grasses and bamboos added a certain hardy range as well.[25]

By 1864 the term 'phyllomania' could be coined, and the *Gardeners' Chronicle* grumbled that 'flowers, at one time the greatest favourites, are after a few years of popularity no longer looked at'. During the 1860s, the name most often given to this new style was 'picturesque bedding'; however, as early as 1860 foliage bedding was being praised for creating 'tropical-looking gardens', and, especially in the wake of Battersea Park, the term 'subtropical bedding' became standard.[26] By this time a trend toward harder-leaved plants could be observed, fuelled by reports of Barillet-Deschamps's experiments in bedding in the Paris parks, using not merely *Canna* and *Coleus* but *Caladium*, *Dieffenbachia*, *Philodendron*, shrubby solanums, and bananas. It was to Paris that gardeners like John Gibson and John Fleming looked for a model.[27]

Gibson was superintendent of Battersea Park, which he had laid out over a decade before. By 1864 his new attraction was the subtropical garden: a lawn of irregular outline studded with tree ferns, with planting ranging from formal patterned beds of *Solanum* and *Canna* species to isolated specimens of such large and imposing shrubs as *Montanoa bipinnatifida* and *Wigandia caracasana*, two of the prizes of the subtropical movement.[28] Meanwhile, at Cliveden, John Fleming was planting cannas and giant solanums in open glades in outlying portions of the estate.[29]

In 1867, the young William Robinson went to Paris as *The Times* gardening correspondent to cover the Exposition Universelle, and devoted portions of three books to the merits of subtropical gardening.[30] The associations of foliage bedding were transferred decisively from Germany to France. By 1875, Shirley Hibberd could write of 'an importation from Paris, of limited, and indeed almost questionable value'.[31] Robinson, however, claimed for subtropical gardening the merit of a more refined range of colours, and indeed the replacement of colour by form as the keynote of interest. In this he was followed by many gardeners, who found foliage groups 'poetry itself' compared with ribbon borders.[32]

Gibson remained, for most gardeners, the great innovator and model of subtropical expertise; Robinson, however, had moved to the attack by the 1870s, and condemned Gibson's use of tender plants. Preference ought to be given to hardy plants, to bamboos, pampas grasses, ivies, *Heracleum*, gourds and the like, although as late as the first world war Robinson was still reprinting his expressions of delight over seeing *Musa ensete* growing outdoors at Park Place. Similar proposals for hardy foliage bedding were advanced by Shirley Hibberd, but as a continuation of the tradition of winter bedding; for summer bedding the gardening community as a whole resisted Robinson's claims, and continued to use tender and half-hardy plants.[33]

Subtropical gardening retained its enthusiastic following until the turn of the century. There were those, of course, who objected to its prominence. D. T. Fish became involved in a controversy with Robinson in 1868 when he objected to over-indulgence in green. Another writer plainly felt that flower gardening was under threat:

> If it is to be converted into a greenery, a Kale-yard, or a place for the vulgar exhibition of meaningless masses of coarse foliage plants, sub-tropical or otherwise, then let us boldly call it a leaf garden at once, and at least find a place somewhere for our lovely flowers to exhibit their beauty by themselves . . .[34]

His complaint was premature, however, for 1868 was to see the beginning of a movement that was to carry the use of foliage to an extent previously unimagined.

Carpet Bedding

Not all the plants popularized by subtropical gardening had large and showy leaves; by the late 1860s, a range of dwarf foliage plants had become available, including species of *Iresine* and *Alternanthera* from South America, and were being tried out in gardens. These new plants acted as

ground covers, and a surface as uniform and even as a carpet could be created by careful clipping.[35]

60 A carpet bed at Kew, 1870. A raised mound was a favourite expedient for avoiding problems of perspective in viewing a carpet pattern.

At first this was seen as one more novel form of subtropical bedding; but the possibilities were also seen by the makers of embroidered beds. The innovator was John Fleming of Cliveden, who in 1868 laid out a bed with the monogram of Harriet, Duchess of Sutherland, the HS pattern composed of *Arabis*, *Echeveria*, and *Sempervivum* species on a background of sedum of different colours. A leader in the *Gardeners' Chronicle* suggested the name 'carpet-bedding' for this new effect, and recommended it for experiment in other gardens during the coming season.[36] By 1870 the new system had penetrated the fastness of Kew, resulting in the *Chronicle*'s first illustration of a carpet bed.[37]

The following year, William Robinson's *Alpine Flowers for Gardens* drew attention to the new style:

> The way in which these plants have hitherto been found most useful in flower-gardens is in the making of edgings, borders, &c.; but when people begin to be more familiar with their curiously chiselled forms, they will use them abundantly for making small mosaic beds.[38]

Before long it seemed as though every garden in the kingdom was experimenting with it. The majority of country houses boasted carpet beds at some point during the 1870s, and the fashion spread into suburban villas and town gardens; Henry Cannell's nursery became the leading firm in the country for the relevant plants.[39]

The technical advantages of carpet bedding over the established bedding system were numerous. Evenness of surface after scissoring ensured that no differences of level would interfere with the design. With a range of dwarf or compact succulents (notably *Sempervivum* and *Echeveria*) as dot or edging plants, the means were at hand to create a compact effect hitherto only achieved by moss patterns as recommended by Mrs Loudon. Carpet beds lasted for a longer season and were more weather-resistant than flowers. Their primary disadvantage lay in their absolute flatness: a pattern laid out on a plane needed to have its perspective carefully considered, lest it appear distorted when viewed from any but one particular position. For this reason many carpet beds, beginning with Kew's, were laid out on raised mounds. Within a few years a wide variety of names had been proposed for the new style: embossed bedding, jewel bedding, tapestry bedding, mosaic bedding, artistic bedding, 'a general ransacking of the vocabulary'.[40]

Since both subtropical gardening and embroidery had been seen by some as alternatives to the massing of flowers, it is not surprising that the rhetoric of carpet bedding in its early days emphasized its opposition to the bedding system. Fleming's monogram at Cliveden was seen as a continuation of his experiments in the subordination of background colours, and the comparative neutrality of tone of many carpet plants was regarded as a welcome reaction against glare. The colour range of the new plants – greens, yellows, and browns, with some deep reds and purples – was recommended by Robinson and William Wildsmith as subtler than that of flower bedding.[41] Wildsmith eventually tried to establish the bedding of dwarf succulents as a separate form of gardening, using shades of green and blue-green only, to be called 'neutral bedding', but this usage did not become widely established, despite publicity in Robinson's anthology *The English Flower Garden*.[42]

Alexander Forsyth regarded carpeting as a refinement of Nesfieldian embroidery, hitherto led astray by experiments with ground glass, and he suggested that 'Tunbridge ware, Torquay marble ware, and Matlock ware' be looked to as sources for designs. As so many carpet beds were laid out on circular raised mounds with arabesques, one wonders how many Adam or other ceiling patterns were transferred to the ground during the 1870s and '80s.[43] A few experiments were made in informal carpet bedding: John Gibson laid out a bed of *Antennaria tomentosa* in Battersea Park, which Robinson praised as an imitation of the appearance of snow on mounds, and some enthusiasts put carpeting plants to use on rockwork.[44]

In 1875, however, George Thomson, superintendent of Crystal Palace Park, prepared the most arresting carpet display yet seen: a series of six beds in the shape of butterflies, with small decorative infill beds between them. The butterflies were realistic portrayals of particular species, the wing colours copied as faithfully as possible. (The design seems not to have been Thomson's own.) In 1878, Thomas Moore published the plan of one of the butterflies in his revised edition of Thompson's famous textbook *The Gardener's Assistant*; they had already been imitated in Victoria Park.[45] Despite mockery and scepticism from some quarters, the idea spread; even bigger and better butterfly was a featured exhibit at the Exposition Universelle at Paris in 1878, and zoomorphic beds quickly became as popular on the continent as in England.[46]

61 Hampton Court, a carpet bed. This lithograph from Götze's *Album for Teppichgärtnerei*, *c.* 1900. Such beds became a popular feature at Hampton Court, and their suppression after the First World War proved controversial.

In the wake of Thomson's butterflies, a resurgence of interest could be seen in the portrayal of monograms and heraldic emblems in carpet beds. In 1878, R. C. Kingston's carpet beds at Brantingham Thorpe, near Hull, incorporating the device of the Prince of Wales's feathers, were illustrated in the *Gardeners' Chronicle*; by the same year, the grounds of Petworth House had been graced with a dragon cut out in the turf – carpet bedded in the summer and planted with bulbs in the spring. John Noble had a mosaic bed in the shape of a vase in his garden at Park Place in 1879.[49] Similar devices spread thereafter, as aristocratic families dabbled with the new method of displaying their insignia. 'The gardeners are now trying their skill in designs on their carpet-beds, and names, mottoes, coats of arms, and other frivolities, are becoming common', wrote H. A. Bright in 1881, claiming that emblematic carpet bedding was a revival of sixteenth-century French practice, the 'quaint devices in flowers' of Henri IV's court.[48]

But while the country house gardener tended to accept the constraints of history and use devices with family or national associations, there were in effect no limits to the subject matter available to others. As early as 1876 the press noted with dismay the appearance of a hundred-yard-long carpet display proclaiming the name of the newspaper 'Glasgow Herald'.[49] Names of towns and slogans of civic crests were more acceptable ways in which lettering could form part of the carpet bed, supplemented before long by commemorative notices, announcements of centenaries, and the like; and gradually, portraits, human figures, and the full range of animal and emblematic shapes became part of the park superintendent's stock in trade.

62 A monogram bed of 1910 in an unidentified garden: the use of emblematic motifs in carpet bedding.

By the 1880s, emblematic carpet bedding had settled in as part of standard practice, although the three-dimensional beds of the Edwardian period had yet to appear. It could appear to a veteran gardener like George Eyles that the bedding system was now finally complete. The horticultural experiments of his youth, channelled by his successive instructors, Paxton and Nesfield, had now emerged in a permanent form, and the flower garden had reached its highest stage of development.

> This system has gone on improving ever since, until our flower gardens have become real works of art, and a pleasure to look upon for the whole of the summer and autumn. No doubt the carpet bedding in our parks and public gardens, as well as in many private gardens when the necessary time can be bestowed upon its proper keeping, is as near perfection as can well be. Indeed, I think it very doubtful whether the next generation of horticulturists will witness such a startling revolution, or see such a marked improvement in flower garden decoration as the last has done.[50]

Revivalist Planting

The variety of fashions for foliage plants constituted one form of reaction against the bedding system; another lay in the revival of old-fashioned plants. Increasing knowledge of garden history brought with it a better understanding of the chronology of plant use; as early as 1855, the *Cottage Gardener* ridiculed Maclise for including an 1840s hybrid fuchsia in a painting depicting a scene from *As You Like It*. Part of this knowledge, however, was a realization that today's old traditional plants had been the exciting exotics of the past: 'Even Lord Bacon's list is largely made up of importations from abroad'. If the Tudors had had access to the modern range of plants, they would have used them; so why exclude them now? Despite the hesitations of a Loudon or a David Gorrie about the use of modern plants in a surviving ancient garden, the general attitude of High Victorian gardeners was that period accuracy in design brought with it no commitment to period accuracy in planting.[51]

The eventual change in this attitude began with the mixed border. 'A garden without a border for mixed flowers is seldom to be met with', said Donald Beaton at the end of the 1850s, and the importance of the border increased steadily over the course of the ensuing decades; Shirley Hibberd asserted that borders were a necessity, bedding merely an embellishment.[52] As a result, border plants gradually lost the associations of unsophisticated artlessness that they had had in Errington's time. Some of them came to be regarded as poets' flowers, largely because of their use in Tennyson, although Shakespeare, Milton, Herrick, and Spenser also functioned as sources of allusions. Tennyson, at least until the 1860s, preferred the garden planting of his youth to the new Victorian styles; his poem 'Amphion', published in 1842, was a protest against the use of exotics, and his repeated invocation of sunflowers, hollyhocks, tiger-lilies, and the like surrounded these flowers (exotic novelties to former generations) with an atmosphere of haunting suggestion. (In his later years, at Aldworth, Surrey, Tennyson had an Italianate terrace with vases of pelargoniums to give a red touch to the distance, but it was his poetry, not his own practice, that was influential.)[53]

After poetic associations came associations of age and tradition, as the phrase 'mixed border' gradually gave way to 'herbaceous border', a phrase used by the Loudons and George Johnson when referring to seventeenth-century practice. 'Herbaceous borders' were shown as early as 1846 on a plan of the new gardens at Arley Hall, Cheshire, where they accompanied topiary hedges. By the 1870s, the borders at Newstead Abbey were being claimed as a direct survival from monkish times, although there is no evidence for such continuity.[54] Also in the 1870s an attempt was made to identify old-fashioned flowers with 'Queen Anne', the popular but inappropriate name for a new architectural style based on seventeenth-century Anglo-Dutch precedents; names like 'Queen Anne's double daffodil' (first recorded 1873) and 'Queen Anne's lace' (even later) may show the influence of this label.[55]

63 Engraving of a herbaceous border. Noel Humphreys offered this view in *The Garden*, 1872, as a preferable alternative to a formal design. The engraving was later used by James Kelway and Son in their catalogues of herbaceous plants.

Associations of antiquity were reinforced by suggestions of loss and rescue. By the 1880s a mythology was being created of the wholesale disappearance of herbaceous plants from gardens, and their rediscovery around humble cottages. William Robinson did more than anyone else to propagate this myth, which became more extreme as the decades passed; here is an 1876 version:

> When in nearly every private garden in the land orders to adopt bedding-out in all its severity were given, and the old flowers were consigned to the rubbish-heap without a protest, who saved our precious collections of hardy flowers? Why, mainly nurserymen, independent enough to have their own way in spite of fashion – the Backhouses, Hendersons, Osborns, Lawsons, Wheelers, and the botanic gardeners like Moore, McNab, Niven, Bain, and others.

By 1913, Robinson was claiming to have revived interest in herbaceous plants almost single-handed.[56] Herbaceous perennials, however, far from dying out, had remained available in the nurseries: 'the old plants, if out of fashion, can yet generally be procured'.[57] The genuine losses from cultivation fell into two categories: old florists' flowers, and exotic introductions of the 1820s and 1830s which had been superseded too rapidly in the hectic rush of new plants. H. H. Dombrain and Harpur-Crewe in particular attempted to recover these plants; attempts were made to revive daffodils, hollyhocks, and seventeenth-century roses; one of Mrs Ewing's popular stories of the 1880s has as its theme the rescue by some children of a hose-in-hose carnation.[58]

64 Blickling, the terrace garden. Lady Lothian had this arrangement of disconnected herbaceous beds laid out in place of Nesfield's proposed parterre, *c.* 1872.

Finally, Henry Arthur Bright, propounding the theory that associations were primarily called up by the sense of smell, called for the revival of the old scented garden, and condemned the emphasis on colour planning and 'scentless plants, to which no association attaches'.[59]

The 1860s and 1870s, then, saw the creation of a mystique attaching to herbaceous plants. Many gardeners were irritated by the new rhetoric of sudden rediscovery; Robinson was attacked as 'an eminent "arm-chair" gardener' who 'in the seclusion of his study, has discovered that hardy plants are beautiful', while his elders had been experimenting with mixed borders for a generation. D. T. Fish, echoing Donald Beaton, claimed that he had never seen a well-planted border; the landscape painter Frank Miles, in rebuttal, offered his border to Robinson, who featured it as a model in his *Hardy Flowers* (1871).[60] The rules of symmetrical growth and arrangement that had been regarded as essential in the 1850s were rejected by the new enthusiasts, who tended to value individual combinations of plants above overall effect. 'In the management of herbaceous borders', wrote Hibberd, 'details are everything, and principles next to nothing'.[61]

But the herbaceous style was also beginning to spread beyond the border, into the parterre. At Blickling, Norfolk, about 1870, Lady Lothian overruled Nesfield's plans for the layout of his new terrace garden, and instead of an arabesque in box, created an intricate pattern of disconnected beds of herbaceous plants. Early reports of 'this new, or shall we not say, revived old style of planting' emphasized the absence of blazing colour.[62]

Ironically, while Blickling initiated a trend for replacing bedding by herbaceous planting in the parterre, observers noted an increasing tendency for small cottage gardens to go over to bedding:

> It is often amusing to trace a fashion as it percolates downwards. By the time it has reached the far-away sleepy country villages something quite new and entirely opposite is really the rage amongst the upper ten thousand. Cottagers now try to fill their little plots with geraniums and calceolarias, which they are obliged to keep indoors at great inconvenience to themselves and loss of light to their rooms. Meantime my lady at the Court is hunting the nursery grounds for London Pride and gentianella to make edgings in her wilderness, and for the fair tall rockets, the cabbage roses, and the nodding columbines which her pensioners have discarded and thrown away.[63]

The Old-Fashioned Garden

By the 1870s, for the first time, it was possible to suggest an historical revival simply by the choice of plants, independently of the design of the garden. But a new phase in revivalist design was emerging to accompany the herbaceous revival. An interest in enclosure rather than prospect had been developing for some years, with Biddulph Grange showing how the internal subdivision of the garden could temper the effects of contrast; but during the 1860s this interest was to be expressed in architectural form. Andrew Murray provided the first indication of the coming change:

> Another consequence of this ribbon craze is the doing away with the walls of the garden. Having destroyed the garden, why retain the walls? Perhaps it has not just reached this stage, but it certainly has come to this – that in new places the garden walls are dispensed with, and the garden itself is represented by the shrubbery in front, diversified by ribbon beds. Our neighbours across the Channel speak of this style in terms of high commendation: 'It not only allows the view of the owner to extend to a distance, but also permits the eye of the passer-by to plunge with admiration within.' And it is natural they should like it. So much of their life is passed in public, that I do not believe they understand what seclusion or retirement are; or at any rate if they do, they are utterly insensible to their charms. For my part I have been brought up an Englishman ... There is a sense of snugness and security in a walled garden which is not to be found in any shrubbery, however much closed in.[64]

During the 1870s, this sense of enclosure was reintroduced into the bedding system in a number of establishments. At New Tarbet, Ross-shire, the Duchess of Sutherland developed what was called 'stall bedding', subdividing a ribbon border by fuchsia hedges. Hibberd extended this to recommend 'a series of courts or gardens, divided and bounded by hedges of Yew or Holly or Privet', modelled on the style of mid-century rosaries. Gardens like Hoar Cross and Beaudesert, both in Staffordshire, screened their parterres with yew hedges, although continuing to employ formal bedding; at Beaudesert the patterns were modelled on 'the Hyacinth and Tulip beds of a former age'.[65]

Hedges and topiary, by the 1870s, were being promoted instead of geometric parterres, as necessary to provide an architectural setting for the house. 'Many modern mansions are dropped as it were in the middle of a park – the turf comes up to their walls. This we consider very bad taste.' The box hedges of Castle Bromwich (a mid-century restoration) were commended for their old-fashioned atmosphere, and the admixture of bedding condemned.[66] The more figurative forms of topiary, generally proscribed hitherto, began to find a more appreciative audience. There were yews cut into rings in the parterre at Baron Hill, Anglesey, by 1873, and Rossetti purchased a topiary armchair, 30 years old, for his garden in 1866. William Morris cut one of his hedges at Kelmscott Manor into the shape of a dragon, named Fafnir after the Icelandic sagas he was translating at the time.[67]

At Hardwick Hall, where herbaceous borders and an emblematic bedding scheme (the letters ES) were mingled on the western court, Lady Louisa Egerton laid out an eight-acre enclosure on the south side of the house in the late 1860s.

> It is divided into four parts by avenues of Yew and Hornbeam hedges running north and south and east and west, the grass walks between them being 20 feet wide and in excellent condition. The first part contains the croquet ground, surrounded by fine evergreens and Conifers ... The second part, which is in close proximity to the house, is a fruit orchard, and Apples, Pears, and Plums are well presented. The third is chiefly taken up with Filberts and other fruit trees; and the fourth is entirely devoted to vegetables.[68]

This mixture of fruit and flowers, later sometimes called a 'medley garden', was also promoted by George Devey in the gardens of Penshurst Place, where an orchard was made the basis of many of the hedged compartments. Reginald Blomfield, following in Devey's steps, earnestly recommended a greater use of fruit trees for ornament:

> Nothing can be more beautiful than some of the walks under the apple-trees in the gardens at Penshurst. Yet the landscape gardener would shudder at the idea of planting a grove or hedge of apple-trees in his garden. Instead of this he will give you a conifer or a monkey-puzzle, though the guelder-rose grows wild in the meadow and the spindle-tree in the wood, and the rowan, the elder, and the white-thorn; and the wild cherry in autumn fires the woodland with its crimson and gold ... It is only since nature has been taken in hand by the landscapist and taught her proper position that these have been excluded.

By the end of the century, nut walks were becoming popular as ornamental features, and many enclosures in art-and-crafts gardens functioned as orchards.[69]

These generalized trends were coming by the early 1870s to crystallize around a common theme: the Baconian garden. Sir Francis Bacon's essay on gardens had been invoked in order to praise the Royal Horticultural Society's garden at Kensington; but within a few years a writer in *Fraser's Magazine* had invoked it specifically on behalf of rectilinear design, perennial planting, and a restraint in visual display.[70] Gardens of the Tudor period had weathered the accusations of primitivism and clumsiness which Lindley had levelled at them; they were now works of art contemporary with Shakespeare, the period 'when English wits and English taste were confessedly at their brightest and best'.[71]

The revival of the enclosed garden was not primarily a scholarly movement, however. Such gardens were displayed in the paintings of Frederick Walker and many of the Pre-Raphaelite circle; Disraeli's novel *Lothair* ended with the rejection of the parterres of Trentham for an enclosed scented garden; impressionistic writers like George Milner and Mrs Francis Foster held up the Elizabethan ideal, but without distinguishing it very carefully from the mediaeval, the Wordsworthian, or the Tennysonian.[72] Furthermore, the later Stuarts were coming to receive the same attention as the Tudors, and Philip Webb was starting to promote Georgian models for smaller houses. Thackeray, whose novels were creating an aesthetic interest in the eighteenth century, had a Georgian-style brick house built for himself in Kensington in 1860. The later 1860s saw the emergence of the so-called 'Queen Anne' style of architecture, which took the florid brick architecture of the seventeenth century as its model, and was at first associated with Eden Nesfield and Norman Shaw. Through Eden Nesfield, the precedent of Witley Court, with its parterre of clipped shrubs, was added to the repertoire of models for gardens. In practice all these periods were conflated in the garden. As a result, attempts to find a general stylistic label were failures, and the unspecific epithets 'old-fashioned', 'old-world' and 'pleasaunce' became generally current.[73]

The stylistic features of such gardens had been stabilized by the end of the 1870s. Walled or hedged enclosures provided the basic structure, dividing the garden into a sequence of self-contained rooms which did not impinge on each other's views. Where walls were used, they tended to be planted with ivy, Virginia creeper, or other climbing plants. The enclosures were paved, and trees were often planted in tubs. Herbaceous borders were an inevitable feature; when beds rather than borders were used, they were edged with stone or tiles.[74] Philip Webb's modest garden for William Morris at the Red House, Bexley, was a prototype of such gardens, and important later representatives included Morris's hedged garden at Kelmscott Manor (which formed the setting for his novel *News from Nowhere*), and The Downes, Hayle, laid out on sloping ground in a series of dwarf, tile-edged terraces by John Dando Sedding.[75]

The garden which did most to popularize the old-fashioned style was Huntercombe, Buckinghamshire, where the Hon. Mrs Evelyn Boyle, who wrote under the name of E.V.B., began redesigning the garden in 1871. A seventeenth-century lime avenue, some specimen elms, walls, and a square lawn with beds comprised the garden that she found, but this had been radically altered by the time she published a detailed account of her garden in 1882.

> These 'gardens on a flat' are transformed. There are now close-trimmed Yew hedges, some of those first planted being 8 feet 6 inches high, and near 3 feet through, while others are kept low and square. There are Yews cut in pyramids and buttresses against the walls, and Yews in every stage of natural growth . . . The borders are filled with the dearest old-fashioned plants . . .
>
> There are green walks between Yew hedges and flower borders, Beech hedges, and a long green tunnel – the *allée verte* . . .

Bedding was not utterly banished, but much more of her effort went into experiments with naturalized bulbs, a woodland plantation, and a lavender border.[76]

65 Huntercombe, a view of cones and hedges of yew in an influential 'old-fashioned' garden of the 1870s.

Huntercombe alerted the general public to the delights of the old-fashioned garden, but in the long term the greatest influence on design was Penshurst Place, Kent. George Devey, an architect who catered for an aristocratic clientele, had by the 1860s developed a method of incorporating into his buildings an apparent history of changing styles over the generations. He began the restoration of the house about 1850 for the first Lord De L'Isle, and continued intermittently for thirty years; and during the course of these works he restored the parterre to the form indicated in Kip's illustration of the early eighteenth century. Penshurst was held up as a model by turn-of-the-century architects like Reginald Blomfield and Walter Godfrey, and through their advocacy helped to purify the old-fashioned garden of its eclectic character.[77]

The Reaction in Landscape

The general philosophy of High Victorian landscaping, reduced to its lowest common denominator, was summed up by Shirley Hibberd in his *Rustic Adornments:*

> It should be borne in mind by every cultivator of taste in gardening, that a garden is an *artificial* contrivance, it is not a piece scooped out of a wood, but in some sense a continuation of the house. Since it is a creation of art, not a patch of wild nature . . . so it should everywhere show the evidence of artistic taste, in every one of its gradations from the vase on the terrace, to the 'lovers' walk' in the distant shrubbery.

This may be seen as the philosophy of Loudon, M'Intosh, and their coevals reduced to commonplace, but it differs from the early Victorian theory in its comparative tightness of handling; Hibberd's ideal envisaged the 'subordinating of every detail to the production of a *complete effect*'.[78]

During the 1860s, however, a reaction was gradually building up against the character of artistic treatment assumed necessary in the previous decade. Nesfield's prominence meant that his work was most often singled out for attack. In the Royal Horticultural Society itself, a reaction took place against the Kensington garden; Prince Albert's great cultural schemes were felt to have resulted in an inappropriate dominance of sculpture and other arts at the expense of horticulture. The Society eventually vacated the Kensington site in 1889, and Nesfield's garden became the site of the Science Museum and the Imperial Institute.[79]

Nesfield did not live to see this. Nonetheless, his reputation underwent a sudden decline. His last gardens were a series of defeats, his planting schemes rejected by the owners; many of his gardens were being altered and simplified; his parterre at Kew was ripped out and redesigned the year before his death in 1881. His obituaries were brief and unenthusiastic; even George Eyles was damned by association, for on his death in 1887, it was found appropriate that he should die at the same time that the Kensington garden he had helped to lay out was being abandoned.[80]

Nesfield's offences were the gravel parterre and the quantity of stonework associated with the Italian garden. His gardens began to attract descriptions like 'Nesfield's abominations', and 'frittered and childish, though costly, suggesting the idea of playing at gardening with unsuitable materials'.[81] French Renaissance parterres were not for our time; 'we have to deal with the future', wrote William Robinson, and 'the coloured gravel, terrace wall, water-squirt pattern bed properties have nearly served their turn.'[82]

The broader issue, however, was the relation of the house and garden. The arguments of Lindley and Joshua Major against period design in the garden were now revived.[83] A variety of approaches, ranging from the simple substitution of carpet beds for box parterres to the repudiation of all architectural accompaniments, competed for favour during the 1870s.

At Thoresby Hall, Nottinghamshire, Salvin's last country house (1865–76), the attribution of the garden is uncertain, a range of designers from Nesfield to Broderick Thomas having successively produced plans. The eventual outcome was a series of terraces with carpet beds of simple design, some cut in the grass, others set within massive stone curbs.[84] Carpet beds

66 Cardiff Castle, the moat garden. Originally designed by William Burges to include sculpture and fountains, but executed by Andrew Pettigrew in a more informal style, 1871–91.

like these, and massive beds of the sort popularized by Linton Park, continued the tradition of architectural gardening through the 1870s.

Stone-edged beds formed part of a more eclectic scheme at Cardiff Castle, William Burges's feudal extravaganza. Work on the gardens began in 1871 under the new head gardener Andrew Pettigrew. Burges produced plans for turning part of the moat into a garden; along the base of the outer wall would run a series of raised beds with dwarf stone walls and trelliswork for climbing plants. The moat garden was not completed until 1891, and in a reduced style which brought Burges's plan into keeping with the informal landscape style that Pettigrew employed in planting the pleasure ground within the walls; in lieu of the fountains and statue that Burges originally envisaged, a sloping lawn was ornamented with large circular beds.[85]

The early 1870s found Broderick Thomas landscaping the new estate of the Prince of Wales at Sandringham, Norfolk, and greatly reducing the architectural framework of the terrace garden. A grass slope led down from the new house to a parterre laid out on a lawn, which led with no architectural separation to open glades beyond, and thence to the new lakes and rock garden.[86] Even Noel Humphreys, twenty years after his demand for formal terracing as essential for any garden, became a prominent spokesman for the informal 'home landscape'.[87]

The debate also affected the public park. Warrington Taylor fulminated against the competition for Sefton Park and wished instead for a 'human design' based on Kip or Versailles: 'broad allées, grand avenues, shrubberies, woods with grand straight walks through them'. Similarly, when Alexander McKenzie and Joseph Meston laid out the gardens on the new Victoria Embankment, the architectural press lamented the lost opportunity for creating an urban garden with a screening wall and central avenue instead of 'meaningless paths', an arboretum instead of a parterre.[88]

The lawn became the touchstone of the new anti-architectural taste, which condemned its 'cutting up' for flowerbeds. Joseph Newton emerged in the 1860s as a spokesman for the lawn, offering Hyde Park as a model for what public parks ought to be: 'what our citizens want is plenty of room for grass promenading, and that cannot be had where notices are put up to the effect that "Visitors are requested to keep off the grass"'. A 'broad grassy surface, skilfully planted, would be a greater boon ... than expensive earthworks, with finely kept surfaces'.[89]

The resurgence of the lawn was to become the hallmark of a movement that saw itself as returning to the principles of the gardenesque, before it had been subverted by the arrival of the Italian style. One of the famous practitioners of the 1830s was still active: Robert Marnock, since 1840 curator of the Royal Botanic Society's garden in Regent's Park, which he had designed. Newton described this garden, with 'its array of shrubs, its varied lawn, its range of glass and botanical collections', as being in 'the old English style' – that is, the English landscape style as improved by nineteenth-century horticulture;[90] and this view corresponded closely to Marnock's own conception of his work. In the 1860s his reputation was to soar as the leading landscaper of the post-Nesfield period.

Marnock wrote little, and the most concentrated exposition of his views is to be found in a series of extracts from his letters, made after his death by Mungo Temple, who had implemented some of his plans at Impney Hall, Worcestershire, in the 1870s. Among the things that Marnock found objectionable were:

> 'Formal lakes with long, meaningless curves, and studded with islands in the centre', 'rockwork of a mean, paltry character', 'walks with many unnecessary windings, and whose crooks and bends were seen from the dwelling, his maxim being that no walk should be brought into view where it could be obscured' ... 'The dotting of trees and shrubs on lawns like sentinels ... or placing anything on a lawn at all which in any way interrupted the view or defaced the space' ... 'The formation of terraces or other artificial work, where no building or anything else required such aid;' 'cutting up open space for beds or borders, where a clean well-formed lawn would have enhanced the beauty of the demesne;' 'abrupt slopes'; 'planting in hollows;' ... 'covering up with soil gnarled surface-roots of old trees;' 'forming beds for flowers or shrubs among or near old trees;' ... 'formal avenues, where they could be easily dispensed with;' 'roads to the dwelling-house, taking long out-of-the-way turns, where they could be concealed and the distance shortened....'[91]

Many of the prohibitions in this list depended on circumstances. Thus, scepticism about formal avenues did not prevent Marnock from making a copper-beech avenue as the approach to the garden at Rousdon, Devon; and terraces with parterres featured in several of his gardens, Impney Hall

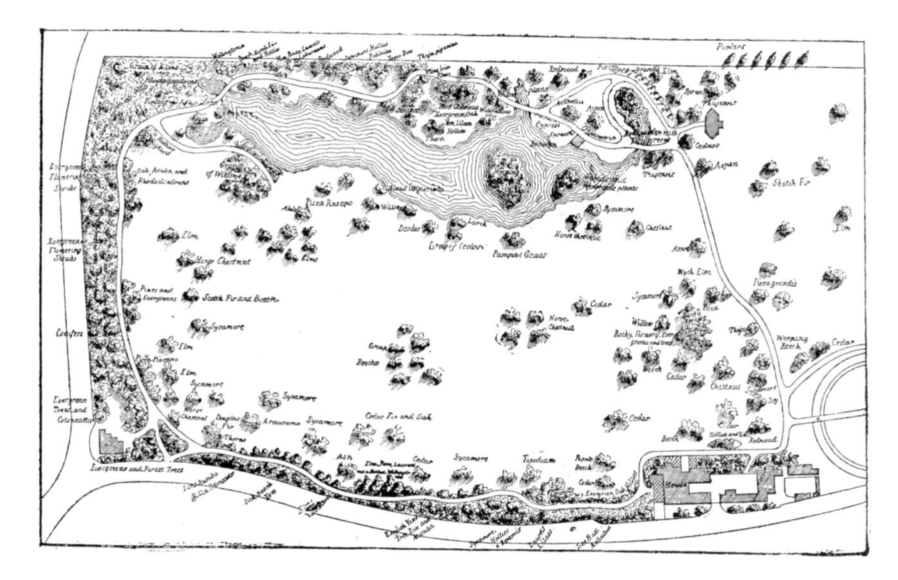

67 A garden plan by Robert Marnock, published in William Robinson's *English Flower Garden* (1883). A re-assertion on the gardenesque principles of the 1830s and 1840s.

among them. Marnock's flower gardens, the most notable of which was the parterre at Warwick Castle, had their own recognizable style – 'the absence of the numerous geometrical figures and beds usually considered indispensable', wide box edgings, and a low centre 'so as to bring greater surface into sight'. This Beatonian subordination of the centre also characterized Marnock's tree grouping: 'instead of placing trees of bold or peculiar habit in the centre of clumps', wrote Burbidge, 'he usually plants them on their outer and most prominent edge . . . In due time, these trees, instead of forming an almost unnoticed unit, in a more or less formal mass, stand forth boldly'.[92]

Marnock gathered around himself a group of pupils and protégés to carry his ideas further, among them Alexander McKenzie, Joseph Meston (who eventually inherited Marnock's practice), and William Robinson, his assistant at Regent's Park, whose garden at Gravetye Manor Marnock helped to design in his last years.[93] The key event for the Marnock group was the founding in 1871 of the magazine *The Garden*, in order to advocate 'pure horticulture of the natural, or English, school, free from rigid formalities, meretricious ornaments, gypsum, powdered bricks, cockle-shells, and bottle-ends'.[94]

Marnock's style was adapted from Loudon's pictorial gardenesque: predominantly exotic planting, planned for colour effect and botanical variety, employing a scatter of distinct specimens where important views would not be affected.[95] Its positive features, however, were less important for Marnock's followers than its repudiation of the architectural gardening of the 1850s; for some, Marnock was in effect a half-way stage in the revolt against all forms of 'style'. By the 1870s, McKenzie and Robinson were moving beyond Marnock to an assertion of the absolute independence of garden design from architectural style.

Landscape Principles in Conflict

In 1867 a competition was announced for the design of Sefton Park, Liverpool. Edouard André, one of the designers of the Paris parks, collaborated with a local architect, Lewis Hornblower, on an entry; Markham Nesfield, then at the peak of his fame in the wake of his Regent's Park alterations, was the adjudicator. André and Hornblower won the premium, beating Edward Milner and Joseph Newton among other competitors.

André accorded the highest importance in design to tracing 'the lines of vistas between the greatest number of attractive points'. In the Paris parks, this meant that a complex geometry was projected onto the ground: a network of paths in overlapping circles and ellipses, their locations determined less by the contours of the ground than by the need to open up multiple vistas.[96] The plan for Sefton Park was basically Parisian, with archery and croquet grounds, a deer park, and an aviary, Moorish kiosk and windmill as eyecatchers.

Marnock's circle was noted for a degree of Francophilia – Robinson made his name with two books on the merits of French gardening, and McKenzie drew up proposals for the replanning of London in the manner of Haussmann.[97] Sefton Park was to prove a test case for French ideas; '[we] are now . . . to receive from our pupils the Gallicised version of the Jardin Anglais'.

> The radical defect of the plan is . . . that it is sadly frittered away by roads and walks, by useless buildings, objects, or compartments, and by an attempt to utilise or render ornamental a very insignificant streamlet, breaking it up into pools and impracticable cascades. The roads and walks, indeed, often run nearly parallel with each other, at short distances apart, and curving in the same direction; thus cutting up the ground into narrow and ugly strips, with very long acute corners, and presenting, as a whole, the appearance of a network of railways . . .[98]

Many of these criticisms resemble those levelled at Joshua Major's parks twenty years earlier; in both cases, the designers were accused of needless proliferation of detail at the expense of unity of expression. Markham Nesfield, in his adjudicator's report, complained that the vistas cut up the view: 'Such an arrangement not only produces confusion, but instead of variety, by an excess of variety produces monotony.' Marnock, reviewing André's *Art des Jardins* later, condemned the indifference to 'breadth of effect' displayed in the multiplication of vistas, and repudiated 'the idea that there is anything English in this style of monotonous circles'; André, in reply, accused Marnock of being interested in creating views from the terrace only.[99]

The concern with unified effect remained a dominant concern of English landscape gardeners, although in the years after Sefton Park something of its abstract geometry filtered into the plans of John Shaw at least, in his Churchtown Botanic Gardens, Southport, and Stamford Park, Altrincham.[100] Joseph Newton found a similar emphasis on multiple views in German sources, particularly Rudolph Siebeck, a volume of whose plans he adapted for the English audience; he adopted this principle in his garden

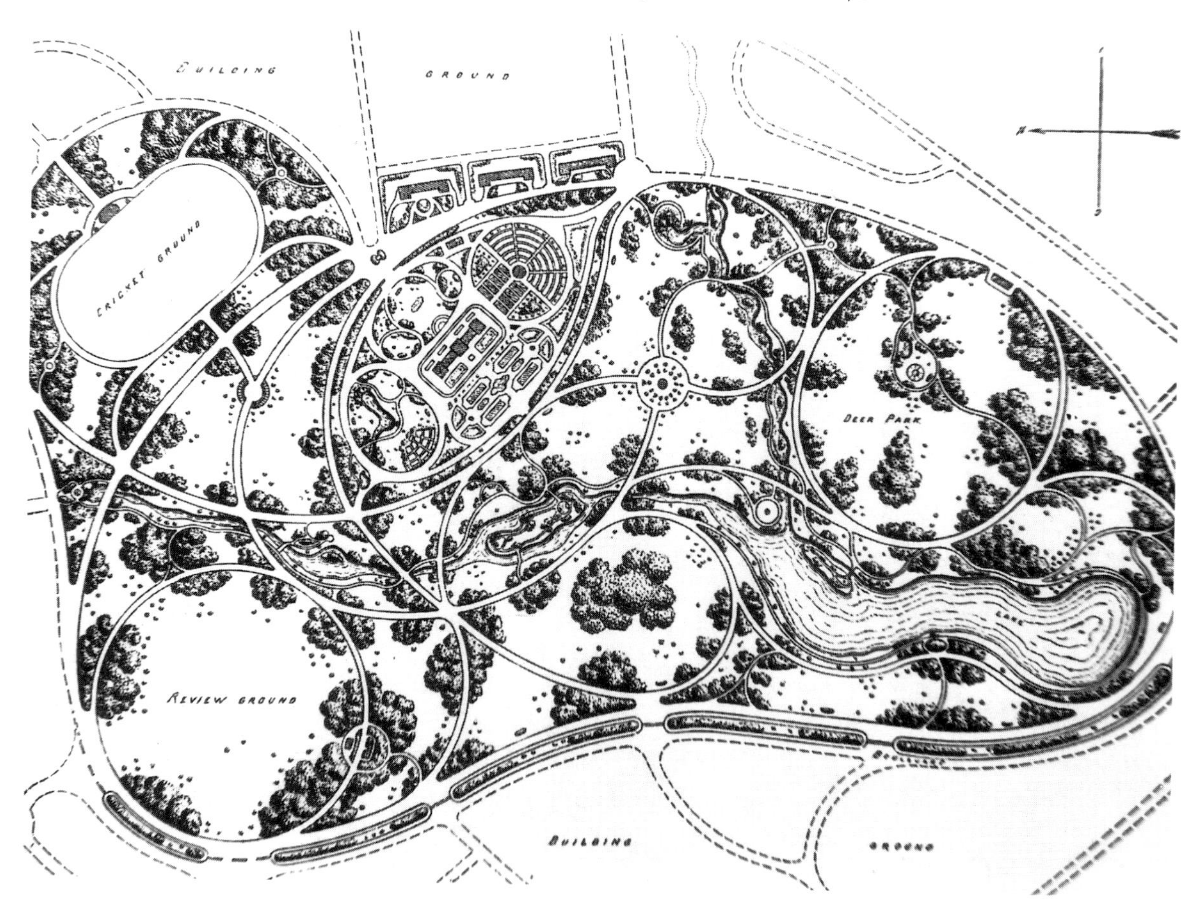

68 Sefton Park, plan. An abstract geometry of circles and ellipses: Edouard André's application of French landscape principles to an English site, 1867.

at Hatton, near Hounslow, where he 'so contrived the outline of the water ... that in passing round it a series of panoramic views occurred at short distances apart, each being so varied as to be distinct in character.'[101]

André's possible influence was checked, however, by a native innovation. By the 1870s, William Barron was well advanced into his second career as a professional landscape gardener, and in a pair of municipal parks he made his mark as the innovator of a new style. In Locke Park, Barnsley (1875–77), the focal point of the park was an ornamental fountain, reached by a serpentine path through a dell, which provided a strong visual axis for part of the park; a few years later, in Abbey Park, Leicester (1878–80), the entire park was laid out axially, with parallel paths advancing toward a chain of lakes at one end.[102] By the time Abbey Park was finished, the Birmingham gardener R. H. Vertegans had taken axiality a stage further, by making an emphatic central walk bisect the park.[103] Barron died in 1891, but his firm went on to a prolific career of park and garden designs stretching well into the twentieth century.

The Paxtonian tradition, of the penetration of the landscape by the garden, was carried on after his death by two of his protégés, Edward Kemp and Edward Milner. Kemp's major works of the 1860s were Hesketh Park, Southport and Stanley Park, Liverpool, in both of which rocky outcrops and plantations were used to create enclosures, while

69 Locke Park, Barnsley, view in the dell. The serpentine path illustrates the axial tendency that William Barron brought to his parks in the 1870s.

Stanley Park employed an architectural terrace in the manner of Paxton's late parks.[104] So did Milner's Lincoln Arboretum of 1872; but Milner was to prove more innovative, beginning with his Preston parks (1862–67). Here, a railway viaduct formed the boundary line of the adjacent Miller and Avenham Parks, connected by an archway under the viaduct, and the base of the structure was turned into a series of rocky outcrops to make the transition into the undulating parkland. This relationship between the obviously artificial and the supposedly natural was maintained in Milner's in a number of ways, ranging from the steep formal terracing of a garden like Bodnant to the Paxtonian gesture of extending a long serpentine walk across the middle of an otherwise 'naturalistic' tumbling lawn at Rangemore Hall, Staffordshire.[105]

Milner left no body of writing, but in 1890, six years after his death, his son Henry Ernest Milner published *The Theory and Practice of Landscape Gardening*, and this may be taken as an indication of his views. Henry Ernest's own works were on a less heroic scale than his father's, and the rhetoric of the book often matched Edward Milner's works better than his own. The informing vision was a modified version of the heroic gardener of Paxton's day; the landscape gardener was conceived of as a counterpart to creative nature, transforming the landscape through an understanding of the underlying principles of geological change.

Water was seen as the main agent of geological action: 'It has scooped out valleys and modified the hills ... With the subsidence of the water, wide grassy valleys have been formed; wherein are seen long vistas of lawn running up till they are lost in the obscurity of the forest.' The practical consequences for the landscape gardener were spelled out in a long series of partially disconnected aphorisms.

> A valley appears deeper by not being planted, as a hill appears higher than it really is by being planted to its summit. Single trees emphasize falling ground, and they, like the shadowy regions of a wood, conduce to a sensation of mystery, subtly stimulating imagination. They induce an idea of possible shelter that bestows pleasurable sensations ... The idea of spaciousness can be artificially promoted, particularly by the breaking of continuous lines and hard boundary lines, and by providing various objects for the eye to count, just outside the direct line of sight ...
>
> The created character of a water-feature must be consonant with the surrounding land; for fitness to surrounding conditions is a measure of beauty to both. A lake expresses spaciousness; but much of its charm is due to its outline. A river expresses action.[106]

Edward Milner's gardens made provision for the formal effects standard at the time, on the principle that everything about the terrace should show the hand of man;[107] it was beyond the terrace that the geological imagination found its fruition, in the creation of landscapes that suggested a history of geological development. Howard Park, Glossop, for example, was laid out on a steep declivity, and found its focal point in a stream that pursued a largely direct course down the slope, diving underground at intervals. In the gardens of the Buxton Pavilion, on the other hand – where Milner designed a domed pavilion and a Dutch garden, as well as a rose mount reminiscent of the Crystal Palace – the landscape occupied a largely flat site with rocky outcrops, and the main feature was a lake with a stream snaking from it, as though about to erode into an oxbow lake.[108] Even at Iwerne Minster, Dorset, where a flat site dictated one of the most completely formal gardens that Milner created, a geological history for the site was implied by terracing and graduating the ground to make it impossible 'to detect that the house has not been built on a knoll'.[109]

During his last years, Milner directed the Crystal Palace School of Gardening; when he died in 1884 he was Marnock's principal rival as the country's most eminent landscape gardener.[110] But while the approaches of the two men could be exaggerated into opposing principles – on the one hand the artist as heroic counterpart of creative nature, on the other the self-effacing observer of the 'genius of the place' – they nonetheless shared many common elements. Both approved of lawns as essential features, and adopted the standard picturesque principles of tree massing and plantations with bold recesses. Both criticized the French approach of denying a formal treatment to the immediate environs of the house.[111] In practice their results are not always immediately distinguishable. At Impney Hall, for example, Marnock's great lake and cascading stream dominated the grounds, but his formal terrace between house and lake (especially after William Goldring added a second terrace) is as architectural a creation as one might expect from the creator of Bodnant or the Lincoln Arboretum. Conversely, Milner's lawns and lake at Rangemore Hall,

70 Rangemore Hall, the serpentine walk cutting across Edward Milner's landscape garden of the 1870s.

now that the serpentine walk has been removed, could pass for an example of Marnock's work.

But a further model for landscape gardening was emerging in the work of Alexander McKenzie. By 1863, he was laying out the grounds of Alexandra Palace, his stated aim one of non-interference with the natural landscape. Alexandra Park, as it appeared on its opening, was in diametrical contrast to the Crystal Palace Park south of the river. Terracing was confined to the creation of a level platform for the Palace, from which the ground fell away informally; the approach road cut diagonally across the main vista from the entrance, in a position where Paxton or Milner would have created some axial feature. Patches of informal bedding marked the conjunctions of some of the paths, but the major visual element was the irregularly grouped deciduous tree cover; McKenzie opposed the introduction of flowerbeds into parks.[112]

The ideal of nature expressed in Alexandra Park found expression elsewhere by the end of the 1870s. At Bear Wood, where Robert Kerr erected a French-style chateau for John Walter, proprietor of *The Times*, James Tegg created a landscape which was praised for its avoidance of straight lines; the planting choice for the shrubberies – rhododendrons, Ghent azaleas, *Berberis*, *Philadelphus*, *Escallonia*, roses – could have come from McKenzie's articles; even its wellingtonia avenue was not inconsistent with McKenzie's ideas.[113] McKenzie himself continued his career as a landscape gardener while acting as superintendent of the Palace, eventually becoming the superintendent of Epping Forest, where he had a more 'natural' landscape to look after.[114]

71 Battersea Park, the rock garden. Rocky outcrops in artificial stone, constructed by James Pulham and Son, 1866–70.

Landscape in Rock

By the 1860s, rockwork was playing an increasing role in the organization of gardens. Biddulph Grange had shown the use of rockworks as a structural framework, and this principle was exemplified in some of the gardens laid out under its influence. Highbury, Birmingham, the garden of Joseph Chamberlain (begun by Edward Milner) incorporated 'a series of gardens on different levels, many of them backed by neat shrubberies or rockworks, and approached by winding walks'.[115] More spectacularly, by 1870, E. W. Cooke's garden at Glen Andred was replete with rocky dells and combes, passageways, and mounts, and was being planted with aid from Harry Veitch and William Robinson. By 1872 Cooke was even speculating about having the rocks lit up at night.[116]

The most important qualities to be sought when rockwork assumed such a key role in the garden were massiveness and boldness. Among the most prestigious natural rock gardens of the 1860s were Sydnope Hall, where a rockery composed of massive blocks of stone formed a passageway between the house and the terraced parterres, and Osmaston Hall, where rocks were arranged to form a naturalistic bluff.[117] Neither of these, however, could compete for sheer scale with Stancliffe Hall, whose gardens were laid out by Edward Milner in 1871; here a cliff was excavated from the hillside to form a massive arrangement of boulders and outcrops where 'the difficulty is not to create a rugged outline, but to find a foothold for plant-life of any description'.[118]

These were also the years of James Pulham's most celebrated rockeries. His firm's reputation for accuracy in replicating geological effects reached its highest point when the naturalist Roderick Murchison mistook his artificial stone at Lockinge, Berkshire, for the natural sandstone of the area. At Sandringham, under Broderick Thomas's direction, he created an extensive series of rocky outcrops around the new lake, with squat blocks of orange carstone forming a support for large horizontal slabs of Pulhamite stone; the boathouse also was roofed in Pulhamite. At Madresfield Court, he designed a rock garden on three separate levels, even signing one of the rocks. But most in the public eye was the rockwork at Battersea Park, constructed partly as a screen to conceal the view of Clapham Junction; the boulders were arranged by the lakeside to 'appear as if there had been a "fault" near the lake, and the tip of the strata is seen to be inland. This rockwork is to have basins and ledges for the growth of alpine and other suitable plants, and there are to be some small waterfalls'.[119] By the 1870s Pulham's style was so well established that the gardening magazines began to offer advice on how amateurs could construct cement rockeries.[120]

The planting of such rock gardens was generally required to be as bold as the rocks themselves; at Stancliffe the boulders were carpeted with ivies, cotoneasters, and *Pernettya*, while brooms, gorse, rhododendrons, hollies, pyramidal conifers, and a small range of alpines were planted in the interstices. This taste for coniferous and shrubby planting as appropriate in scale for major rockworks continued long after the fashion for alpine flowers had set in; Edward Luckhurst recommended hollies, yuccas, silver birch and mountain ash for planting on stratified rockworks in the 1890s,

and well into the twentieth century pines, junipers, thorns and gorse were suggested by George Dillistone.[121]

During the 1860s, however, interest was growing in the cultivation of alpine flowers. At Belvoir Castle, William Ingram created a stratified rock garden suggesting the appearance of an old quarry bank, and here the stones were covered with saxifrages and *Sedum*, *Aubrieta*, *Myosotis*, and *Epimedium*.[122] The most influential of early alpine gardens was that erected by James Backhouse in his nursery at York in the late 1850s. This rock garden, however, was not realistically stratified, but contained 'several distinct chasms or valleys, above which rise great angular pinnacles, grouped in a natural and effective manner; while, in the deepest parts, small sheets of water occur, in which some of the boldest portions of the work are reflected with charming effect'. Backhouse's firm became the leading authority on the cultivation of alpines, a wide range of which were featured in their catalogues from 1857; Backhouse himself contributed notes on their culture to William Robinson's *Alpine Flowers for Gardens* in 1871, the first detailed book on the subject, and one which was

72 Stancliffe Hall, the rock garden. Edward Milner excavated this massive cliffside rock garden in the 1870s, and complemented it with bold coniferous planting.

recommended by Pulham for advice on planting.[123]

Backhouse's rockery was singled out by C. P. Peach as a demonstration that realistic geological stratification was unnecessary to the rock garden: 'there is no attempt to put every stone on its right bed, or to make believe that it is a natural stratified rock pushed through contrary to Nature.' Peach criticized Ingram for wasting his time at Belvoir, arranging the rocks in their natural beds, on the grounds that in nature alpine flowers would be found most readily not on rock faces but on moraines: 'in the natural dells formed by the disintegration of rock, and which is the nearest approach in Nature to such a garden as that at Belvoir, the stones would not be found in their natural beds'. He therefore opened an argument against the existing tradition of rock gardening, including Pulham's works: 'Rockwork does not want to be an attempt to deceive, but a picturesque place to grow Ferns and Alpines.'

Pulham replied with a defence of the structural, rather than the horticultural, use of rockwork, pointing out that if 'it is a mistake to try and imitate cliffs and stratification, then all our leading landscapists are wrong, as Mr. Broderick Thomas, Mr. E. Milner, Mr. Marnock, Mr. Kemp, and Mr. Gibson'. He quoted Wordsworth and Scott on the inspiring effect of rocky features, and concluded:

> No such effects can be produced by simply scattering stones and *débris* in the way 'C.C.P.' desires. There must be the origin apparent, cliff or mother rock . . . It is all very well, pleasing and interesting, to grow the pretty little Alpines or Ferns, and it is in the screens or *débris* at the base of the cliff they will do well and will be seen best; but for the rugged and bold picturesque effect or grandeur we must have the noble cliff, if only as high as our heads . . .[124]

The 1870s, then, saw attitudes toward the rock garden diverge: on the one hand, those who regarded it as a setting for alpine flowers, its construction to be subordinated to their requirements; on the other, those who regarded it as a picturesque feature whose planting was to be dictated by its construction. The story of the rock garden in the last years of the century was to be the gradual triumph of horticultural over compositional needs.

Landscape with Ruins

Despite the condemnation of artificial ruins since the days of Loudon, in the gardens of the middle classes they refused to go away; Shirley Hibberd was still advocating small-scale ruins as a model for rockwork in the 1860s and 1870s.[125] In the 1870s even some of Pulham and Son's commissions, particularly the fairy cave at the Brighton Aquarium, subordinated geological realism to fanciful decoration. At the same time, their commissions began to include more buildings within the rock garden ambience, like the Sandringham boathouse, the Denmark Hill caves for Henry Bessemer, or the artificial ruins in Sir Henry Tate's garden in Streatham.[126]

In 1875, the botanical artist Worthington G. Smith suggested that as prehistoric cromlechs were continually disappearing, they 'could easily be moulded and reproduced in concrete . . . and set up in our better rock-gardens and parks before all traces of the originals are utterly lost'. S. P. Oliver of the Royal Artillery immediately proposed the erection of a model stone circle at Alexandra Palace; the head gardener Adam Hogg set up two Druidical stones at the Buxton Pavilion Gardens; and a stone circle was erected in Cathays Park, Cardiff, at the turn of the century.[127] Once again, after half a century of abuse, sham ruins were returning to the garden as ornamental features. In 1882, a proposal was published for a garden house based on ruins at Chichen-Itza, bearing a roof covering of subtropical plants to give it the effect of a temple discovered in the Mexican rain forest.[128]

Accompanying the revival of sham ruins was an exploitation of genuine artefacts. As early as 1841, the remains of the York Minster screen had been incorporated into the rock garden at Escrick Park; by the 1870s the use of genuine ruins was on the increase. At The Plantation, Norwich, Henry Trevor salvaged a Gothic window removed from a local church for use in his garden, while erecting a large fountain in the shape of a Gothic ruin; his terrace walls held an assemblage of builders' fragments. The demolition of the Temple for the erection of the new Law Courts in the 1870s provided a golden opportunity for antiquarian gardeners: Joseph Newton used a portion of the ruins of the Old Temple Church as eyecatchers in a Hounslow garden, and the entire structure of Temple Bar was removed to Theobalds Park to stand as a folly.[129]

The use of ruins as a setting for the currently fashionable mode of flower gardening was on the increase as well by the 1870s. At places like Ashby-de-la-Zouch and Devizes Castle, carpet beds were introduced within the curtilage of the ruins. Thomas King, the gardener at Devizes, created a rampart walk bordered with Irish and golden yews, planted a wellingtonia and other conifers in the grounds, and covered a bank and various walls with ivy, in addition to planting the carpet bed within sight of the main windows.[130]

Such attitudes made for a confused approach when dealing with ruins that came into public ownership, as is shown by the case of Kirkstall Abbey, which after a spirited campaign found its way into the hands of Leeds Council by 1893. Joseph Cheal, the Kentish nurseryman and landscape gardener, was commissioned to lay out the grounds for public use. An irregular triangle of land adjacent to a river was turned into a park with games areas and a bandstand, with an avenue leading from the bandstand to the centre of the ruins.

> The Cloister Court is treated in a formal style in unison with its environment, and it is therefore laid out with straight paths and flower beds of formal design, with a few conifers, &c., interspersed. The fountain in the centre is in keeping with the surroundings, especially as the basin is to be constructed with rough rockwork corresponding with the building.[131]

This approach, a hybrid between national monument and pleasure garden, could not be long sustained, and a counter-ideology grew up in the later years of the century which emphasized associations of age and antiquity. Noel Humphreys attacked the landscaping of the grounds of Rochester Castle for its 'desecrative impiety' in dividing up the grounds with curving paths and shrubberies. For Humphreys, this approach made the ground seem like a private garden, and destroyed 'every association connected with the history of the place'; the whole central space ought to have been left open except for a few choice trees.[132]

But while Cheal's ornamental features may have conflicted with the historic associations of Kirkstall Abbey, his approach at least respected the materials of the building. Humphreys's approach, on the other hand, in order to promote associations of antiquity, meant that the visual impression of a ruin had to be augmented; he therefore recommended that plants be sprinkled in the crevices of the Castle, with ivy and herbaceous perennials along the base of the walls. William Robinson included a section on 'ruin and wall gardens' in his *Alpine Flowers for Gardens* (1870). In 1890, a contributor to *The Garden* put the case forcibly against Loudon's views on the removal of vegetation from historic architecture, offering as an alternative the wild scenes shown on early nineteenth-century prints of famous ruins, before they were cleaned up. Fountains Abbey, for example, was now inappropriately 'neat, trim, and bare'. He therefore called for a landscape gardener for 'our picturesque old ruins', one who would add touches 'quite easy and naturally suggesting themselves to the landscape gardener, but never to the beautifiers of ruins' – things like roses, ivy, and bramble, which could grow over the stonework and ornament it. The subordination of history to horticulture was here carried to its furthest extreme; it was in this context that Mrs Earle attacked the use of creepers on historic buildings.[133]

Colour in the Landscape

An interest in the colour planning of the wider landscape had grown slowly since the early years of the century. On most estates it was long confined to autumn colour; the enthusiasts of the pure picturesque avoided spring and summer colour as beautiful, and thus inconsistent with a picturesque landscape. C. H. J. Smith, for example, while appreciative of furze and broom, 'designedly omitted the abnormal tints', by which he meant purples and variegation, from the landscape; his colour planning was limited to the contrast of darker and lighter shades. Joshua Major abandoned his early attempts at colour grouping. Edward Kemp, however, had suggested greater possibilities, and George Fleming's experiments at Trentham in the 1850s finally put into practice the idea of extending colour planning into the landscape.[134]

The basic preconceptions of the picturesque had still to be fought, however. Sefton Park provides a revealing example of this process. Edouard André proposed the planting of dark-leaved oaks, beeches, elms and limes along the margin of the park: 'Loose-growing and light-coloured trees reserved for centre of Park, and near the water whiter-leaved trees are to be placed. Thus along the drives will be noticed a succession of colours decreasing towards the centre of the Park.' This planting scheme was entirely in line with the advice of picturesque theorists about the blue distance, but Markham Nesfield rejected this basic premise:

> Dark colours, as reflecting less light, naturally retire of themselves, while light colours come forward ... When near at hand, light or cut-leaved foliage is

73 Bulstrode Park, tower and flower garden. The fashion for clothing buildings in vegetation returned in the 1870s.

> seen to greater advantage against dark foliage, as regards relief of outline and colour; but for the purposes of perspective the distinction is inappreciable as applied to park-planting, as perspective is entirely dependent upon the state of the atmosphere, and is continually varying according to the weather or the hour of the day. This produces what the artist calls effects, but it is quite out of the range of landscape gardening.

André replied indignantly that Nesfield was ignorant of the basic laws of landscape gardening, which he regarded as identical with the laws of landscape painting:

> tasteful artists, either in pictures for the selection of their scenery or in landscape gardening ... prefer for their background tenderly-coloured leaves, which at a distance naturally blend with the uncertain tints of the horizon.

This dependence on landscape painting as a model, however, was precisely what English gardening had been trying to throw off for the past generation. Nesfield, in effect, was repudiating the picturesque conventions that had hitherto governed landscape gardening, and applying to the planning of the landscape the same colour principles that his generation applied to the flower garden.[135]

Most early colour grouping depended on flowering shrubs, especially rhododendrons and azaleas, which formed the characteristic vegetation of gardens from Bedgebury to Inverewe.[136] In the wake of Fleming, however, William Paul, the celebrated Waltham Cross nurseryman, attempted to take the matter a step further. In a series of articles in the *Gardeners' Chronicle* in 1864, he urged gardeners to cast their eyes beyond ephemeral flower colour, to the use of colours other than green as permanent features. Several different categories of trees, from those of pyramidal or weeping form to those with purple, golden or silver leaves to those with coloured bark for winter effect, he assembled under the label of 'pictorial trees'.[137]

The excitement generated by Paul's ideas can be measured by the sudden eruption of proposals for landscape colour over the next decade. James Bateman lectured to the Royal Horticultural Society on coloured-leaved trees in 1865; Joseph Newton was urging the grouping of trees by families by 1870; George Abbey was campaigning for the purple beech and the introduction of colour grouping in woods; Joseph Forsyth Johnson was planning the distribution of gold-tinted foliage to impart a glow to woodlands; Charles Lee was to propose richly-coloured avenues arranged in multiple rows.[138] By 1870, when he repeated his injunctions in a public lecture, Paul found ready support from such listeners as William Barron and D. T. Fish; the latter commented at the end of the talk that the 'ruin of our landscapes had been the mixed system of planting, sufficient attention not having been paid to distinctness of colour', and recommended a diminution of green.[139]

Fish went on to launch a campaign against existing shrubberies, which had been planted either in monochrome blocks or in a mixing style analogous to that of the mixed border. 'The best thing that could happen to many of them would be their improvement off the face of the landscape.' Many people, he reported, were already trying 'to cut through the dead sea of monotony with the knife', and weed out their shrubberies to make room for specimens; George Paul performed such an operation at Rougham Hall in the 1880s, clearing new vistas and glades in the coniferous landscape. This treatment, however, could never equal intelligent massing for colour effect. Fish, as a devout Ruskinian, would have appreciated his hero's planting on his estate at Brantwood, Coniston, where in the 1870s he planted a rhododendron bank and interspersed other flowering shrubs among the woods.[140]

From the 1870s, then, we can trace a number of themes in landscape colour gradually developing toward the turn of the century. The overwhelming trend was a rejection of conifers as the basis of park planting, and a revival of interest in deciduous trees, more especially flowering shrubs.[141] The leading horticulturists continued to share the enthusiasm for autumn colour, and there was an enormous expansion of interest in purple trees, especially with the new introductions of Japanese maples and *Prunus* × *pissardi*; the purple-leaved hedge was to become a feature of Edwardian gardens such as Hidcote.[142]

Variegated foliage equally became an obsession with late Victorian plantsmen. Barnes of Bicton was an authority on its planting, and Sir Frederick Pollock built up a collection of variegated plants, which he told D. T. Fish were more perfect than green ones: 'another step towards higher evolution and more perfect development of plant life'. At Ascott, a Rothschild garden in Buckinghamshire, golden privets and variegated plants made up the featured planting:

> Variegated maple, copper beech, silver variegated privet, are effectively planted, copper beech and maple in particular ... it is essential to so group or associate the various kinds that no spotty, mosaic-like effect results from the mixtures.[143]

To see how attitudes had changed in regard to woodland planting, we need only compare Cockerell's 1854 plan for turning Hampstead Heath into a park with William Paul's 1880 proposals for Epping Forest, which had recently been saved for public use by the City of London. Paul stressed that it would be inappropriate to turn the forest into a landscape garden or an arboretum; he envisaged 'single trees, groups of trees, groves, avenues, thickets, interspersed and relieved with open glades and wide stretches of pasture', using exotics while preserving the character of an English forest.

> The colours of the trees now existing in the Forest are, for the most part, a uniform green; and, however correct it may be to use such as the groundwork of our operations, it is desirable to secure every shade of colour, from grass green and silvery grey to inky black ...

Accordingly, he suggested introducing scarlet oaks, Norway maples, Douglas firs, cypresses, cedars, birches, limes, and wellingtonias; *Rhododendron ponticum* should abound. J. T. Boscawen, who was busy introducing Australian trees into his Cornish garden, responded favourably to Paul's proposals, but argued that all conifers should be excluded.[144]

'Strong colours are like the voice of Nature speaking to mankind in tones that all can hear', wrote J. F. Johnson in the 1870s, and the enrichment of the English landscape by strong colour seemed then to be the irresistible current of the future.[145] Even before the end of the century, however, the colour planning of the landscape began to meet the same criticisms that the colour planning of the flower garden had. Mrs Loftie thought that 'the plants natural to a country' were adapted to harmonize with that country's general tone of vegetation and skies, so that in Britain, where 'the grass is bright and the sky often grey', flower colours were properly subdued; similar views were urged by Grant Allen. A debate on the different roles of colour in tropical and temperate landscape took place in the pages of the *Garden* in 1881. William Robinson was to recommend the use of northern hemisphere exotics, which were hardy and had subdued colours appropriate to the English landscape.[146]

Probably the most influential critic of arboricultural colour was Alexander Dean, who at the turn of the century launched an attack on positive colour in trees, in favour of green, 'by far the most neutral, restful, and pleasing hue, and, so far as I can judge, the most pleasing hue for extent'. It was primarily variegation that he wished to proscribe:

> A garden largely planted with variegated trees, Golden and Silver Hollies especially, all cone-shaped, variegated Conifers, Aucubas, Euonymuses, and various other distorted-leaf trees and shrubs, is a horror from which anyone with taste soon escapes. Let us have flowering trees and shrubs in abundance, plenty of natural and graceful growth, but keep the pepper-box variegated things to delight the denizens of Brixton and Clapham.[147]

(This was probably a reference to Brockwell Park and its collection of *Acer negundo*.)

Dean had powerful opponents, most notably D. T. Fish, but he was not alone, and the planting of purple beeches nearly ground to a halt in the 1890s.[148] Twentieth-century interest was to turn back to 'Capability' Brown and the landscape park, and the cult of green gained an ascendancy over the cult of colour.

7

The re-creation of nature

During the 1860s 'nature' and 'the picturesque' were emerging once again as positive values, in large part through the fashion for the subtropical garden. During the 1860s and 1870s the new aesthetic of foliage invaded flower arrangement, interior decoration, window gardening, and flower-show planning.[1] Of greatest significance for the future was the work of the nurseryman and decorator John Wills, whose displays in the Royal Horticultural Society's ballroom in the 1870s took the form of depictions of exotic scenery, ranging from the tropics to the arctic.[2]

For a generation, it had been an aesthetic commonplace that one should not imitate the effects of nature; but now the boundaries of art and nature were shifting. The experiments of Wills in replicating foreign landscapes were soon paralleled in the garden proper, and imitative scenery was to become a major theme in British gardening during the last third of the century.

The Landscape in the Conservatory

The subtropical movement had a great impact on the arrangement of conservatories. The balance of opinion was already shifting decisively in favour of planting in beds rather than pots for greenhouse plants; in 1860 the larger palms in the Palm House at Kew were removed from their tubs and recessed in the floor.[3] The shade-tolerance of many subtropical plants made them useful for underplanting the larger trees. In the late 1860s, as a result, the character of conservatory planting began to change from collections of specimens to scenic displays of foliage plants.

The provision of rockworks in glasshouses, for the cultivation of ferns, became common in the 1860s. James Pulham entered the field with a fernery at Poles Park in 1865–66; his major commission in this manner was the furnishing of the Brighton Aquarium in 1872, with a fernery, waterfalls, and fairy cave. (A surviving specimen can be seen at Old Warden House, where in 1876 he gave a stalactite ceiling to two corridors of a cruciform glasshouse.)[4] By the 1870s Pulham was facing competition from Dick Radclyffe, a South Kensington decorator, and Harpham of Edgware Road. Radclyffe, less concerned with geological accuracy than Pulham, took ruins as his model, and composed his scenes of stone stairways, arches, and tumbled heaps of masonry.[5] An important amateur effort was Henry Harland's magic grotto, which exploited the effect of different colours of glass in the roofing of various compartments of a conservatory divided by rockworks.[6]

The call for 'natural' landscape in the conservatory, like the subtropical movement in general, had a French source. Edouard André's views, broadcast in the first volume of Robinson's journal *The Garden*, were a development from Dillwyn Llewellyn's experiment at Penllergare a quarter of a century before; his main aim was to suppress from view as many reminders as possible of the artificial character of the building, by encouraging climbers to hide the supporting columns, undulating the walks around the periphery of the house, and filling the centre with a studied irregularity of terrain, asymmetrical tree grouping, and a lawn of ground covers and carpet-bedding plants to conceal the soil.

André's ideas were promoted enthusiastically by Robinson – 'it is not a mere question of taste between conservatories arranged in the ordinary way and in the natural manner; one is right and the other wrong' – but did not meet with uncritical acceptance. Thomas Baines criticized the scheme for its reliance on permanent planting, thus abandoning the attempt to provide year-round colour by moving things seasonally.[7] Through the advocacy of F. W. Burbidge and others, the tropical landscape at Penllergare was gradually adapted to the needs of the temperate house,[8] but it was usually contained within the limits of some degree of framing artifice. Where the entire conservatory was laid out as one picturesque scene, either the emphatic architectural character of the glazed structure or the bold patterning of the walkways remained to set off the vegetation.

The greatest example of the French influence was at Oakworth House, Keighley, where the rockery was constructed in natural stone and concrete by the Parisian designer Aucaunte, and boasted mosaic floors laid by Italian craftsmen. At one end, a natural rock face was hewn into a series of grottoes and cascades; this effect was then continued along the side wall by a mixture of natural stone and concrete extending to the roof. Here the French influence made itself felt, for Oakworth marked the introduction into England of concrete rusticwork, already familiar in the Parisian parks. Outside in the grounds, benches and a summerhouse were fashioned in concrete, cast to resemble logs of unbarked wood. Within the winter garden, the most arresting feature of this sort was a dead elm in concrete, its branches apparently lopped; the elm itself was hollow and contained a staircase, from the top of which the visitor followed a tortuous path over stones and gullies to the head of the cascade. André had held that 'to imitate the forests of Brazil by compelling the spectator to scramble over the rotten remains of trunks of fallen trees, rough stones, and withered fern fronds, would be the height of absurdity', but that was the sort of experience offered at Oakworth.[9]

The restraining presence of conspicuous artifice was reduced even further in the fernery at Ascog Hall on the Island of Bute, where natural rock, collected from the seashore, was banked up to allow a waterfall to flow through the house.[10]

The last development of the conservatory landscape was the attempt, toward the turn of the century, to link glasshouse and open-air rockeries in one coherent unit. Ellen Willmott's garden at Warley Place had a fern house set in a declivity amongst the rocks; but far more elaborate was the

rock garden at Merrow Grange, Guildford, a Pulham construction of the 1890s. A walk wound through a series of artificial rockworks of increasing elaboration to a grotto with a glazed roof, forming a large cavity crossed by a bridge. Here obvious artifice, the deceptively natural, and the genuinely natural met: the landing of the bridge had a mosaic floor; artificial stalactites concealed heating pipes; the outer walls were of Pulhamite stone, but the sunken chamber was lined with tufa in which ferns could root.[11]

74 Ascog Hall: view in the conservatory. The glasshouse as a replica of a tropical jungle, from an engraving of 1879.

The Alpine Rock Garden

The debate over the imitation of natural features had been a perennial theme in the history of rockwork. In the wake of the Backhouse rock garden, the idea was spreading that the cultivation of alpines was more important than the structure of the rocks: 'Rockwork does not want to

75 Oakworth, view of the rockworks formerly part of the conservatory display. This dead elm in concrete concealed the staircase to the upper level.

be an attempt to deceive, but a picturesque place to grow Ferns and Alpines.'[12] Planting choice was changing from the conifers and evergreen carpeting plants of the 1850s and 1860s to a new emphasis on flowering plants. So complete was the reversal that a later generation tried to explain High Victorian plant choice as the unintended consequence of a failure to grow alpines properly:

> Times have wholly changed the rock-garden. Fifty years ago it was merely the appanage of the large pleasure ground. In some odd corner, or in some dank, tree-haunted hollow, you rigged up a dump of broken cement blocks, and added bits of stone and fragments of statuary. You called this 'the Rockery,' and proudly led your friends to see it, and planted it all over with Periwinkle

> to hide the hollows in which your Alpines had promptly died. In other words, you considered only the stones, and not the plants that were to live among them.[13]

Thus Reginald Farrer, with his usual disregard for historical niceties; but it was a prevailing attitude during the early twentieth century.

By the 1870s, Messrs Backhouse of York were specializing in the design of rock gardens in natural stone, their chief rival being Robert Veitch and Son of Exeter, whose rockwork expert, F. W. Meyer, wrote a standard work on the subject in the Edwardian period.[14] Pulham and Son continued to construct their Pulhamite rock gardens well into the 1890s, but this method became increasingly controversial. Robinson condemned the use of artificial rockwork, even though Pulham recommended his *Alpine Flowers* as a guide to planting and Robinson's *English Flower Garden* included advice on alpine cultivation by Latimer Clark, the owner of a Pulhamite rockery. By the turn of the century, a reaction was apparent. James Pulham died in 1898, and under the direction of his son, James R. Pulham, the firm gradually abandoned the use of artificial stone, and the name 'Pulhamite' came to be a label for their terracotta instead.[15]

Under the impact of the cultivation of alpines, the tradition of the rock garden splintered into a variety of approaches. At one extreme, the rocks were discounted except as an aid to cultivation. 'In the Alps,' wrote Robinson, 'we find alpine flowers by thousands growing on the level ground', and he recommended growing alpines on open banks, with but a small amount of largely buried rockwork. This mode of cultivation was to be associated with E. A. Bowles, whose rock garden at Myddelton House was criticized by Frank Crisp for reducing the visible rocks to a nullity.[16]

Peach had commended the Backhouse rockery for its indifference to geological arrangement, for the way in which stones were 'improperly' bedded, and many rockeries of the next generation followed this example. Even Pulham and Son, so strongly associated with the principle of stratification, created such rock gardens as Gatton Park, Surrey, where rocks emerged from a bank in unrelated ways, even standing on end. Farrer was to characterize such construction as the 'almond-pudding' and 'plum-bun' systems. Peach had recommended moraine cultivation as a variant of his styleless approach, but during the Edwardian period Farrer was to change the image of the moraine by insisting on its artistic status: 'it is not "natural": this is the word, the fatal word, that has deluded so many into thinking that ... you just drop the stones all over the place, and it comes right'.[17]

Moraine construction was still being opposed well into the present century by the supporters of imitation strata: 'let the stones of which it is to be composed', said Walter Godfrey, 'resemble in some degree the natural stratification of the quarry, for Nature seldom tosses her material in a confused heap, save in her angry and volcanic moods.' Godfrey, indeed, wanted to see geometrically designed rockeries, but S. Arnott made a more fruitful suggestion when he proposed creating rockeries in the form of terraces. The most celebrated example of this style was the Royal Horticultural Society's rock garden at Wisley, built in 1911 by Pulham and Son. Using natural stone, it descended a large embankment in a series of shelves.[18] In 1882 a new rock garden was constructed at Kew in imitation of a Pyrenean stream-bed, giving prominence to the idea of the rock garden as an excavation instead of a raised contruction. About the same time Backhouse and Son were carving out a gorge for Ellen Willmott's rock garden at Warley Place, and gardeners began to excavate their rock gardens where once they had built them.[19]

In the wake of the Kew rock garden, the imitation of exotic scenery, largely dormant since the 1840s, was revived. During the succeeding quarter-century, the major works in this style were the Khyber Pass in East Park, Hull, built by E. A. Peak in artificial stone; the thirty-foot scale model of the Matterhorn at Friar Park, Henley-on-Thames; Mount Fuji in the Japanese garden at Fanhams Hall, Ware; and, shortly before the First World War, the Mappin Terraces in the Regent's Park Zoo, modelled in concrete after the Atlas Mountains of Morocco, as a home for mountain-dwelling animals. This same passion for geological imitation found a humbler but more prevalent issue in the sand trap, introduced by Reginald Beale to replace the more stylized bunkers of the early English golf courses, and modelled on the sandpits of the original Scottish links.[20]

Scale-model scenery did not meet with universal favour, of course, and Reginald Blomfield was only one of several who poured ridicule on it:

> To suppose that love of nature is shown by trying to produce the effects of wild nature on a small scale in a garden is clearly absurd; any one who loves natural scenery will want the real thing; he will hardly be content to sit in his rockery and suppose himself to be among the mountains.[21]

Nonetheless, associations of exactly this sort did determine aesthetic responses to the rock garden, and we find one writer defending the inclusion of a summer house in the rock garden on the grounds that there were rest houses in the Himalayas and chalets in the Alps.[22]

The greatest of all rock gardens was undoubtedly Friar Park. Successive portions were added by the period's main designers: Pulham created a waterfall and rocky banks to a lake; Backhouse made an alpine landscape for the main body of the rockworks; Harpham of Edgware Road designed a network of caves underneath; and the final touch, the Matterhorn, was the work of Crisp's own gardener Knowles. Crisp indulged his sense of humour by adding cast-iron chamois to the upper slopes to improve the Swiss effect. But its fame spread as much for its planting as for its extravagant structure; Crisp was an expert on alpines and eventually became a partner in Waterer's nursery, using the Matterhorn as a symbol for their alpine department. Some 2500 species were grown in broad masses amid the rocks. Robinson had recommended the planting of alpines 'in little colonies or carpets' to give effect to their bright colours, and he regarded Friar Park as the milestone in good planting: 'The Friar Park garden is by far the best natural stone rock garden I have ever seen. It shows the way for all good work in that direction. ... The lesson was much needed, as the dotty, spotty way of planting was so common.'[23]

Reginald Farrer, however, opposed this sort of colour grouping, and stood up for the dotting system Robinson condemned; 'better a hundred yards of Arabis than half a dozen vernal Gentians', was his summary of Robinson's approach. In a preface to E. A. Bowles's *My Garden in Spring*

76 Gatton Park, the rock garden. Rocks arranged without reference to stratification and natural bed: constructed by Pulham and Son for Jeremiah Colman at the turn of the century.

(1914), he aimed a barbed attack at an unnamed rock garden:

> But what a display is here! You could do no better with coloured gravels. Neat, unbroken blanks of first one colour and then another, until the effect indeed is sumptuous and worthy of the taste that has combined such a garden. But 'garden' why call it? There are no plants; there is nothing but colour, laid on as callously in slabs as if from the paint-box of a child. This is a mosaic, this is a gambol in purple and gold; but it is not a rock garden, though tin chamois peer never so frequent from its cliffs upon the passer by, bewildered with such a glare of expensive magnificence. This is, in fact, nothing but the carpet-bedding of our grandfathers, with the colour masses laid on in pseudo-irregular blots and drifts, instead of in straight stretches . . .[24]

Crisp, scenting a vein of insult, indulged in discreditable vituperation against the innocent Bowles, thus effectively tarnishing his own reputation for later generations. But the question at issue – the colour-planting of rock gardens – was not to be resolved by a personal quarrel. Colour

77 Friar Park, the 'Henley Matterhorn'. Sir Frank Crisp's scale-model construction, praised by William Robinson as 'the best natural stone rock garden I have ever seen'.

schemes and planting in drifts went on being recommended despite Farrer's rhetoric, and as Edwardian bedding came to insist on ever more rapid changes in the flower garden, a similar pace was envisaged for the rock garden:

> It is quite possible, with the material at disposal, to make a rock garden that changes its colour every three or four weeks, based on the idea that a garden may well reflect the dominant colour found in the pastures of the Alps, and produced by the plants each season.[25]

Spirits of Nature

Sir Charles Isham's rock garden at Lamport Hall, begun in 1848, had continued to develop throughout his lifetime, and was still changing in the 1890s. As the aesthetic of imitative scenery developed, its terms were invoked to interpret the structure, one visitor being reminded of 'the extinct volcanic regions of the Auvergne'.[26] But something new was being added. In 1881, an engraving was published showing a toy monkey swinging from one of the miniature trees, and by the 1890s the rockery was swarming with miniature china figures, mostly gnomes, of continental provenance. Strange as it may seem to the modern reader, some of them were grouped to represent striking miners (presumably in the wake of the miners' strike of 1894).

78 Hull Botanic Garden, the lake. On the island in J. C. Niven's short-lived garden can be seen giant *Heracleum* specimens, a tradition still followed in the Hull parks.

This is the first recorded appearance of gnomes in an English garden, and the motive for their addition was religious. Isham was an ardent spiritualist, and, like Conan Doyle, extended his occultism to include a belief in the existence of fairies as spirits of nature. Not all the figures were miniature, though. Seated upon a rock there was a life-size female figure in terracotta, 'invariably mistaken for an actual person', and probably representing the guardian spirit of the rockery; this was added after the death of Isham's wife, whom he had married the year he began the rockery.[27]

The second recorded appearance of gnomes was also in a rock garden, this time at Friar Park, where they peopled the underground cave. Crisp's gnomes were probably dictated by the same sense of humour that had visual puns about friars carved into the terracotta of his house; but in one of his guidebooks Crisp recorded incidents of a possibly supernatural significance in his life, and the gnomes of Friar Park may have had a layer of spiritualist meaning as well as those of Lamport.[28]

The fashion for gnomes began to spread rapidly in the Edwardian period. In 1908 *The Connoisseur* featured an advertisement by Ernest Wahliss, the source of Crisp's specimens, claiming (probably fraudulently) to offer gnomes based on rococo German models.[29] This suggests that their early popularity may have been associated with a form of eighteenth-century revivalism.

79 Lamport Hall, gnomes in the rock garden. Sir Charles Isham's rockwork, begun in 1848, was peopled by porcelain gnomes by the 1890s.

The Wild Garden

The principle of creating replica landscapes was to have repercussions in other departments besides the rock garden, and during the 1880s it was to transform the image of the wild garden.

When William Robinson published his book *The Wild Garden* in 1870, he coined a catchy new label, but the practices he described were long-established: woodland embellishment, the naturalizing of exotics in the landscape, on the one hand, and on the other an admixture from the subtropical garden, with its emphasis on foliage grouping. This mingling of the two traditions remained the basis of wild gardening throughout the 1870s and early '80s.

But while the practices were not new, something of the rhetoric accompanying them was. To a great extent, wild gardening derived its aesthetic effect from a series of exclusions: the elimination of formal beds, of recognizable pattern, the avoidance of those categories of plants most associated with the bedding system. His cherished effects, illustrated by Alfred Parsons in the later editions of *The Wild Garden*, consisted of choice groupings of individual plants - often achieved with great effort; William Taylor, who made Longleat into a paradigm for wild gardening from 1868, recalled: 'one where Snowflakes were growing in the grass amongst Rhododendrons, where I carefully cut away a twig at a time in such a stealthy manner that Nature herself scarcely found it out, formed a never-to-be-forgotten picture'.[30]

When wild gardening was practised on a large scale, however, individual combinations like these had to be supplemented by plants which could spread themselves in large masses. 'To do it rightly,' wrote Robinson, adapting an argument advanced by the defenders of bedding, 'we must group and mass as Nature does.'[31] The massing of naturalized bulbs proved the most popular method; in 1876 a press controversy arose over the propriety of plundering large quantities of daffodils from woodlands for transplanting into the garden.[32] Many wild garden favourites became the bane of later generations because of their spreading propensities; Robinson and his coevals boosted *Oxalis* and willow-herb (*Epilobium*), launched the Japanese knotweed (*Polygonum*) on its successful career, and went into raptures over the giant hogweed (*Heracleum mantegazzianum*). This last is particularly interesting as an enduring legacy of the subtropical garden. James Craig Niven exulted in the 'perfect ideas of exuberant health' the plant conveyed, and recommended it 'as admirably adapted for planting on an island in a lake, where the watery surroundings would arrest their roving population, and where their tall spectral stems might remain during the winter.' This was indeed his own practice at the Hull Botanic Garden, and the tradition of islands stocked with giant hogweed continues in the Hull parks to the present day.[33] The bog garden proved another way of maintaining the customs of the subtropical garden, with *Gunnera* achieving rapid popularity for bog and lakeside during the 1880s.[34]

All this was simply an extension of Robinson's principles on a larger scale. But during the 1880s, as the vogue grew for creating replicas of foreign scenery, new and different ways of naturalizing exotics were tried. None was more startling than the attempt to create a Mexican landscape of cacti, first made at Eythrope, Buckinghamshire, in the late 1880s; but by the Edwardian period the possibilities of hardy cacti were being tried more widely by gardeners like E. A. Bowles.[35]

More widespread was the rhododendron forest. The experience of reading Joseph Hooker's *Himalayan Journals*, with their accounts of the colourful rhododendron forests of Nepal, gave British gardeners an incentive to recreate such Himalayan scenery at home, by planting hillsides with masses of rhododendrons. At Cragside, Northumberland, by the 1890s, 'several hundred thousands have been planted ... forming impenetrable thickets, and blooming so profusely as to light up the whole hillside with their varied colours'.[36]

In reaction against this colonization of entire landscapes by Asiatic forests, a new concern developed for the indigenous British flora, and this too came to be referred to as 'wild gardening'. Robinson's wild garden had been a place for the naturalizing of exotic species, rather than for native plants, but as early as the 1870s, John Robson and others began to draw attention to the ornamental uses of natives. At the same time the Hull parks became noted for their wildflower collections, which eventually served as a model for other parks. Revivalist architects like J. D. Sedding and Reginald Blomfield were among the promoters of native plants, which they felt to be historically appropriate for old-fashioned gardens.[37]

And so the wild garden emerged into the twentieth century a fragmented concept, encompassing exotics and natives, rhododendron thickets and wild-flower meadows, but still regarded with suspicion by the older landscape gardeners like George Abbey, who defended the principle of the recognition of art, but conceded that wild gardens might be allowable to contrast with the urban environment.[38] It could even accommodate small-scale replicas as eccentric as the Lamport gnomes: Selfe-Leonard had garden seats 'modelled in the shape of giant and coloured fungi'. These, however, did not achieve the popularity that gnomes did, and he was forced to admit that 'they are uncomfortable on the one hand, and the suggestion is disagreeable on the other'.[39]

The Landscape of the Imaginative Ideal

Robert Marnock retired in 1879, leaving his business to Joseph Meston, and died in 1889; Edward Milner died in 1884, his last years having been devoted to the Crystal Palace School of Gardening. Their passing left H. E. Milner and William Goldring as the major figures in landscaping. As the 1890s began, the progressive tendency in landscape design could be said to be a new reserve, a quieter, 'better mannered' style.

Milner's *Art and Practice of Landscape Gardening*, published in 1891, made him the standard authority to be recommended to students and liberally cribbed from.[40] Most of the work described in the book was his father's and the principles expounded in it had a more obvious relevance to his father's work than his own; the same vision, of the landscaper emulating the forces of geological change, informed the son's work, but its exercise was gentler and more restrained. Where Edward Milner created the dramatic terraces of Bodnant, Henry Ernest seemed more excited by a lower-key project of his father's last years, the creation of the low knoll on which Iwerne Minster stood. Where Edward Milner had worked with waterfalls and rapids, Henry Ernest seemed more interested in effects like the separation of groups of trees to suggest the course of vanished streams. In gardens like Yeatton Peverey, where he provided a setting for Aston Webb's house, his landscaping was analogous in its restraint to the unflamboyant architecture.[41]

William Goldring turned professional in 1887, after eight years of visiting gardens for *The Garden*.[42] Goldring inherited Marnock's mantle; indeed, one of his early works was the addition of a new terrace to Marnock's Impney Hall; but just as Milner's style was a toning-down of his father's, so Goldring in his early years presented a chastened version of Marnock's. His rose garden at Coleorton Hall was quiet and restrained compared with Marnock's formal parterre at Warwick Castle; a Goldring park like the Dorchester Public Garden, while continuing such Marnockian traits as the contouring of ground to obscure paths from each other's view, was designed to fit unobtrusively into place, its major tree planting chosen to echo the town's existing selection of street trees.[43]

A rather more dynamic approach to landscape could be found in some of the nurseries which offered garden design as part of their services – for instance, the firm of Backhouse of York, whose designer Simeon Marshall, at Thornbridge Hall, created a dramatic conjunction of a formal terrace

80 Friar Park, the terrace garden. An engraving from Henry Ernest Milner's *Art and Practice of Landscape Gardening* (1890), showing Frank Crisp's house and terrace.

garden with a rock and water garden sloping down the hillside. The most explicit juxtapositions of art and nature since Paxton, on the other hand, were achieved by the firm of Veitch and Son in their series of gardens in Buckinghamshire for the Rothschild family: for instance at Halton House, where a rocky stream and waterfall were brought immediately up to the lawn and flower garden.[44] But for the most part, the atmosphere of restraint prevailed; even the work of William Barron and Sons became more conventional after old Barron's death in 1891, and younger designers like Thomas Baines and A. G. Jackman (the latter a desciple of Edouard André) abandoned formal design altogether and placed their emphasis on the creation of views across the countryside.[45]

It is against this background that the debate which began in the 1890s about the formal garden should be seen, for if taken at face value, many of the statements it generated do not make sense. Thus Reginald Blomfield and Inigo Thomas, both architects by profession, portrayed William Kent and 'Capability' Brown as the archetypes of the modern landscape gardener, and the 'natural' style as dominant since the early eighteenth century. On grounds of historical accuracy, they were an easy mark for William Robinson, who pointed to the Crystal Palace and the gardens of Nesfield to show that the 'formal' garden had been the dominant mode of the nineteenth century. In part, no doubt, Blomfield's strange omission sprang from a wish to dissociate himself from Nesfield's baroque excesses, as from the elaborately patterned terrace gardens still being created by provincial architects like Edward Boardman. But his inaccuracy was

81 Letton Hall, plan for the garden. An undated plan by Edward Boardman, probably 1880s, and altered in execution: a continuation of the mid-century tradition of flowerbeds in architectural patterns.

further compounded by picking on H. E. Milner as a figurehead of the 'natural' school; Milner, after all, emphasized the importance of fitting the terrace garden to the architectural character of the house, and explicitly recommended the formal garden in his lectures. 'Very innocent of prevalent knowledge', was one reviewer's comment.[46]

But beyond the questions of historical accuracy and period preference, the question of the relationship of art to nature was once again at issue. The subordination of garden to prospect, the vogue for creating replicas of landscape scenery, seemed to be substituting imitation for 'exalted idealization' in a manner similar to that which Loudon and his contemporaries had attacked in the eighteenth-century landscape garden: 'the crudest forms in Nature being placed on a higher pedestal than the finest forms purified by man's imagination.'[47] And so the battle was resumed on the old ground, using Kent and Brown as the symbols of modern naturalism.

A significant new vocabulary was appearing, though. The imitators of nature were accused of 'materialism', as opposed to the 'idealism' of sixteenth- and seventeenth-century gardeners.[48] This rhetoric of the ideal characterized much turn-of-the-century discussion of aesthetics; it performed for the younger generation of gardeners the same function that the rhetoric of art had for the early Victorians, but was free from association with those aspects of Victorian gardening that were now unfashionable. For the gardening world its major locus was in the writings of J. D.

Sedding, whose *Garden-Craft Old and New* was published posthumously in 1891.

> A garden is man's transcript of the woodland world: it is common vegetation ennobled: outdoor scenery neatly writ in man's small hand. ... It is man's report of earth at her best. It is earth emancipated from the commonplace.[49]

Sedding's idealism had a religious basis, and can be seen to some extent as an attempt at a Christian aesthetics: he spoke of the garden as summoning up 'Eden-memories', as hinting to man of his unfallen condition, and phrased his rejection of nature as a model in religious terms – the artist-gardener, 'knowing good and evil', could not 'present things indiscriminately' like 'untaught, lawless Nature'.[50] Once the rhetoric of idealism was established, however, it could function independently of such Christian underpinnings. Sir George Sitwell, in contradiction to Sedding, proclaimed that man was 'a part of nature, not a supernatural being who has been suddenly intruded into a garden'; yet nothing essential was changed when he substituted evolutionary memories for Edenic ones, and justified formality in psychological terms instead.[51]

The rhetoric of idealism pervaded the gardening literature at the end of the century. Its major proponents, Sedding, Mawson, and Sitwell, used it in the cause of formal design, conceived as man's imaginative counterpart to the forms of nature; and with H. E. Milner proclaiming the virtues of formality, and even Goldring late in his career remarking on 'the beauty and dignity of straight lines',[52] the direction of 'idealist' formalism was the dominant one in landscaping during the early twentieth century. It was not without opposition, however; once the rhetoric of idealism had been established, its applications could not be controlled, and W. F. Rowles could use its vocabulary to condemn formal work 'as a sacrilegious defacement of natural beauty'.[53] An informalist idealism began to be preached during the Edwardian period, and its major channel was to be through the cult of the Japanese garden.

The Japanese Garden

Despite the interest in national styles in the first half of the century, there had been no attempts to recreate a Japanese garden in England. The reason for this was simple ignorance: European contact with Japan had been suspended for over a century, and it was not until Commodore Perry's mission to Japan in 1853 that it became possible for first-hand information about Japanese culture to reach the west. What information had trickled back to England during the years of exclusion came from Chinese sources, and it proved difficult, even after better sources were available, to disentangle concepts of Japanese gardening from Chinese.

When the English gardener of this period thought about Japanese garden-craft, he thought first about bonsai. Robert Fortune had drawn attention to the Chinese art of dwarfing trees in his books of travel, and John Lindley mentioned the practice in his *Theory of Horticulture* (1840).[54] Yet even in that age of the proclaimed triumph of art over nature, such dwarfing roused little enthusiasm, especially with such a wide range of sizes available among the newly introduced shrubs. Despite the interest in root-pruning, and Sir Charles Isham's experiments in dwarfing at Lamport Hall, the same prejudice that discouraged topiary militated more successfully against bonsai. Indeed, the two were often conflated, as in John Robson's description of the topiary at Elvaston Castle as being in the Japanese–Chinese taste.[55]

The technical skill was there, however, and toward the end of the century it gradually emerged. In 1872, for a banquet given in Liverpool for the Japanese embassy, the young G. A. Audsley, later an important authority on Japanese art, supervised a display of British-trained bonsai.[56] As topiary became more popular, bonsai was looked upon more favourably; by the Edwardian period it had already become a cult, particularly associated with such patrons of horticulture as Joseph Chamberlain at Highbury.[57]

A knowledge of the Japanese arts gradually spread, especially after the International Exhibition of 1862 featured a Japanese court.[58] The younger architects of the 1860s and '70s, led by Burges, saw in Japanese artefacts a parallel to mediaeval craftsmanship, and it was not long before plans were being prepared for garden buildings in the Japanese style. E. W. Godwin exhibited plans for a Japanese conservatory, and Thomas Jeckyll designed a cast-iron pagoda in the Japanese style, which he exhibited at Philadelphia and Paris before eventually erecting it in Chapel Field, Norwich, in 1880.[59]

Of greater significance for gardening, however, was the Vienna exhibition of 1873, which included a miniature Japanese village, reassembled afterwards as a permanent feature in the grounds of the Alexandra Palace.

> The village stands in the midst of grounds laid out by a Japanese landscape gardener. There is the little mound, the bridge, the stream with which we are familiar on the Chinese and Japanese plates and dishes – we seem only to want the Weeping Willow to make it complete.

The willow-pattern plate had, twenty years earlier, been invoked as the model for James Bateman's Chinese garden at Biddulph Grange; but by that time Chinoiserie was already on the decline, tainted by its eighteenth-century associations. No such taint clung to things Japanese.

This scale-model approach dominated most early attempts at Japonaiserie in the garden. The 'Japanese' garden at Ivy House, Shipley Glen, laid out in the 1880s by a Yorkshire restaurateur named Thomas Hartley, contained a miniature lake and islands, one carrying two pagodas, but on the other stood a miniature castle with no Japanese connotations.[61] After the publication of Josiah Conder's books about Japanese gardening in the early 1890s, however, such naïvety was proscribed.[62] The wealthier and more sophisticated sought to create more authentic effects by bringing genuine Japanese gardeners to Britain, and by 1905 their advice was being offered in the gardening magazines.[63] The best publicized of these attempts was at Tully, in County Kildare, laid out by the gardener Tass Eida and his sons from 1906. The garden was laid out according to a symbolic plan, representing the journey of life from womb (cave surmounted by flowering cherry) to tomb (weeping trees), and decorated with stone lanterns, bonsai, and a miniature village. By 1910 the garden was announced as complete, and the Tully Nursery Company was established to keep the garden-making community together. At Fanhams Hall, a scale model of Mount Fuji was erected.[64]

By the time of the Japan–British Exhibition in 1910, with bonsai exhibits and two miniature gardens created by Japanese gardeners, the public was ready to respond to the scale-model taste with delight.[65] In the wake of the exhibition, Walter P. Wright recommended the adoption of the Japanese style on a wide scale, listing among its features an irregular lake, waterfall, rustic bridge, waterside planting, and 'Alpine regions, perhaps planted with Firs, and with foothills that are clothed with miniature Pines'.[66] And so the Japanese garden was assimilated to the existing tradition of the rock and water garden; the distinguishing elements were the use of ornaments such as stone lanterns, Japanese plants – notably irises – and subdued colour schemes, with the use of dark backgrounds to create a sense of mystery.[67] Gardens of this sort flourished during the Edwardian period, both on private estates like Holland House, Newstead Abbey, Hinchingbrooke, and Friar Park, and in public parks like Battersea and Abbey Park, Leicester.[68] Reginald Farrer completed the process by recommending an oriental inspiration as a corrective to the rock garden of his day: 'A Chinese or Japanese garden set with European alpines is my ideal.'[69]

There was, however, an alternative approach to the Japanese garden, one which began by rejecting any attempt at daintiness or miniaturization. In the 1860s, both Robert Fortune and John Gould Veitch had taken advantage of Japan's new accessibility to explore the country for plants, and their introductions sparked off a wave of interest in Japanese plants. Edward Luckhurst proposed that the American garden, that old staple of gardening practice, should now be supplemented by a 'Japanese garden – that is to say, a garden containing only plants and trees introduced from Japan'.[70] His plea was taken up by Algernon Freeman-Mitford, later Lord Redesdale, a former diplomat in Japan, and an enthusiast for most aspects of Japanese culture, but who had no respect for the idea of the miniature landscape. His garden at Batsford Park, Gloucestershire, was laid out in the early 1890s as an arboretum of Japanese conifers and maples, with oriental statues positioned as ornaments among the glades; but it was arranged as an 'English' garden on Marnockian principles, with a special area given over to the cultivation of bamboos, on whose classification Freeman-Mitford became an authority.[71]

The most widely publicized garden in this tradition was created at the turn of the century by James Hudson, gardener to Leopold de Rothschild at Gunnersbury Park. This was basically a wild garden devoted to Japanese plants; its most formal feature was a bamboo avenue, and it was studded with Japanese lanterns and stepping stones. The model was a Japanese-style garden in north Italy, which Hudson saw as an alternative to the more architectural Italian gardens that had been popular earlier in the century; throughout the Edwardian period he promoted a hybrid Italian–Japanese style as an alternative to the formal garden.[72]

Thus, thanks to Hudson, the Japanese influence was assimilated to the tradition of the wild garden; but the major impact of this taste lay not in its vegetation – even though bamboos, maples, and flowering cherries

82 Hinchingbrooke, the Japanese garden. A miniature landscape with lake and stream, stone lantern, sculpted birds and tea-house.

formed an immediately recognizable style, and launched the successful career of the nurseryman V. N. Gauntlett – but in its rhetoric. Japanese precedent could be cited for everything from an iris parterre to the use of native plants in the garden, but above all it gave a new feeling of vigour and dynamism to the proponents of informality in the garden, at a time when the formalists seemed to have the upper hand. To a propagandist like P. S. Hayward, Japanese inspiration would bring vitality and transforming power to the English garden:

> There is no need to be afraid of the idea. It is virile, throbbing with life and beauty. The possibilities stretch out beyond the horizon full and free, only waiting for the wit and brain and energy of the younger generation of garden makers to use them to the highest degree.[73]

8

Horticulture adrift from history

In the Wake of Carpet Bedding

The dominance of carpet bedding lasted from 1870 until the later 1880s, but while it filled the niche previously occupied by the embroidered parterre, the bolder and simpler forms of massing continued unaffected by its sway, and a composite foliage-and-flower style was quick to develop. An early important indication of this new approach was the 'tessellated colouring' of Mason, superintendent of Prince's Park, Liverpool, using colours 'repeated in small blotches, with sharp dividing lines to separate the groups, like a series of dotted ribbons placed side by side'. This was, in effect, a partial return to mixed colouring, and Shirley Hibberd found it 'wanting in decidedness when viewed from a distance'.[1]

The mixing of colours, which had faded from topical importance during the 1860s with the acceptance of both herbaceous borders and bedded parterres, was about to emerge once again as a key issue. Frances Jane Hope, in Edinburgh, mixed or shaded some of her beds, but it was William Wildsmith of Heckfield Place who became the figurehead of the campaign. By 1880 he had emerged as the most celebrated gardener of his generation, the author of regular columns in both the *Gardeners' Chronicle* and the *Garden*; Heckfield was repeatedly discussed in the magazines, and was opened to the public for a week every year, thus making his experiments accessible to a wide audience. In 1883, he wrote the chapter on summer bedding for Robinson's *English Flower Garden*, and for two decades his views circulated under Robinson's imprimatur.[2]

Wildsmith presented himself as a pluralist in his bedding preferences, distinguishing four styles that could be judiciously employed:

> There are four types of summer flower gardening. 1, the massing (the oldest); 2, the carpet; 3, the neutral, quiet and low in colour, mainly through use of succulents; and 4, the sub-tropical, in which plants of noble growth and graceful foliage play the chief part. To my mind, a mixture of the four classes, skilfully worked out in conformity with the surrounding architecture, landscape scenery, and ground formation, is the beau ideal of flower gardening.[3]

The notion of conformity to the surroundings was decisive. The 'colour-massing or grouping style' was adapted for parterres set against a background of evergreens to provide relief from the glare of colours; where the parterre was open to the landscape, neutrality of colouring, hues that blended with the prevailing tone, became important. For Wildsmith, whether in the beds or in the landscape planting, the highest achievement

83 Heckfield Place, the parterre. This photograph, published in 1888, shows the complex shrubby style which William Wildsmith hoped would replace carpet bedding.

of art was to make it impossible 'to determine what tint predominates in the entire arrangement'. In bedding, this meant a dominance of softer colours over stronger, an avoidance of sharp transitions between colours, and a great variety of plants for the beds. Indeterminate colouring was felt to give greater repose to the eye:

> if any colour at all may predominate, it is what gardeners know as 'glaucous,' that is, a light grey or whitish green. Of such a colour the eye never tires, perhaps, because it is in such harmony with the predominant tints of the landscape, and particularly of the lawn.[4]

Sedding attacked this attitude as scorning the picture for the sake of the frame.[5]

Wildsmith's views on colour had a wide influence during the 1890s, but it was not in colour mixing alone that Heckfield served as a model for younger gardeners. By the 1880s, Wildsmith's 'mosaiculture', the use of dot plants and patches of herbaceous flowers to give variety to the surface of carpet beds, was moving in the direction of a deliberately ragged, shrubby, and cluttered bedding, intended to stimulate associations of profusion rather than control. This is how the stone baskets and beds on the terrace at Heckfield were planted in 1882:

> They were filled chiefly with the intensely bright double Cactus Dahlia Juaresii, and the rich single variety Paragon, not formally staked, but each plant affording support to the other, the whole forming a great tangled mass of flowers. These were relieved by groups of white and golden Marguerites,

> Heliotropes, &c., with Tropaeolums scrambling among them and falling over the sides here and there, as if escaping from an overladen receptacle. The plants appear to have been inserted, and then as regards their floral outline left to take their chance. Their growth has been a floral struggle as if to represent the survival of the fittest; and the freedom, almost wildness, of the arrangement was not only pleasing in itself, but by force of contrast the trim and highly finished compact beds were shown to great advantage.[6]

It had been a criticism of the old-fashioned herbaceous border that plants were left to support each other and ended up killing each other,[7] but in the post-Darwinian era the metaphor of struggle for existence could turn what would previously have been regarded as waste and neglect into an aesthetic merit.

For twenty years, Wildsmith made Heckfield a celebrated training centre, and many of the famous gardeners of the next generation passed through his hands; as they gradually moved on, so Wildsmith's influence began to radiate outward from Heckfield.[8] Gradually, a formula was evolved: the bedding of shrubby plants, a three-dimensional effect created by emphasizing disparities between layers of vegetation, bedding that broke the traditional rules about neatness and straggled beyond its edging lines. Before his death in 1890, Wildsmith was able to draw attention to his pupils' work at other Hampshire gardens: to Trinder's beds 'filled in with every conceivable mathematical design worked out in flowers or foliage plants' at Dogmersfield, or, even better, to Jones's work at Elvetham Park. Here he found a 'unique effect' – immense beds of formal design, but planted in 'such a loose, natural manner as to completely destroy all formality'. This was a step in the direction of the ideal which Wildsmith left to the younger generation: 'A more radical alteration is still required, and must be carried out by young and thinking men, and that is the abolition of geometry itself.'[9]

The Re-Assertion of Colour

The English Flower Garden was not so much one man's book as an anthology of the gardening practice of its generation. This is nowhere more clearly shown than in its treatment of colour schemes, for it offered conflicting advice from three different authors: while Wildsmith advocated colour mixtures in the chapter on summer bedding, two different approaches to the massing of colours were put forward in another chapter, by 'J.D.' (J. Dundas?) and Gertrude Jekyll.

The year before *The English Flower Garden* was published, J.D. had become involved in a lengthy argument about complementary colours in the pages of the *Garden*.[10] He traced the idea of complementary planting back to Chevreul, whose baneful influence was still being propagated by art schools, though his opponent claimed that the truth of complementarity was independent of Chevreul's discredited theory. J.D. developed an alternative argument, based on Maxwell's new wave theory of light; each colour, according to this theory, was characterized by a distinct wavelength, and therefore, reasoned J.D., it was incorrect to divide colours into primaries and composites:

> No colour is produced by any combination of colours. White is not a mixture of colours, but a thing apart. Red and yellow do not form orange, even orange-scarlet is not scarlet with a little orange in it, but a distinct colour produced by a distinct rate of colour waves, so that even were M. Chevreul's reasoning correct, all and every tint in the rainbow would have to be present in order to produce harmony.[11]

J.D. was confusing the perception of colour with the physical transmission of light, but in this he was hardly unique.

J.D.'s practical advice was a recapitulation of that of George Field, Owen Jones and Sir Gardner Wilkinson; like them, he held up Moorish and Hindu colouring as a model of taste. In particular, he restated the idea that colours should be presented in the same proportions in which they appeared in the rainbow.[12] He further argued that colours only really harmonized with those that lay nearest to them in the spectrum (whereas forty years earlier, D. R. Hay had claimed that only colours widely separated in the spectrum harmonized):

> Three pure colours much separated in the rainbow are almost the worst combinations that can be made. Red, blue, and yellow are enough to produce lunacy ... Colours harmonise when their place in the rainbow is very close, as crimson, pink, and scarlet, scarlet and orange, orange and yellow, yellow and lemon, turquoise blue and pure blue, &c.[13]

Colours should therefore be separated by neutral backgrounds.

It is difficult to say how influential J.D.'s theories were; his ideas about the harmony of spectrally adjacent colours may have had a share in the Edwardian fashion for one-colour gardens. The influence of Gertrude Jekyll, on the other hand, has been amply attested to.

Jekyll came late to gardening; she had been trained in the schools of art in the early 1860s, and had built up a reputation as a painter and decorator by the 1870s. Her worsening eyesight made close work steadily more difficult, however, until she was forced to abandon her intended career, and turned progressively instead to gardening, where the larger scale of activity made the blurring of visual detail less of a handicap. She had refashioned her mother's garden at Munstead, Surrey, by the 1880s, and was contributing advice about colour planning to Robinson's magazine by 1882.[14] 'Splendid harmonies of rich and brilliant colour and proper sequences of such combinations' were her recommendations to the readers of *The English Flower Garden*.

To understand the degree to which Jekyll's planting schemes were innovative, they must be seen against the double legacy of the herbaceous border and the bedding tradition. The traditional mode of planting borders was in uniform lines often for ease of maintenance; already in the 1870s, however, 'some prefer to plant their borders in groups, and the effect is, perhaps, less formal than it otherwise would be'. Jekyll's advice followed this latter plan: plants were to be grouped in masses, 'large enough to have a certain dignity', and these masses were to be arranged informally, in drifts, rather than in geometrical figures. Under Jekyll's influence, though she does not appear to have been the originator, informal drift planting came to dominate the herbaceous border by the turn of the century.[15]

These masses were to be arranged in graded sequence with due attention

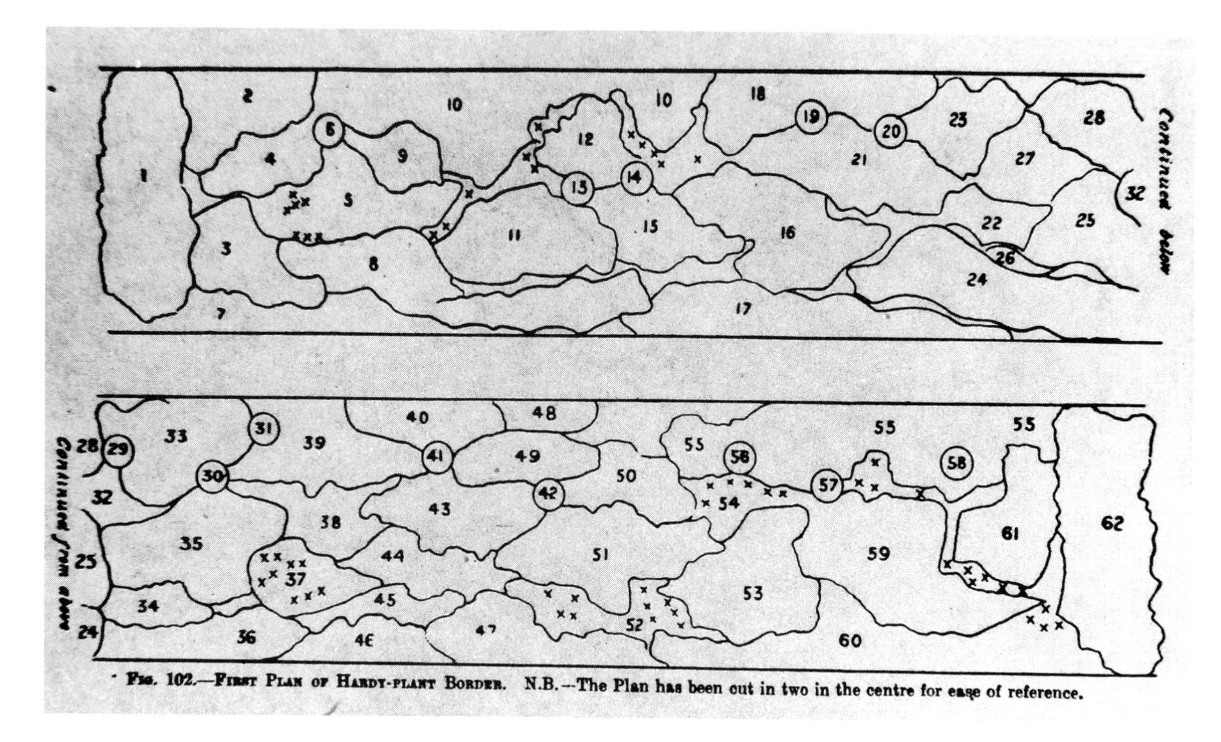

84 Plan for a herbaceous border, by Gertrude Jekyll. 1, 62, *Yucca*; 2, *Polemonium*; 3, 16, 22, 59, irises; 4, *Phlox*; 5, 7, anemones; 6, 13–14, 19–20, 27, 29–32, 41–42, 56–58, *Canna* or *Dahlia*; 8, 60, *Hosta*; 9, 50, hollyhocks; 10, 49, 55, delphiniums; 11, paeonies; 12, *Veratrum*; 15, 58, *Hemerocallis*; 17, 47, *Bergenia*; 18, 40, *Thalictrum*; 21, 25, 33, *Kniphofia*; 23, 28, *Helianthus*; 24, 35, poppies and *Gypsophila*; 26, 34, *Lychnis*; 36, Heuchera; 37, 52, 54, lilies; 39, *Echinops*; 43, *Buphthalmum*; 44, 46, *Oenothera*; 45, *Monarda*; 48, *Verbascum*; 51, *Eryngium*; 61, *Polemonium*. x marks Madonna lilies.

paid to the effects of foreshortening when seen from one end of the border. In this, her planting bears a great resemblance to the shading originated by Fleming and Beaton; William Goldring praised her border and Munstead for its 'soft and sensible transition from one mass of colour to another'. Shading was still in the air at the time, and being practised at Castle Ashby, which Jekyll later praised highly.[16]

Jekyll's principal innovation in this respect (apart from the choice of plants) was the replacement of uniform progression of hue by an interrupted sequence:

> Warm colours are not difficult to place; scarlet, crimson, pink, orange, yellow, and warm white are easily arranged so as to pass agreeably from one to the other . . .
>
> A progression of colour to be recommended in a mixed border might begin with strong blues, light and dark, grouped with white and pale yellow, passing on to pink. Then rose colour, crimson, and strongest scarlet, leading to orange and bright yellow. A paler yellow followed by white would instantly connect the warm colours with the lilacs and purples, and a colder white would combine them pleasantly with low-growing plants with cool-coloured leaves.[17]

Her great border at Munstead had a mass of scarlet in the middle, moving to drifts of grey and white at either end, intended, by 'the law of complementary colour', to provide relief to the eye saturated with the warm colours of the centre.[18]

On specific colour combinations, Jekyll's advice sometimes contradicted J.D.'s; the reader of *The English Flower Garden* could find two radically opposed notions about the association of pink and lilac five pages apart.[19] Contrasts of colour she felt to be ineffective at a distance, or when interspersed, and were therefore to be used 'sparingly as brilliant accessories rather than trustworthy principles'. By these means, Jekyll solved the problem posed thirty years before by Donald Beaton; 'If we could but teach, or rather unteach, the system of planting herbaceous plants, we might hope to succeed in learning the true art of flower-gardening at last'.[20]

Jekyll showed little awareness of the principal gardeners of her youth, although she referred approvingly to William Ingram and John Fleming. She emphasized, by contrast, her role as an artist, and as early as 1882 was proclaiming that gardening was 'painting a picture': 'the colours should be placed with careful forethought and deliberation, as a painter employs them on his picture, and not dropped down in lifeless dabs, as he has them on the palette'.[21] Certainly it was from her training in art school that she derived her lifelong interest in colour theory. But it should be noted that the works she studied there in the early 1860s were precisely those being argued over by the gardeners of the day: Chevreul, Wilkinson, and Owen Jones, whom Beaton held up as providing instructions for bedding.[22] Her art training, in effect, would have confronted her with the same ideas about colour that the masters of the bedding system were using.

In her earlier books, Jekyll insisted strongly on her opposition to the bedding system. Nonetheless, her first published statements on colour planning were greeted by the advocates of mixing as a restatement of the bedding tradition..

> There is far more of the mere bedding-out ring in your correspondent's article than is agreeable ... The one set of plants is no more objectionable than the other if it be true that 'splendid harmonies of rich and brilliant colour, &c., should be the main rule' in setting out a garden, and that 'one of the most important points in the arrangement of a garden is the placing of flowers with regard to their colour effect.' This has always been the creed, pure and simple, of the bedding-out fraternity, and 'G.J.' seems only to be attempting in another way, and with greater variety of materials, what the bedding man has been aiming at all along.

Jekyll replied with a splutter of indignation, but not altogether a convincing one, since she had given explicit instructions for the adaptation of her colour schemes to the uses of bedding, and was to enlarge this section for *The English Flower Garden*. This exchange revealed the ambiguity of the anti-bedding stance. The proponents of the old-fashioned garden saw the bedding system in terms of its rejection of traditional herbaceous plants; the proponents of mixing saw it in terms of its segregation of plants by colour; from either of these points of view, Jekyll, whose stated objection to bedding was its use of geometric pattern and who did not base her choice of border plants on historical criteria, could be regarded as falling into the bedding category.

As she grew older she came to extend a more tolerant hand to bedding. At Renishaw, in 1911, she even planted a scheme of marigolds in rectangular and circular beds in what the 1850s had known as the promenade style;[24] and in *Garden Ornament*, the major book of her last years, she produced a moving tribute to the bedding system which she is often credited with having destroyed:

> Beautiful examples of the good treatment of parterres existed a few years ago at Castle Ashby, and it is to be hoped that the same tradition is maintained.

> They were delightfully planned for colour harmony, so that each department formed a satisfying picture. Such intelligent employment of the summer plants showed the best possible utilization of the bedding system, which, in these large parterres, was, and always is, absolutely in place.[25]

Sculptural Bedding

By the 1890s, carpet bedding was on the retreat, but it obstinately refused to disappear. Its use diminished on country estates, as the claims of historical revivalism were pressed, but it continued in the small surburban garden into the 1920s, and remained consistently popular in municipal parks. Even here, however, its opponents gained power, and carpet bedding was discontinued in Hyde Park in 1904. 'Up to the last', it was remarked,

> these beds attracted the greatest attention of the visitors, and when at length but one such carpet or mosaic bed was left in a public garden, so great was the attention devoted to it that iron guards had to be erected to preserve the grass near it.[26]

As the fashion for carpet bedding passed its peak on the country estate, some gardeners looked for comparable substitutes. In 1890 William Sherwood of Scarborough announced a method of imitating carpet bedding with 'minerals in six distinct colours, broken up small to the substance of rather small gravel. The materials are dark blue glass, light blue ditto, sand, gravel, ochre, black brick, red and green glass'. Whether Sherwood was really unaware of the precedents for this method is unknown, but the similarity to Nesfield's gravel parterres was noted in the press.[27] This model was openly avowed in the case of William Miller, head gardener at Coombe Abbey, who had worked there with Nesfield in the 1860s; in the late 1890s he designed a new parterre, consisting of tracery beds cut out of turf in the shape of

> an idealistic tree growing from an ornamental vase . . . spreading in fanciful curves over the space the garden covers, some of the beds terminating in little beds, similar in form to the Shamrock leaf; and others resemble the flower-head of a Thistle.

The planting of this new 'free and easy' parterre was seasonally alterable, though a 'semi-carpet-bedding style' was recommended for summer use. On leaving Coombe Abbey in 1899, Miller went into business as a landscape gardener, displaying one of his parterre designs at the Paris Exhibition in 1900, and publishing in the *Gardeners' Chronicle*.[28]

Miller and Sherwood intended to supersede carpet bedding, but unexpected life was still to be found in the style. The new development took place at Halton House, one of the Rothschild estates in Buckinghamshire, where by 1889 a series of extraordinary beds had extended carpet bedding into a vertical dimension: 'a cushion-bed planted to represent a huge ottoman with cords and tassles, two large vases covered with succulents and other plants, just as a Dresden China vase may sometimes be seen studded with shells.'[29] These effects were probably achieved with a frame of galvanized wire on which the plants could be packed with their roots

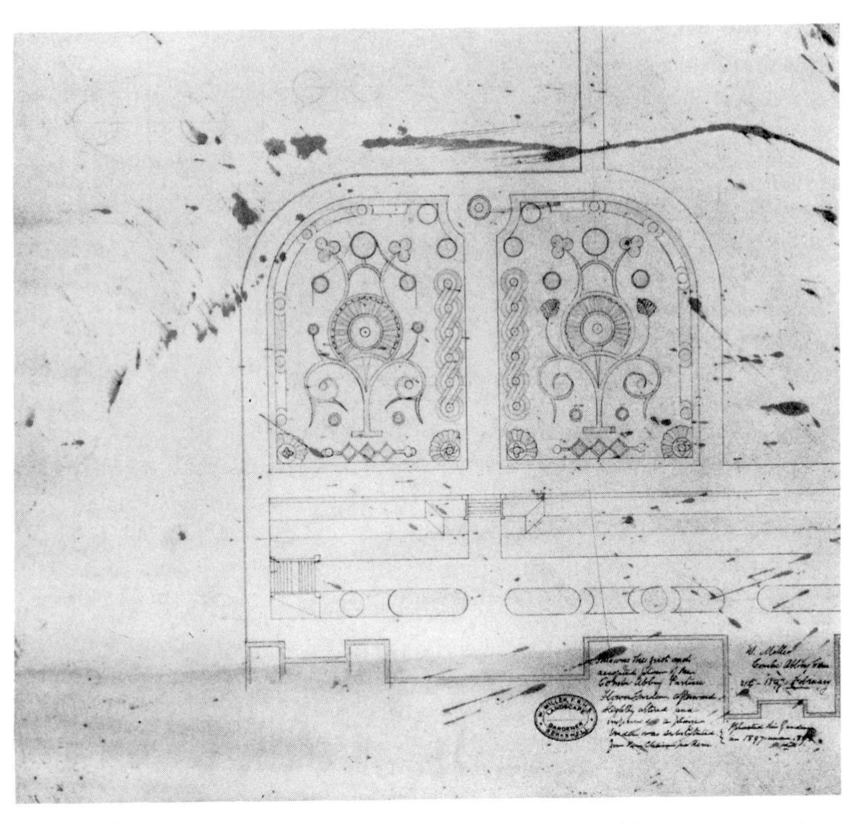

85 Coombe Abbey, plan for the parterre. William Miller's 'free and easy' alternative to carpet bedding: tracery beds cut in the turf.

in peat or soil masses. Gardeners like Edward Luckhurst greeted 'the growing predominance of fanciful display' with outrage, and Halton remained the only country house at which such three-dimensional bedding structures were publicized. There was certainly a long gap between Halton and the further development of the principle in England; in the intervening years, reports came from America of similar three-dimensional experiments, and were usually greeted with pious wishes that an art so debased should never reach the English shores.[30]

When the first wire-frame bedding sculpture was erected in an English park is difficult to say. Perhaps the earliest, certainly the wittiest, consisted of taking the phrase 'carpet bed' literally; first reported in Pearson Park, Hull, in 1907, it represented 'a roll of stair carpet, with a length of carpet unrolled'.[31] Thereafter the possibilities of galvanized wire frames began to be realized in earnest, as park superintendents in several parts of the country tried their hands at creating this new form of vegetable sculpture. By the First World War such bedding displays were becoming a well-known feature of municipal parks. Some of the motifs may have been modelled on the known devices of topiary – crowns, for instance, were familiar as a topiary feature from gardens like Levens and Elvaston, and the coronation of George V sparked off a series of experiments with floral crowns.[33] Three-dimensional bedding may have been the horticulturist's alternative to topiary – sculptural effect obtained in a novel, rather than an historically revivalist, medium. In the postwar years, the park superintendent's repertoire of effects more than rivalled the topiarist's: staircases, an organ, a complete suite of furniture, even a cenotaph were fashioned

86 Halton, the floral vase. The first galvanized-wire floral structure in England, 1889.

in carpet-bedding.[33]

The most popular and enduring of all such forms was introduced by John M'Hattie, formerly the Duke of Wellington's gardener at Strathfieldsaye, but from the late 1890s superintendent of parks in Edinburgh. A bed was laid out in the shape of a clock face, with numbers and a decorative pattern in carpet bedding, arms covered with succulents, and a functioning clockwork mechanism set in the ground underneath. The horticultural press greeted this development with a cough of reservation; M'Hattie, wrote one reporter on its inauguration, 'is exciting the horticultural tastes of the dwellers in the Modern Athens, providing floral beauties for some, arborescent displays for others, and floral freaks to attract yet others'.[34] It was not, actually, M'Hattie's invention; he probably got the idea from a floral clock that had been exhibited in Paris.[35] Once it had been displayed in Edinburgh, however, it was taken up widely, and became perhaps the most significant of all interwar fashions in the parks.

New Directions in the Public Park

The role of the park superintendent was gradually changing. As municipal parks multiplied, they began to take over the entertainment functions once provided by the commercial pleasure gardens. After the example of the Royal Horticultural Society's garden at Kensington, bandstands became a common feature; drinking fountains were appearing by the 1860s, and refreshment pavilions by the 1870s; by the turn of the century most large parks had at least one conservatory. But the provision of facilities for sports and games was to have the greatest impact on the

87 Carpet bedding taken literally: a floral carpet at Alexandra Gardens, Weymouth.

appearance and management of parks.

Joshua Major, an early advocate of 'innocent athletic games', included areas for archery, quoits, bowls, and gymnasia in his Manchester parks of the 1840s.[36] Despite Major, however, provision for sports in the parks was largely *ad hoc* until 1880, when the idea of the sports park was introduced. West Park, Wolverhampton, and Stamford Park, Altrincham, were both opened in 1880 to considerable publicity, and set the trend for much that was to follow.

West Park, the more original composition, was the work of the Birmingham nurseryman and landscape gardener Richard H. Vertegans. It intensified the axial layout promoted by Barron: one major avenue bisected the park, and crossing paths divided two-thirds of the park into cricket grounds, archery ground and bowling green, their boundaries planted with widely spaced single trees, and shrubberies at corners.[37] Stamford Park, by the John Shaw father-and-son team in Manchester, was in many ways more conventional: instead of an immediately tangible central avenue, an implied axis lay through the centre of two large oval lawns. Nonetheless, it went further than West Park in terms of its sports provision; the main lawns were set aside for cricket and football – now losing its traditional reputation for violence and becoming respectable as a result of public schools and church groups[38] – with a bathing pond, playgrounds, and grounds for lawn tennis and croquet in additional enclosures.[39]

The trend thus established continued and eventually grew dominant. The more sedate sports, that occupied more circumscribed areas, could be adapted without strain to the horticultural goals of the park: bowling greens in the early twentieth century, for example, were laid out with alpine or herbaceous borders around their perimeters; early tennis courts were frequently enclosed by hedges. Football, however, tended to devour space, and gave an open-lawned character to the parks it colonized, relegating horticultural display, and indeed walking space, to a position of secondary importance.

88 Philips Park, Manchester, in 1913, during a visit by the Parks Committee. A model for bedding for parks superintendents of the early twentieth century.

Park superintendents, however, saw bedding as essential, especially in inner-city areas, where air pollution placed limits on what could be achieved in landscaping. In the 1920s, W. W. Pettigrew, superintendent of parks in Manchester, published statistics on Philips Park, one of Major's creations, then in the worst-polluted district. The average life-span of rhododendrons was three years, and flowering was only reliable the first year; poplars lasted 'somewhat longer'; each year, some 7000 trees and shrubs had to be planted to replace the annual losses.[40] When even the structure planting of the park could not be expected to grow to maturity, seasonally renewable bedding remained the superintendent's best means of beautifying an inner-city park, and often had to act as a substitute for the more permanent effects of landscape gardening. Pettigrew, the author of the first British textbook on the subject, saw his role as reconciling the horticultural tradition of the parks with the increasingly strident cry for sports facilities.[41]

As the demand for parks increased, local authorities, short of open space in built-up areas, increasingly began to acquire existing estates as they came on the market, for conversion to park use. The scope available to the landscape designer for originality varied considerably as a result. In South London, for instance, Colonel Sexby made almost no changes of design in converting the Brockwell estate into a park, but had a greater opportunity to display his skills in knocking three separate gardens together to make Ruskin Park. The annexation of sites of natural beauty, from Hampstead Heath to Jesmond Dene, Newcastle, and the conversion of small parcels of land into recreation grounds, were further aspects of this attempt to meet the demand for open space.

The Attack on the Gardener

William Barnes, the famous 'Barnes of Bicton', retired in 1868, worn down in health by years of arduous work. Shortly afterward, his late employer, the Baroness Rolle, claimed in two letters that he had left the gardens in a disorderly condition on his departure, and Barnes sued her for libel. The jury awarded him £200. In one sense, this was a culminating vindication of the professional status of the head gardener, and was perceived as such in the gardening press.[42]

Complaints had been occasionally heard about the tyranny of gardeners, some of whom made themselves easy targets for reaction by their ostentatious refusal to bend their professional standards to their employers' wishes. Samuel Wood, for example, recalled being instructed that his employer had no interest in floral display; 'I took no notice of what was said, but proceeded, as was my wont, with the getting up of stock for a full display of flowers both indoors and out' – in this case to win his master over.[43] In the wake of Barnes *v.* Rolle, however, the employers began to fight back, and the 1870s heard the first stirrings of a campaign against gardeners' professional standing – coming, predictably, not from the nobility but from the aspiring middle classes. The first notable contestants were 'John Latouche' (O. J. F. Crawfurd), Henry Arthur Bright, and Mrs Loftie, who called for 'a crusade against the modern gardener, a tyrannical and prosaic creature'. Their attack was centred on two points: competitions and the bedding system.[44]

The flower show and horticultural competitions were rightly seen as central to the position of the gardener. They were where he tested his skills against his peers, where he appeared in the public eye; it was through them that he hoped 'to educate the taste of the public', in the words of John Wills, who looked forward to the day 'when a flower show will be held in every village in the United Kingdom'.[45] Henry Arthur Bright complained that

> nothing can be more spoiling to the gardener than these flower-shows so constantly are. In the first place, the prize-ticket generally asserts that the prize is adjudged to 'Mr ---, gardener to ---.' The owner of the garden is nobody, and the gardener is almost everything. The prize is in almost every case regarded as the unchallenged property of the gardener, who has, nevertheless, won the prize by his master's plant, reared at his master's expense, and at the cost of time which has made him too frequently neglect much more important matters.[46]

Such buffets, however, were ineffective against the professional organization that lay behind the shows. Wills's hope of seeing flower shows in every village seemed likely to be achieved until, shortly before the First World War, rivalry from the cinema suddenly cut flower-show attendances.[47]

The second point of attack was the bedding system, in whose place the complainants elevated the old-fashioned garden, in which horticultural experiment was of subordinate importance if not simply discouraged. Loftie contrasted the gardener, 'whose only knowledge of plants has been acquired by working in a nursery-ground', with the 'real lover of flowers'; Jekyll defended the 'garden-artist' against being relegated by the architect to the status of a builder, but she was thinking of someone like herself, not her gardening staff. Edith Chamberlain, in the 1890s, added a feminist element by complaining about 'the undiscriminating male gardener' who looked for visual qualities instead of fragrance in plants. (The role of women such as Lady Middleton in advancing the bedding system, and Donald Beaton's insistence on the role of 'the ladies' in deciding on colour schemes, were conveniently overlooked.)[48] Underneath the stylistic reform ran a heavy undercurrent of snobbery, emerging on occasion into an overt desire to strengthen class boundaries which some felt the gardeners were eroding. 'Have you no proper spirit left, that you submit to be dictated to by a servant?' cried Latouche to his country house audience. The new country-house journalism responded to the call; *Country Life* systematically overlooked the gardener, attributing everything to do with the garden to the owner, so that, for instance, Lord Eversley rather than Wildsmith was given credit for the terrace gardening at Heckfield Place.[49]

What then was to be the role of the gardener? In the place of a professional whose qualifications might overshadow his master's, Loftie proposed to employ uneducated labourers, who would do exactly as they were told without getting ideas above their station. Bright seconded this notion: 'It is not necessary to understand every matter of detail . . . but at least we may make up our mind as to what we want to have done, and then take care that the gardener carries out our orders.'[50]

On the great country estates, where skilled gardeners occupied a useful tier in the management hierarchy, such proposals roused little interest, but they were better received in the world of the smaller country house. Charles Wade laid out his garden at Snowshill, Gloucestershire, to a design by Baillie Scott just after the First World War. At his father's house in Yoxford, he recalled, a retired coachman had become the gardener.

> But he became such an autocrat, it ceased to be our garden any more, it became his garden in which we were allowed to walk. If asked to move a plant, we were always told it was the wrong time of year, or the plant was too old or too young, or the moon not old enough, in any case it would die if moved. He ordered all the seeds and plants and put them where he wished, our only part was to pay.
>
> I took warning from this when I came to Snowshill, preferring to have my own garden and not a gardener's garden in which I was allowed to walk. When the workmen were here repairing the old house I noted a labourer who was a good worker and very tidy in all he did. I liked his name, which was Hodge, his hat, which was mauve, and having asked him, I was satisfied that he knew nothing about gardening beyond cabbages and cauliflowers, so here

> was my very first man. The garden has remained my garden these 25 years, and at my wish plants are moved in spite of the time of year, in spite of their age or the age of the moon, nor do they invariably die, but flourish abundantly.[51]

From Paxton to Hodge: the gardener was one craftsman on whose behalf the proponents of the arts-and-crafts movement did not concern themselves. From Mrs Loftie to Miss Jekyll, throughout the writings of architects and opponents of bedding in the late nineteenth and early twentieth centuries, there runs a vein of denigration of the gardener, dismissing him as merely mechanical, inartistic by comparison with the country-house owner, fit only to take instruction. In place of the Victorian myth of the heroic gardener, the new century was to substitute the myth of the amateur plantsman, of aristocratic or at least wealthy extraction, whose garden was informed by his own artistic sensibility, and whose gardeners have disappeared without trace in the horticultural literature.

The Edwardian Flower Garden

Gardening, wrote F. W. Burbidge at the beginning of the new century, 'formerly aristocratic, conservative and secretive, is now democratic, more generally diffused, and more liberal'. The consequences of this democracy and liberalism were feared by some, but helped to make the Edwardian period one of great excitement for others.[52] Variety, on a scale not seen since the 1860s, was the keynote of the period. The greatest degree of eclecticism was to be found in the public parks, whose most famous superintendents, like Moorman and Pettigrew, openly defended all possible aspects of the horticultural tradition – from ribbon borders to alpine rockeries, from carpet bedding to naturalized bulbs.[53] But the same spirit of experiment could be found on many private estates as well.

The gardens designed by Robert T. Veitch and his landscaper, F. W. Meyer, between the 1880s and the Edwardian period displayed a revival of interest in the dramatic contrast of art and nature; discussions of Halton, Ascott, and Minley Manor continually stressed the juxtaposition of geometric gardens and naturalistic scenery, topiary and rock gardens, smooth lawns and rivulets. Minley Manor, Hampshire, was the site of their most innovative geometric garden: a complex parterre, laid out in the form of the family crest, but employing for the purpose a mass of miniature conifers. Retinosporas (juvenile cypresses) were arranged in a scroll pattern against a groundwork composed of 80,000 seedling yews; panels of dwarfed hollies in different colours were added to provide a nocturnal effect, their foliage shining under electric light. 'Some of our readers', predicted the *Gardeners' Chronicle*, 'may throw up their hands at this reversion to a style which has not only gone out of fashion, but entails vigorously-expressed disapproval on the part of some writers'.[54] Nesfield's work was also experiencing a revival of interest: William Sherwood's gravel parterres and William Miller's 'free-and-easy' scroll designs were products of the 1890s; a box parterre in the 1850s manner was laid out at Gosford House, Lothian, after 1890. Nesfield's parterre at Broughton Hall, quiescent as a bowling green for over twenty years, was restored, without the polychrome gravels, at the turn of the century.[55]

The Minley parterre reveals another fashion of the period: the use of dwarfed trees as bedding plants. Contemporary with the first flush of interest in bonsai came experiments with dwarfed trees as bedding plants – conifer parterres, a revival of dwarf oak edgings, *Euonymus* and similar shrubs trained as carpet plants for geometric beds.[56] On the other hand, the vertical dimension was provided for by a new interest in standards. In the words of a critic of the style,

> the public are treated to a series of beds full of tall pillar or pyramid-like plants, 4 to 5 feet in height, ranged with all the stiffness, formality, and regularity seen in a regiment of soldiers.

Fuchsias, heliotropes, and weeping roses were among the plants trained to 'break the flatness' of beds, although sweet peas – which, through Henry Eckford's breeding programme, were yielding a greater variety of colours than any other plant – soon became dominant.[57]

Aldenham House, the successor of Heckfield as the period's most-discussed virtuoso garden, made extensive use of formal shrub beds, while geometric azalea gardens, such as the oval enclosure William Goldring designed at Elvetham Park in 1912, became popular.[58] The period also saw waves of enthusiasm for tubbed plants, promoted by James Hudson, for planting on walls and in the interstices of paving, and for the use of spiky and ball-headed plants in flowerbeds, a trend that culminated immediately before the First World War with Reginald Cory's attempt to revive the dahlia as a garden flower by holding trials at his garden, The Dyffryn.[59]

The old quarrel between the advocates of bedding and those of the herbaceous garden dragged on, but the dominant tone of the period was one of reconciliation. A noteworthy representative of this tolerant temper was Alfred Austin, the Poet Laureate, who deserves to be remembered for his series of gardening narratives beginning with *The Garden that I Love*.[60] His garden at Swinford Old Manor, which mixed display bedding with herbaceous borders, was held up by H. H. Dombrain as a model of temperance:

> Some persons throwing off one system rush to the other extreme; the place where bedding out has been carried to its fullest extent is all at once so changed that no trace of it is to be found. Now this, while very English, is very unwise; therefore one is glad to see a combination of both systems.[61]

Visitors sometimes expressed surprise on seeing scarlet pelargoniums in Gertrude Jekyll's garden, but she replied that the plant was not to blame for the uses to which it had been put.[62]

The respective claims of mixing and matching, of neutral bedding versus vibrant colour schemes, continued to be debated. The followers of Wildsmith still contended for the elimination of contrast within the beds, for the subordination of bright to tender colours;[63] but the dominant trend was away from Wildsmith's influence, towards both massing and a renewed use of stronger colours. 'Why', asked one critic,

> do our park gardeners persist in the subordination of warm brilliant colours to cold tints – yellows and greens? ... Where a colour design is arranged on

> a lawn and where there are trees and shrubs as background the warmer the colours are the better.[64]

Similar complaints against 'greenery-yallery' combinations eventually won the day; by 1911 *The Times* could comment:

> The ordinary amateur, who learned most of his art from the epoch-making canons of 'The English Flower Garden,' suffers a painful shock when he hears his lavish beds, with their mixture of opulent colour, crudely called a muddle, and compared to a kaleidoscope or a crazy-quilt ...

The dotted texture of Wildsmithian bedding, once thought of as tranquil and soothing, was condemned as restless, and 'the reign of mass, harmony, and repose' was ushered in once more, as in the early days of the bedding system.[65]

The most striking indication of the return to the massing of colour was the fashion for one-colour gardens, for which grey, blue, pink and white were the colours most frequently used. Early exemplars of this style kept rigorously to the one colour chosen, although Jekyll regarded such limitation as pointless, and urged the incorporation of other colours as punctuation marks within the scheme.[66] Where this extreme was not adopted, the establishment of a dominant tone for a bedding system was still frequently emphasized, and as the First World War neared, many bedding schemes were restricted to a couple of hues for maximum impact. Scarlet and red were the colours most often chosen as keynotes, and the impact of poppies in a cornfield was adduced as a model for bedding to follow.[67] Much Edwardian planting, from flame nasturtiums to the orange and red tones of dahlias, was directed towards imparting a warm red glow to the landscape, although Reginald Farrer and E. A. Bowles reacted by campaigning against magenta hues.[68]

Roses sprang to new-found popularity as bedding plants. The unflamboyant hues of the roses then available had led them to be segregated from the main display, and Jekyll was still writing, after the turn of the century, that 'a Rose garden can never be called gorgeous ... The gorgeousness of brilliant bloom, fitly arranged, is for other plants and other portions of the garden.' But the first rose beds had started to appear in public parks in the 1890s, and their popularity soared in the new century, as breeders introduced new strains of flaming orange colour in the 1920s.[69]

The bedding system, meanwhile, seemed to be drawing towards a climax, as it was finally developed into a system that spanned the entire year. The naturalization of spring bulbs was carried out on an ever-increasing scale, though a pundit like Alexander Dean condemned the taste for such massing.[70] The complaint was now growing, however, that both spring bedding, as developed by Fleming, and winter bedding, as practised at Heckfield, were inadequate, because both still left a dull period in the beds at different times of year. The merits of plunging in pots and of continual transplanting for ensuring a genuine all-season display were debated in the 1890s.[71]

The attempt to secure continuous year-round effects quickly led to an impatience with the customary periods allotted for the bedded-out plants to burgeon and to die back. In 1898, a reporter called attention to a new departure in gardening in Regent's Park:

89 Lockinge Park, the flower garden. The post-Wildsmith garden using contrasting levels of planting: box-edged beds, standards and dwarfs in a flower garden designed by William Fyfe, the head gardener.

> There is no waiting for effect, but when a bed is cleared of plants that have become bare of bloom, others in full flower at once take their places. Plants the most unlikely to remove safely are transplanted with no bad effect ensuing, as for instance, in the case of Hollyhocks.[72]

Little more than a decade later, this 'intermittent bedding-out' was a recognized vogue, with greenhouses being worked to provide a steady supply of new plants for turning into beds and borders as soon as they reached flowering stage.

> Compared to this up-to-date system of summer bedding, with its endless planning and forethought, the massed bedding of the 'thirties–'sixties was child's play. Even the graceful and stately sub-tropical gardening which began at Battersea, at Gibson's hands, in 1864, has a permanence and a simplicity that seems elementary in comparison, for once the beds were filled and the palms and Bananas were plunged in due order in the grass, the 'bedding,' as such, was all over. Under the newer system the 'bedding' never can be said to have terminated. It is bedding all the while.[73]

The Edwardian period exulted in the rhetoric of struggle, and an aura of heroic endeavour could be created in unexpected contexts:

> I dream of a sweet-pea garden. This has no old-time flavour. It does not steal into my winter musings with an association of grey, staid orcharding, or of stiff yew alleys and sleepy sundials. It is modern, strenuous, fiercely vital. The flower is in the fire of transformation by the florist, and new varieties pour out hotly, like the editions of evening newspapers.[74]

The vigour of Walter P. Wright's image was slightly compromised when he went on to speak of the delicacy and grace of the flowers; but no such danger of incongruity attached itself to the latter developments of the bedding system. The strong colours of the immediate pre-war years lent themselves easily to a rhetoric of bold assertiveness. The 'futurist and post-expressionist painters have helped to create the prevailing craze for vivid hues', noted one commentator in 1913, and gardens were to exhibit 'correspondingly gorgeous contrasts'.[75] As English painting accommodated the vibrant colours of Charles Ginner and Spencer Gore, the horticultural community found that the new aesthetic was already being practised in the English garden, in the recovered tradition of bedding.

9

In search of a vernacular

In 1892, H. E. Milner laid out the grounds of an exhibition at Earl's Court. His aim was to fill the limited space with a conspectus of historical national styles. Part of the grounds was laid out for Buffalo Bill's wild west show; in other parts there stood a Japanese garden, an Indian tea garden, an Egyptian garden, and a Roman garden with 'terraces and statuary as Pliny described them about 1800 years ago'. Above all, there was a sequence of English styles: a Georgian garden, a Jacobean garden, and a Tudor mansion and garden, 'intended to be as true to Nature and Art as are producible'. There was no section devoted to the nineteenth century, but, said Milner, 'we have our Victorian age amply represented – not in a special garden to itself, but in the thousand and one evidences of floral beauty scattered over the Exhibition generally'.[1]

Standing behind this exhibition layout can be seen the influence of Biddulph Grange – especially in the concept of an Egyptian garden. And the continuing influence of Biddulph, in terms of geographical and historical organization, could still be seen at the turn of the century in gardens such as Friar Park and Iford Manor, functioning in their different ways as digests of the history of civilization. But something new can also be seen in Milner's arrangements: the heavy emphasis on the sequence of English historical styles. In the gardening world, no period style had ever attained the apparent dominance that Gothic had in public architecture during the mid-nineteenth century, but even the Gothic consensus had fallen apart by the 1870s as younger architects began to look sympathetically on the styles that had succeeded it. The question of revivalist gardening had furthermore opened a debate over period planting – whether it was appropriate to use recently introduced plants in historical re-creations – and this was exacerbated by the complete novelty of such forms of planting as the extremes of carpet-bedding. During the last years of the nineteenth century, accordingly, the central theme in historical revival became the attempt to identify and promote the English vernacular – the truly English style.

From Italian to Dutch

As architectural interests shifted forward through the sequence of seventeenth-century styles, as Board Schools and fashionable houses filtered Anglo-Dutch motifs thoughout the country, a change of terminology can be noticed, beginning in the 1880s and becoming steadily more dominant. Networks of geometric beds, box or stone edgings, clipped conifers, even pounded brick and coloured gravels, all those features which at mid-century would have identified a garden as 'Italian', gradually started to be referred to as 'Dutch'.[2] It was, admittedly, unusual for a garden which had already become familiar as 'Italian' to change its label to 'Dutch', although this happened at Lyme Park. But turn-of-the-century commentators often expressed puzzlement over earlier generations' use of the epithet 'Italian', and the revised terminology was readily applied to newly-designed gardens.[3]

Once 'Dutch' had become a term of praise, there arose a need to identify genuinely Dutch elements for emulation. Dutch architectural motifs in garden buildings were one obvious hallmark; the use of bulbs was another. The most celebrated illustration of a Renaissance Dutch garden – the frontispiece to Crispin de Pas's *Hortus Floridus* (1614) – showed a symmetrical pattern of beds of fanciful shapes, and to such shapes gardeners began to return after years of propaganda for simplicity – beginning with scrolls and proceeding to tear-drops and even the heart-shaped beds of Lady Wolseley's 'surprise gardens'.[4]

There was also a return to gravel rather than grass as the groundwork for flower-beds, but with a great increase in the proportion of gravelled to flowered area. Sedding praised the Dutch gardener for creating beauty from the most confined and unpropitious circumstances, and many Dutch gardens of the Edwardian period seemed to aim at a similar impression by having box-edged beds emerge from the midst of a dominating expanse of gravel.[5] In 1898, the *Gardeners' Chronicle* depicted bare grass panels in the new terrace garden which Simeon Marshall was laying out at Thornbridge Hall, Derbyshire; the publication of these pictures may have influenced a trend towards the appreciation of turf panels for their own sake as a further aspect of the Dutch garden.[6]

The terrace at Thornbridge also featured hedges, pyramids and standards of yew and holly, both green and golden; clipped evergreens were perhaps the most obvious association called to mind by the Dutch garden, which to many people was synonymous with topiary.[7] Well into the 1870s, the taste for topiary was largely confined to its architectural forms. Despite the general discouragement of the gardening press, however, an interest in the more figurative and emblematic forms was growing, and a few, like 'John Latouche' and Sedding, began to perceive that topiary had been an ancestral English habit, not one belatedly introduced by the Dutch.[8] Sedding indeed emerged as the first explicit champion of representational topiary:

> I have no more scruple in using the scissors upon tree or shrub, where trimness is desirable, than I have in mowing the turf of the lawn that once represented a virgin world. There is a quaint charm in the results of topiary art, in the prim imagery of evergreens, that all ages have felt. And I would even introduce *bizarreries* on the principle of not leaving all that is wild and odd to Nature outside of the garden-paling; and in the formal part of the garden my yews should take the shape of pyramids or peacocks or cocked hats or ramping lions in Lincoln-green, or any other conceit I had a mind to, which vegetable sculpture can take.[9]

Sedding's views were vigorously attacked by William Robinson, who had lost the partial tolerance for topiary he demonstrated in the 1870s.[10] In this instance, however, his fulminations were singularly ineffective, for the topiary revival caught fire during the decade after Sedding's book was published.

The garden that, more than any other, was responsible for creating a favourable image for figurative topiary was Ascott, a Rothschild estate in Buckinghamshire. George Devey began expanding an old half-timbered house in the 1870s, keeping to the style of the orginal building; the landscaping, by the firm of Veitch, left the old trees and orchard untouched. Within that framework, however, a garden for autumn and winter interest was created, which by 1890 boasted an unsurpassed collection of golden yews: 'animals and birds of almost every kind, with tables, chairs, churches, and other objects'. The eventual gem of the collection was a massive topiary sundial. Much of this topiary was placed in striking juxtaposition with naturalistic features: a fountain surrounded by scroll beds and corkscrew yews, for example, backed up against the face of a rock-garden.[11]

The popularizing of figurative topiary with the wider public was primarily the work of two nurserymen, Joseph Cheal and Herbert J. Cutbush. Of Cutbush it was said that he knew the Netherlands better than Dutch nurserymen did, and he toured the towns and rural areas in search of specimens; he bought hundreds for his nursery, and staged exhibits of topiary at the later Temple Shows and their successor, the Chelsea Flower Show, under the fetching title 'Cutbush's cut bushes'. In 1904 C. H. Curtis completed the initial stages of the revival by publishing *The Book of Topiary*, although it was not until the 1920s that a step-by-step manual appeared (Nathaniel Lloyd's *Garden Craftsmanship in Yew and Box*).[12]

From Friar Park, where a topiary garden with animal figures was planted in the 1890s, through a generation of hedged enclosures and Cotswold peacocks, to the truncated hedges of Headley Court and Mapperton Manor and the aerial hedges of Hidcote in the years immediately before the First World War, topiary spread irresistibly. Its progress was not even significantly affected by a rearguard campaign from William Robinson, the later editions of whose *English Flower Garden* were organized around Lloyd and his fellow topiarists as the new enemies to defeat.[13]

Predictably, topiary provided a rich subject matter for debates over the priorities of art and nature in the garden. Curtis, the major Edwardian publicist, was ambivalent in his attitude toward the perceived conflict. On the one hand, he endorsed the nineteenth century's characteristic elevation of art over nature:

> In the carrying out of the Topiary work, Man is striving to a very great extent against Nature, and Nature is never an easy adversary to fight. Natural beauty, therefore, must not be considered too deeply in the formal laying out of a Topiary garden . . . Hence nature must occasionally be relegated to a secondary position.

Only occasionally, however; Curtis still tried to reconcile the apparent opposites. With Levens Hall evidently in mind, he recommended combining topiary with the flower garden, using bedding plants (so as to keep herbaceous plants from contact with yews), and particularly favouring the scarlet *Lobelia cardinalis*.[14]

Other topiarists refused such compromise: while the architectural forms of topiary – hedged enclosures in particular – continued to lend themselves as settings for flower gardens, the more complex and figurative patterns often had no accompaniment beyond naked turf. Blomfield dismissed objections to the art, pointing out that it was only by adopting a narrow and partial definition of 'nature' that one could condemn topiary as 'unnatural'. Tress were no less subject to the laws of nature after clipping than before; 'it is no more unnatural to clip a yew-tree than to cut grass.'[15]

The Old English Garden

By the end of the century, young architects were looking seriously at the wide range of Renaissance forms that had succeeded Gothic during the Tudor period. As early as 1884, the architect G. Richards Julian was lecturing at the Crystal Palace School of Gardening on the 'Free Renaissance' style, a label which was coming to be accepted for the stylistic range of the sixteenth to eighteenth centuries.[16]

As can be expected from such an umbrella label, 'Free Renaissance' design offered a wide range of possibilities for the designer to select from. Discussing pierced screens and parapets, for example, Julian recommended 'any form of piercing, beautiful in itself, ... provided that it be not of distinctly Gothic or of Oriental character', and even suggested the Palladian bridge at Wilton as a model. As houses in this wider range of Renaissance styles began to appear, the question of the appropriate style of garden to accompany them became a pressing one. The problems and possibilities confronting the designer can be illustrated by three gardens, of which the most important was Hewell Grange, Worcestershire, the garden of Robert George Windsor-Clive, later the Earl of Plymouth.

Hewell Grange was rebuilt in a Jacobean style by Thomas Garner between 1884 and 1891. The site of the new house, on the advice of one of the Milners, was oriented to the presence of an existing flower-garden, already laid out symmetrically as four quarters of lawn with a few flower beds. The redevelopment of the gardens was placed in the hands of Andrew Pettigrew, the head gardener.[17] The first stage was the transformation of the flower garden, each of whose quarters was outlined with lime hedges and arches, and filled with a fantastic elaboration of box arabesques and herbaceous plants. (This garden was subsequently referred to as the 'French garden', perhaps from a general similarity to M'Intosh's illustration of a French garden.) But the most original feature at Hewell Grange was an immense series of grass terraces connected by turf steps, modelled on the 1870s hedged terraces of Rous Lench Court; construction began in 1900, and was completed in 1903. In the first years of the new century, a pair of rose gardens, a turfed forecourt, and a maze were added to complete the ensemble.[18]

90 Compton Wynyates, the topiary garden. An example of the trend towards sculptural topiary in the 1890s.

At Rhinefield, Hampshire, an Elizabethan house built by Romaine-Walker in 1889–90, grass terraces formed the termination to one side of

the parterre, looking out over one of three vistas scooped out of the New Forest – not in the baroque form of a *patte-d'oie*, but rather as three arms of a cross. At Copped Hall, Essex, the stained-glass artist, C. E. Kempe, extended the garden front in the 1890s according to the original eighteenth-century plans, and created a terrace garden which punctuated the view with garden temples in hybrid seventeenth-century style and a series of small obelisks springing from the balustrading – one of the most widely used Free Renaissance features, recommended by Richards Julian. (Kempe's earlier garden at Old Place, Lindfield, was Tudorized after his departure with yew hedges and a mount.)[19]

These were all what might be called free-style approaches, based more on horticultural or architectural individualism than on rigorous historical accuracy. But this was to change: unlike the Dutch garden, which remained comparatively free in style and did not provoke much searching of old books, the English Renaissance garden became an intense focus of historical research. The aim was to distinguish the peculiarly English aspects of Tudor and Stuart gardening, to counter the notion that English gardening had been purely derivative from continental models. The Tudor gardeners, after all, had been the contemporaries of Shakespeare and Drake, the heroes of English culture: surely, asked Sedding, they should inspire the same sort of awe?

> By all the laws of human expression, I say, these old gardens should be masterpieces. The sixteenth century, which saw the English garden formulated, was a time for grand enterprises; indeed, to this period is ascribed the making of England. These gardens, then, are the handiwork of the makers of England, and should bear the marks of heroes.[20]

In 1889 and 1890, Percy Newberry contributed a series of articles on old English gardens to the *Gardeners' Chronicle*; R. P. Brotherston was to contribute a comparable series to the *Journal of Horticulture* a decade later. In 1892 the young architect Reginald Blomfield published *The Formal Garden in England*, with illustrations by his fellow designer Inigo Thomas. They were succeeded by Alicia Amherst,[21] the first English garden historian to draw on manuscript sources, whose *History of Gardening in England* was published in 1895, followed by the writings of Inigo Triggs.[22] Attention was drawn to such gardens as Haddon Hall and Hampton Court, to the balustrading at Montacute and the fishpond at Newstead Abbey (an unornamented fishpond formed the centrepiece of the parterre at Rhinefield).[23] A detailed exposition of precedents was gradually unfolded. 'To my mind,' wrote Inigo Thomas, 'the finest corrective for insanity in design is a knowledge of what great architects have done in the past, and that is what the landscape gardener always seems to have lacked.'[24]

In the short term, *The Formal Garden in England* had the greatest impact; appearing within a year of Sedding's posthumous *Garden-craft*, it proffered advice as well as information, both books arguing forcefully for the superiority of the architect to the gardener. Blomfield's book was a brilliant piece of rhetoric based on sustained misrepresentation. Distortions and non-sequiturs abounded; anything of which Blomfield disapproved was attributed to landscape gardeners rather than architects, from coloured-gravel parterres to a neglect of lawns; his bibliography of gardening

91 Hewell Grange, the 'French garden'. A herbaceous parterre designed in the early 1890s by Andrew Pettigrew to accompany a neo-Jacobean house.

revealed an ignorance or a suppression of the nineteenth-century literature.[25] His enthusiasms ran ahead of his historical knowledge: he paid homage to Arley Hall and Penshurst as the true tradition of modern times, but was taken in by the spurious antiquity of Packwood, Hatfield, and Hardwick.[26] In a similar way Inigo Thomas denounced most nineteenth-century gardens as 'wilderness'. On simple grounds of accuracy, both Blomfield and Thomas were easy marks for William Robinson, who scornfully pointed out that the most celebrated gardens of the century had been formal, from the Royal Horticultural Society's garden to Shrubland Park: 'The only "wilderness" to be seen in these places is a stone out of place.'[27]

Nonetheless, the term 'formal garden' was quickly established as a term to replace the 'geometric garden' of mid-century, but bearing the implication of something more restrained, more historically accurate. The model examples of the genre were provided by Inigo Thomas (Broderick Thomas's nephew). In 1891 he began the restoration of the garden at Athelhampton, Dorset – a project that was eventually to last for thirty years. Here he created a series of compartments, each with its own character; the most notable features were a series of great pyramidal yews, and a long fishpond whose architectural details were modelled on the roof of the hall.[28] An Edwardian garden which may reasonably be attributed to Thomas, Parnham House, also in Dorset, deployed its pyramidal yews in a more open pattern, and used receding levels of terracing instead of enclosures, to look out on a wider prospect. Elaborate hollows were built into the terrace extension to accommodate existing trees without burying their trunks.[29]

Governing Thomas's work was a familiarity with the gardens, such as Montacute (on which some of the details of Parnham were based), which he had illustrated for Blomfield. Simplicity and restraint were among its most obvious qualities, and precisely those which Blomfield had held up as characteristic of the English, as opposed to the continental, garden. Marble statuary was Italian (leadwork was more suited to England), parterres were French, topiary Dutch: 'Those who attack the old English formal garden do not take the trouble to master its very considerable difference from the continental gardens of the same period.' Remove these un-English elements, and what is left is the formal framework: 'a place of retirement and seclusion', an architectural setting outdoors.[30]

Despite the emphasis placed by Blomfield and Thomas on architectural precedent, Bacon's essay on gardens continued to dominate the general notion of the old English garden as it had done for most of the century.[31] But after a generation of being held up as a corrective against the excesses of the High Victorians, Bacon's essay began to attract criticism in the 1890s. George Gordon mounted an attack in 1898:

> But what are the facts? . . . [Bacon may reject knots but] suggests that there should be arches in the hedge with a turret over every arch with a cage for birds, and 'over every space between the arches some other little figure with broad plates of round coloured glass, gilt, for the sun to play upon.' He further advises that the fountain be 'embellished with coloured glass and such things of lustre.' . . . It will thus be seen that whatever may have been the merits of the Tudor gardens they had their defects, and were certainly not superior to those of the Victorian era, as some writers would fain have us believe.[32]

Another commentator noted that 'if carpet-bedding had been invented at that time, it would have found favour'.[33] Blomfield, however, had already found an alternative model in William Lawson, whose *New Orchard and Garden* of 1632 offered more the sort of simplicity and restraint that he required.[34] The recommendation of Lawson brought with it a new emphasis on trelliswork for architectural effect in the flower garden, and its use was promoted by architects like John Belcher.[35]

The search for models was nowhere carried further, or more accurately, than in Sir Frank Crisp's garden at Friar Park, where, in addition to its rock and Japanese gardens, there developed a series of period gardens. By 1910 there were a Dutch garden (scroll beds with dwarf shrubs and brick borders); a topiary and sundial garden based on the plan of the Labyrinth of Versailles; a garden based on details from the *Roman de la Rose*; a knot garden based on the initials of Crisp and his wife; a herb garden and 'nosegaie' garden, the planting choice based on sixteenth-century sources; and an Elizabethan garden based on an illustration from the *Gardeners Labyrinth* of 'Didymus Mountaine', featuring trelliswork, raised beds,

92 Hewell Grange, the grass steps, constructed in 1900–1903 to connect a series of terraces.

and a planting style based on Crispin de Pas.

Within a few years additional gardens had been added, based largely on mediaeval and Renaissance illustrations, which Crisp reproduced in his guidebook so the visitor could judge his re-creations: a wattle garden, a Boccaccio garden, a castle garden, and a Mary garden based on plants named after the Virgin Mary.[36] Interest was growing in the antiquarian folklore of plants, and one fringe of the Anglo-Catholic movement was attempting to revive mediaeval religious associations of flowers; Crisp's Mary garden was a rare (and tongue-in-cheek) application of this interest to the garden. The Countess of Warwick tried to create a similar emblematic border at Easton Lodge, but failed to distinguish between ancient folk meanings and the 'Language of Flowers' popular in the early nineteenth century.[37]

The major theorists of the old English garden stressed the opposition between its architectural qualities and the horticulture of the day. This opposition was to emerge as a public issue with the restoration of Hampton Court, where J. A. Gardiner, curator from 1897 to 1907, had tried to bring the gardens into 'conformity with wild nature' and where the carpet beds had continued a popular attraction. At the outbreak of the great war, the beds were grassed over; but while public agitation for their renewal began after the armistice, the formalist Avray Tipping wrote in *Country Life* that their removal had been an improvement and urged more yew planting. A compromise scheme was devised by a committee of architects and horticulturists: a reduced number of beds was allowed, but the central and radial walks were to be restored to their period standard, reinstating many lost yews. Ernest Law later augmented the historical effect by laying out an 'Elizabethan' knot garden.[38]

The Horticultural Vernacular

The primary emphasis of Blomfield, Thomas, and their associates was on the architectural features of the garden; most of their advice on horticultural planning was negative – the avoidance of features obviously modern. Meanwhile, however, the cult of the old-fashioned flowers grew apace, as horticulturists pursued their own quest for a vernacular style of gardening. The 1880s saw the launching of Peter Barr's campaign to recover all the old daffodils described by Parkinson and Gerard, which he could not believe had died out, and the foundation by Mrs Ewing of the Parkinson Society, dedicated to the recovery of vanishing garden flowers. The floral cottage garden had by now become so well-established that the younger generation began uncritically to swallow spurious claims for its antiquity. Inigo Thomas directed architects to the cottage garden for an example of vernacular form; Robinson and Jekyll directed gardeners there for examples of vernacular planting, thus ensuring that the mixed style of the 1840s and 1850s was adopted by the twentieth century as the heritage of unmeasured antiquity.[39]

Apart from cottage gardens, the major source drawn on for horticultural vernacularism was the works of Shakespeare. H. N. Ellacombe's *Plant-lore and Garden-craft of Shakespeare* went through three editions in the last quarter of the century, and was followed by a small flood of books and articles about Shakespeare's flowers.[40] As interest in Shakespeare the gardener grew, the use of the flowers named in his plays to dictate the planting of the garden had a striking vogue. The Countess of Warwick planted a 'Shakespeare border' at Easton Lodge, which inspired Walter Crane's whimsical little book *Flowers from Shakespeare's Garden*. After this was publicized, similar Shakespeare borders multiplied, although at The Pleasuance, Overstrand, Lady Battersea generalized the concept into a 'Tudor' border.[41]

In 1892 the London County Council converted the Brockwell estate at Herne Hill into a public park. Instead of demolishing the old walled kitchen garden, Colonel Sexby retained it as a geometric garden, planted with all the flowers mentioned in Shakespeare's plays. (Alicia Amherst criticized it for misleadingly containing modern plants as well.) It proved unexpectedly popular, and Sexby included 'old-fashioned' gardens in all his schemes after that, ranging from a pergola and bowling green in Ruskin Park to rusticwork in Peckham Rye Park (which latter was known in his honour as the Sexby garden).[42] During the Edwardian period municipal parks elsewhere began to feature old-fashioned gardens, and eventually even Stratford-upon-Avon replaced the 1860s informal pleasure ground at New Place with a Shakespeare garden: in 1920 Ernest Law laid it out in an Elizabethan style, planted with old-fashioned flowers, and based on models from Bacon, Lawson, and 'Didymus Mountaine'.[43]

93 Parnham House, the terrace garden. This Edwardian formal garden, probably the work of Inigo Thomas, used architectural motifs based on those of Montacute.

'Shakespeare' gardening extended the old-fashioned garden of the 1870s into the public domain, but a more genuinely novel form of horticultural revivalism was to emerge at the same time, in the form of the herb garden.

The traditions of herbalism had increasingly been attacked by the medical profession since Paracelsus in the sixteenth century, but it was not until the nineteenth, and the rapid development of experimental chemistry and bacteriology, that herbalism had finally been pushed to the rural fringes of society. No sooner had educated opinion declared the tradition dead than interest in it began to revive. An antiquarian interest in herbalism had found expression in Robert Southey's *The Doctor* in the 1830s, although in the year of Southey's death the *Gardeners' Chronicle* could reply to a correspondent, 'We do not know what you mean by a Herbal. The term is disused.'[44] By the 1890s, researches into sixteenth- and seventeenth-century horticultural literature were focussing attention on the medicinal basis of the Tudor garden. The emphatic reintroduction of herb beds into the kitchen garden can be dated at least from Thomas Baines's advocacy in the 1870s, and was being advocated by writers like Gertrude Jekyll and Hugh Maule at the turn of the century; there was a herb garden at The Flagstaff, Colwyn Bay, a Mawson garden of 1900.[45]

The most important step in the herb garden revival came with Broughton Castle, Oxfordshire, laid out just after the turn of the century. Here the herb garden was no longer a subordinate part of the kitchen garden, but an ornamental unit in its own right, with the words 'Ye herbe garden' spelled out in clipped santolina at its entrance. Clipped herbs could thus carry a double meaning: on the one hand carrying intrinsic associations of the old-fashioned garden (there was a topiary sundial elsewhere in the garden), their use for lettering meant that they could function as the revivalist's alternative to emblematic carpet-bedding. This dual utility helps to explain the enthusiasm with which herb gardening was taken up in the early years of the century.[46]

In 1907, Jekyll produced a plan for a geometric herb garden for Knebworth, which however was not carried out until recently. Apart from their use in clipped patterns, the primary mode of grouping herbs until the mid-century was in informal borders – Jekyllian outlines with a different style of planting. Despite the example of Friar Park, the widespread attempt to base the design, as well as the plant selection, of herb gardens on Tudor precedents had to wait for the 1920s and the work of Eleanour Sinclair Rohde; but once established, it became one of the dominant modes of British gardening up to the present day.[47]

Arts and Crafts

Of all the ways of searching for a vernacular style, the most widespread (because most commonly used for smaller gardens) were those which gained the label of 'arts and crafts', which looked to surviving rural traditions rather than to histories.[48] In architecture, the label implied a study of vernacular building techniques and materials. Local brick and stone; thatch or slates, depending on locality; dry-stone walls in Yorkshire, rubble walls in East Anglia, roughcast in Scotland – each region had its own traditions, and this variety caught the imaginations of young architects who had been raised on Pugin, Ruskin and Morris, and learned 'the Gothic principles of evolving our homes out of local conditions and requirements'.[49] The ideal was to make the house look of a piece with the older buildings of its area, even to the extent of copying the textures of age-worn materials. Despite the warning of Inigo Thomas that Jacobean gardens 'were not originally picturesque and old, but bright and new',[50] a speedy patina of age was a merit in the eyes of many young designers.

In the garden, the first signs of the new tendency can be seen in the revival of interest in rusticwork. Rustic bridges and arbours began to multiply from the 1860s, in the work of architects like Edward Boardman and gardeners like William Barron; J. Caven Fox exhibited rustic buildings in the Royal Horticultural Society's garden in 1874; bridges, arbours, trelliswork, and pergolas in unbarked wood multiplied throughout the public parks.[51] Eventually authorities like Thomas Mawson rebelled anew against rusticwork as inauthentic – a falsely generalized rather than a regional style – but it foreshadowed their interest in unsophisticated building techniques that was to come.[52]

Mawson can serve usefully as a guide to the new interests. In his *Art and Craft of Garden Making* (1900), he drew attention to vernacular styles of fencing, praised cobbled paths over the smooth technology of asphalt and cement, and condemned cast-iron furniture, urging instead the use of local carpenters and antique models.[53] There eventually arose an ambiguity

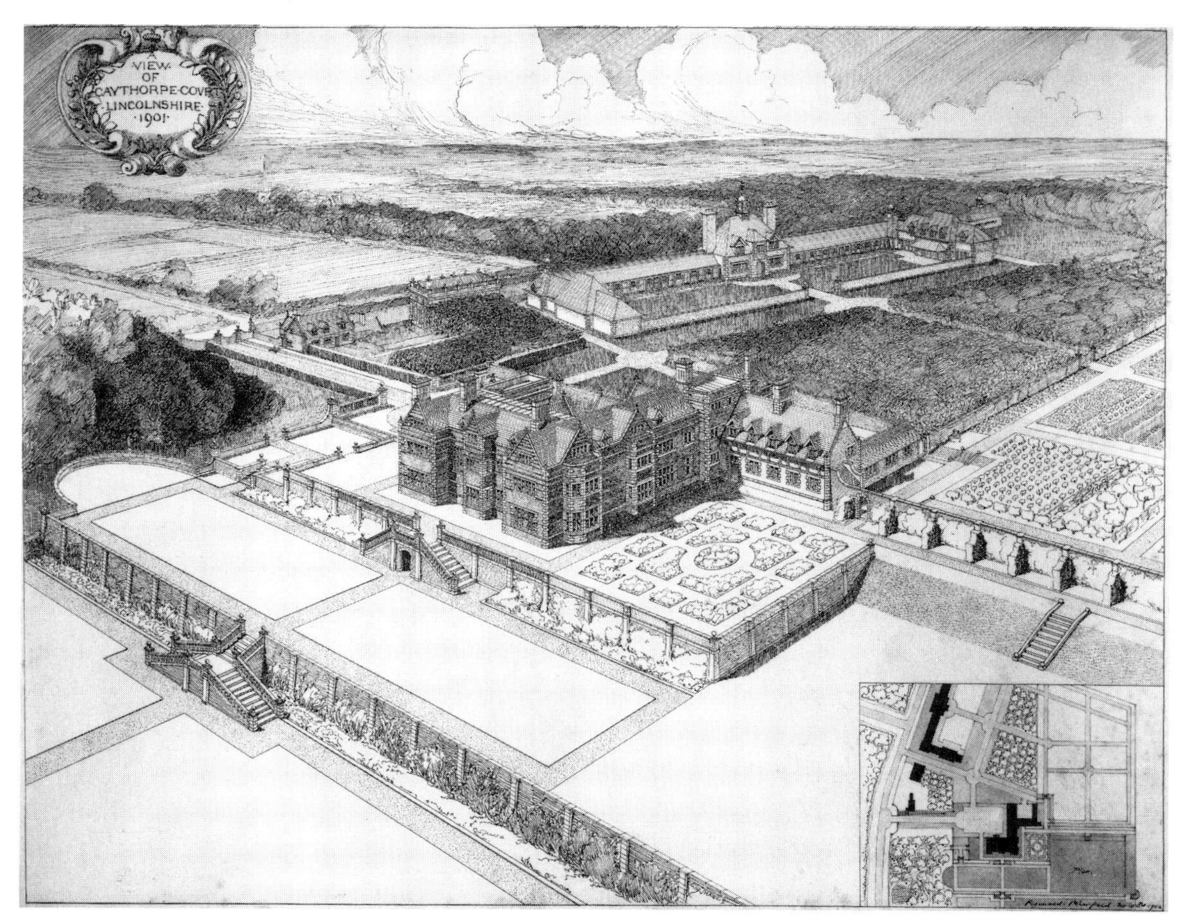

94 Caythorpe Court, Lincolnshire. A garden plan of 1901 by Reginald Blomfield, showing his ideal of the English Renaissance garden, free from continental accretions.

out of such vernacularism, though. The use of compacted earths for building fascinated many in the arts-and-crafts movement: Ruskin's last protégé, Detmar Blow, studied cottage building from sun-dried mud in Wiltshire; Lutyens used compressed chalk to build Marsh Court; between wattle-and-daub and concrete no fine distinction was drawn. Many designers, Mawson included, turned progressively to the use of artificial composition stone, and as they did so their works lost their vernacular appearance.[54]

Mawson had begun his career in Westmorland in the late 1880s. He acknowledged the influence of Repton and Kemp, and his early designs set formal terraces amidst informal pleasure ground very much in Kemp's early manner – differing basically in his use of the Free Renaissance style for detailing. During the 1890s, however, his work developed a strong axial tendency, probably influenced by Barron, and sequences of terraces and compartments advanced on the landscape.[55] This development reached its most dramatic point in 1898 at Broadleys, where the architect C. F. A. Voysey perched a low-slung house on the hillside looking down over Windermere, and Mawson laid out the slope in a series of narrow descending terraces giving way to a rhododendron-covered bank.[56] Mawson coined the term 'landscape architect' to describe himself, and held throughout his career that an English vernacular must be rooted in an awareness of the landscape, that building should be integrated within the wider

95 Broughton Castle, the herb garden. The revivalist's alternative to carpet bedding: a text in clipped santolina.

context of planting.[57]

The alternative tradition which fed into the arts-and-crafts movement was that of the old-fashioned garden, enclosed and independent from the broader landscape. A large number of architects were, by the 1890s, designing gardens in this manner to accompany their houses; some of them had been trained in the offices of Norman Shaw, George Devey, or Ernest George; many of them were members of the Art Workers' Guild, which had been founded in 1884 to try to reunite architecture with the other arts. Edwin Lutyens, Robert Lorimer, E. S. Prior, Ernest Newton, Guy Dawber, Detmar Blow, Charles Mallows, Weir Schulz, Halsey Ricardo, Arnold Mitchell and Baillie Scott were among those who proуced distinguished garden designs; books such as Mawson's *Art and Craft of Garden Making* and Jekyll and Weaver's *Gardens for Small Country Houses* served as anthologies of their work. The vernacular building style provided the context against which their gardens were to be seen; the relation of

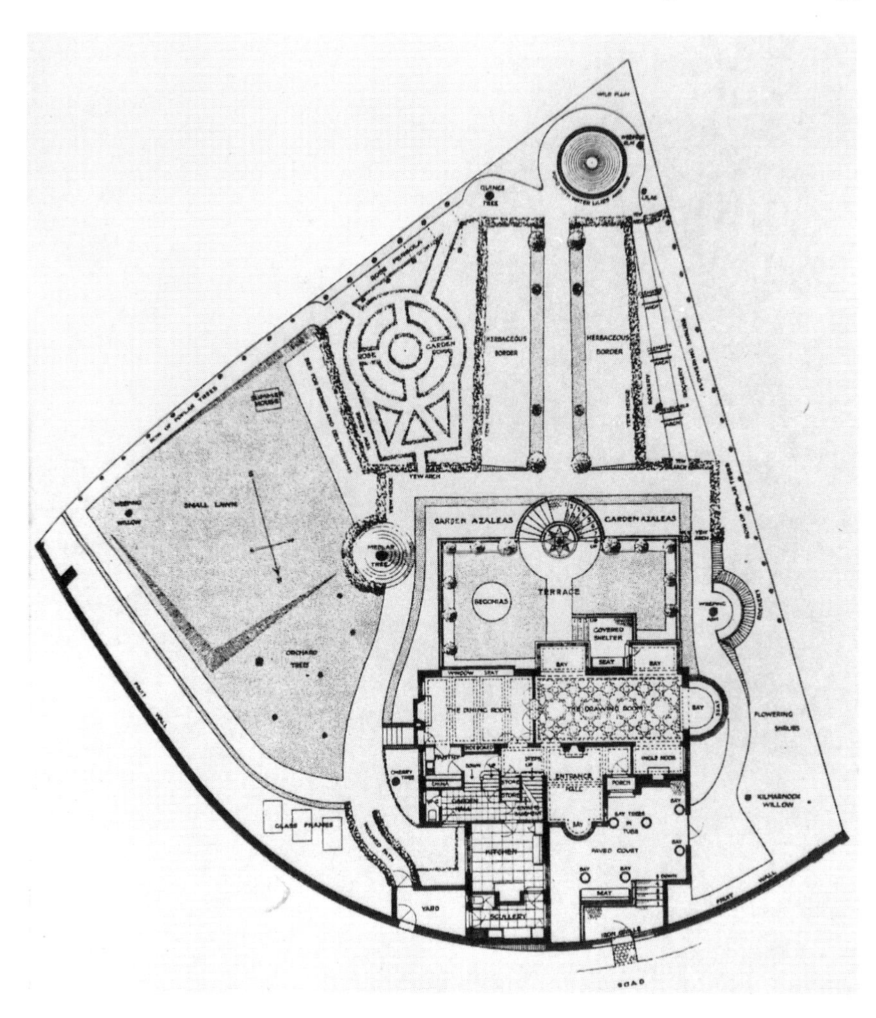

96 The Orchard, Harrow, plan for the garden. The garden of the architect Arnold Mitchell, a model of the arts-and-crafts manner adapted to a small suburban site.

the house to the garden was more important than that of the garden to the landscape. House and garden were constructed from the same materials; garden buildings often reflected the roofs or other details of the house; pergolas or covered walks continued the plan of the house into the garden as a structural feature.[58]

Of all these architects, the one who stood most prominently as a rival to Mawson was Edwin Lutyens.[59] With his first important garden, Woodside, Buckinghamshire (1893), many of his stylistic trademarks were already apparent: brick paving, a flat surface of water, a strong axial plan, geometrical patterns using different levels. The centrepiece of the garden was a circular pond within an octagonal pergola, around which were grouped octagonal beds with stone edgings. Ironically, much of his early fame was based on Munstead Wood, which he built for Gertrude Jekyll, for its informal setting was mostly of her design; Lutyens' gardens tended more toward geometrical intricacy, expressed not only in details like circular steps but, in gardens like Grey Walls, Hestercombe, and Ammerdown, a play with diagonal axes as the basis for the garden's organization.

As his career developed, Lutyens's historical range broadened; in 1897–

97 Rivernook, near Staines. Thomas Mawson's garden for a house by Thomas Collcutt, *c.* 1890: a terrace imposed on grounds formerly in 'the naturalesque or landscape style', and decorated with perennial beds and clipped yews and junipers.

98 he was even able to mimic Nesfield's style in a parterre planned for Eaton Hall (where Nesfield's garden was still intact).[60] Continuing into the garden Devey's practice of building into a house the apparent evidence of a long history of change, he refused to be tied too closely by the style of any particular period; Avray Tipping wrote admiringly of Hestercombe:

> Yet there is no dull subservience, no mere copying. The whole realm of formal gardening, Italian, French and English, has been industriously and intelligently surveyed. But that having been understood and absorbed, the designer of the Hestercombe gardens has then thought for himself. He has weighed the full possibilities of the site, the peculiar character of the local materials, the manifold modes of modern gardening, the particular traits of modern life ... It is the work of a particular man in a particular place.[61]

The ethos of the arts-and-crafts movement lay in its hopes of reuniting the arts, but this aspiration emerged in two distinct forms: on the one hand, attempts to restore the supposed community of the crafts and return the craftsman to his rightful position; on the other hand, architects who tried themselves to master all the relevant crafts, and impose one man's vision on every detail of the house from chimneys to handrails. In neither of these approaches did the gardener as craftsman figure significantly. Lutyens studied vernacular horticultural traditions as well as building ones, exemplified in his use of pleached limes at Knebworth,[62] but most of his gardens came equipped with detailed planting schemes by Gertrude Jekyll that left no function to the gardener other than obedience. And Lutyens

98 Woodside, pergola in pond court. Lutyens's first important garden, 1893, already showing a complex pattern of interlocking architectural beds and the use of a flat surface of water.

was by no means the only architect of the movement to avail himself of her plans, often in later years drawn up for correspondents without ever visiting the site.

The concept of nature was deeply ambiguous in arts-and-crafts rhetoric. In architectural terms, 'natural' could stand as an agreed synonym for 'vernacular', the natural house being one that blended indistinguishably into the pattern of existing building; or it could refer to the use of stylized patterns derived from the natural world for interior decoration, in the work of Baillie Scott and others;[63] or it could be carried further, as with E. S. Prior, to amalgamate the textures of stone and wood and the marks of the craftsman's tools thereon into an assertion of harmony between man and nature.[64] But while any of these usages could be comfortably applied to garden architecture, their application to planting created problems. The *Gardeners' Chronicle* questioned the aesthetic standards of one like Mawson, who swallowed topiary but gagged at the monkey-puzzle as a 'freak of nature'.[65] For most designers, the problem was solved by adopting the cottage garden as a model of vernacular planning and planting at once; its claims to antiquity were promoted by such diverse figures as Sedding, Mawson, Jekyll and Inigo Thomas.[66]

The arts-and-crafts aesthetic grew steadily stronger throughout the Edwardian period. Mawson's *Art and Craft of Garden Making* went through four editions before the war; *Country Life* gave great publicity to the movement, and to Lutyens in particular; Baillie Scott's trelliswork and garden furniture designs were produced commercially by John P. White and Company. As the movement progressed, it diversified. In one direction lay the pursuit of a purer eighteenth-century style; Mawson and Lutyens led in another direction toward a style of abstract monumentalism, and the 'great game' of classicism.[67]

The Italian Garden Reinterpreted

As the older meaning of the Italian garden modulated into Dutch, a blank was left waiting to be filled. What indeed was the Italian garden when the Victorian misconception had been drained away? The early years of the twentieth century saw a variety of new conceptions put forward.

James Hudson was primarily associated with the Japanese garden, but it should not be forgotten that he derived his inspiration for it not from direct experience of Japan, but from a 'Japanese' garden near Lake Como. Among the Italian lakes he found several gardens to approve: not Isola Bella, where the architecture was too obstrusive, but Bellaggio and the Villa Carlotta, whose green terraces and comparative lack of stonework made them acceptable models for England. It is difficult to say how much influence Hudson's advocacy may have had on gardens avowedly Italian, but his recommendations for the use of tubbed plants on terraces – *Agapanthus*, scented pelargoniums, sweet bay, *Phormium tenax* – met with an encouraging response.[68]

The name 'Italian garden' could also be used, as at Sledmere in 1911, for what was little more than a paved terrace dotted with sculptures after the antique. Such an austerity of approach seems to have spelled 'Italian' to many Edwardians: when Lutyens built the gaunt terrace at Nashdom, Buckinghamshire (1909), Lawrence Weaver, praising the 'masculine disposition' of the design, responded by invoking 'Italian examples, such as the great Roman palaces' as models. Analogous to this in some respects was Cathays Park, Cardiff, laid out by W. Harpur, the borough engineer, between 1904 and 1909: a green rectangle, divided by avenues, flat and unornamented, around which were built those showpieces of Edwardian baroque, the Welsh government offices. Young architects came to be overwhelmed by the buildings, and carried back with them the memory of the most rigidly geometrical park yet created in Britain.[69]

This enthusiasm for austerity was not arbitrary. An immediate justification for it lay in the perceived contrast between the Victorian garden, blazing with the colours of exotic flowers, and its Italian prototypes, dependent on design alone, their only colours green and white. (In fact, the Victorians had followed better than they knew, for seventeenth-century Italian gardens had been ornamented with the exotics of the day – the tulips, irises and fritillaries being imported from Constantinople.) To concentrate rigorously on those design features that had survived to be studied was therefore a way of correcting the errors of one's forebears, and a redirection of the garden away from the Victorian concern with colour planning in favour of the values of form.

An international interest in the gardens of the Italian Renaissance began in the 1880s with Tuckermann's *Gartenkunst der Italianischen Renaissance-*

99 Iford Manor, ascending the terraces from the lily pond. Harold Peto designed his garden in a Renaissance style as a setting for a collection of antiquities.

Zeit, and continued with historical works by Edith Wharton and Inigo Triggs, and impressionistic ones by Vernon Lee and Sir George Sitwell.[70] For continental designers, the exploration of the Italian heritage was a rediscovery of their common past; much of Harold Peto's work was carried out in the south of France. Already by 1910 an English designer, Cecil Pinsent, had become so proficient at the Italian manner that he was launched on a career of making imitation-Renaissance gardens in Italy itself.[71]

Harold Peto's gardens were both the most proficient examples of the new architecturally authentic Italian garden, and the culmination of the encyclopaedic tradition inaugurated by Biddulph Grange. Easton Lodge, which he remodelled for the Countess of Warwick, combined American, Japanese, and Italian gardens and a bosquet on continental models; the Italian garden was a paved terrace with an oval balustraded lily pond.[72] In his own garden at Iford Manor, Wiltshire, which he bought in 1899, he created an outdoor museum of European history on a hillside site laid out in terraces. Groupings of Etruscan, Greek, and Roman remains along the north walk; a Romanesque arcade; Byzantine objects from early Venetian palaces on the east walk; remains of Gothic Italy along the south walk, including a pair of fourteenth-century red marble lions – all culminated in a section devoted to artefacts of the Renaissance.[73]

A parallel development took place at Hever Castle in Kent. The castle was bought in 1903 by the American millionaire William Waldorf Astor, who had it restored, and a Tudor-style village created alongside, by Frank Loughborough Pearson; the gardens were laid out by the firm of Cheal's of Crawley over a four-year period. The first stage was to recreate gardens suitable for Anne Boleyn, who had once lived there; between the inner and outer moats Joseph Cheal, an expert on topiary, created a series of compartments within yew hedges, including a maze and a set of topiary chessmen based on Tudor models. Beyond the outer moat, the ground was laid out as an Italian garden, a long rectangle of lawns extending to a loggia overlooking a 35-acre lake dredged out of boggy ground; this was studded with antiquities brought back by Astor from Italy (he had also bought the balustrade of the Villa Borghese and installed it at Cliveden). Along one wall Pearson and Cheal, who shared Astor's enthusiasm for Italian gardens,[74] created a gallery modelled on the avenue of fountains at the Villa d'Este, the wall faced with boulders, divided into sections by stone buttresses, and planted with shade-tolerant plants; on the opposite side ran the 'Pompeiian Wall', its bay crammed with statues and fragments of buildings, planted to suggest that vegetation was taking over.[75]

In its scale, its dramatic use of a flat site, its loggia and lake, Hever Castle was an exact counterpart to Trentham – the Edwardian answer to Barry. But in the intervening years, the historical assumptions that underlay Trentham had broken down; no longer could it be confidently assumed that the authentic English style was a derivative of the Italian. And so at Hever the two antecedents were separated, the Italian garden lying perpendicular to an old English garden of more studied accuracy, as though to signal the parting of the ways.

Towards a Neo-Georgian Style

At the close of the nineteenth century, architecture seemed to be engaged on the enterprise of recapitulating its past: the country houses of the younger architects seemed to show a straightforward and predictable chronological progression in style, from the Elizabethan and Jacobean houses of Ernest George, to the late-seventeenth-century 'Wrennaissance' style of Reginald Blomfield, to early eighteenth-century models in the work of Mervyn Macartney.

Several forces were converging on Neo-Georgian as the coming style. An interest in the eighteenth-century arts had been growing steadily since Thackeray; at the same time, some arts-and-crafts architects were coming to accept Georgian houses as part of the English vernacular, esteeming them for their lack of outward display; the ideal Georgian house, even more than the ideal arts-and-crafts house, sat quietly in the landscape without calling attention to itself. The first showpiece of the Georgian revival was provided by Norman Shaw in 1894 with the completion of Bryanston, Dorset; but its departure from the Victorian tradition of asymmetricality was not widely followed for several years. Indeed, it was not until after the First World War that 'Neo-Georgian' was widely adopted as a stylistic label.[76]

The question now arose, what sort of garden should accompany a Neo-Georgian house? The earliest attempts simply repeated the existing practice of the arts-and-crafts movement. Lutyens accompanied his Neo-Georgian extension to Folly Farm with one of his typical geometric gardens. At Houndsell Place, built immediatedly before the great war, the young architect Alwyn Ball drew up plans for an elaborate layout of topiary alleys, but these were never carried out.[77]

But those more seriously dedicated to Neo-Georgian looked for something less flamboyant, something partaking of the symmetrical solidity of the style. Mervyn Macartney attempted to provide guidance by publishing an anthology of selected plates from Kip, Knyff, and Badeslade, contending that these early eighteenth-century views showed how the gardens of that period 'carried out the contentions of some modern architects as to the necessary relation of the house to its surroundings'.[78] In particular he emphasized symmetry of design, both in house and garden. Two additional points which emerged from the illustrations were the scale of such gardens – the way in which the compartments were not clustered around the house, but spread out in additive progression across the landscape – and the impression of vista that they gave. The geometric enclosures seemed not to be visually self-contained, in the manner of the old-fashiond garden of the 1870s, but to provide a much greater openness of prospect. The design of Edward White's Moreton Paddox, carried out immediately before the First World War – a symmetrical pair of parterres immediately before the house, each sub-divided by low interrupted hedges – was probably inspired by illustrations such as that of Westbury Court.[79]

As the Edwardian period gave way to a new Georgian age, many architects foreswore the ostentatious brilliance of a Lutyens and observed a symmetrical restraint in their parterres; and a new fascination with open prospect settled in to characterize the advanced gardening. In 1909, for example, Reginald Blomfield laid out new gardens for Mellerstain, an Adam house in Berwickshire; from the base of the terraces a long channel of lawn, separated from the surrounding plantations by hedges, swept down the hillside to the lake. This lake had been in the form of a Dutch canal, but Blomfield enlarged it and reduced the regularity of its outline; only the end nearest the house retained its formal shape, around which the hedges curved in a crescent – a solution reminiscent of Nesfield's in the pond at Kew, and one which showed an interesting advance over the rigid formalism of Blomfield's most famous book.[80]

Open prospect was one thing, but it was as yet too early to carry it to the extremes of the original Georgian period. When Lutyens was confronted by a late eighteenth-century house like Wyatt's Ammerdown, he had no hesitation about designing a formal garden to complement it, full of topiary hedges. The idea of accompanying an eighteenth-century house with an eighteenth-century landscape park was too radical a break with the Victorian tradition. Yet, a model for such an endeavour had already been provided, with the first prominent example of the Neo-Georgian style.

Norman Shaw was not allowed to design a garden to accompany Bryanston House; most of the landscaping work devolved on the head gardener, and consisted of an attempt to graft the new work seamlessly onto the old. The new house was perched on high ground, the level having been artificially raised up to ten feet in places, and an immense labour of planting and transplanting was required to blend the newly banked areas with the existing pleasure-ground. The formal basis for the house was restricted to a paved terrace, connected by a double staircase to a further reduced terrace and pool. Beyond that, the grass slopes extended informally, dotted with specimen trees and shrubberies.[81] Bryanston thus accidentally set a precedent for informal landscape as a setting for a Neo-Georgian house, and helped to influence a new appreciation of the eighteenth-century landscape park.

In the short term, however, a greater impact was probably made by the golf course. It was not until the Edwardian period that courses began to appear in large numbers in England; their major elements were broad expanses of lawn, and clumps or belts of trees to separate fairways – exactly the features commonly associated with the eighteenth-century landscape park. 'Capability' Brown was, in fact, a good designer of golf courses,[82] and a Brown park like Edgbaston Hall required little alteration to turn it into a course between the wars. The presence of such large-scale informal trees-and-turf parks on the outskirts of most towns and cities by the 1920s helped to create an atmosphere in which the reputation of Brown, despised by most architects as recently as the First World War, could once again rise to a position of respect and eminence.

And thus, with an exquisite irony, the Victorian garden completed its circular progress. The rebellion against the eighteenth-century landscape park at the beginning of the nineteenth century had resulted in attempts to bring back the gardening styles of the past; and after a century of experiments in this historical revivalism, the movement ended by resurrecting the very style it had begun by reacting against.

100 Mellerstain, proposal for the gardens. Reginald Blomfield laid out the terrace garden and channel of lawn in 1909.

MELLERSTAIN
Col. Lord Binning CB
BIRDS EYE VIEW
OF NEW GARDENS from HOUSE to CANAL
Reginald Blomfield ARA Architect.
invenit 1910.

Acknowledgements

When I first began researching the history of Victorian gardens, there was a general consensus that the Victorian period was the nadir of British gardening. The force that helped to change this attitude was the Victoria and Albert Museum's exhibition, 'The Garden', in 1979; since then interest in the period has been growing steadily. If I am now able to argue that it was in fact the golden age of British gardening, this is in large part because I have been able to share in the researches of many people over the last decade or so.

The first major source of accurate information about Victorian gardens was the National Trust, as a result of its efforts to restore gardens of the period. I should like especially to thank its garden advisers, past and present: Graham Thomas, Paul Miles, and John Sales.

I should like to thank also my colleagues in the Victorian Society, especially Jill Allibone, Nick Antram, Roderick Gradidge, Hermione Hobhouse, Peter Howell, Paul Joyce, John Maddison, Hugh Meller, and Teresa Sladen; and my colleagues on the Council of the Garden History Society, above all Mavis Batey, Peter Goodchild, John Harvey, Peter Hayden, David Jacques, and the late Kenneth Lemmon. This book is dedicated to his memory.

Many additional people have provided information and assistance; I am particularly grateful to those who have allowed me to visit their gardens or investigate their archives. Some of these gardens I have been unable to bring into this book; I apologize to the owners concerned. In some cases I have used the notes to acknowledge help with information about particular people or estates. Here may I briefly acknowledge the following: Phillada Ballard, Krisia Bilikowski, Marcus Binney, Patrick Bowe, Mike Calnan, Susan Campbell, Charles Carus, Merrick Denton-Thompson, Susan Denyer, Edward Diestelkamp, Kate and Duncan Donald, Gilly Drummond, Sally Festing, Patrick Goode, Richard Gorer, John Harris, Sandra Higgins, Toni Huberman, John Kenworthy-Browne, Audrey le Lievre, Dodie and Standish Masterman, Graeme Moore, Joan Morgan, Stefan Muthesius, Charles Nelson, Bryony and Vic Nierop-Reading, David and Susan Reid, Anne Scott-James, Richard Simpson, Penny Smith, D. G. C. Tudor, and Tony Venison.

I owe considerable debts to Peter Stageman and Barbara Collecott, my colleagues, past and present, at the Lindley Library. All members of my family have contributed in various ways: my mother, by giving continued support and assistance; my wife, Frances Clegg, by helping with photography and transport; my son David, by explaining the mysteries of the word processor; and Rega, by lying on my paperwork and dangling his tail in front of the VDU.

The author and publisher acknowledge with thanks permission from the following to reproduce illustrations (roman numerals denote colour illustrations). British Architectural Library: 3, 26, 27, 85, 94, 100; His Grace the Duke of Buccleuch and Queensberry: Ib, 25; Cardiff City Council: 66; Christie's Fine Art Services: V; Dr Frances Clegg: 75; *Country Life:* 64, 65, 72, 91, 98, 99; Hull City Museums and Art Galleries: 78; London Library: 5; Mrs Robert Maxwell: 45; Norfolk Record Office: 57, 81; Publisher's collection: 7, 11, 24, 54, 90, 93; Royal Commission on the Historical Monuments of England: 73, 76, 95; Royal Horticultural Society, Lindley Library: front and back covers, Ia, Ic–d, III, IV, VII, X–XII, 1, 2, 4, 6, 8, 9, 12, 13, 16–19, 28–31, 34–37, 40–44, 49–52, 55, 58–61, 63, 67–69, 74, 77, 79, 80, 82–84, 86, 88, 89, 96; The Cadland Trustees: VI; Victoria and Albert Museum: 46.

Author's collection: II, VIII, IX, 10, 14, 15, 20–23, 32, 33, 38, 39, 47, 48, 53, 56, 62, 70, 71, 87, 97.

List of Illustrations

Colour
Front cover: Elvaston Castle, lake and rockworks (RHS)
Back cover: Arley Hall, the herbaceous borders (RHS)
Between pp. 120 and 121
I a Colour scheme by John Caie (RHS)
b Colour scheme for Drumlanrig Castle (His Grace the Duke of Buccleuch)
c Colour scheme by Gardner Wilkinson (RHS)
d Spring bedding colour scheme for Cliveden (RHS)
II Baron Hill, the topiary garden (author)
III Belvoir Castle, spring bedding (RHS)
IV Bowood, the terrace garden (RHS)
V Atkinson Grimshaw, 'In the Pleasaunce' (Christie's International)
VI Drummond Castle, the terrace garden (The Cadland Trustees)
VII Enville Hall, the great fountain (RHS)
VIII Chatsworth, the rock garden (author)
IX Cannon Hill Park, Birmingham, the floral crown (author)
X Trentham, the Italian garden (RHS)
XI Shrubland Park, the fountain garden (RHS)
XII The Willows, Ashton-on-Ribble (RHS)

Black-and-white

1 The ideal of the English landscape garden (RHS)
2 The counter-ideal: proposals for the revival of Renaissance formality (RHS)
3 Kiddington Hall: J. C. Loudon's plan for a rosarium (British Architectural Library)
4 William Barron transplanting the Buckfast Abbey yew (RHS)
5 Barncluith, the formal garden (London Library)
6 Hendon Rectory (RHS)
7 Chatsworth: Paxton's Great Stove (Publisher's collection)
8 Woolverstone Park, view in the conservatory (RHS)
9 Redleaf, the 'English garden' (RHS)
10 Bicton, the monkey-puzzle avenue (author)
11 Alton Towers, view of the valley garden (Publisher's collection)
12 Regent's Park, plan of the Royal Botanic Society's garden (RHS)
13 T. J. Ricauti, sketch for rustic building (RHS)
14 Glendurgan, the maze (author)
15 Old Warden, the circular lake (author)
16 Joshua Major and Son, plan for rococo revival flower beds (RHS)
17 Hoole House, view of the rock garden and lawn (RHS)
18 A fountain in a garden in Peckham (RHS)
19 Birkenhead Park, plan (RHS)
20 Levens Hall, topiary figures (author)
21 Virginia Water, ruins (author)
22 Clumber Park, the terrace (author)
23 Lews Castle, Stornoway (author)
24 Gawthorpe Hall (Publisher's collection)
25 Drumlanrig Castle, proposals for the gardens (His Grace the Duke of Buccleuch)
26 Buckingham Palace, sketch for the formal garden (British Architectural Library)
27 Buckingham Palace, proposed parterres (British Architectural Library)
28 Worsley Hall, the terrace garden (RHS)
29 Kew, plan of the Royal Botanic Gardens (RHS)
30 Wilton House, the Italian garden (RHS)
31 Shrubland Park, view from the upper terrace (RHS)
32 Chatsworth, the weeping willow fountain (author)
33 People's Park, Halifax, the fountain (author)
34 Elvaston Castle, Mon Plaisir (RHS)

35 Elvaston Castle, the Alhambra garden (RHS)
36 Bedford Lodge, plan of the garden (RHS)
37 Trentham, the lake (RHS)
38 Chatsworth, the rock garden (author)
39 Pencarrow, the rock garden (author)
40 Biddulph Grange, plan of the garden (RHS)
41 Albert Memorial, proposed conservatory (RHS)
42 Welton Place, the wilderness (RHS)
43 Hardwicke House, the rosary (RHS)
44 Poles Park, the parterre (RHS)
45 Headington Hill Hall, the terraces (Mrs Robert Maxwell)
46 Crystal Palace, Sydenham Hill (Victoria and Albert Museum)
47 Wellington College, view from the lakes (author)
48 Sudeley Castle, topiary (author)
49 Plan for a flower garden (RHS)
50 Putteridge Bury, the floral avenue (RHS)
51 Pelargonium pyramid (RHS)
52 Heckfield Place, the terrace garden (RHS)
53 Hardwick Hall, west front (author)
54 Holkham Hall, the parterre (Publisher's collection)
55 Royal Horticultural Society garden, Kensington (RHS)
56 Witley Court, the parterre (author)
57 Crown Point, plan for the garden (Norfolk Record Office)
58 Castle Ashby, the parterre (RHS)
59 Subtropical plants (RHS)
60 Kew, carpet bed (RHS)
61 Hampton Court, carpet bed (RHS)
62 Unidentified garden, monogram bed (author)
63 Herbaceous border (RHS)
64 Blickling, the terrace garden (*Country Life*)
65 Huntercombe, the old-fashioned garden (*Country Life*)
66 Cardiff Castle, the moat garden (Cardiff City Council)
67 Garden plan by Robert Marnock (RHS)
68 Sefton Park, plan (RHS)
69 Locke Park, Barnsley, view in the dell (RHS)
70 Rangemore Hall, the serpentine walk (author)
71 Battersea Park, the rock garden (author)
72 Stancliffe Hall, the rock garden (*Country Life*)
73 Bulstrode Park, tower and flower garden (Royal Commission on the Historical Monuments of England)
74 Ascog Hall, view in the conservatory (RHS)
75 Oakworth, view of the rockworks (Dr Frances Clegg)
76 Gatton Park, the rock garden (Royal Commission on the Historical Monuments of England)
77 Friar Park, the 'Henley Matterhorn' (RHS)
78 Hull Botanic Garden, the lake (Hull City Museums and Art Galleries)
79 Lamport Hall, gnomes in the rock garden (RHS)
80 Friar Park, the terrace garden (RHS)
81 Letton Hall, plan for the garden (Norfolk Record Office)
82 Hinchingbrooke, the Japanese garden (RHS)
83 Heckfield Place, the parterre (RHS)
84 Plan for a herbaceous border (RHS)
85 Coombe Abbey, plan for the parterre (British Architectural Library)
86 Halton, the floral vase (RHS)
87 Alexandra Gardens, Weymouth, carpet bed (author)
88 Philips Park, Manchester, the flower beds (RHS)
89 Lockinge Park, the flower garden (RHS)
90 Compton Wynyates, the topiary garden (Publisher's collection)
91 Hewell Grange, the 'French garden' (*Country Life*)
92 Hewell Grange, the grass steps (*Country Life*)
93 Parnham House, the terrace garden (Publisher's collection)
94 Caythorpe Court, garden plan (British Architectural Library)
95 Broughton Castle, the herb garden (Royal Commission on the Historical Monuments of England)
96 The Orchard, Harrow, plan for the garden (RHS)
97 Rivernook, the formal garden (author)
98 Woodside, pergola in pond court (*Country Life*)
99 Iford Manor, the terraces (*Country Life*)
100 Mellerstain, proposal for the gardens (British Architectural Library)

Notes

Where names introducing the notes are printed in capitals, the reader should refer also to the Bibliography for further information.

Chapter 1

1. For a study of eighteenth-century aesthetics, see E. L. Tuveson, *The Imagination as Means of Grace* (1960), despite its confusion over the use of the term 'romanticism'; see also Marjorie Hope Nicolson, *Mountain Gloom and Mountain Glory* (1959); D. J. Engell, *The Creative Imagination* (1982); HIPPLE 1957; and J. D. Hunt, *The Figure in the Landscape* (1977). There is as yet no adequate study of nineteenth-century aesthetics, but see M. H. Abrams, *The Mirror and the Lamp* (1953); Morse Peckham, *Beyond the Tragic Vision* (1961); Chris Brooks, *Signs for the Times* (1984).
2. George Mason, *An Essay on Design in Gardening*, rev. ed. (1795), p. 204, quoting Shaftesbury.
3. PRICE 1842, p. 254.
4. William Marshall, *Planting and Rural Ornament*, 2nd ed. (1796), pp. 1–3, 247–8. Serpentine lakes: see PRICE 1842, pp. 256, 284; I am indebted to the researches of Robin Chaplin on their origin.
5. John Locke, *An Essay concerning Human Understanding*, Book II, chapter i.
6. See for instance William Chambers, *A Dissertation on Oriental Gardening* (1772).
7. See HIPPLE 1957; CARTER 1982, pp. 34–41; JACQUES 1983, pp. 121–5, 144–56.
8. Thomas Love Peacock, *Headlong Hall* (1816), chapter 4.
9. ALISON 1811, vol. I, pp. 8–11, 14–19, 81–96, 111–13. See HIPPLE 1957, pp. 158–81.
10. The association of ideas was derived from Locke, who invoked chance associations as an explanation for the emergence of erroneous ideas. It had become a staple of eighteenth-century psychology, an ever more encompassing explanation of human behaviour; but while the notion of the passive mind held people in thrall, there had been a continual tendency to turn it into an inherent and deterministic process. In Alison's hands it led to quite different conclusions.
11. ALISON 1811, vol. I, pp. 5–6; and see pp. 71–2.
12. Francis Jeffrey, *Contributions to the Edinburgh Review* (1844), vol. I, pp. 1–32; much of his essay is extracted in Lauder's introduction to PRICE 1842.
13. PRICE 1842, pp. 6–8, 51–2; for the theory of visual perception implied, see p. 29, and below, chapter 2.
14. SITWELL 1909, pp. 48, 55–61, 77; William James was the inspiration behind Sitwell's ideas.
15. PRICE 1842, p. 2. Lauder's interpolations were ridiculed at length in GC 1847, pp. 301, 699–700, and 1848, pp. 99–100, 235–6, 267, 315–16, but were more favourably received elsewhere.
16. PRICE 1842, p. 38.
17. Ibid., pp. 53–5.
18. See, for example, M'INTOSH 1838, p. 3; MANGLES 1839, p. 30; KEMP 1850, p. 1; Ellacombe in *Garden* II (1872), p. 551; and see Fish in *Garden* IX (1876), p. 540.
19. Humphry Repton, *Designs for the Pavillon at Brighton* (1808), frontispiece (REPTON 1840, p. 374).
20. FLETCHER 1969.
21. Foremost of the colour-plate magazines was Curtis's *Botanical Magazine* (1787–1983); its principal rivals were Edwards's *Botanical Register* (1815–47), Loddiges's *Botanical Cabinet* (1817–33), and the various part-works of Robert Sweet, most notably *The British Flower Garden* (1823–38). See DESMOND 1977; for Robert Sweet, see E. J. Willson, *West London Nursery Gardens* (1981), pp. 94–6.
22. For a survey of the rise of local botanic gardens, see BALLARD 1983, pp. 11–13.
23. For the life of Loudon, see TAYLOR 1951; Bea Howe, *Lady with Green Fingers* (1961); GLOAG 1970; and MACDOUGALL 1980, which reprints Jane Loudon's memoir from LOUDON 1845.
24. Paxton: *Horticultural Register* (1831–36 – the later volumes edited by James Main), *Paxton's Magazine of Botany* (1834–49). Harrison: *Gardener's and Forester's Record* (1833–36), *Floricultural Cabinet* (1833–59) – continued as the *Gardener's Weekly Magazine*, 1860–65, and then as the *Gardeners' Magazine*, 1865–1916. Marnock: *Floricultural Magazine* (1836–42), *United Gardeners' and Land Stewards' Journal* (1845–48).
25. See DESMOND 1977. For Glenny, see TJADEN 1983, and Ray Desmond, 'Loudon and nineteenth-century horticultural journalism', in MACDOUGALL 1980, pp. 77–97. Beaton's hope for peace: *CottGard* V (1850), p. 19.
26. QR LXXXIX (1851), p. 20. As the *Journal of Horticulture*, the magazine ran until 1915.
27. Hibberd: *Floral World* (1858–80); *Amateur Gardening* (1884–); from 1861 until his death he also edited the *Gardeners' Magazine*, formerly Harrison's *Floricultural Cabinet*. Robinson: *The Garden* (1871–1927),

Gardening Illustrated (1879–1956), *Flora and Sylva* (1903–5).
28. he gardener was William Wildsmith. *JHort* V n.s. (1882), p. 430.
29. For the life of Paxton, see MARKHAM 1935; CHADWICK 1961; ANTHONY 1973; and John Kenworthy-Browne's forthcoming biography. For his reputation, see e.g. *CottGard* VIII (1852), pp. 334–5, and *Garden* V (1874), p. 68.
30. Horticultural Society, 'Handwriting of Gardeners' notebook (Lindley Library).
31. GC 1881 i 89–90.
32. See Beaton's autobiography, in *CottGard* XIII (1853), pp. 153–8; and GC 1866, pp. 588–9.
33. GC 1872, p. 540; see also ELLIOTT 1984b.
34. Some examples on each issue. Education: GM IV (1828), pp. 461–2; XIII (1837), pp. 49–55. Wages: GM I (1826), pp. 141–4; *Florist's Journal* 1841, pp. 5–11; GC 1874 ii 269–70. Gardeners' houses: GM XI (1835), pp. 64–6, 173–4. Relations with employers and working conditions: GM III (1827), pp. 156–7, 291–2; *Gardener's and Forester's Record* I (1833), pp. 196–7; JRHS XVIII (1895), pp. 86–95; J. R. B. Evison, 'The changing face of the greenhouse world', in K. Beckett, ed., *The Love of Gardening* (1980), pp. 43–50.
35. GC 1875 i 655–6.
36. *CottGard* IV (1850), pp. 186, 366. For a glimpse of the competitive atmosphere, see William Taylor's reminiscences, esp. *JHort* LXIII n.s. (1911), pp. 128–9.
37. Elisabeth Cunnington, *Cunnington Family History* (1978: privately printed), pp. 146–7; *GardMag* XLV (1902), p. 282.
38. GC 1869, p. 1305.
39. Lawn mower: see K. N. Sanecki's chapter on the lawn in G. S. Thomas, ed., *Recreating the Period Garden* (1984); and D. G. Halford, *Old Lawnmowers* (1982). Budding's patent: GM VIII (1832), pp. 34–36. Advantages: see Beaton in *CottGard* III (1849), p. 108.
40. Too much to footnote adequately. M'Intosh's verge cutter: GM I (1826), pp. 139–40. Forsyth's plumb-line and level: FP XI (1872), pp. 136–7. Watering pots: *JHort* XXIV (1873), pp. 429–32. Paxton garden tools: GC 1877 ii 688. Revolving frames: GM III (1827), p. 170. John Fountaine's greenhouse railway: GC 1873, p. 11.
41. Scotland to London plant transport: *JHort* XXX (1876), pp. 352–4. Motorcar: *JHort* XLI n.s. (1900), p. 377.
42. Pond-concreting competition: challenge issued by J. Holliday, artificial pond maker, in the Welbeck Lakes papers, Nottinghamshire Record Office, DD.4P 62/101/11.
43. FRANCIS 1977.
44. Asphalt: a thriving literature from GM XV (1839), pp. 188–9, until the 1850s. Tiles: see MURRAY 1863, pp. 144–7.
45. John Gloag, *A History of Cast-Iron in Architecture* (1948); Raymond Lister, *Decorative Wrought Ironwork in Great Britain* (1957).
46. GC 1850, p. 548.
47. See GC 1849 passim for Hartley's glass; for the burning effects of the old sheet glass, see GC 1848, pp. 334, 348, 364, etc.
48. *JHort* I (1861), pp. 171–2, for a retrospective view on glass since 1845. The abolition of the glass tax provoked copious commentary in GC 1845; and see GC 1847, pp. 717, 766, for the effects on price.
49. For orchard-houses, see Thomas Rivers, *The Orchard House* (1850), and subsequent editions to 1873 at least. For Ewing's glass walls at Bodorgan, see GC 1851, pp. 755, 771, 790, and GC 1852, pp. 423, 486–7 for their trial by the Horticultural Society at Chiswick. For the rivalry of the two systems, see GC 1852, pp. 3, 4, 6, 37, 54, 70, 166, 485, 828. See also *Garden Companion* 1852, pp. 28–9, for a glass-wall scheme by Spencer of Bowood.
50. For general histories of glasshouse technology, see LEMMON 1962; HIX 1974; E. W. B. van den Muijzenberg, *A History of Greenhouses* (1980); ELLIOTT 1983a. Polmaise heating: GC 1845, p. 871, and 1846–48 passim; UGLSJ 1846, p. 821, and 1847, pp. 65–6; JHS II (1847), pp. 49–71; PMB XIV (1847), pp. 154–5. Double glazing: *CottGard* IX (1852–53), pp. 55–6, 455–6; *Floral World* IV (1861), pp. 279–80; *JHort* XI (1866), pp. 45–6; Samuel Wood, *The Forcing Garden* (1881), pp. 13–16. The earliest large-scale architectural use of double glazing I know of was by S. S. Teulon at Elvetham Hall, Hants (1859–62). Greenhouse watering systems: *TransHS* III (1817), pp. 14–16. Hygrometers and other greenhouse equipment: *Memoirs of the Caledonian Horticultural Society* III (1825), pp. 165–73. See also LOUDON 1817, pp. 52–72.
51. Nathaniel Bagshaw Ward, *On the Growth of Plants in Closely Glazed Cases* (1842). See also Ray Desmond, 'The problems of transporting plants', in HARRIS 1979, pp. 99–104, and ALLEN 1969.
52. Hibberd in *GardMag* 1883, p. 163; Beaton in *CottGard* XXIII (1860), p. 313; Robson in *JHort* XXI (1871), pp. 481–4. Propagation: *CottGard* III (1850), p. 276; XII (1854), pp. 432–4. (See also Beaton's technical rules for bedding out, *CottGard* XII (1854), pp. 114–15.)
53. GC 1875 i 720.
54. *CottGard* VIII (1852), pp. 305–6. Hardiness: *TransHS* I (1805), pp. 21–5; GM VI (1830), p. 330. Aquatics in heated tanks: M'INTOSH 1838, pp. 31–2. 'Geothermal gardening': *Florist's Journal* 1842, pp. 4–8; *JHort* V (1863), pp. 493–5; IX (1865), p. 257. George Fleming's achievements in forcing: *CottGard* XIII (1855), p. 372. Vineyard revival: A. Pettigrew in JRHS XVII (1895), pp. 95–104; Hugh Barty-King, *A Tradition of English Wine* (1977), pp. 117–45.
55. Soil sterilization: UGLSJ 1846, pp. 165–6; *CottGard* VII (1852), pp. 387–8, on burning versus charring. David Thomson first became known for a large-scale exercise in soil burning at Dyrham Park, Barnet: see *JHort* XXXIV n.s. (1897), pp. 204–5. Rothamsted: A. D. Hall, *The Book of the Rothamsted Experiments* (1905).
56. See E. C. Large, *The Advance of the Fungi* (1940).
57. Pruning: GM VI (1830), pp. 43–7; Lindley's impact: *CottGard* III (1849), pp. 140–1. Cordon training: see the series on this subject in *GardMag* XIX (1876); but English gardens seldom boasted results as elaborate as those of Germany, as illustrated in Nicolas Gaucher, *Handbuch der Obstkultur* (1902). Root-pruning: *CottGard* III (1849), p. 27, for Lindley's impact; and see the account of a master root-pruner, Mungo Temple, in *GardMag* XXXVI (1893), p. 481.
58. Root control: *CottGard* III (1849), pp. 152–4; IV (1850), pp. 144–5. (See Beaton's account of how he was first taught to plant a tree, *CottGard* III (1849), pp. 40–42.) Dynamite: *JHort* XXXIII n.s. (1896), p. 325.
59. Forsyth: see Guy Meynell, 'The

personal issue underlying T. A. Knight's controversy with William Forsyth', *J Soc. Biblphy. nat. Hist.* IX (1979), pp. 281–7. Caie: *CottGard* XI (1853), pp. 177–9.
60. *GardMag* XXV (1883), p. 164. For pre-Victorian hybridization, see Conway Zirkle, *The Beginnings of Plant Hybridization* (1935). For Rollisson's work, see GC 1843, p. 461; for William Herbert, see *TransHS* IV (1820), pp. 15–50, and JHS II (1847), pp. 1–28, 81–107.
61. STEUART 1828; and cf. Main's review, GM IV (1828), pp. 115–126. For other pre-Barron experiments, see GM XIV (1838), pp. 505–10; PMB I (1834), pp. 46–48. Even Barron, however, was surprised at William Tillery's successes in transplanting at Welbeck Abbey: see Nottingham City Record Office, DD.4P. 72/68, and Portland MSS, PwK 4079 (Nottingham University Department of Manuscripts).
62. BROOKE 1857, 'Elvaston Castle'; BARRON 1852; *Garden* VI (1874), pp. 571–2.
63. *CottGard* IV (1850), pp. 328–9. For post-Barron innovations in transplanting, see GC 1863, p. 149; 1864, p. 914; *JHort* XXI n.s. (1890), pp. 448–9.
64. Buckfast Abbey yew: GC 1880 i 556–7, *et seq.* intermittently for the next two years.

Chapter 2

1. For general surveys of gardening in the Regency period, see LOUDON 1822; JACQUES 1983, pp. 170–205. See also Melanie Simo in *Journal of Garden History* III (1983), pp. 59–63.
2. GM IX (1833), p. 515.
3. Hall Barn, LOUDON 1822, p. 1233; Marble Hill and Strawberry Hill, p. 1226; Southgate Lodge, GM XV (1839), pp. 512–13; White Knights, GM VI (1830), pp. 654–5.
4. ALISON 1811, vol. I, pp. 120–2. See also Joshua Major's views in GM VI (1830), p. 611, and P. F. Robinson's instructions for beautifying cottages, in *Designs for Farm Buildings* (1830), pl. XXXV.
5. Mavis Batey, 'Nuneham Courtenay: an Oxfordshire eighteenth-century deserted village', *Oxoniensia* 33 (1968), pp. 108–24; for the removal of villages generally, see DARLEY 1975, pp. 2–16, 19–20.
6. See for instance GM I (1826), pp. 275–7; II (1827), pp. 19–24, 271–3; III (1827), pp. 162–7; VI (1830), pp. 139–208; VIII (1832), pp. 263–4; LOUDON 1836.
7. PRICE 1842, pp. 75–6, 398; Loudon, 'Remarks on the improvements proposed to be made at Linton Place' (1825), Maidstone Record Office, pp. 11–12.
8. PRICE 1842, p. 71; GC 1875 i 50.
9. John Martin Robinson, *Georgian Model Farms* (1983).
10. For famous instances of flowery kitchen gardens, see Culford Hall, GC 1866, pp. 903, 926–8, and Heckfield Place, GC 1872, pp. 1524–5. For an insistence on the intrinsic beauty of the kitchen garden, see *JHort* XXIII (1872), p. 173; *Gardener* 1874, pp. 327–8.
11. MAJOR 1852, p. 121. See also R. H. Cheney, QR XCVIII (1855), pp. 210–11.
12. For accounts of the picturesque debate, see HIPPLE 1957; JACQUES 1983, pp. 150–56; CARTER 1982, pp. 34–41.
13. PRICE 1842, p. 64, 69–70, 77–89. REPTON 1840, pp. 106–8, 111–14, 116; see SOUTHEY 1848, pp. 256–9, for a Reptonian bias.
14. PRICE 1842, pp. 83, 149, 166–75; REPTON 1840, pp. 76–7, 234, 337, 374.
15. LOUDON 1838; CARTER 1982, p. 38. For Loudon's changing attitude to Price, see his accounts of his garden at Foxley, in LOUDON 1822, p. 1238, and GM XIV (1838), pp. 217–18. For a differing view of Loudon's relation to Repton, see TURNER 1982.
16. LOUDON 1822, pp. 1226, 1238.
17. REPTON 1840, pp. 398–400; GM X (1834), p. 559. See also TURNER 1982, but I think this account exaggerates Quatremère's dependence on Platonism.
18. QUATREMERE 1837, pp. 29–30; and cf. pp. 11–14, 121–2, 170–1.
19. Ibid., pp. ix–x; LOUDON 1838, pp. 137–9; M'INTOSH 1853–55, vol. I, pp. 604–5.
20. REPTON 1840, pp. 398–400.
21. LOUDON 1815, pp. 10–12.
22. For M'Intosh's life, see GC 1864, p. 50; for glimpses of his reputation, see *Annals of Horticulture* 1846, pp. 228–33, and GC 1866, p. 436.
23. COUSIN 1848, pp. 121–2, 128–9, M'Intosh expected Cousin to supplant Locke and the British empiricists as the standard author on the human mind: see M'INTOSH 1838, p. 8.
24. For an example of Price's picturesque restated with a more transcendentalist rhetoric, see the series of articles by 'Gr.' in GC 1844, pp. 51, 83, 115, 131, 211, 331. See also *HortJ*, n.s., I (1838), pp. 72–9.
25. WORDSWORTH 1951, pp. 118–19. *Letters of William and Dorothy Wordsworth: the Later Years*, p. 1056 (Wordsworth to J. T. Coleridge, 1840).
26. NOYES 1968, pp. 101–35. N. Clutterbuck, Dove Cottage guidebook (198–). Rydal Mount: GM VII (1831), pp. 551–2; E. S. Dixon, QR LXXXIX (1851), pp. 24–6; Christopher Wordsworth, *Memoirs of William Wordsworth* (1851), vol. I, pp. 18–26; Ken Lemmon, CL CLXXV (1984), pp. 1240–42. Coleorton: *Letters of William and Dorothy Wordsworth: the Middle Years* (1937), vol. I, pp. 90–99; Wordsworth, 'To Lady Beaumont' (1807) and 'A flower garden' (1824); Russell Noyes, 'Wordsworth and Sir George Beaumont's family', *Times Literary Supplement*, 10 August 1962, p. 614.
27. *Letters: Middle Years*, op. cit.; *The Excursion* III 520–31; E. S. Dixon, op. cit., pp. 21–2, 24–6.
28. Edna A. Shearer, 'Wordsworth and Coleridge marginalia in a copy of Richard Payne Knight's Analytical Inquiry into the Principles of Taste', *Huntington Library Quarterly* I (1937), pp. 63–94; Wordsworth, *Prose Works*, ed. W. J. B. Owen and J. W. Smyser (1974), vol. III, p. 349. For a discussion of Wordsworth and the picturesque, see W. M. Merchant's preface to WORDSWORTH 1951, pp. 9–32; see also NOYES 1968, and V & A 1984, pp. 77–91, a work which mixes aperçus and solecisms in roughly equal proportions.
29. WORDSWORTH 1951, p. 107.
30. *Letters: Middle Years* op. cit., vol. I, pp. 90–99; vol. II, p. 467.
31. WORDSWORTH 1951, pp, 96–8, 112–23; H. D. Rawnsley, *Reminiscences of Wordsworth among the Peasantry of Westmoreland* (1968), p. 20.
32. Noyes, 'Wordsworth and Sir George Beaumont's family', op. cit.
33. *The Excursion* IV 588–92. See 'Effusion in the pleasure-ground on the banks of the Bran' (published 1827); 'This lawn, a carpet all alive' (published 1835).

34. William Wordsworth, *Prose Works*, op. cit., vol. III, p. 343.
35. Nikolaus Pevsner, *North Lancashire* (1969), p. 265.
36. I am grateful to Susan Denyer for inroducing me to the estates at Wray Castle and Monk Coniston. For the course of post-Wordsworth developments in the Lakes, see MAWSON 1900; Ellen E. Frank, 'The domestication of nature: five houses in the Lake District', in KNOEPFLMACHER 1978, pp. 68–92; V & A 1984, pp. 101–31.
37. LOUDON 1824, p. 3; MANGLES 1839, p. 28; KENT 1823 (later editions 1825, 1831); GM XIV (1838), pp. 220–34.
38. Welton Place: *JHort* V (1863), pp. 493–5; IX (1865), p. 257. M'INTOSH 1838, pp. 31–2.
39. LOUDON 1824, p. 3.
40. Mackenzie: *TransHS* II (1815), pp. 171–7; LOUDON 1817, pp. 15–16.
41. Chiswick: KEMP 1851, p. 107; *CottGard* XV (1855), pp. 69–70, 108–9. I am grateful to Robert Thorne for tracking down the identity of the architect of the Chiswick conservatory.
42. GM V (1829), pp. 680–1.
43. *HortReg* I (1832), pp. 134–5; IV (1835), pp. 19–23, 88–92; V (1836), pp. 71–4; PMB II (1836), pp. 80–85, 244–59 passim; VIII (1841), pp. 255–9.
44. LOUDON 1817, p. 49.
45. FM II (1838), p. 467; *Gardener and Practical Florist* III (1844), pp. 276–7.
46. LOUDON 1824, pp. 36–7, 131.
47. GM I (1826), pp. 105–12; II (1827), pp. 170–71; GC 1845, p. 691. French and English: GC 1850, pp. 147–8.
48. JHS I (1846), pp. 5–8 and frontispiece; repr. in *CottGard* XVI (1856), pp. 208–9.
49. Ward's garden: GMB III (1851), pp. 148–50. H. N. Humphreys, 'On the picturesque in hothouses', ibid., pp. 1–4; repr. in *JHort* III (1862), pp. 316–17.
50. GM III (1827), pp. 245–7; IV (1828), p. 304. Bowood: GC 1845, p. 755; JHS IX (1853), p. 43. See also *Gardener and Practical Florist* III (1844), pp. 208–9; *CottGard* IX (1852), p. 103; XXII (1859), pp. 216–17. For advice on the point from Thomas Appleby and Robert Errington, see *CottGard* II (1849), p. 66, and *Florist's Guide* 1850, pp. 150–1.
51. GM IX (1833), pp. 50–9; XIII (1837), 206–11; XIV (1838), pp. 80–1; *CottGard* VIII (1852), pp. 4–5.
52. *CottGard* III (1849), p. 62. For the most recent account of × *Laburnocytisus adami*, see Peter Barnes in JRHS CXI (1986), pp. 44–5.
53. *JHort* III (1862), pp. 132–3.
54. LOUDON 1838, pp. 140–1; see pp. 136–170 generally. SCOTT 1836, pp. 84–87.
55. PRICE 1842, pp. 201, 269–70. Dropmore: GC 1868, pp. 464–5; E. V. Boyle, 'Dropmore', *National Review* XXXIII (1899), pp. 302–16. For accounts of the progress of arboriculture and lists of arboreta, see UGLSJ 1847, p. 177, and M'INTOSH 1853–55, pp. 584–7; LOUDON 1835–38, vol. I, pp. 117–32.
56. FORBES 1820, p. 10; GM VI (1830), p. 602; XI (1835), pp. 155–6; SMITH 1852, p. 31.
57. *Midland Florist* II (1848), pp. 128–9, 185–6; IX (1855), pp. 15–17, 39–41. For a lavish use of a weeping tree, see NIVEN 1838, reproduced in MALINS 1980b, p. 37; H. J. Elwes and A. Henry, *Trees of Great Britain and Ireland*, vol. IV (1909), p. 238. See Miles Hadfield, 'Weeping beeches', *Quarterly Journal of Forestry* (1970), pp. 303–8.
58. GM I (1825), pp. 16–20, 116–18.
59. GM VIII (1832), p. 701.
60. GM IX (1833), p. 7; X (1834), pp. 531–2; XII (1836), p. 332; see also LOUDON 1835–38, vol. I, pp. 117–32.
61. LOUDON 1838, pp. 164–6. For a differing account of the emergence of the gardenesque, see TURNER 1982.
62. GM XIX (1843), pp. 166–7.
63. Ibid.; see also REPTON 1840, pp. viii–ix. Loudon's sense of 'gardenesque' was still in occasional use at the turn of the century: see George Abbey, *JHort* LIX (1909), pp. 295–6.
64. PUCKLER-MUSKAU 1832, vol. III, p. 55.
65. GC 1841, p. 53.
66. GM XVI (1840), p. 534; GC 1844, p. 318.
67. Kensington: GM XIII (1837), pp. 146–8. Bicton: *Florist* 1857, p. 145. Elvaston: GM XIV (1838), pp. 76–9; see also GM VIII (1832), p. 486.
68. Marnock: J. D. Bassett, *The Plantation, Leighton Buzzard* (1872), pp. 2–3; *Garden* II (1872), pp. 470–1.
69. GM I (1826), pp. 336–7; V (1829), pp. 585–8; VII (1831), pp. 364–5; IX (1833), p. 10; XIII (1837), pp. 109–11; XIX (1843), pp. 239–40. See also REPTON 1840, pp. viii, 466–8.
70. FM IV (1840), p. 176; Reinagle, GM III (1827), pp. 247–52; GILPIN 1835, pp. 63–4; SMITH 1852, pp. 76–8.
71. GM XVI (1840), p. 620.
72. For Errington's early articles, see GM VIII (1832), pp. 151–2; XIX (1843), pp. 118–19. He later became a regular columnist for the *Cottage Gardener*; see *CottGard* XVI (1856), pp. 118–20.
73. Errington, 'A further glance at modern flower-gardens', *Florist's Guide* 1850, pp. 149–51.
74. GM XI (1835), pp. 233–7; XII (1836), pp. 513–15; XIV (1838), pp. 33–5. For Glendinning's life and infuence, see GM XVI (1840), pp. 626–7; apart from Bicton, where he was head gardener, his major works were Poles Park and the rearrangement of the Horticultural Society's arboretum at Chiswick (see GC 1850, p. 167; GC 1851, p. 263; KEMP 1851, pp. 55–6).
75. Bicton: GM XVIII–XIX passim; GC 1841, pp. 799–800; GC 1842, p. 128; *JHort* XVII (1869), p. 302; XXI (1871), pp. 201–3; GC 1871, pp. 1515–16; and for James Barnes' criticisms, see FP XI (1872), pp. 78–9.
76. George Collison, *Cemetery Interment* (1840), pp. 314–408. Loddiges's nursery: LOUDON 1835, p. 1217; LOUDON 1835–38, pp. 130–1.
77. Loudon's scheme: LOUDON 1830, part II, pls. 6–8. Chatsworth: GM XI (1835), pp. 385–95.
78. See Dora Wiebenson, *The Picturesque Garden in France* (1978).
79. GM VII (1831), pp. 390–5.
80. Ibid.; GM XVI (1840), p. 580; (1841), pp. 41–2; BROOKE 1857; GC 1869, p. 416; *JHort* XIX (1870), pp. 287–90, 307–10; GC 1873, pp. 811–12; FP XII (1873), pp. 174–5. The Earl eventually dismissed the Protestant Forsyth; see Royal Botanic Gardens, Kew, English Letters XXV letter 376 (11 December 1847) for Nesfield's efforts on his behalf.
81. GM VII (1831), p. 399; XV (1839), pp. 210–11; XVII (1841), pp. 350–3; XVIII (1842), pp. 162–4. For Thomas Rutger's villa plans, see GM XI (1835), pp. 163–71, 509–17, 561–3; XII (1836), pp. 66–9, 121–3, 175–6, 180–81, 230–33, 470–74, 564–6; FC XXIV (1856), pp. 194–5, 287–8, 344. Rutger was a former gardener at Longleat; see FC XXII (1854), p. 77.
82. Letter from Mary Wordsworth to Edward Quillinan, 1824, in the possession of the Trustees of Dove

Cottage. I am grateful to Mrs Nora Lowe for bringing this letter to my attention, and for showing me what remains of Samuel Barber's garden.
83. GM VII (1831), p. 551.
84. REPTON 1840, pp. 525–32. Woburn: GM I (1825), pp. 26–9, 112–16; XII (1836), pp. 292–4; FM III (1838), pp. 55–7; Clive Aslet, 'Park and garden buildings at Woburn', CL CLXXIII (1983), pp. 860–63. See the great sequence of Woburn publications: George Sinclair, *Hortus Gramineus Woburnensis* (1816); *Hortus Ericaeus Woburnensis* (1825); James Forbes, *Salictum Woburnense* (1829); *Hortus Woburnensis* (1833).
85. *Civil Engineer and Architect's Journal*, 1840, pp. 173–4.
86. *Annals of Horticulture*, 1846, p. 15; 1847, pp. 367–9; *Garden* I (1872), pp. 234–6; CHADWICK 1966, pp. 96–7; MEYNELL 1980.
87. FM IV (1840), p. 177.
88. CL, CXXXIX (1966), pp. 944–8; JACQUES 1983, p. 143; WATKINS 1982, p. 64.
89. PAPWORTH 1823; GM XI (1835), pp. 12–13; XIII (1837), pp. 161–6; FM IV (1839), pp. 8–11; PMB IV (1837), pp. 61–4; *Florist's Journal* 1846, pp. 192–6; M'INTOSH 1853–55, vol. II, pp. 705–15. Rustic baskets: GC 1855, pp. 551–2; *CottGard* XXII (1858), p. 269; *JHort* II (1861), pp. 218–19.
90. LOUDON 1838, pp. 166–8.
91. RICAUTI 1842; reviewed in GM XIV (1840), pp. 355–6, 519. Howlett: GMB III (1851), p. 70: *Cottage Gardener* V (1851), p. 300; VIII (1852), p. 122. I have not succeeded in tracing a copy of his *Practical Rustic Work* (1852).
92. Mosshouses: GM X (1834), pp. 532–7; LOUDON 1840a, pp. 352–6.
93. Humphreys: GMB I (1850), pp. 132–4. Bowes' Manor: GC 1850, p. 631. Knowle Cottage: HARVEY 1837; GM XIX (1843), p. 239.
94. Complaints which have continued ever since to be levelled at those exhibits. For the best discussion of the rococo revival to date, see Simon Jervis, *High Victorian Design* (1983), pp. 37–57.
95. GM VII (1829), p. 389; William Marshall, *On Planting and Rural Ornament* (1803), vol. I, p. 301.
96. REPTON 1840, pp. 445–52; CARTER 1982, pp. 58–60. Ross Priory: Scottish Record Office, GD47/575.
97. Masey: LOUDON 1830, part II, pl. 5; GM XII (1836), pp. 341–7. Laxton: see MEYNELL 1980.
98. Errington: GM VIII (1832), pp. 562–6. Glendurgan: National Trust Garden Survey, Glendurgan (1982).
99. STEUART 1828, pp. 422–3; for the opposition, see GILPIN 1835, pp. 50, 94–111, and GM VIII (1832), pp. 700–702.
100. LOUDON 1830, part II, pls. 6–8. Kiddington House: plans in RIBA Drawings Collection. See *CottGard* XVIII (1856), p. 223, for the use of circular clumps of shrubs at Warwick Castle.
101. GC 1841, p. 99 (Errington); GC 1842, p. 236; FC XIII (1845), pp. 50–53; *Gossip for the Garden* I (1851), p. 25. Charles Dickens, *Great Expectations*. See also *CottGard* V (1851), p. 403.
102. GM III (1828), pp. 257–63; VI (1830), pp. 423–4.
103. For examples, see JACKSON 1822. Lewis Wyatt had designed a kidney-shaped flower-garden at Tatton Park by 1814; see National Trust Garden Survey, Tatton Park.
104. Loudon: GM XI (1835), pp. 237–47, 284–9, 352–8, 449–59. HIBBERD 1857, p. 340. MAJOR 1861.
105. M'INTOSH 1838, pp. 3–5. I am grateful to Priscilla Allderidge for the information about William Rollinson at Bethlem Hospital (now the Imperial War Museum). See also GC 1842, p. 305.
106. HIBBERD 1857, 1870.
107. LOUDON 1838, pp. 141–2.
108. REPTON 1840, pp. 160–3; PRICE 1842, pp. 96, 189–90, 267.
109. GM VI (1830), p. 491; VII (1831), pp. 426–7. HARVEY 1837, p. 25. GC 1844, p. 391; 1856, pp. 631–2.
110. GM XIV (1838), pp. 463–4; GC 1845, pp. 562, 591–2; PRICE 1842, p. 267.
111. GM III (1827), p. 248; *Florist's Journal* 1845, pp. 56–9; LOTHIAN 1845.
112. GORER 1979; MANGLES 1839, p. 125; LOTHIAN 1845; GM XIV (1838), pp. 362–3. Cassiobury: PUCKLER-MUSKAU 1832, vol. III, p. 196; John Britton, *The History and Description . . . of Cassiobury Park* (1837), pp. 29–30.
113. GM X (1834), pp. 103–4.
114. GM XIV (1838), pp. 353–63.
115. *CottGard* V (1851), p. 240; GM XIV (1838), pp. 102–3.
116. M'INTOSH 1838, p. 24; KEMP 1851, pp. 118–19.
117. GM XV (1839), pp. 353–79, esp. pp. 370, 374–9, GMB II (1850), pp. 164–6; III (1851), pp. 44–5, 171–3; GC 1875 ii 324–5. See Frederick Goodall, *Reminiscences* (1902), pp. 117–26, 172–3.
118. James Meader, *The Planter's Guide* (1779).
119. John Locke, *An Essay concerning Human Understanding*, Book II, chapter 8. George Berkeley, *An Essay towards a New Theory of Vision* (1709), para. 158.
120. MORRIS 1825, pp. 66; JOHNSON 1874, p. 24.
121. REPTON 1840, pp. 312–9, 452–5, for a presentation of Milner's theory of colours.
122. PRICE 1842, pp. 130–32, 136–7; Rawnsley, op. cit., p. 20.
123. PRICE 1842, p. 139; NICOL 1810, p. 10; GILPIN 1835, p. 185; SMITH 1852, p. 102.
124. REPTON 1840, p. 106; PRICE 1842, pp. 66–8; GC 1849, p. 373; MAJOR 1852, p. 121; R. H. Cheney, QR XCVIII (1855), pp. 210–11.
125. For surveys of the changing attitudes to colour in British painting, see GAGE 1969; J. A. W. Heffernan, 'The English romantic perception of color', in K. Kroeber & W. Walling, eds., *Images of Romanticism: Verbal and Visual Affinities* (1978), pp. 133–48; W. F. Axton, 'Victorian landscape painting: a change in outlook', in KNOEPFLMACHER 1978, pp. 281–308.
126. PRICE 1842, pp. 136–43; REPTON 1840, p. 221.
127. Major: *CottGard* XXI (1859), pp. 248–9, 276. MANGLES 1839, p. 62. See also GM II (1827), pp. 33–34.
128. GC 1841, p. 685. See GM X (1834), p. 60; XVII (1841), p. 36; XVIII (1842), pp. 592–3.
129. University of Durham, Dept. of Palaeography & Diplomatic, Grey Papers (20 June 1847); MANGLES 1839, p. 35; GC 1841, p. 685.
130. GM I (1825), pp. 12–13.
131. HUNT 1840, pp. 7–8 ('Colour'); pp. 14–15 ('A flower for your window').
132. GM II (1827), pp. 309–10.
133. Windsor: GM IV (1828), pp. 177–8. Whitmore Lodge: GM V (1829), pp. 564–7. Dropmore: GM III (1827), pp. 257–9. For the priority of Frost in bedding, see GC 1880 i 267; *National Review* XXXIII (1899), p. 308; TAYLOR 1952, pp. 70–79.
134. PUCKLER-MUSKAU 1832, vol. II, pp. 204–5, talking about Blaise Castle.
135. Waldershare Park: North MSS (C147/21), Maidstone Record Office.

Kew Annual Report, 1 January 1870, p. 4. Defence of the working classes: E. S. Dixon, QR XC (1851), p. 61; BURRITT 1868, pp. 305–7.
136. LOUDON 1822, p. 1186. I am grateful to Patrick Goode for drawing my attention to the open-space crisis of the 1830s. See also F. Baltazavek and R. Schediwy, 'The economic origins of Europe's largest city parks', *Parks and Recreation*, July 1981, pp. 15–20, August 1981, pp. 35–42.
137. For inn gardens, see GM V (1829), p. 481; VIII (1832), pp. 96–101; IX (1833), pp. 524–5; XII (1836), p. 516. For the pleasure gardens, see Warwick Wroth, *The London Pleasure Gardens of the Eighteenth Century* (1896), and James Stevens Curl, 'Spas and pleasure gardens of London . . . ', *Garden History*, VII no. ii (1979), pp. 27–68. Belle Vue Gardens: *Midland Florist* IV (1850), pp. 83–90.
138. GM XVI (1840), pp. 521–45, later republished in LOUDON 1843. See also James Stevens Curl, *A Celebration of Death* (1980).
139. For florists' societies, see the work of Ruth Duthie, 'English florists' societies and feasts in the seventeenth and first half of the eighteenth centuries', *Garden History* X (1982), pp. 17–35, and 'Florists' societies and feasts after 1750', ibid., XII (1984), pp. 8–38
140. CHADWICK 1966, pp. 37–52; Richard Iliffe and Wilfred Baguley, *Victorian Nottingham*, X (1973), pp. 31–49.
141. Birmingham: BALLARD 1983. Gravesend: GM XII (1836), pp. 13–26; TURNER 1984. Derby: GM XVI (1840), pp. 59–63, 73–81, 521–45, later published as LOUDON 1840b. The Gravesend park was built over in the 1870s, but the Derby Arboretum survives today.
142. GC 1843, p. 742; 1847, p. 603; Frederick Law Olmsted, *Walks and Talks of an American Farmer in England* (1852), pp. 78–82; *Garden* X (1876), pp. 550–551; CHADWICK 1966, pp. 68–89.
143. Ipswich: FC XIX (1851), pp. 174–5.
144. Wordsworth, *Prose Works*, op. cit., III, pp. 360–61.
145. CHADWICK 1966, pp. 111–36. Victoria Park: COLE 1877, pp. 27–30, and see Stephen Rettig's forthcoming discussion in *Garden History*.

Chapter 3

1. For the survival of this version of garden history, see Irvin Eller, *The History of Belvoir Castle* (1841), pp. 337–9.
2. REPTON 1840, pp. x-xi. See also *HortReg* IV (1835), pp. 220–26; HUGHES 1866, pp. 30–42 on styles. See Georg Germann, *Gothic Revival* (1972), pp. 24–7, for the replacement of the older term 'manner' by 'style'.
3. MORRIS 1825, p. 17; REPTON 1840, pp. 398–400. See MALINS 1980.
4. LOUDON 1822, pp. 1–111; JOHNSON 1826. For Johnson's articles, see e.g. *CottGard* I (1848/9), pp. 49–50, 217; II (1849), pp. 31–3. I am grateful to David Jacques for information on Forsyth.
5. Important examples: *HortReg* IV (1835), pp. 220–26; *Floral Cabinet* III (1840), pp. 41–4, 57–60, 73–5, 107–8, 121–4; *Gardener's and Forester's Record* III (1836), pp. 221–8; *HortJ* n.s. I (1838), pp. 72–9; *Gardener; Florist and Agriculturist* 1847, pp. 56–7, 75.
6. GM XII (1836), pp. 114–16; the garden was Haffield House.
7. REPTON 1840, pp. v-vi.
8. *Scottish Gardener* III (1854), pp. 41–2, 264; GMB II (1850), p. 59; *Garden* XV (1879), p. 447. See also THOMPSON 1859, pp. 687–8; KERR 1864, pp. 334–6.
9. M'INTOSH 1838, pp. 9–23. See also M'INTOSH 1853–55, pp. 1–10.
10. REPTON 1840, pp. 231–241, 326; M'INTOSH 1853–55, pp. 573–8; J. S. Barty's review of M'Intosh, *Blackwood's Magazine* LXXIII (1853), p. 141.
11. Busbridge, GM IX (1833), pp. 481–2; Knole, LOUDON 1822, p. 1231; Bilston, ibid., p. 1239; Wroxton, ibid., p. 1236; Holme Lacy, ibid., p. 1238.
12. PRICE 1842.
13. JACQUES 1983, pp. 140–1; PRICE 1842, pp. 184–5; MORRIS 1825, p. 48; GILPIN 1835, p. 27; GC 1843, p. 57; SMITH 1852, pp. 32–3, 82–3.
14. For the general history of attitudes to ruins, see Michel Baridon, 'Ruins as a mental construct', *Journal of Garden History* V (1985), pp. 84–96, and DELLHEIM 1982.
15. MORRIS 1825, p. 69; GM IX (1833), p. 12; REPTON 1840, p. 129; PRICE 1842, pp. 134–5; GC 1847, pp. 155–6, 172.
16. *Ladies' Magazine*, p. 361.
17. *White's 1845 Norfolk* i.e. *History, Gazetteer, and Directory of Norfolk* (1969), pp. 151–2.
18. Bayham Abbey: LOUDON 1822, p. 1230. Battle Abbey: GM XVIII (1842), pp. 611–13. Farnham Castle: GM XI (1835), pp. 503–5. Bury St Edmunds: GM VII (1831), p. 674; *Garden* V (1874), pp. 140–1. Leicester: GM VII (1831), p. 425; GC 1865, pp. 1063–4. Canterbury: GC 1847, p. 343. York: FM II (1837), p. 86.
19. Dryburgh Abbey: GM XVIII (1842), p. 578. Berry Pomeroy: GM XVIII (1842), pp. 536–7. Melrose Abbey: *Ladies' Magazine*, pp. 288–9. Lochleven: ibid., p. 320; GM XVIII (1842), p. 587.
20. *CottGard* XIV (1855), pp. 120–22.
21. GM VII (1831), p. 550.
22. *Scottish Gardener* III (1854), pp. 263–6. For Barncluith, see also GM XVIII (1842), pp. 342–3; *Ladies' Magazine*, p. 260; PRICE 1842, frontispiece.
23. William Gilpin, *Observations on Forest Scenery* (1792), remarking that the garden was neglected; John Britton, *Beauties of England & Wales* (1814). I am grateful to John Harris for drawing these references to my attention.
24. GC 1874 ii 263–6; *Garden* XXII (1883), p. 565; TRIGGS 1902, pp. 27–8; Guidebook. FORBES 1820, his one book, makes no mention of topiary, so it is uncertain whether he had yet begun its restoration then.
25. TRIGGS 1902, p. 17.
26. GC 1898 i 121.
27. REPTON 1840, p. 452; CARTER 1982, pp. 58–60; JACQUES 1983, pp. 162–4.
28. GM XVI (1840), p. 567; XIX (1843), pp. 252–3; PRICE 1842, pp. 169–74; GC 1864, p. 679; *JHort* XXXI (1876), pp. 122–4.
29. PAPWORTH 1818, p. 60; PAPWORTH 1823. MORRIS 1825, pp. 29–31. PHILLIPS 1823.
30. PRICE 1842, p. 167, and see also pp. 299–300; HOPE 1808, reprinted in GM XVIII (1841), pp. 157–64; GILPIN 1835, p. 37; SCOTT 1836, pp. 80–84..
31. REPTON 1840, pp, 416–17, 534–6. GILPIN 1835, pp. 44–5, 69, 81; see also GM XIX (1843), pp. 242–3 for Heanton Park. To see what they were reacting against, see MORRIS 1825, p. 27. For Page's use of railings see GM XI (1835), pp. 332–3; Gilpin's drawing for a wall and vases at Montagu House, London, is in the Scottish Record Office, RHP 9715/34.
32. *CottGard* XX (1858), pp. 2–4.
33. REPTON 1840, p. 525.
34. LOUDON 1822, p. 1229; GM III (1827), pp. 124–5.
35. GM III (1828), pp. 261–2; IV

(1828), p. 435; VI (1830), pp. 226–7; VII (1831), pp. 432–6; VIII (1832), pp. 155–7; XII (1836), pp. 520–5; XIX (1843), pp. 371–3. *HortReg* II (1833), pp. 16–17.
36. FM III (1838), pp. 32–3.
37. WILKES 1980, pp. 38, 57.
38. Gardens criticized for lack of terraces include: Hatfield House, GM V (1829), p. 672; Prospect Hill, GM IX (1833), pp. 669–70; Nuneham Courtenay, GM X (1834), pp. 97–8; Belvidere, GM XVI (1840), p. 583.
39. GILPIN 1835, pp. 41–2, 45–6. See BARRY 1867, pp. 269–71, for Barry's abortive plan for Clumber.
40. PRICE 1842, p. 314; see also pp. 305–7, 325. M'INTOSH 1853–55, pp. 1, 592–3.
41. Scottish Record Office RHP 14447/2. Drummond Castle: *Garden* V (1874), pp. 442–4; GC 1877 i 663, 688–9; *JHort* IX (1884), pp. 528–30; TAIT 1980, pp. 234–7. I am grateful for the assistance of Lady Jane Willoughby, Mrs Gilly Drummond, Miss E. J. Willson, and David Jacques in enquiries about Drummond.
42. DENNIS 1835, pp. 85–6; see also A. A. Tait, 'Loudon and the return to formality', in MACDOUGALL 1980, pp. 61–76.
43. MAJOR 1852, pp. 18–19. See GM IV (1828), pp. 85–90, 211–14; V (1829), pp. 604–7, 673; VIII (1832), pp. 155–7; XV (1839), pp. 457–8; *Florist's Journal* 1841, pp. 55–8; JHS III (1848), pp. 1–15.
44. Robert Southey, *Sir Thomas More* (1829), vol. I, pp. 173–4; Thomas Babington Macaulay, 'Southey's Colloquies', *Works* (1897), vol. V, p. 342.
45. For the changing significance of 'cottage', see John Woodforde, *The Truth about Cottages* (1969); SCOTT-JAMES 1981; George H. Ford, 'Felicitous space; the cottage controversy', in KNOEPFLMACHER 1978, pp. 29–48; JACQUES 1983, pp. 196–201. For late nineteenth-century statements about the historical importance of cottage gardens, see William Robinson, *The English Flower Garden*, 2nd ed. (1889), pp. 8–9; *Garden* XXXIX (1891), pp. 285–6; *GardMag* XXXIX (1896), p. 105; Marcus B. Huish and Helen Allingham, *Happy England* (1903), pp. 113–50.
46. *GardMag* XXVII (1894), p. 798; XXXVIII (1895), p. 89 (and see p. 137 on cottage planting); *JHort* XXII n.s. (1891), p. 197.
47. Thomas Bernard, *An Account of a Cottage and Garden near Tadcaster* (1797). Cobbett noted ornamental cottage gardens in the home counties: COBBETT 1830. The evidence for genuine cottage gardens is rehearsed in DARLEY 1975, pp. 2–3, 13–14.
48. DARLEY 1975; Walter L. Creese, *The Search for Environment* (1966). See the references in Chapter II, note 6.
49. Tom Taylor, *Birket Foster's Pictures of an English Landscape* (1863), poem xviii.
50. GC 1872, pp. 864–5.
51. William Busfeild Ferrand, *Allotment of Waste Lands* (1838).
52. GM XVI (1840), pp. 337–42.
53. DARLEY 1975, pp. 18, 21, 24. P. F. Robinson, *Rural Architecture*, 2nd ed. (1826), p. viii; *Designs for Park Buildings* (1830), esp. pl. xxxv, showing Italian, Swiss, and old English cottages together.
54. Robert Adamson, *The Cottage Gardener* (1851), p. 10; J. S. Barty, *Blackwood's Magazine* LXXIII (1853), p. 133.
55. *CottGard* VII (1852), p. 289.
56. Pugin, *True Principles of Pointed or Christian Architecture* (1841), pp. 48–9. Lews Castle: George Henry Hely Hutchison, *Twenty Years' Reminiscences of the Lews*; I am grateful to Peter Cunningham for providing me with this reference.
57. Dalkeith Palace: M'INTOSH 1853–55, vol. I, pp. 364–6 and plate xv. Harlaxton: GIROUARD 1979, pp. 92–102.
58. GC 1899 i 304–5; *JHort* XXVII (1874), p. 301.
59. FM IV (1839), pp. 263–4; *GardMag* LIII (1910), p. 490.
60. GC 1841, p. 231; 1843, p. 859; 1845, p. 839; FC XIV (1846), pp. 44–7; *Annals of Horticulture* 1847, p. 289; GC 1858, p. 860; *JHort* XIX (1870), pp. 432–4; HIX 1974, pp. 89–91.
61. GM XV (1839), pp. 145–7; XVI (1840), pp. 591–2; *GardMag* XXIII (1880), pp. 517–18.
62. DESMOND 1972; DIESTELKAMP 1982.
63. KEMP 1851, p. 37.
64. GOODHART-RENDEL 1953, pp. 57–8; HITCHCOCK 1954, vol. I, pp. 8, 15–18; Mark Girouard, 'Attitudes to Elizabethan Architecture, 1600–1900', in John Summerson ed., *Concerning Architecture* (1968), pp. 13–27; John Martin Robinson, *The Wyatts* (1979), pp. 60–65.
65. GIROUARD 1979, pp. 43–8, 103–9.
66. SCOTT 1836, pp. 80–86; GM XVIII (1842), p. 440; *Ladies' Magazine*, pp. 359–60; John Gibson Lockhart, *Memoirs of Sir Walter Scott* (1900), vol. IV, pp. 266–76; GC 1884 ii 583–4; MELLER 1975, pp. 8–11; TAIT 1980, pp. 203–211.
67. Drumlanrig Castle Muniments 9677/24 for Barry's plan; 9677/5 and 9677/7 for a plan of the gardens in 1840 and details of a compartment GM IX (1833), pp. 1–4; *JHort* III (1862), pp. 571–3; BARRY 1867, p. 142; *JHort* XVI (1869), p. 258; *Garden* III (1873), pp. 123–4; *JHort* XXXIII (1877), pp. 195–8; MELLER 1975, p. 98; TAIT 1980, pp. 204–6, 236.
68. REPTON 1840, pp. 56–60, 295; see KEMP 1850, p. 140 (KEMP 1864, p. 210).
69. PRICE 1842, pp. 305–7, 325; M'INTOSH 1838, pp. 86–98; PMB IV (1838), pp. 59, 206.
70. Phoebe Stanton, *Pugin* (1971), p. 28. TURNER 1842. See also 'Elizabethan Gardening', *Fraser's Magazine* LXX (1864), p. 179. The assimilation of Tudor to the Gothic tradition carried on as late as Barry's building of the Houses of Parliament, which were called Gothic although very much in a Tudor idiom; Pugin tried to cut Tudor off from Gothic altogether, and criticized the Parliament buildings as 'Grecian' to emphasize the point.
71. RICHARDSON 1837, pp. 10–11; *Fraser's Magazine* LXX (1864), p. 179.
72. Scotish Record Office GD 52/198/18/4–5 (1853).
73. GM XVI (1840), pp. 329–42; GC 1855, p. 823; GIROUARD 1979, pp. 91–102.
74. HITCHCOCK 1954, vol. I, pp. 220–58, for Vintners and other castellated houses of the period.
75. BARRY 1867, pp. 138–40; CL XXXIII (1913) pp 670–4; THOMAS 1979, p. 137.
76. GC 1853, p. 535; THOMAS 1979, pp. 170–72; Montacute House guidebook (1983), pp. 25–6.
77. GM V (1829), p. 672; XII (1836), p. 294; GC 1850, pp. 743, 759, 775; 1869, pp. 844–5; *JHort* XXI (1871), pp. 299–303; TRIGGS 1902, pp. 18–19; Lord David Cecil, guidebook to 'Hatfield House' (1973).
78. Sir Edward Bulwer-Lytton, undated letter at Knebworth House; I am grateful to Mike Calnan for allowing me to examine the Lytton

correspondence and plans. See *JHort* XVII (1874), pp. 451–3.
79. *Blackwood's Magazine* XXV (1834), pp. 691–2; NASH 1839–49; SOUTHEY 1848. Arley Hall: TRIGGS 1902, pp. 24–5; CL CLX (1976), pp. 950–2.
80. John Lindley, 'On the arrangement of gardens and pleasure-grounds in the Elizabethan age', JHS III (1848), pp. 1–15. See GC 1847, p. 670.
81. For the life of Nesfield, see ELLIOTT 1981b. For Salvin, see ALLIBONE 1977; for Blore, see MELLER 1975. Among gardens where Nesfield is known to have worked are: Arley Hall, Blickling, Broughton Hall, Coombe Abbey, Crewe Hall, Fortis Green, Grimston, The Grove, Holkham, Inverary Castle, Keele Hall, Kew, Latimers, Lynford Hall, Merevale Abbey, Oxon Hoath, the Royal Horticultural Society's garden at Kensington, Stoke Edith, Stoke Rochford, Stoneleigh Abbey, Treberfydd, Witley Court, Wivenhoe Park, Woolverstone Hall, Worsley Hall.
82. ALLIBONE 1977, pp. 135–8.
83. GM XVI (1840), pp. 49–58. Loudon had wanted to publish this in his *Suburban Gardener* in 1838, but the engravings had not been ready in time. See also ALLIBONE 1977, p. 83. For its influence, see a derivative plan by Davidson in *Florist* 1856, pp. 16-17.
84. *Gardener* 1874, pp. 408–10.
85. GC 1846, p. 807; BROOKE 1857; *CottGard* XXI (1859), p. 400; XXII (1859), pp. 285–7; *JHort* VII (1864), p. 130; GC 1875 ii 70–71; *JHort* XXXI (1876), pp. 214–16, 237–9; MELLER 1975, p. 35.
86. KEMP 1851, p. 117; THOMAS 1979, pp. 191–2.
87. FERRIS 1837.
88. *CottGard* IX (1852), pp. 67–8; VIII (1852), p. 414; GMB I (1850), pp. 13–14.
89. SMITH 1852, pp. 47–8. Somerleyton: *Florist* 1857, pp. 327–9, 368–70; 1858, p. 29.
90. Royal Botanic Gardens, Kew: English Letters, vol. XXII, letters 129–140; vol. XXIII, letters 517–18; vol. XXIV, letters 432-3; vol. XXV, letter 376; vol. XXVI, letters 403–7; vol. XXVII, letters 126–8; vol. XXXV, letters 338–9; vol. XXXVIII, letter 429; vol. XL, letter 165. W. A. Nesfield, 'Report on the formation of a National Arboretum at Kew', 20 July 1845, in Kewensia: Pleasure Grounds 1845–1911, pp. 214–15, and see also pp. 218, 227–9. KEMP 1851, pp. 35–50. FC XXIV (1856), pp. 158–9; *CottGard* XVIII (1857), pp. 388–90; XXI (1858), pp. 1–3; XXIV (1860), pp. 367–70.
91. W. A. Nesfield, Manuscript report on the gardens proposed to be annexed to Buckingham Palace, RIBA MSS; GC 1850, pp. 595–6; John Harris et al., *Buckingham Palace* (1968), pp. 30–34, 97, 99.
92. For the development of the Italianate style, see GOODHART-RENDEL 1953, pp. 65, 110–11; HITCHCOCK 1954, I, pp. 162–90; PEVSNER 1972, pp. 69–71.
93. LOUDON 1822, p. 1228; GM V (1829), pp. 589–93; XI (1835), p. 508; *JHort* XXX (1876), pp. 252–4; WATKIN 1968, pp. 158–92.
94. GM XII (1836), pp. 509–13; GC 1845, pp. 738–9; BROOKE 1857; Wiltshire Record Office 2057 A2/9–10, H2/4, H3/32–3.
95. GM IV (1828), pp. 211–14; IX (1833), pp. 9–10; XV (1839), p. 462; M'INTOSH 1838, p. 10; *Annals of Horticulture* 1848, pp. 475–7; GC 1848, p. 687; 1851, pp. 131–2; M'INTOSH 1853–55, pp. 573–4; and see KEMP 1864, pp. 172–203.
96. BARRY 1867, pp. 15–63.
97. LOUDON 1822, p. 1239; GM XVI (1840), pp. 580–1; GC 1848, p. 867; *CottGard* VII (1851–2), pp. 167–8, 195–6; BARRY 1867, pp. 113–15; TRIGGS 1902, pp. 26–7; CL CXLIII (1968), pp. 178, 228.
98. MANGLES 1839, pp. 28, 31; M'INTOSH 1838, pp. 10–11.
99. *CottGard* XXI (1858), pp. 7–8.
100. Osborne: GC 1897 i 396–9; Cyril Ward, *Royal Gardens* (1912), pp. 61–72. Hermione Hobhouse, *Thomas Cubitt, Master Builder* (1971), pp. 373–93, esp. 391–2.
101. GC 1845, p. 755; JHS IX (1853), pp. 42–5; *Florist* 1854, pp. 155–6; BROOKE 1857; *JHort* XIII (1867), pp. 345–6; *JHort* XXI (1871), p. 309–11; TRIGGS 1902, pp. 16–17.
102. GC 1879 i 747–8, 779–80; *JHort* V n.s. (1882), pp. 478–80; XL n.s. (1900), pp. 219–24.
103. WYATT 1854, p. 35.
104. KERR 1864, p. 345; GC 1864, pp. 1201–2; MALINS 1980b, pp. 82–95.
105. *Florist* 1857, pp. 42–5; BROOKE 1857; GC 1863, pp. 919–20; BARRY 1867, pp. 117–18; *GardMag* XXXIX (1896), pp. 271–8; Carol Kennedy, *Harewood* (1982), pp. 84–5.
106. GC 1853, p. 263; JHS IX (1853), pp. 40–41; GC 1856, pp. 55–6; FLEMING 1864; BARRY 1867, pp. 119–22.
107. *CottGard* V (1850), pp. 328–9; VI (1850), pp. 190–1; X (1853), pp. 495–7; XI (1853), pp. 5–7; GC 1855, p. 583; *CottGard* XVI (1856), pp. 452–4, 469–71; XVII (1856), pp. 39–41; *Florist* 1856, pp. 151–5 (repr. in GC 1856, pp. 322–3); BROOKE 1857; BARRY 1867, pp. 118–19; GC 1867, pp. 1099–1100, 1123, 1170–72; 1868, pp. 9–10, 31; FP VII (1868), pp. 221–4; *Garden* I (1872), pp. 350–1.
108. GC 1867, p. 1123.
109. Rhianva: *Garden* XVII (1880), pp. 364–5. Linton Park: *JHort* II (1861), p. 186.

Chapter 4

1. *Florist* 1852, pp. 151–3, of Elvaston Castle: 'so noble a creation ... We say creation, because all that is wonderful about it must be ascribed to the inventive genius of man, and chiefly to that of Mr Barron.'
2. For accounts of Paxton's life, see reference note 29 to chapter 1. For accounts of Chatsworth, see GC 1842, pp. 3, 20, 51–2, 67–8, 107–8, 187; GC 1844, p. 734; MAJOR 1852, pp. 125–8; *Garden* V (1874), pp. 5–7, 26–7; *JHort* XXVI (1874), pp. 149–50; *GardMag* XXXIX (1896), p. 463; *GardMag* XLIV (1901), pp. 804–8; Francis Thompson, *A History of Chatsworth* (1949); CHADWICK 1961, pp. 19–43.
3. GM VII (1831), pp. 395–7.
4. *HortReg* I (1832), pp. 132–3. Loudon's later more favourable views: GM XV (1839), pp. 450–3.
5. GC 1842, p. 3. For the history of the willow, see George Hall, *The History of Chesterfield* (1839), pp. 420–21; I am grateful to M. A. Pearman, archivist at Chatsworth, for this reference.
6. GM XV (1839), p. 451.
7. *HortReg* IV (1835), pp. 57–8; MAJOR 1852, p. 125; GC 1883 ii 176.
8. There is a 'Description of the Great Fountain at Chatsworth', dated 1844, among the Paxton papers at Chatsworth; for published accounts, see PMB XI (1844), pp. 223–7; GC 1844, p. 734; ROE 1845, p. 13.
9. *HortReg* I (1832), p. 133.
10. GC 1842, p. 20; MAJOR 1852, pp. 125–6.
11. *JHort* XVII (1857), p. 487.

12. PMB I (1834), pp. 254–60.
13. MAJOR 1852, pp. 127–8.
14. GC 1842, p. 3.
15. *JHort* VII (1864), p. 395; BROOKE 1857.
16. Enville: BROOKE 1857; BURRITT 1868, p. 308. Arundel Castle: GC 1855, p. 567. See also ELLIOTT 1986b.
17. *CottGard* XVI (1856), p. 217. The original jet fountain at People's Park was replaced by a sculptural group brought from Somerleyton at the turn of the century.
18. For Barron's life, see GC 1891 i 522–4.
19. GM XV (1839), p. 458; GC 1849, p. 773; BARRON 1852, pp. 1–3; *Horticulturist* 1857, pp. 211–12.
20. BARRON 1852, pp. 5–6, 26–48; GM XV (1839), pp. 458–60; GC 1849, pp. 84, 789; GC 1850, p. 84.
21. GM XV (1839), pp. 458–60; GC 1849, pp. 773, 789; 1850, p. 4.
22. Mark Girouard, *The Return to Camelot* (1981), pp. 88–9.
23. GC 1849, pp. 773, 789, 820–21.
24. GC 1850, p. 4.
25. GM XV (1839), pp. 458–60; GC 1849, p. 805; *CottGard* XXI (1859), p. 211. Marot's design is reproduced in Frank Crisp, *Mediaeval Gardens* (1924), vol. II, plate clxix.
26. GC 1849, p. 773; *CottGard* VIII (1852), p. 244; *Horticulturist* 1857, p. 211. Glendinning's account: GC 1849, pp. 773, 789, 805, 820; 1850, pp. 4, 21, 36, 53, 69, 84, 100.
27. GC 1864, pp. 937–8; *JHort* VII (1864), p. 130; GC 1876 ii 838. Baines's prediction came true; 'Mon Plaisir' finally collapsed in the 1960s, and the garden is now a country park.
28. GM III (1828), pp. 485–6; GC 1862, p. 1218.
29. John Caie, 'Descriptive notice of Bedford Lodge', GM XIV (1838), pp. 401–11. For the debate over the priority of Caie and Philip Frost, see GC 1880 i 224, 267; TAYLOR 1952, pp. 70–79.
30. GC 1879 ii 442, 489, 534; also *CottGard* V (1850), pp. 158–9, XII (1854), p. 336, and VI (1851), pp. 112–13 for Beaton's praise and indebtedness.
31. John Caie, 'On a proper arrangement of plants, both as to their height and the colour of their flowers, being indispensably necessary in a flower-garden ', GM XIII (1837), pp. 301–4. GMB I (1850), pp. 51, 105, 153, 198–9 (this article was reprinted in the *Florist's Guide* 1850, pp. 54–55, and in *JHort* III (1862), pp. 84–5), 202, 267, 316; II (1850), pp. 51, 195.
32. M'INTOSH 1838, p. 33; *Florist's Journal* 1841, pp. 289–90; PMB XIV (1847), pp. 158–62; KEMP 1850, p. 127 (KEMP 1864, pp. 166–7); MAJOR 1852, p. 33.
33. HAY 1845. For a discussion of Hay, see GM XIX (1843), pp. 130–33.
34. UGLSJ 1845, pp. 441, 443.
35. MANGLES 1839, pp. 41–3.
36. *CottGard* V (1850), p. 158; X (1853), p. 20; XIV (1855), pp. 156–7. See also John Robson, 'The rise and progress of the bedding geranium', *JHort* XXI (1871), pp. 481–4; GORER 1975, pp. 71–91; GORER 1978, pp. 128–49.
37. Beaton, *CottGard* IV (1850), p. 76. For the progress and future of bedding, see Caie: GMB II (1850), pp. 244, 292; Beaton: *CottGard* IV (1850), pp. 158–9; (1851), pp. 289–90.
38. For Fleming's life, see *CottGard* XIII (1854), pp. 33–7. General accounts of Trentham: UGLSJ 1846, pp. 197–8, 213, 229–30; BROOKE 1857; and the anonymous guidebook *Trentham and its Gardens* (1857).
39. *CottGard* XIII (1854), pp. 35–6.
40. GC 1848, p. 687, 703, 719, 751, 783; *Florist* 1854, p. 102.
41. BROOKE 1857; GC 1848, p. 87.
42. Ribbon borders: UGLSJ 1846, p. 198; BROOKE 1857; GC 1856, pp. 692–3; but see also Beaton's claim for the priority of Shrubland Park, *CottGard* XVI (1856), p. 454, 470.
43. Shading: *CottGard* V (1851), p. 290; XVI (1856), p. 470.
44. BROOKE 1857.
45. GC 1848, p. 703.
46. Ibid.; KEMP 1851, pp. 120–21.
47. *CottGard* X (1853), pp. 364–5; XIV (1855), pp. 405–6.
48. *CottGard* X (1853), p. 364; BROOKE 1857.
49. For the subsequent history of the garden see ELLIOTT 1984 b.
50. Bagshot: GM IV (1828), p. 303; V (1829), pp. 570–71. Caen Wood: LOUDON 1822, p. 1226; GM III (1828), p. 486; GC 1841, p. 471.
51. GM V (1829), pp. 570–71.
52. GC 1841, pp. 52, 85, 135.
53. *Builder* XI (1853), pp. 417–18; GC 1853, pp. 436–7.
54. Dropmore: GC 1868, pp. 464–5; *National Review* XXXIII (1899), pp. 302–16.
55. GC 1882 ii 75–6; see also GC 1887 ii 463–4.
56. PRICE 1842, pp. 211–12; GC 1841, p. 183; *CottGard* II (1849), p. 18; *JHort* III n.s. (1881), p. 40.
57. GC 1865, pp. 626–7; *Garden* II (1872), pp. 234–5.
58. GC 1868, p. 459; *Floral World* 1867, p. 307; *GardMag* XLV (1902), p Linton Park: Maidstone Record Office, U24 A12, for John Robson's planting of a snowdrop field in 1873.
59. Barr and Sugden catalogue, 1862.
60. ROBINSON 1870b, p. 7.
61. MAJOR 1852, p. 40; THOMPSON 1859, p. 693.
62. GC 1845, p. 327; *CottGard* IV (1850), p. 232.
63. GC 1842, p. 560; *JHort* XXXIV (1878), pp. 69–71; GC 1909 i 234; *GardMag* LII (1909), p. 103.
64. BARRON 1852, pp. 71–77. Glendinning: GC 1850, pp. 21, 36. Robson: *CottGard* XXI (1859), p. 212.
65. GC 1844, p. 734; M'INTOSH 1853–55, vol. I, pp. 701–5; *CottGard* X (1853), p. 423; XVII (1857), p. 427.
66. MAJOR 1852, p. 128; *Garden* I (1871), p. 50; *Garden* V (1874), p. 26.
67. GC 1850, p. 663.
68. GC 1844, pp. 115, 211; KEMP 1850, pp. 159–60 (KEMP 1864, pp. 272–3); KEMP 1851, pp. 118–119; SMITH 1852, p. 53–4; R. H. Cheney, QR XCVIII (1855), p. 213. See also Robson in *JHort* II (1861), pp. 102–3.
69. GC 1850, p. 37.
70. *CottGard* XXIII (1859), pp. 84–6; *JHort* XXII (1872), pp. 501–3; *JHort* XXV n.s. (1892), p. 50.
71. GC 1843, p. 134. For a survey of the Portland cements, see James Pulham, 'On cements, artificial stone, and plastic compositions', *Builder* III (1845), p. 160, and FRANCIS 1977.
72. For the history of Pulham and Son, see PULHAM 1877; R. G. Freeman, 'The house that James built', *Hertfordshire Countryside*, September 1966 (ex info A. T. Crow); FRANCIS 1977, pp. 91–109; FESTING 1984; ELLIOTT 1984a.
73. GC 1842, pp. 607–8.
74. FESTING 1984. I am grateful to Graham Stuart Thomas for first showing me how to identify Pulham stone in the field.
75. Lindley's articles: GC 1847, pp. 83, 99, 115, 133–4, 155–6, 172, 187–8, 203–4, 219, 235, 251–2, 267, 283, 301–2,

339–40, 355, 371, 387–8, 403, 419, 435–6, 452, 523–4, 539, 587–8, 603, 619, 635, 651–2, 683, 699–700, 747, 763–4, 795, 813–14, 835–6; GC 1848, pp. 3, 67, 83–4, 99–100, 133–4, 155–6, 171, 187–8, 203–4, 219, 235–6, 267, 300, 315–16, 331–2, 363, 379–80, 419–20, 435. See also replies from correspondents: GC 1847, pp. 749, 767; GC 1848, pp. 22, 205, and additional letters on Queen's Park Manchester, listed in note 86 below.
76. Smith: TAIT 1980, p. 208; see GC 1852, p. 614.
77. Gorrie: *Scottish Gardener* III (1854), pp. 9–12, 41–3, 102–4, 134–8, 177–9, 263–6, 328–31; IV (1855), pp. 11–13, 107–10, 208–10, and see also 255–9. For Gorrie's career, see *CottGard* XVI (1856), pp. 98–9.
78. GC 1853, pp. 183, 197.
79. MAJOR 1852, pp. 41, 125–9.
80. SMITH 1852, pp. 44–5; KEMP 1850, p. 32 (KEMP 1984, pp. 37–8).
81. GC 1847, pp. 172, 683, 747.
82. SMITH, p. 53. See also KEMP 1850, pp. 32–3 (KEMP 1864, p. 38).
83. SMITH 1852, p. 135; MAJOR 1852, pp. 82–3; Lindley, GC 1847, p. 115.
84. *Scottish Gardener* III (1854), p. 41.
85. Lindley: GC 1847 passim; JHS III (1848), pp. 1–15.
86. GC 1847, pp. 191, 236–7, 267, 325, 780, 817. See also ELLIOTT 1986a.
87. SMITH 1852, p. 61.
88. *Scottish Gardener* III (1854), p. 9; see also *Florist's Journal* 1840, pp. 67–9, and 1845, p. 262.
89. *Scottish Gardener* IV (1855), p. 256.
90. MAJOR 1852, p.126.
91. KEMP 1850, p. 101 (KEMP 1864, p. 125).
92. Glendinning, GC 1850, p. 37.
93. For accounts of Bateman's life, see GC 1871, pp. 1514–15; P. Hayden, 'James Bateman: plantsman and garden designer', *Staffordshire History*, I (1984). His major works were a pamphlet on cool orchid growing, *A Monograph of Odontoglossum*, and his major work, *The Orchidaceae of Mexico and Guatemala* (1840), a cumbersome folio with Mayan decorations on its title page, illustrations by Cruikshank and Mrs Withers, and an account of the tropical orchids being introduced by George Ure Skinner and other collectors.
94. *CottGard* XV (1855), pp. 461–2. For the extract from Cooke's diaries, see below.
95. Mavis Batey, 'Edward Cooke, landscape gardener ... ', *Garden History*, VI no. i (1978), pp. 18–24; HAYDEN 1978. Peter Hayden has deposited in the Lindley Library a copy of his transcript of garden-related entries from Cooke's diaries (originals in the National Maritime Museum, Greenwich); all citations are taken from this.
96. For an account of Biddulph Grange, see Edward Kemp's articles: GC 1856, pp. 679, 695, 711, 727–8, 775–6, 807–8; also p. 821 for Bateman's letter specifying Cooke's role; then GC 1862, pp. 478–80, 527–8, 575–6, 670–2, 712–20. Kemp released separately a pamphlet based on these articles, 'Description of the gardens at Biddulph Grange' (1862). Cf. also GC 1876 ii 236–7; JRHS CII (1977), pp. 193–6; HAYDEN 1978.
97. For previous stumperies, see GM III (1828), p. 481; GC 1841, p. 300; *Birmingham and Midland Gardeners' Magazine* 1853, pp. 47–8; *CottGard* XIV (1855), pp. 461–2 (at Knypersley).
98. WIGHTWICK 1840, pp. 39, 51–2.
99. James Bateman, 'Substance of two lectures on the final and universal triumph of the Gospel' (1848), pp. 43–4; quoting from *Churchman's Monthly Review* (1844), p. 473.
100. GC 1856, p. 695; 1862, p. 527.
101. Home House, Worthing: GC 1890 ii 243, 246; 1894 ii 345.

Chapter 5

1. GC1851, p. 19; BARRY 1867, pp. 284–5; CHADWICK 1961, pp. 104–36; HIX 1974; Anthony Bird, *Paxton's Palace* (1976).
2. Nesfield to Paxton, 8 July (1850); Paxton Papers 582, Chatsworth.
3. GMB III (1851), 269–72; *Florist* 1851, p. 169.
4. *Illustrated London News*, 6 July 1850, p. 13.
5. GC 1851, pp. 707–8.
6. *CottGard* VIII (1852), p. 175; GC 1851, p. 19.
7. *JHort* VII (1864), pp. 375–6.
8. *CottGard* XII (1854), pp. 443–5.
9. Sydenham: CHADWICK 1961, pp. 137–59. Enville: *JHort* VII (1864), pp. 375–6; BROOKE 1857. It is difficult to determine which partner was responsible for the design; Ormson used the building in his advertisements after the break-up of the firm, but it was Gray who received the payment. Kew: DIESTELKAMP 1982.
10. *Garden* VI (1874), pp. 368–9.
11. Crystal Sanitarium: *CottGard* VIII (1852), pp. 15–16; CHADWICK 1961, pp. 137–8.
12. *GardMag* XXIII (1880), pp. 517–8. See GC 1877 ii 108–9 for Gothic versus Queen Anne conservatories.
13. GC 1877 i 373, 436.
14. Winter gardens. Edinburgh: GC 1872, pp. 465–6. Bournemouth: GC 1877 i 77. Folkestone: *Gardening World* I (1885), p. 649; GC 1885 i 576–7. See *Floral World* II (1859), pp. 98–9, for the Owen Jones/John Spencer scheme for a People's Palace in North London.
15. Alexandra Palace: *Garden* III (1873), pp. 386, 390; GC 1873, p. 811; *Garden* V (1874), p. 178; *JHort* XXXI (1876), pp. 468–70. The Alexandra Palace burnt down again in 1980 (the water towers were empty), and is being restored.
16. GC 1851, p. 773.
17. *Florist* 1853, pp. 274–6; GC 1853, pp. 583, 739–40; *CottGard* XII (1854), p. 422, 490–2; *CottGard* XIII (1854), pp. 14–15, 38–40, 49–50; WYATT 1854, pp. 34–39; *Phillips' Guide to the Crystal Palace* (1854); GC 1855, pp. 7, 263–4; *CottGard* XVI (1856), pp. 217, 450–2, 467–8; XVII (1856), pp. 21–2, 42–3; GC 1856, pp. 419–20, 454; COLE 1877, pp. 53–8.
18. ROE 1845, pp. 19–34.
19. FC XXIV (1856), pp. 158–9. People's Park: *Florist* 1858, p. 22; *CottGard* XXI (1859), p. 108.
20. *CottGard* XXIV (1860), pp. 337–40.
21. KERR 1864, p. 345. Poles Park: *CottGard* II (1849), pp. 252–3; VI (1851), p. 94; XIX (1857), pp. 128–30, 143–4; WILKINSON 1858, pp. 366–7; *JHort* XXII (1872), p. 527; XXIII (1872), pp. 14–16. For Robert Fish's dream of a terrace garden, see *CottGard* XIV (1855), p. 371; XVIII (1857), pp. 376–7.
22. SMITH 1852, pp. 8, 29, 38–39; KEMP 1864, p. 172–203.
23. *Garden* XVII (1880), pp. 364–5; ROBINSON 1883, pp. xxii–xxiv.
24. *CottGard* XXI (1858), pp. 100–1; *JHort* XXXV (1878), pp. 450–2; GC 1901 ii 111. Baxter also designed the short-lived Royal Victoria Horticultural and Botanical Gardens in Bath; see HANHAM 1857.

25. Humphreys: GMB I (1850), pp. 124–6, 132–4, 164–6, 220–2. PAUL 1855, pp. 9–10, 24–27 and see ELLIOTT 1987a.
26. Fish: BEETON 1862, p. 9. HIBBERD 1857, pp. 334–8. HUGHES 1866, pp. 37–42.
27. *CottGard* XII (1854), pp. 491–2.
28. KEMP 1850, pp. 140–3 (KEMP 1864, pp. 210–214). For Grecian: lime, beech, birch, Turkey oak, larch, yew, cypress, deodar, araucaria; for Gothic: sycamores, horse chestnuts, laurels, aucuba, magnolias, hollies and ivy.
29. SMITH 1852, pp. 26–7; HUGHES 1866, pp. 18–26. 'E.g. approach at Pynes truly frightful', wrote the Exeter nurseryman and landscape gardener Robert Pince, whose annotated copy of SMITH 1852 is in the Lindley Library.
30. SMITH 1852, pp. 2–10; GC 1858, pp. 20–21; *CottGard* XXII (1859), pp. 80–81; HUGHES 1866, pp. 2–10.
31. GILPIN 1835, p. 185; SMITH 1852, p. 102; KEMP 1850, p. 122 (KEMP 1964, p. 160).
32. *JHort* XXX (1876), pp. 192–4; KEMP 1864 pp. 288–302.
33. *JHort* V (1863), pp. 493–5.
34. HIBBERD 1857, pp. 334–46.
35. KEMP 1850, pp. 41, 82–94 (KEMP 1864, pp. 46, 91–120); M'INTOSH 1853–55, pp. 693–701; THOMPSON 1859, pp. 687–8; HUGHES 1866, p. 1.
36. HIBBERD 1857, p. 340.
37. KEMP 1850, p. 82 (KEMP 1864, pp. 91–2); THOMPSON 1859, pp. 688–9.
38. *CottGard* XXIII (1860), p. 250.
39. *CottGard* VIII (1852), p. 358; WOODBRIDGE 1976.
40. BARRON 1852, pp. 10–11; PAUL 1855, pp. 17–21. See also ELLIOTT 1987a.
41. LOUDON 1835–38, vol. I, pp. 117–32. Hartweg: JHS IV (1849), pp. 211–20. Veitch: VEITCH 1906. See also GORER 1978; Sir George Taylor, 'The contribution from America to British gardens in the early nineteenth century', in MACDOUGALL 1980, pp. 107–23. Cedar and araucaria: *Annals of Horticulture* 1848, pp. 449–52, 543–6.
42. JHS V (1849), pp. 173–5; *CottGard* XII (1854), pp. 272–3; XXI (1858), p. 100.
43. Glendinning, 'On the introduction of new coniferous trees into park scenery', JHS VII (1849), pp. 173–5; Errington, 'On style and expression in certain trees and shrubs', JHS VII (1852), p. 193–8, esp. p. 196; John Cox, 'On conifers as ornamental plants', FP XI (1872), pp. 155–7; Masters, JRHS XIV (1892), pp. 1–18, esp. p. 10. See also Edward James Ravenscroft, *Pinetum Britannicum* (1863–84).
44. BARRON 1852, pp. 78–89; *Florist* 1852, pp. 151–3; HANHAM 1857, pp. xxx–xxxvii.
45. SMITH 1852, pp. 52–6. Appleby, 'Grouping trees in parks', *CottGard* XX (1856), pp. 245–6.
46. GC 1843, p. 57; *CottGard* VIII (1852), p. 358; HUGHES 1866, p. 24. For Bayfordbury, see GM XVI (1840), pp. 588–90; GC 1842, pp. 543–4.
47. *CottGard* VIII (1852), p. 358; XX (1858), pp. 377–8. KEMP 1864, p. 141; HUGHES 1866, p. 25. See GM XI (1835), pp. 57–9; KEMP 1851, pp. 30–3.
48. *JHort* XXV n.s. (1892), p. 507.
49. GC 1875 ii 785; 1899 i 50; *Garden* XXIX (1888), p. 49; *JHort* XVIII n.s. (1889), p. 278.
50. Welbeck: GC 1891 ii 185–6, 215–16; *GardMag* LIII (1910), pp. 449–53. Kew: BEAN 1908.
51. Kew: *CottGard* XVIII (1857), p. 388. SMITH 1852, pp. 248–50. Bowood: JHS IX (1853), pp. 42–5: M'INTOSH 1853–55, vol. I, pp. 584–90.
52. Royal Botanic Gardens, Kew: Kewensia (Pleasure Grounds 1845–1911), lvs. 214–15 ('Report on the formation of a National Arboretum at Kew', 1845), 218; English Letters, vol. XXII, letters 131, 133, and vol. XXIII, letter 517.
53. Eastnor: *Gardener* 1870, pp. 39–41, 165–8; GC 1875 ii 517; GC 1878 i 76–8, 107–8, 170–1; *Gardening World I* (1884), p. 93; *Garden* XXXIII (1888), pp. 357–8; GC 1908 i 143; 'Some Trees of Eastnor Castle' (University of Birmingham, 1977).
54. Earl Somers at Eastnor, the Earl of Ducie at Tortworth Court, Lord Delamere at Vale Royal, Sir Philip Egerton at Oulton Park, and R.S. Holford at Westonbirt formed an informal association for the mutual exchange of new exotic trees. Tortworth Court: *JHort* XXV (1873), pp. 155–8. Oulton Park: *JHort* XIII (1867), pp. 152–3. Westonbirt: *JHort* L (1873), pp. 81–4; XLVIII n.s. (1904), pp. 205–9.
55. GILPIN 1835, pp. 51–2.
56. GM XIII (1837), pp. 249–56.
57. *JHort* III (1862), p. 132: *CottGard* III (1849), pp. 61–2.
58. Florence Hopper, 'The Dutch Régence garden', *Garden History* IX no. ii (1981), pp. 118–35.
59. H. Noel Humphreys, 'On the effect of clipped trees in decorative gardening, and how far they are admissable', GMB II (1850), pp. 59–62.
60. Sudeley Castle Guidebook 1977; Emma Dent, *Annals of Winchcombe and Sudeley* (1877), pp. 77, 322. Castle Combe: BROOKE 1857; *Florist* 1857, pp. 291–3; GC 1857, pp. 711–12.
61. M'INTOSH 1853–55, pp. 579–80; *Blackwood's Magazine* LXXIII (1853), pp. 141–2; *JHort* XXIX (1875), p. 229.
62. KEMP 1864, pp. 222–3.
63. I am grateful to Mr G. Mander for information on the probable dating. No topiary scheme is mentioned in the accounts of Owlpen in either Rudder's or Fosbrooke's histories of Gloucestershire (1779 and 1807).
64. Packwood: BLOMFIELD 1892, pp. 72–4; THOMAS 1979, pp. 192–3. Heslington Hall: FM I (1837), pp. 213–14; TRIGGS 1902, p. 28; CL XXXIV (1913), pp. 90–7.
65. TRIGGS 1902, p. 24; J. Bosworth et al., *Bridge End Gardens: an historical study and proposals for their renovation* (1983). The attribution to Chater is based on GC 1885 ii 155.
66. GC 1867, p. 1123.
67. GC 1841, pp. 182, 189. Hatfield: BLOMFIELD 1892, p. 151.
68. MURRAY 1863, pp. 174–9.
69. KEMP 1864, pp. 232, 274, 276. See ROBINSON 1883, pp. lv–lviii, for an attack on stumperies.
70. WYATT 1854, p. 39.
71. R. C. Turner, *Mellor's Gardens* (Cheshire County Council, n.d.). The 1880s visitors were from the Manchester Field Naturalists and Archaeologists; see their *Report and Proceedings*, 1885, pp. 28–9. I am grateful to Mrs Ruth Humphreys for providing this reference.
72. GC 1862, p. 719.
73. KEMP 1864, pp. 184–6 for Daylesford Hall; see also Edward Kemp, 'Memoranda explanatory of plan for rearranging the approach to the mansion at Wynyard Park', Durham County Record Office.
74. KEMP 1864, pp. 180–183 for Leighton Hall; 239–42, 371–4 for Underscar.
75. SMEE 1872, p. 37.
76. Extracts from E. W. Cooke's diary 1866–70; see note 95 to chapter IV.

77. George Field, *Chromatography* (1835); HAY 1845; Goethe, *Theory of Colour*, transl. Charles Eastlake (1840); CHEVREUL 1854. For the general history of colour theory, see Wilhelm Ostwald, *Colour Science* (1931), and Faber Birren, *Principles of Colour* (1969). There has not so far been an adequate study of the impact of colour theory on the Victorian arts; but for a brief survey of the thought available to the Victorian gardener, see William Keane in *JHort* IV (1863), pp. 199–200.
78. See, e.g., *CottGard* III (1850), p. 321. See HIBBERD 1857, pp. 347–82; much of the Beaton-derived material, however, was dropped in the third edition of 1870.
79. Falkland: Scottish Record Office, GD 152/53/4/11, and GD 152/53/5/Bundle 10/1–2. The plans: *CottGard* IX (1852–53), pp. 67–8, 147–8, 289; X (1853), pp. 14–15, 293, 353–4, 433–4; XI (1853–4), pp. 153–4, 213, 393–4; XII (1854), pp. 89–90.
80. *CottGard* X (1853), pp. 353–4. The Paxton attribution is first found in S. L. Ollard, 'Bainton Church and Parish – some notes on their history' (1930), and was afterwards repeated by Pevsner; I am indebted to Mr C. Huddleston for showing me the plan of Bainton Old Rectory.
81. GMB II (1850), p. 195; *CottGard* IV (1850), p. 20.
82. *CottGard* XIV (1855), p. 20.
83. Caie, GMB II (1850), p. 51. Beaton, *CottGard* IV (1850), pp. 186–7; VI (1851), p. 397.
84. GC 1853, p. 173. Erasmus Darwin: *Zoonomia* (1796), vol. I, pp. 538–76. GAGE (1969), pp. 173–88.
85. GC 1841 p. 291; see also p. 685.
86. Simultaneous contrast: GC 1849, pp. 787–8. Examples of colour schemes from Chevreul: pp. 803–5, 819; GC 1850, pp. 4–5, 36, 116–17, 165, 181. Some of Lindley's discussion was reprinted in FC XVIII (1850), pp. 7–12, 58–60. CHEVREUL 1854, pp. 286–345.
87. *CottGard* III (1849), pp. 53–4; ibid. (1850), p. 333; KEMP 1850, p. 75; M'INTOSH 1853–55, pp. 599–603; and see Crace Calvert's lectures on Chevreul, published in both GC 1857, pp. 596–7, 788, and *CottGard* XIX (1857), pp. 204–5; ibid., pp. 183–4.
88. *CottGard* XXI (1858), pp. 17–19. See also *CottGard* III (1850), p. 333; X (1853), p. 59; XIX (1857), p. 106; XX (1858), p. 143.
89. GC 1843, p. 173; GC 1849, p. 819; see also SMITH 1852, pp. 45–7.
90. *Florist* III (1850), pp. 59–60.
91. GC 1857, p. 382; GC 1859, p. 216. See *CottGard* XXI (1858), pp. 17–19, for the history of the rivalry. For Beaton's role at Kew, see *CottGard* XX (1858), pp. 357–8.
92. *CottGard* XXI (1858), p. 18; see also XXI (1859), p. 377 for further jesting at Lindley's expense.
93. Ostwald, op. cit., pp. 12–13. Red and sea-green, for instance, are true complementaries.
94. WILKINSON 1858, esp. pp. 58–64, 72–4, 91–3, and the section on gardens, pp. 360–388.
95. On Owen Jones: *CottGard* V (1851), p. 227; see also p. 212. On T. C. March: *JHort* III (1862), pp. 757–9. See MARCH 1862.
96. Owen Jones, 'An atttempt to define the principles which should regulate the employment of colour in the decorative arts', in *Lectures on the Results of the Great Exhibition of 1851* (1853), pp. 255–300; see especially pp. 258–9, 272–4. JONES 1856; Field's chromatic equivalents are as follows. Primaries: yellow 3, red 5, blue 8; Secondaries: orange 8, purple 13, green 11; each secondary is harmonized by the remaining primary in equal proportions. Thus, equal masses of orange and blue will harmonize, or yellow and purple in a proportion of 3 to 13. See FIELD 1817.
97. Jones, 'An attempt', op. cit., p. 261.
98. *CottGard* XII (1854), p. 491; see also p. 422.
99. GC 1849, pp. 341–2.
100. *JHort* V (1863), p. 169. For nineteenth-century attitudes to Rubens, see PRICE 1842, p. 116, and GAGE 1969, pp. 62–4.
101. HUGHES 1866, pp. 94–5.
102. *CottGard* XV (1856), p. 328; see also XX (1858), p. 306.
103. These beds are shown on Tuelon's watercolour perspective of his new building, now hanging in the house.
104. *CottGard* XIX (1857), p. 1. See also HIBBERD 1857, pp. 347–50.
105. *CottGard* IV (1850), pp. 158–9; XV (1855) pp. 66–7; XX (1858), pp. 142, 306, 357–8.
106. For the origin of ribbons, see GC 1856, pp. 692–3. Here follows a sampling of the most important writers on the subject. Robert Errington: *Midland Florist* XI (1857), pp. 5–9. Donald Beaton: *CottGard* XV (1855), pp. 214–15, 254–6; XX (1858), 95–7; XXIII (1859), p. 2; XXIV (1860), pp. 95–7; *JHort* I (1861), pp. 57–8. John Robson: *JHort* II (1862), pp. 400–402, 416–17. Shirley Hibberd: HIBBERD 1857, pp. 368–70.
107. Robert Errington: *Midland Florist* XI (1857), pp. 5–9. Beaton: *CottGard* XV (1855), pp. 66–7; XIX (1857), pp. 1–2.
108. *CottGard* XIX (1857) p. 1; XX (1858), pp. 307–8; XXII (1859), p. 162; XXIV (1860), p. 65–7.
109. E.g. at Hemstead Park: *JHort* III (1862), pp. 626–7.
110. *CottGard* X (1853), pp. 433–4; XXIII (1859), p. 3.
111. *JHort* III (1862), p. 778, *CottGard* XXII (1859), p. 285; see also FP III (1864), pp. 40–41.
112. George M'Ewen, 'A plea for pyramidal pelargoniums', *JHort* III (1862), pp. 28–9. Beaton: *CottGard* XII (1854), pp. 472–3; *JHort* III (1862), pp. 132–3.
113. Early floral cones: FC III (1835), pp. 274–5; IV (1836), pp. 193–5; GM XIII (1837), pp. 1–2, 6–7; GC 1845, p. 819. Hibberd and associates: *Floral World* I (1858), pp. 138–9; 1866, pp. 131–4. See also *JHort* XIV (1868), p. 278; GC 1872, pp. 1362, 1423–4, 1624–5; *Garden* III (1873), p. 158.
114. Forsyth: FP XIII (1874), pp. 203–4: XVI (1877), pp. 127, 155. Circles vs. cones: *CottGard* XXIII (1860), p. 279.
115. *JHort* XI (1866), pp. 222, 278–9.
116. *CottGard* XVI (1856), pp. 271–2; XVIII (1857) 388–90; XXIII (1859), pp. 1–3; HIBBERD 1857, pp. 350–3.
117. Scott: *CottGard* XVI (1856), p. 408. Thomson: *JHort* II (1862), pp. 451–2.
118. For the rise of massiveness in High Victorian architecture, see Stefan Muthesius, *The High Victorian Movement in Architecture* (1976), and Edward N. Kaufman, ' "The weight and vigour of their masses": mid-Victorian country churches and "The Lamp of Power" ', in J. D. Hunt, ed., *The Ruskin Polygon* (1979), pp. 94–121.
119. R. H. Cheney, 'Landscape gardening', QR XCVIII (1855), p. 214. Beaton: *CottGard* XV (1856), p. 328.
120. John Robson, 'Flower gardening on a new principle', *CottGard* XXI (1859), pp. 396–7. See the following accounts of Robson's bedding practice:

CottGard XXII (1859), pp. 143–5, 160–3: *JHort* I (1861), pp. 185–8, 218–20, 238–40; II (1862), pp. 227–8; V (1863), pp. 145–6. One of Robson's bedding plans (1863) is preserved in the Maidstone Record Office (U24 E25), along with his garden diaries; I am grateful to Joan Morgan for drawing my attention to these.
121. GC 1845, p. 560; ROBINSON 1870b, p. 5.
122. Beaton: *CottGard* XXII (1859), p. 2; see also VI (1851), pp. 331–2; VIII (1852), p. 318; XX (1858), p. 112. Anderson: *JHort* III (1862), pp. 777–8. See *JHort* XII (1867), pp. 9–10, for Barlaston, celebrated for bedding and borders together.
123. *CottGard* XI (1854), p. 498. Annuals, if anything, underwent a greater eclipse than perennials.
124. *CottGard* XV (1855), pp. 254–6; see also pp. 214–15, and XX (1858), p. 112.
125. Robert Errington, 'On clumping out flowers', JHS III (1848), pp. 304–7.
126. Errington, 'A few observations on styles in flower gardening', *Midland Florist* XI (1857), pp. 5–9. See also Errington, 'A glance at modern flower-gardens', *Florist's Guide* 1850, pp. 137–8, and in *CottGard* XVIII (1857), p. 375.
127. *Garden Companion* (1852), p. 27; also pp. 93–4, 130–1.
128. GC 1849, pp. 341–2, and reply by Henry Bailey, p. 373; Errington, *Midland Florist* XI (1857), pp. 5–9. See also MAJOR 1852, p. 33.
129. GMB I (1850), p. 153.
130. Neutral beds: *CottGard* V (1850), p. 187; VI (1851), p. 397. Shot-silk beds: *CottGard* V (1850), p. 33; see also VI (1851), p. 397; X (1853), pp. 20–1; *Garden Companion* (1852), p. 27.
131. *CottGard* V (1850), p. 33; VII (1851), p. 396.
132. *CottGard* IX (1852), p. 60; XV (1855), p. 84; *Garden I* (1872), p. 440.
133. WILKINSON 1858; HIBBERD 1875, pp. 201–4; ELLIOTT 1986b.
134. *JHort* III (1862), pp. 777–8; KEMP 1850, pp. 157–8 (KEMP 1864, pp. 242–4); 'Elizabethan gardening', *Fraser's Magazine* LXX (1864), pp. 182–4, 186–7; MORRIS 1882, p. 127.
135. *CottGard* XV (1855), pp. 214–5; see also X (1853), p. 59; XIII (1854), p. 20; XX (1858), p. 112. HIBBERD 1857, p. 368.
136. *CottGard* XXI (1858), p. 18.
137. *Times* 25 November 1859, p. 5. I am grateful to John Kenworthy-Browne for drawing my attention to Paxton's speech.
138. GC 1859, p. 726; 1860, pp. 49–50; 1866, pp. 879–80.
139. GC 1865, pp. 889–90; 1866, pp. 879–80; COLE 1877, pp. 19–24.
140. GC 1866, p. 880.
141. Heckfield GC; 1872, pp. 1524–5. Culford: GC 1866, pp. 903, 926–8; GC 1875 ii 261; *JHort* XXVIII (1875), pp. 164–6.
142. BRIGHT 1879, p. 63; but see BURRITT 1868, p. 303 for a rhapsody occasioned by empty beds at Enville.
143. Annuals: *Midland Florist* V (1851), pp. 70–72; *CottGard* XII (1854), p. 336. Plunging: HIBBERD 1875, pp. 238–45; WOOD 1881, pp. 130–5.
144. GC 1855, pp. 823–4; 1857, pp. 759, 792; 1858, pp. 108, 816; thereafter references too copious to itemize. See also BRIGHT 1879, pp. 10–11.
145. Standish & Noble, 'Suggestions for employing evergreens as a winter decoration in flower-gardens', JHS IX (1854), pp. 275–7. See also FLEMING 1864, pp. 1–2.
146. Basing Park: *CottGard* XVIII (1857), p. 275–7. Derby Arboretum: the beds are sketched and identified in Nesfield's annotations on his copy of LOUDON 1840b; I am grateful to Major C. Wace Roberts for allowing me to consult this copy.
147. Frances Jane Hope: 'Winter aspect of trees', GC 1873, pp. 254–6 (HOPE 1881, p. 58–64); 'Winter flower gardening', GC 1863, pp. 125, 148–9 (HOPE 1881, pp. 273–6, 277–82); 'The garden in winter', GC 1874, pp. 13–14 (HOPE 1881, pp. 267–72); 'Winter gardens', ibid., pp. 59, 146–7 (HOPE 1881, pp. 283–90, 291–7). See also Alexander Forsyth, FP XVI (1877), pp. 248–50, and Alexander Dean, JRHS XXI (1897–8), pp. 67–8.
148. Heckfield: GC 1884 i 372–2, 379. For accounts of some other winter bedding schemes, see *CottGard* XXI (1858), pp. 166–7 (The Dell and Cooper's Hill); *JHort* VI (1864), pp. 331–3 (Linton Park). See also GC 1868, p. 1189 (a winter ribbon bed); *JHort* XV (1868), pp. 477–8, 499–501; GC 1870, p. 1022; GC 1879 ii 552.
149. BURGESS 1854 (comprising articles from GC 1846–9). The Northamptonshire Record Office has an 1847 plan for a French garden using spring bulbs, in the Garden Book for Thorpe Hall: Strong Collection S(T) 319.
150. *CottGard* IV (1850), pp. 107–9; XVIII (1857), pp. 32–3.
151. Early references to Fleming's work: GC 1856, pp. 55–6; *Florist* 1857, pp. 177–8; GC 1858, pp. 439–50; GC 1859, pp. 447–8; *JHort* III (1862), pp. 336–7 and plate; GC 1863, pp. 535–6; FLEMING 1864 (reprinted 1870). Reports follow almost annually until the late 1860s, and frequently but more irregularly thereafter. For Fleming's life see GC 1883 ii 701.
152. Niven: *Garden* III (1873), pp. 378–81. See also *Gardener* 1874, pp. 328–31; DIVERS 1909. For Ingram's life, see GC 1875 i 336; 1894 i 50. The earliest detailed account of his spring bedding is in FP IV (1865), pp. 119–20, but the use of bulbs is mentioned briefly in GC 1855, pp. 759–60.
153. GC 1867, p. 459; *Garden* II (1872), p. 235.
154. *Gardeners' Record* 1869, pp. 326–8; *Gardener* 1869, pp. 365–70; GC 1870, pp. 1284–6.
155. HUGHES 1866, pp. 148–152.
156. GM V (1829), p. 683; XIX (1843), pp. 243–4; *Gardeners' and Foresters' Record* I (1833), pp. 193–7 (Marnock).
157. Trentham: BROOKE 1857. Alton Towers: GC 1869, p. 416. SMITH 1852, p. 47.
158. HUGHES 1866, p. 149; KEMP 1864, p. 272.
159. FLEMING 1864, pp. 33–4; see also *JHort* XXVIII (1874), pp. 497–500, for the 'polychrome parterre' at Langton Hall, Lincolnshire.
160. Broughton Hall MSS: W. A. Nesfield to Sir C. Tempest, 15 June 1857; for the qualities of the blue spar, 22 June, and for those of the white, 25 June. I am grateful to Mr H. R. Tempest for allowing me to use these documents. See also GC 1859, p. 791.
161. Scottish Record Office, GD 152/53/4/Bundle 27/letter 9. Letters in this bundle reveal that Roos was working at Auldbar, Falkland, Gask, Whitehill, Drayton, Revesby, Seacroft, and Southam in the 1840s.
162. BRIGHT 1881, pp. 17–18. Nesfield monograms: ELLIOTT 1981b; GC 1880 ii 231–2; *JHort* LXII (1879), pp. 509–10. See CL CLXII (1977), p. 21, for an early monogram parterre at Aldenham

Park, Shropshire, probably of the 1840s.
163. *CottGard* XVI (1856), pp. 314–17.
164. KEMP 1864, p. 224.
165. Beaton: *CottGard* IX (1852), pp. 67–8. On segregation, see *JHort* IV (1863), pp. 97–100.
166. *JHort* XXXIX (1875), pp. 581–4; XXX (1876), p. 6.
167. GC 1862, pp. 379–80.
168. *Florist* 1860, p. 146; see also George Abbey, *JHort* IX (1866), pp. 417–18, 498–500.
169. For the history of the RHS Garden, see MURRAY 1863, pp. 45–52; COLE 1877, pp. 11–14; FLETCHER 1969, pp. 184–96; *Survey of London*, vol. 38: *The Museums Area of South Kensington and Westminster* (1975), pp. 124–32.
170. MURRAY 1863, pp. 117–79. *Floral World* III (1860), pp. 110–11; IV (1861), pp. 125–8. *CottGard* XXIV (1860), p. 81.
171. GC 1862, pp. 379–80. *CottGard* XXV (1861), pp. 299–300; *JHort* I (1861), pp. 373–5.
172. *Floral World* IV (1861), p. 126; *CottGard* XXV (1861), pp. 299–300; *JHort* III (1862), p. 26; QR CXII (1862), pp. 180–2.
173. *Athenaeum* 1861, p. 766; *Floral World* IV (1861), p. 125.
174. MURRAY 1863, pp. 68–72; *JHort* III (1862), pp. 585–6. For Albert's hopes for the reunification of the arts, see Hermione Hobhouse, *Prince Albert: His Life and Work* (1983), pp. 90–114.
175. GC 1863, pp. 221–2, 651.
176. RHS Kensington Garden Committee Minutes, 8 December 1862, pp. 179–186.
177. GC 1864, pp. 391–2, 412, 533.
179. GC 1862, p. 809.
180. Coombe Abbey: GC 1864, p. 991; *JHort* VIII (1865), pp. 441–2; XVII (1869), pp. 126–7; Robin Moore, *A History of Coombe Abbey* (1983), pp. 76–80.
181. Witley Court: GC 1864, pp. 1111–12; 1872, p. 766; 1873, pp. 846–7, 812–13, 919; *JHort* XXIV (1873), pp. 11–14. Kinmel: GIROUARD 1979.
182. GC 1864, pp. 889–90; 1865, pp. 867, 915: *Garden* III (1873), pp. 474–5.
183. Markham Nesfield's gardens included Glanusk Park, GC 1876 i 301–2; unexecuted plans for Longleat; and Ogston Hall, *JHort* XXVI (1874), pp. 204–6 – I am indebted to Mr G. Wakefield for the attribution and to Miss P. Bosanquet more generally.
184. *Gardener* 1873, pp. 123–4; GC 1873, pp. 295–6. Balmoral: GC 1876 ii 519–20.
185. GC 1871, pp. 1323–5; 1875 ii 388–9.
186. GC 1875 i 655–6; William Miller, 'Landscape Gardening' (1901), p. 9.
187. GC 1871, p. 1325.
188. Gardens where Thomas worked include Sandringham, Crown Point, Felbrigg, Powerscourt, Bishop Burton, Sedgwick, Thoresby Hall, Holker Hall, and Castle Ashby.
189. HUGHES 1866, pp. 96–7; see pp. 38–9 for his views of Le Nôtre. See Tasso's *Gerusalemme Liberata* XVI ix.

Chapter 6

1. *Floral World* VII (1864), p. 196; *Gardener* 1880, p. 200; *JHort* IX n.s. (1884), pp. 168–9.
2. JONES 1856, pp. 1–4; *GardMag* XXIII (1880), p. 1.
3. MURRAY 1863, p. 171; GC 1862, pp. 1218–19 (identified as Murray's by being in a volume of his collected articles in the Lindley Library).
4. *JHort* VI (1864), p. 178; GC 1877 i, Supplement to 12 May, p. i; *Garden* II (1872), p. 409; HIBBERD 1875, p. 17.
5. GC 1873, pp. 611–12. Colour blindness was first used thus in GC 1868, p. 543.
6. *Garden* XI (1877), p. 232; XXIII (1883), p. 3–4; BRIGHT 1881, pp. 34–5.
7. Chevreulian or complementary theories: *Floral World* III (1860), pp. 185–9; *Gardener* 1882, pp. 426–30. Chromatic theory: GC 1868, pp. 545–6; and see D. T. Fish's attempt to quantify a colour theory in GC 1867, pp. 683–4. Maxwell's theory: FP 1884, pp. 46–7.
8. GC 1877 i, Supplement to 12 May, p. i; *JHort* IX (1866), pp. 417–18, 498–500; XII (1867), p. 369; JOHNSON 1874, pp. 21, 123. Cattermole: GC 1866, p. 945.
9. *Floral World* III (1860), pp. 185–9; VII (1864), p. 196. *JHort* I n.s. (1880), p. 76; *Garden* XXIV (1883), p. 182.
10. WATSON 1872, pp. 198–200; GC 1866, p. 945; GC 1880 i 176; John Pope, 'Contrast and harmony, with special reference to flowers', in Birmingham Gardeners' Association, *Practical Papers on Gardening* (1887).
11. Stevens: GC 1972, p. 506; ELLIOTT 1984b.
12. BRIGHT 1879, pp. 39, 64–55; Hope: *Garden* V (1874), pp. 114–16 (HOPE 1881, pp. 102–12). HIBBERD 1875, pp. 41–5.
13. GC 1868, p. 574; *Garden* II (1872), p. 504; GC 1873, p. 612; JOHNSON 1874, p. 109; HIBBERD 1875, pp. 44–5; GC 1877 i, Supplement to 12 May, p. i; *Gardener*, 1880, pp. 414–15.
14. WATSON 1872, pp. 121–2, 149–50, 136–7; see also *Garden* II (1872), pp. 333–4. For a reply, see *Gardener* 1880, p. 464.
15. WATSON 1872, pp. 172–232, esp. 178–80. See also FOSTER 1881, p. 21.
16. Beaton: *CottGard* XVIII (1857), pp. 114–15. For an early appearance of the paint analogy, and Beaton's reply, see *CottGard* XVIII (1857), pp. 177, 199; for the revival of the paint analogy, see GC 1868, p. 658; *Garden* II (1872), p. 384.
17. To appreciate the development of Robinson's views, read in sequence GC 1864, pp. 580, 916; *Garden* II (1872), pp. 406–10.
18. Peach: *Floral World* 1872, pp. 297–301; reprinted in *JHort* XXIII (1872), pp. 5–6, 38–9. Robinson: *Garden* II (1872), pp. 265–6, 287–8, 333–4, 406–10; Peach's reply, ibid., pp. 503–5; Ellacombe, ibid., p. 551.
19. GC 1848, p. 703.
20. *JHort* III (1862), pp. 712–713. Charles Kingsley, *Glaucus* (1855), pp. 3–4. For a general history of the fern craze, see ALLEN 1969, but correct it for the later years of the century with N. A. Hall, 'W. and J. Birkenhead: ferns a speciality', *Garden History* XII (1983), pp. 79–85.
21. *Florist* III (1850), pp. 234–5; *CottGard* IX (1852), p. 63; GC 1864, p. 703.
22. *CottGard* VIII (1852), pp. 82–4; XII (1854), pp. 236–7; Peter Grieve, *A History of Variegated Zonal Pelargoniums* (1868). Ivy: *Floral World* I (1858), pp. 131–8; HUGHES 1866, p. 86; Shirley Hibberd, *The Ivy* (1872). Moss: *CottGard* XXII (1859), pp. 87–9; *Floral World* 1869, p. 39.
23. Moore: JHS VI (1851), pp. 115–17. Robson: *JHort* III (1862), pp. 712–14. Hope: GC 1863, p. 125 (HOPE 1881, pp. 273–6). Gourds: *CottGard* XXIII (1860), p. 319.
24. *CottGard* VIII (1852), pp. 62–3; GC 1864, p. 937; GC 1889 ii 380.
25. *CottGard* XXI (1859), p. 209; XXIII

(1860), pp. 296–8; XXIV (1860), p. 193.
26. *CottGard* XXIII (1860), p. 319; GC 1864, p. 703; 1865, p. 937; THOMSON 1868, pp. 118–40, 328–30; WOOD 1881, pp. 100–110.
27. GC 1864, p. 703. Paris: Adolphe Alphand, *Les Promenades de Paris* (1867–73).
28. GC 1863, pp. 915, 963–4, 986–7; 1864, pp. 843–4, 867; COLE 1877, pp. 31–4.
29. *Garden* II (1872), p. 235.
30. See ALLAN 1982, pp. 52–97, for his Parisian travels.
31. ROBINSON 1868, pp. 1–63; ROBINSON 1869, pp. 182–238; ROBINSON 1871a; HIBBERD 1875, pp. 222–237.
32. ROBINSON 1871a, pp. 3–4; *JHort* VIII (1865), pp. 279–80, 322; *GardMag* XXIII (1880), pp. 1–2; BRIGHT 1881, p. 23.
33. ROBINSON 1868, pp. 120–4; ROBINSON 1871c, pp. 6–8, 13–16, 22–6,
32–4; ROBINSON 1883, p. lxxvi (and subsequent editions up to the 12th, 1913). *Musa ensete* has now been separated from the true bananas, and is called *Ensete ventricosum*. Hibberd: *GardMag* XXIII (1880), pp. 1–2, 91, 241–2. See also GC 1877 i, Supplement to 12 May, p. ii; *Gardener* 1881, pp. 463–5.
34. GC 1868 pp. 518, 789–90, 845, 873; see also Luckhurst, *JHort* XXVII (1874), pp. 183–4.
35. *JHort* IX (1865), pp. 295–6; X (1866), pp. 301–2, 404; XI (1866), p. 1; XIII (1867), pp. 134–5; XV (1868), p. 340. GC 1866, pp. 367–8, 637.
36. Cliveden: GC 1868, p. 487; *JHort* XV (1868), pp. 284–5.
37. GC 1870, pp. 1344–5.
38. ROBINSON 1870a, pp. 38–42.
39. Suburban gardens: *JHort* XXIX (1875), pp. 205–6, 226–8, and most magazines over the next few years, for Ralli's at Clapham; *GardMag* XIX (1876), p. 214, 216–17, 512–14, for Butters's at Hackney; *GardMag* XL (1897), pp. 646–7, for a Chelsea back garden. Cannell: GC 1871, p. 901; *Floral World* 1871, pp. 137–41; *Floral World* 1873, pp. 179–81.
40. GC 1875 i 528–9 (HOPE 1881, pp. 90–95); *JHort* XXXIII (1877), pp. 307–8; *Gardener* 1880, pp. 557–62. See also the debate in GC 1873, pp. 1110–11, 1180–81, 1210–11, 1243.
41. *Gardener* 1875, pp. 175, 265; BURBIDGE 1877, pp. 198–9, 211; BRIGHT 1879, p. 64; BRIGHT 1881, p. 23.
42. ROBINSON 1883, p. cii.
43. GC 1870, p. 1442; FP XVI (1877), p. 147.
44. ROBINSON 1870a, pp. 41–2; *Garden* X (1876), p. 255; GC 1870 p. 1344.
45. GC 1875 ii 238–9, 336; *Garden* VIII (1875), p. 500; GC 1876 i 560; THOMPSON 1878, plate 12, and pp. 790–1. For Thomson's writings on carpet beds, see *GardMag* XVII (1874), pp. 463–5, and his debate with F. J. Hope in GC 1877 ii 599, 629.
46. ELLIOTT 1981a.
47. GC 1878 ii 464–5, 468–9; GC 1878 ii 491–2 for the Petworth dragon, which, I am informed by Miss Ursula Wyndham, survived until the late 1920s. Park Place: *Garden* XVI (1879), p. 572.
48. BRIGHT 1881, pp. 24–5; see also MORRIS 1882, p. 128.
49. *GardMag* XIX (1876), p. 508.
50. FP (1883), p. 146.
51. *CottGard* XIV (1855), pp. 197–8; LATOUCHE 1876, p. 97, and see *Garden* IX (1876), p. 509; GC 1864, p. 1060; FP III (1864), pp. 256–7. Contrast with E.V.B., *National Review* XXVI (1895), p. 184.
52. GC 1857, p. 327 (Acton Green mixed borders). *CottGard* XXII (1859), p. 2. HIBBERD 1875, p. 94. Samuel Wood, *The Bulb Garden* (1878), pp. 1–3, 8–10.
53. Helen Allingham and Arthur Paterson, *The Homes of Tennyson* (1905). Among Tennyson's poems note particularly 'Claribel', 'A spirit haunts the last year's hours', 'Amphion', 'The city child'.
54. Arley Hall: CL CLX (1976), pp. 950–52. See also JRHS CVL (1981), pp. 171–5. Holme Lacy: *JHort* XXXIV (1878), pp. 10–13. Newstead Abbey: *JHort* LVII (1877), pp. 9–12.
55. LOFTIE 1879, p. 65. F.J. Hope, 'Hardy Narcissi in the spring garden', GC 1873, p. 1048 (HOPE 1881, p. 144). I am grateful to Kate Donald for help with Queen Anne's double daffodil.
56. GC 1845, p. 560; *CottGard* XVIII (1857), pp. 177, 199. ROBINSON 1870b, pp. 4–7; *Garden* IX (1876), p. 509; Alicia Amherst, 'Victorian gardening', QR CLXXXVIII (1898), pp. 51–2; Robinson, preface to MARTINEAU 1913.
57. ROBINSON 1871b, p. 1; BRIGHT 1881, p. 45; LOFTIE 1879, pp. 64–5.
58. *Blackwood's Magazine* LXXIII (1853), pp. 132–3; *JHort* XIV (1868), p. 199; GC 1871, p. 1551; *Garden* VIII (1875), p. 168. Juliana Horatia Ewing, *Mary's Meadow* (1883–84). Roses: BRIGHT 1879 pp. 54–5; JRHS XX (1896–97), pp. 53–7. See also George Gordon, 'The hardy plant industry', *GardMag* LVI (1913), pp. 223–7, for an overview of the commercial history of the revival.
59. BRIGHT 1879, pp. 63–4; BRIGHT 1881, pp. 65–6. For later developments of this theme, see CHAMBERLAIN 1892, pp. 46–7.
60. *Gardener* 1881, pp. 72–5. For Frank Miles, see ROBINSON 1871b, pp. 5–7; ROBINSON 1883, pp. xxxix–xli. ELLIOTT 1985. His opposition to Fish is revealed in an undated letter to Robinson, now in the Lindley Library.
61. GC 1868, pp. 321–2; THOMSON 1868, pp. 153–62; ROBINSON 1871b, pp. 3–7; SUTHERLAND 1871, pp. xxviii–xxxii; Humphreys, *Garden* I (1872), pp. 261–2; *Garden* II (1872), pp. 143–4; GC 1873, p. 1210; HIBBERD 1875, p. 97; Luckhurst, *JHort* XXXVIII (1879), p. 103; BRIGHT 1881, pp. 50–54.
62. *JHort* XXIV (1873), pp. 166–7; GC 1894 ii 533–4; *Garden* LXIV (1903), pp. 267–9; GC 1912 i 157.
63. LOFTIE 1879, pp. 64–5. See also *Cottage Gardening: a Practical Manual* (1896), pp. 64–5.
64. GC 1862, p. 1219.
65. *Gardener* 1874, pp. 91–4; *GardMag* XXIII (1881), p. 437. Beaudesert: *JHort* XXII (1872), pp. 387–9; GC 1884 ii 748–9; GC 1893 i 164–5. Hoar Cross: CL XI (1902), pp. 592–600.
66. *CottGard* XXIX (1875), pp. 229, 489–91. Castle Bromwich: *CottGard* XXII (1872), pp. 497–8; GC 1872, p. 833. I am grateful to David Jacques for the dating of the box wilderness.
67. Baron Hill: *JHort* XXV (1873), pp. 137–9. Dante Gabriel Rossetti, *Letters*, ed. O. Doughty and J. R. Wahl (1965). vol. II, pp. 608–10. Kelmscott: information from Margaret Preston.
68. *JHort* XXIX (1875), pp. 582–4; XXX (1876), p. 6.
69. G. S. C., *Gardens of Light and Shade* (1886), pp. 30–9; BLOMFIELD 1892, pp. 227–9. Nut walks: MAWSON 1900, p. 106; *GardMag* XLIV (1901), p. 392.
70. 'Elizabethan gardening', *Fraser's Magazine* LXX (1864), pp. 179–91. See MORRIS 1882, p. 123.

71. LATOUCHE 1876, pp. 97–102, and *Garden* IX (1876), pp. 506–10. See also WATSON 1872, pp. 123–8; G. S. C., op. cit., pp. 1–8.
72. George Milner, *Country Pleasures*, 2nd ed. (1881), pp. 145–52; FOSTER 1881, pp. 13–16, 22–57, 92–8. GC 1874 ii 551; 1876 ii 163–4. Frederick Goodall, *Reminiscences* (1902), pp. 279–87. GIROUARD 1977, pp. 152–9.
73. GIROUARD 1977, pp. 10–37, 152–9.
74. LATOUCHE 1876, pp. 97–102. MORRIS 1882, pp. 128–9.
75. Kelmscott: CL L (1921), pp. 224–9, 256–62; A. M. W. Stirling, *The Richmond Papers* (1926), p. 317. Downes: GC 1898 i 219–20; Alastair Service, ed., *Edwardian Architecture and its Origins* (1975), pp. 260–61.
76. E.V.B., 'A Buckinghamshire Garden', GC 1882–85 passim; the quoted passages are from GC 1882 ii 618 (BOYLE 1884, pp. 8–10). See also CL V (1899), pp. 560–65.
77. Penshurst: *Garden* XIX (1881), pp. 393–5; XLVI (1894), pp. 25–6. TRIGGS 1902, pp. 14–15; CL I (1897), pp. 576–8; V (1899), pp. 336–9; CLI (1972), pp. 514–18, 618–21.
78. HIBBERD 1857, pp. 330–34.
79. TJADEN 1974; FLETCHER 1969, pp. 197–221.
80. Eyles: GC 1887 ii 754; *Garden* XXXII (1887), p. 571. Nesfield: *Garden* XIX (1881), p. 296; GC 1881 i 342; *JHort* II n.s. (1881), pp. 192–3.
81. *JHort* XXXI (1876), pp. 30–2; GC 1872, p. 766.
82. *Garden* VII (1875), pp. 403, 405; XIX (1881), p. 546. JRHS XX (1896–97), p. 99.
83. GC 1870, p. 563; *Garden* V (1874), pp. 25–6; IX (1876), p. 286.
84. GC 1870, pp. 45–7, 77–8; *JHort* XXX (1876), pp. 449–52; *Garden* VIII (1880), pp. 425–9; *GardMag* LIII (1910), pp. 473–4; ALLIBONE 1977, p. 561; CL CLXV (1979), pp. 2082–5; CLXVI (1979), pp. 18–21.
85. CROOK 1981, pp. 262–3; Cardiff Castle Collection of Burges Drawings, folder 28, drawings nos. 8–12. I have followed Mrs Pauline Sargent's interpretation of the dating of the moat garden rather than Crooks's; it is confirmed by *GardMag* XLII (1899), pp. 655–60.
86. *JHort* XXII (1872), pp. 59–62, 103–6; GC 1873, pp. 9, 41; Cyril Ward, *Royal Gardens* (1912), pp. 121–46; Philip Hepworth, *Royal Sandringham* (1978), p. 83. I am grateful to Mr R. S. French of the Sandringham Estate Office.
87. *Garden* I (1871), p. 28.
88. GIROUARD 1977, p. 153; *Illustrated London News*, 22 June 1872; *Garden* III (1873), pp. 18–19.
89. For lawns: FP III (1864), pp. 203–5; *JHort* XXXVIII (1880), p. 495; BRIGHT 1881, pp. 20–22. Against; HUGHES 1866, p. 30; EARLE 1897, pp. 138–40. Joseph Newton, 'Style of public gardens', GC 1864, p. 533; 'Planting park scenery', GC 1870, pp. 417–18, 529–30.
90. GC 1864, p. 533.
91. Mungo Temple, 'Marnock's maxims', GC 1890 i 20. See also *Garden* XXXVI (1889), pp. 489–90; HOLE 1892, pp. 231–2.
92. *Garden* I (1872), pp. 592–3; JOHNSON 1874, p. 82; *Garden* V (1874), p. 78.
93. McKenzie; GC 1893 i 397. Meston: GC 1891 ii 256. Robinson: ALLAN 1982; ELLIOTT 1985. Robinson's MS of *Gravetye Manor* is held in the Lindley Library, and records advisory visits by Marnock which were deleted from the published work.
94. HOLE 1892, p. 249; see also JRHS XX (1896–7), pp. 89–100.
95. For Marnock gardens, see *Garden* I (1871–2), pp. 28–30, 143–5, 592–3; II (1872), pp. 592–3; III (1873), pp. 50–1. Among Marnock's gardens of the 1860s and 1870s were Oak Lodge, Kensington; Berry Hill (begun by Kemp); Possingworth; Rousdon; Eynsham Hall; Hassobury; Taplow Court; Greenlands; Park Place; Park Hill, Streatham; Wimbledon House; Weston Park, Sheffield; and Alexandra Park, Hastings.
96. CHADWICK 1966, pp. 152–62. See John Merivale, 'Charles-Adolphe Alphand and the parks of Paris', *Landscape Design* 123 (1978), pp. 32–7. André's comments are taken form his reply to Markham Nesfield; see note 98 below.
97. ROBINSON 1868, 1869; MCKENZIE 1869, esp. pp. 16–20.
98. André's plan (26 August 1868), Markham Nesfield's report (14 October), and André's reply (20 October), are held in the Liverpool Record Office; I am grateful to Peter Adamson for allowing me to consult these. For Sefton Park, see GC 1867, pp. 432, 460, 490, 924; GC 1868, pp. 1162, 1185, 1212–13, 1235; *JHort* XV (1868), pp. 42–3; *Garden* II (1872), pp. 124–6; GC 1872, pp. 1004–5; CHADWICK 1906, pp. 101–2; Michael Brown, 'Sefton Park: the French connection', *Landscape Design* 139 (1982), pp. 11–14; Sefton Park Civic Society, *Sefton Park* (1984).
99. *Garden* XV (1879), p. 447; XVI (1879), p. 68.
100. GC 1875 ii 229–30; GC 1881 i 44–5.
101. NEWTON 1876; GC 1871, p. 1548. See also Joseph Newton, 'Select examples of scenery', *GardMag* XXV (1883), pp. 632–3, 664–5, 676–7.
102. Locke Park: GC 1928 i 425. Abbey Park: GC 1880 ii 672; *JHort* XXI n.s. (1890), pp. 94–7. For Barron's later career, see GC 1891 i 522–4.
103. GC 1880 i 586–7, 593.
104. Kemp: CHADWICK 1966, pp. 104–6.
105. Milner: CHADWICK 1966; HODGES 1977. Lincoln: GC 1872, p. 1226. Bodnant: GC 1884 i 207. Rangemore Hall: *JHort* XXX (1876), pp. 53–5; *GardMag* XLIV (1901), pp. 403–6.
106. MILNER 1890, pp. 4–7. See GC 1844, p. 115 for an earlier expression of a similar geological imagination.
107. MILNER 1890, pp. 22, 25, 34. See also Jon Carder, 'The work of Edward Milner in Derbyshire', *Journal of the Bakewell and District Historical Society* IX (1982).
108. CHADWICK 1966. For Buxton, see R. Grundy Heape, *Buxton and the Dukes of Devonshire* (1948), pp. 100–3; Christopher E. Fair, 'Buxton Pavilion Gardens: a study of a Victorian public park', *Landscape Design* 108 (1974), pp. 10–12.
109. GC 1881 ii 471; GC 1898 ii 317–18; MILNER 1890, p. 20. I am grateful to David spinney for information on Iwerne Minster.
110. Crystal Palace School: GC 1881, pp. 437, 603–4, 636: *Garden* XIX (1881), pp. 546–7. See also I. W. Leigh, 'Milner White and Partners', *Landscape Design* 156 (1985), pp. 9–13.
111. MILNER 1890, pp. 23, 35, 50.
112. Alexandra Palace: *JHort* V (1863), pp. 66–8, 82–3; XI (1866), p. 185; R. C. Carrington, *Alexandra Park and Palace: a History* (1975). McKenzie's diary for 1868, in the care of Haringey Architects' Department, shows meetings and correspondence with

Marnock and Meston; I am grateful to Peter Smith for allowing me to examine this document.
113. *Garden* XVI (1879), pp. 53–4; CL XI (1902), p. 342.
114. McKenzie worked at Easton Neston in 1876 – see *GardMag* XIX (1876), p. 120; the work is not documented at the house. For his writings, see GC 1870, pp. 171–2; *Floral World* 1874, pp. 329–34; 1875, pp. 74–6, 225–8, 321–5.
115. GC 1884 ii 519–20; Phillada Ballard, '"Rus in Urbe" – Joseph Chamberlain's gardens at Highbury, Moor Green, Birmingham, 1879–1914', *Garden History* XIV (1980), pp. 61–76.
116. For Cooke's diary, see chapter IV, note 95.
117. Sydnope: *JHort* XXVI (1874), pp. 222–4. Osmaston: GC 1873, pp. 1240–41; *Garden* III (1873), p. 331; *JHort* XXIX (1875), pp. 428–30. See John Robson, 'The Rockery and its formation', *JHort* II (1861), pp. 102–3, 128–9.
118. GC 1884 ii 807–8; 1886 ii 210–11; CL XXXIII (1913), pp. 750–2.
119. PULHAM 1877; ELLIOTT 1984a; FESTING 1984. Brian Phillips, 'Violent misadventures in Sheffield Park', *Sussex Genealogist and Local Historian* VI (1984), pp. 111–116. Battersea: *JHort* XV (1868), pp. 298–9. See also *JHort* XXV (1873), pp. 81–4.
120. *GardMag* XVII (1874), p. 135.
121. Edward Luckhurst, 'Tasteful gardening', *JHort* XXVI n.s. (1893), pp. 168–9; Dillistone, CL XXXIII (1913), pp. 750–2.
122. *Garden* III (1873), pp. 380–1.
123. *Garden* VII (1875), pp. 477–8; ROBINSON 1870a, pp. 9–14, 18–19; PULHAM 1877, pp. 61–72; HOLE 1892, p. 238; GORER 1975, pp. 133–7.
124. James Pulham, 'Stratified rockwork', *JHort* XXX (1876), p. 137; C. P. Peach, 'Artificial rockwork', ibid., p. 152.
125. *Floral World* 1867, pp. 3–10; HIBBERD 1870, pp. 336–40; *JHort* XXVI (1874), p. 496.
126. PULHAM 1877. Park Hill: *Garden* XXIX (1886), p. 568; GC 1894 ii 400–1. This survives today, unlike Bessemer's garden or the Brighton Aquarium rockworks.
127. GC 1875 ii 293, 752. Cathays Park: GC 1911 i 245, and supplementary plate for 15 April 1911.
128. *GardMag* XXIV (1882), pp. 198–9.
129. *Ladies' Magazine* 1841, p. 361; GC 1871, p. 1548. See Gertrude Jekyll, 'Gardens and garden craft', *Edinburgh Review* CLXXXIV (1896), p. 177, for a complaint against such uses of ruins. Henry Trevor's garden is currently being restored by the Plantation Garden Preservation Trust. I am grateful to Bryony Nierop-Reading and Stefan Muthesius for explorations of builders' follies in Norwich gardens.
130. GC 1878 ii 240–42, 245; GC 1887 ii 96; *Garden* LXI (1902), p. 96; *GardMag* XLV (1902), p. 282. King had worked at Robert Pince's nursery about the time that Pince was studying the picturesque manual *Parks and Pleasure Grounds* (SMITH 1852), his annotated copy of which is in the Lindley Library. Ashby-de-la-Zouche: GC 1894 ii 161.
131. *GardMag* XXXVI (1893), p. 251; see DELLHEIM 1982 for the story of the Abbey's acquisition by Leeds Council. The grounds have today sunk back into oblivion: the avenue has been felled and the flowerbeds removed.
132. *Garden* I (1872), pp. 140–3.
133. ROBINSON 1870a, pp. 32–8; *Garden* XXXVII (1890), p. 227; EARLE 1897, p. 158.
134. SMITH 1852, pp. 98–102. *CottGard* XXI (1859), pp. 248–9, 276. KEMP 1850, pp. 75, 155 (KEMP 1864, pp. 85–6, 215–16).
135. See note 98 above.
136. HIBBERD 1875, p. 216. Bedgebury: *JHort* XIII (1867), pp. 253–5. Inverewe: Osgood Mackenzie, *A Hundred Years in the Highlands* (1949).
137. GC 1864, pp. 770, 819, 844, 893, 963, 1035, 1131; GC 1866, pp. 1139; GC 1867, pp. 103, 237, 404, 628, 805, 926, 1072 (PAUL 1892, pp. 219–279). See also ELLIOTT 1987a.
138. GC 1865, pp. 605–6; GC 1870, pp. 417–18, 529–30; *JHort* XXV (1873), p. 212; JOHNSON 1874, pp. 19–20, 23–5, 47; GC 1873, pp. 1634–5; GC 1875 i 716–17; QR CXLII (1876), pp. 66–7.
139. GC 1870, pp. 1025–6; *JHort* XIX (1870), pp. 82–4.
140. GC 1874 i 143. Rougham Hall: GC 1896 ii 491–2. For Ruskin's planting, see J. S. Dearden, *A Short History of Brantwood* (n.d.).
141. BRIGHT 1879, pp. 89–91; William Goldring, 'Spring-flowering trees and shrubs', JRHS XII (1890), pp. 409–21; Luckhurst in *JHort* XXII n.s. (1891), pp. 107–8.
142. *JHort* XXV (1873), p. 212; *Garden* XIV (1878), p. 77. Harrison Weir on colour trees, GC 1899 ii 294. *Prunus × pissardi*: GC 1881 i 728; *JHort* XXIX n.s. (1894), p. 471.
143. GC 1877 ii 586; 1890 i 674; 1898 ii 423. Ascott: CL VIII (1900), p. 244.
144. William Paul, 'The future of Epping Forest', *JHort* XXXVIII (1880), pp. 96–8; p. 182 (Boscawen's reply). See G. Shaw-Lefevre, 'The rescue of Epping Forest', *Contemporary Review* XXXIV (1879), pp. 45–59.
145. JOHNSON 1874, p. 109. See also *JHort* LXVIII n.s. (1914), pp. 272–3.
146. LOFTIE 1879, p. 67; see also GC 1897 i 88. Grant Allen: *Cornhill Magazine* XXXVIII (1878), p. 477. Tropical colour: *Garden* XIX (1881), pp. 85, 120, 150, 243, 168–9. William Robinson, 'Exotic trees at Gravetye Manor', *Garden* 1921, p. 290. MILNER 1890, pp. 54–5.
147. GC 1898 ii 445.
148. Fish: *JHort* XXXIV n.s. (1897), p. 392; GC 1898 ii 423.

Chapter 7

1. ELLIOTT 1987b.
2. JRHS XV (1893), pp. 84–5.
3. GC 1860, pp. 289–90.
4. John Robson, 'Ferns under glass', *JHort* I (1861), pp. 260–2; *Garden* IX (1876), p. 5; *GardMag* XVIII (1875), pp. 524–5; PULHAM 1877. Brighton: *GardMag* XIX (1876), p. 210. Old Warden: *GardMag* XXIII (1880), p. 527.
5. Radclyffe: see *GardMag* XIX (1876), p. 210.
6. *GardMag* XIX (1876), pp. 699–700.
7. Edouard André, 'Conservatories in the natural style', *Garden* I (1872), pp. 181–4; and pp. 219, 260, 311–12.
8. F. W. Burbidge, *Cool Orchids* (1874), esp. pp. 34–6; the frontispiece transposes the engraving of Penllergare originally published in JHS 1 (1846). See also ELLIOTT 1983b.
9. *JHort* n.s. I (1880), pp. 240–1, 259–60, 326; *Series of Picturesque Views of Castles and Country Houses in Yorkshire* (1885), published by Bradford *Illustrated Weekly Telegraph*. My thanks to Mr H. Pickles, superintendent of Oakworth Park, and Mrs Garside.
10. GC 1879 ii 523–5.

11. FESTING 1983.
12. *JHort* XXX (1876), p. 152.
13. FARRER 1913, p. 1.
14. F. W. Meyer, JRHS XXIII (1899–1900), pp. 78–95; GC 1906 ii 120; MEYER 1910.
15. FESTING 1983, 1984; ELLIOTT 1984a.
16. ROBINSON 1883, p. lv.
17. Reginald Farrer, 'Rock gardens and garden design', in CORY 1914, p. 13. See also FARRER 1909, p. 172.
18. GODFREY 1914, pp. 201–2. S. Arnott: *JHort* XXX n.s. (1895), p. 247. Wisley: JRHS XXXVIII (1912–13), pp. 225–33.
19. Kew: BEAN 1908. Warley: LE LIEVRE 1980, pp. 47–8.
20. Friar Park: CRISP 1910, pp. 73–8: *GardMag* XLI (1898), pp. 442–4, 754; GC 1899 ii 321–4. See also James Bateman's last garden at Home House, Worthing: GC 1890 ii 246; 1894 ii 345. Sand traps: Reginald Beale, *Lawns for Sports* (1934), pp. 38–40.
21. BLOMFIELD 1892, p. 15.
22. *GardMag* LIX (1916), p. 325.
23. ROBINSON 1883, p. lv; *Gardening Illustrated*, supplement to 23 May 1914.
24. BOWLES 1914, pp. vii–viii.
25. *GardMag* LIX (1916), pp. 108–9.
26. Isham Papers, Northampton Record Office: Book 'Emily' (report by Richard Potter).
27. Ibid.; *Garden* XX (1881), p. 217; *Cosmopolitan* III (1888), pp. 323–34; GC 1897 ii 209–10.
28. CRISP 1906, pp. 68–71, 83–4.
29. *Connoisseur* XXIII no. lxxxvi (1908), pp. xii–xiii I am indebted to Peter Goodchild for drawing my attention to this.
30. *JHort* LXII n.s. (1911), p. 497; see ROBINSON 1894. For Taylor's advice on wild gardening, see *JHort* XXVIII (1875), pp. 485–6, and XXIX (1875), pp. 47–8.
31. *Garden* XVI (1879), p. 485.
32. *Garden* IX (1876), pp. 352, 407.
33. ROBINSON 1883, plant notes passim. Niven: *Garden* XVII (1880), p. 33. Niven's giant cow parsnip, *H. giganteum*, and the giant hogweed, *H. mantegazzianum*, which the nineteenth century distinguished, are now generally held to be synonymous.
34. GC 1886 i 682, 730; *JHort* XII n.s. (1886), p. 400.
35. Eythrope; Bowles in JRHS XXXIV (1909), pp. 24–31.
36. *GardMag* XXXV (1892), pp. 397–
37. Robson: *JHort* XXXVI (1879), p. 463, and XXXVII (1879), pp. 105–6. ROBINSON 1870b, pp. 157–236. Spread of wild-flower gardening: *GardMag* XLVIII (1905), p. 574, and JRHS XXXIV (1909), pp. 418–29. SEDDING 1891, pp. 163, 179. BLOMFIELD 1892.
38. *JHort* LXIX (1909), pp. 295–6.
39. H. Selfe-Leonard, 'Some Talk about Wild Gardens', JRHS XXVI (1901–2), p. 52.
40. Arthur Kettlewell's crib from Milner: *JHort* XX n.s. (1890), pp. 224–5, 260–1, 286; GC 1893 i 567–8.
41. MILNER 1890, p. 55.
42. *Garden* XXXI (1887), p. 107.
43. *JHort* LXVI n.s. (1913), p. 509; *Garden* 1919, pp. 110–11. Among gardens where Goldring worked are Minto House, Elvetham Park, Hackwood, Crown Point, Coleorton Hall, Knowsley Hall, Beaudesert, Dorchester Public Gardens, Impney Hall, Phoenix Park (Dublin).
44. Marshall: GC 1910 ii 169. Meyer: GC 1906 ii 120.
45. Baines: GC 1895 i 307. Jackman: GC 1887 ii 107, 109–110, and 1888 i 805–6.
46. BLOMFIELD 1892. F. Inigo Thomas, 'The garden in relation to the house', *GardMag* XXXIX (1896), pp. 104, 118, 135. J. J. Joass, 'On gardening', *Studio* XI (1897), pp. 165–7. Replies: *Garden* L (1896), p. 482 etc; GC 1892 ii 493. Boardman's plans are in the Norwich Record Office.
47. MAWSON 1900, p. 2.
48. *GardMag* XLIII (1900), p. 399, reviewing and summarizing Mawson.
49. SEDDING 1891, pp. 7–9.
50. Ibid., pp. 11, 18, 186–7. See Godfrey Blount's *Arbor Vitae* (1899) for a related attempt in the visual arts.
51. SITWELL 1909, pp. 49–50.
52. Milner: *GardMag* XLI (1898), pp. 227–8, 245, 270. Goldring: GC 1909 ii 275, in a favourable review of Sitwell.
53. W. F. Rowles, 'An ideal garden', *GardMag* L (1907), pp. 132, 158.
54. For early references to bonsai, see *TransHS* IV (1820), pp. 214–31; Robert Fortune, *Three Years' Wanderings in China* (1847), pp. 90–94: LINDLEY 1840, pp. 262–4; GC 1845, p. 547; FC XVI (1848), p. 308; QR LXXXIX (1851), pp. 30–1; *JHort* I (1861), p. 224; GC 1870, pp. 1191, 1218.
55. *Florist's Journal* 1840, pp. 25–6. *JHort* VII (1864), p. 130; see also Cuthbertson's association of bonsai and topiary in GC 1904 i 74.
56. GC 1872, p. 1386.
57. See GC 1904 i 74; GC 1894 i 140–1; and JRHS XXXIII (1908), pp. 53–70.
58. For a general survey of European interest in the Japanese arts, see Siegfried Wickmann, *Japonisme* (1981). For early English references to Japanese gardens, see GC 1862, p. 22; *Garden* III (1873), pp. 146–8; *JHort* XXVI (1874), pp. 202–3, 221.
59. CROOK 1981; Elizabeth Aslin, *The Aesthetic Movement* (1969), pp. 93–5.
60. *JHort* XXVI (1874), pp. 444–5; *Garden* X (1876), p. 3.
61. David Midgley, 'Japanese gardens of Shipley Glen', *Yorkshire Life* XXXI xii (1977), pp. 82–82.
62. Josiah Conder, *The Flowers of Japan* (1891); CONDER 1893.
63. See JRHS XXIX (1904–5), pp. 82–5.
64. J. Colleran and E. McCracken, 'The Japanese Garden, Tully, Kildare', *Garden History*, V i (1977), pp. 30–41; *JHort* LX n.s. (1910), p. 405. Fanhams Hall: Richard Bisgrove, *The Gardens of England*, vol. III (1978), pp. 74–5.
65. *JHort* LX n.s. (1910), pp. 141, 214.
66. WRIGHT 1912, p. 187.
67. JRHS XXVIII (1903–4), pp. 451–7; *GardMag* LIV (1911), p. 68.
68. Holland House: *GardMag* LIV (1911), pp. 498–9. Newstead Abbey: Hinchingbrooke: *GardMag* XLVIII (1905), pp. 22–4; LIX (1916), p. 273. Friar Park: CRISP 1914, pp. 12–13. Battersea Park: Abbey Park: *GardMag* XLVII (1904), p. 373.
69. GC 1912 i 355; see also FARRER 1907, p. 5; CORY 1914, pp. 17–18.
70. *JHort* XXXIV (1878), pp. 369–70. For a survey of Japanese introductions, see GC 1863, p. 1059.
71. FREEMAN-MITFORD 1896; see also JRHS XIX (1896), pp. 359–74.
72. *GardMag* XLV (1902), pp. 160–1. For Hudson's writings, see 'A Japanese garden in England', JRHS XXXII (1907), pp. 1–10; 'Plants for terrace gardening', XXXIII (1908), pp. 369–77; 'The gardens by the Lake of Como', XXXV (1909–10), pp. 204–12; 'Informal and wild gardening', XL (1914–15), pp. 361–71. For Hudson's life, see GC 1919 i 194.
73. P. S. Hayward, 'The new theory in garden design', *GardMag* LIV (1911),

p. 68. See also his other essays: 'Japanese art in English gardens', *GardMag* LII (1909), p. 187; 'The Japanese ideal', ibid., p. 530; 'The Japanese ideal in practice', *GardMag* LIV (1911), pp. 498–9.

Chapter 8

1. HIBBERD 1875, pp. 30–31.
2. ROBINSON 1883, pp. xvc–cv; Wildsmith's contribution, although abridged, was not eliminated until the thirteenth edition (1921). For Wildsmith's life and reputation, see *JHort* V n.s. (1882), p. 430; *Garden* XXXVII (1890), p. 141; GC 1890 i 171. The literature on Heckfield between 1870 and 1890 is immense; the one important post-Wildsmith article is CL IV (1898), pp. 688–92.
3. ROBINSON 1883, p. cii.
4. Ibid., pp. xvc–xcvi, xcix–c. Part of this section was separately published in *Garden* XXVII (1885), p. 308.
5. SEDDING 1891, pp. 168–71.
6. *JHort* V n.s. (1882), p. 431.
7. *JHort* I n.s. (1880), pp. 387–8.
8. The most famous would include: William Crump of Madresfield; Thomas Turton of Sherborne Castle; Jones of Elvetham; Trinder of Dogmersfield; Edwin Molyneux of Swanmore Park; not to mention Maxim, his successor at Heckfield. *Garden* XXXV (1890), p. 141; *GardMag* XXXIII (1890), p. 70.
9. ROBINSON 1883, p. c. Dogmersfield: GC 1889 ii 246–8; Elvetham: *Garden* XXXVI (1889), pp. 95–6. See also MILNER 1890, p. 53, as an example of the influence of Wildsmithian bedding.
10. R.A.H.G.'s contributions: *Garden* XXII (1882), pp. 477, 521, 566; XXIII (1883), pp. 75–6. J.D.'s replies: *Garden* XXII (1882), pp. 499–500, 543–4; XXIII (1883), pp. 3–4, 21–2, 115.
11. *Garden* XXII (1882), p. 544.
12. ROBINSON 1883, p. cxvi. J.D.'s proportions were different from Field's chromatic equivalents, which Owen Jones had adopted (see JONES 1856, proposition 18); theirs were yellow 3, red 5, and blue 8; J.D.'s were yellow 2, red 3, and blue 5. See also C. T. Druery, 'Colour', *JHort* L n.s. (1905), p. 204, for a restatement of Jones's principles in the Edwardian period.
13. *Garden* XXII (1882), pp. 543–4.
14. For accounts of Jekyll's career, see JEKYLL 1934; MASSINGHAM 1966; BROWN 1982; and TOOLEY 1984. William Goldring published an account of Munstead in *Garden* XXII (1882), pp. 191–3.
15. GC 1873, p. 1208; *Garden* VII (1875), p. 136 (HOPE 1881, pp. 163, 99). For an example of this influence, see Highbury: *JHort* XXXII n.s. (1896), p. 232.
16. *Garden* XXII (1882), p. 191. Castle Ashby: *Garden* XIX (1881), pp. 7–8.
17. Gertrude Jekyll, 'Colour in the flower garden', *Garden* XXII (1882), p. 177; reprinted in ROBINSON 1883, pp. cx–cxii.
18. JEKYLL 1908, p. 52. See also Gertrude Jekyll and H. Selfe-Leonard, 'Hardy-plant borders', JRHS XXI (1897–8), pp. 433–41.
19. ROBINSON 1883, pp. cxi, cxvi. Jekyll thought that purple and lilac should be kept well away from red and pink; J.D. inserted lilac as part of a graded sequence from pink to scarlet.
20. *CottGard* XIII (1854), p. 20.
21. Jekyll, 'Colour in the flower garden', op. cit.
22. TOOLEY 1984, pp. 25–40. Jekyll's copy of FIELD 1817 is preserved in the Lindley Library.
23. *Garden* XXII (1882), pp. 470–1.
24. M. J. Tooley, 'Gardens Designed by Miss Gertrude Jekyll in northern England', *Garden History*, VIII iii (1980), pp. 37–42.
25. JEKYLL 1918, p. 237.
26. E. S. Ashmore, *Flower Beds* (c. 1922); *JHort* L n.s. (1905), p. 53; GC 1907 ii 268.
27. *JHort* XXI n.s. (1890), p. 248; GC 1903 ii 331.
28. William Miller, 'Landscape Gardening' (1907), pp. 12–13; GC 1898 ii 230–1; GC 1904 i 42–3; GC 1909 i 271–2.
29. GC 1889 ii 380.
30. Edward Luckhurst, 'Tasteful gardening', *JHort* XXVI n.s. (1893), pp. 168–9; *JHort* XXXV n.s. (1897), pp. 362, 392.
31. GC 1907 ii 436–7.
32. See *JHort* LXVII n.s. (1913), p. 160, for one of the few reports on a floral crown to appear in the gardening press.
33. Floral staircases appeared in Bridlington and Rugby, the floral organ and floral furniture in Wibsey Park, Bradford, and the floral cenotaph in Brenchley Gardens, Maidstone. The gardening press tended to avert its gaze from these structures, but the evidence survives on contemporary postcards.
34. *GardMag* XLVI (1903), p. 456.
35. Karl Götze, *Album fur Teppichgärtnerei*, 2nd ed. (190–), p. 252.
36. MAJOR 1852, p. 196.
37. GC 1880 i 586–7, 593.
38. Linda Meller, *Leisure and the Changing City* (1976), pp. 225–36.
39. GC 1881 i 44–5.
40. W. W. Pettigrew, 'The influence of air pollution on vegetation', GC 1928 ii 292, 308–9, 335; ELLIOTT 1986a.
41. E. P. Mawson, 'Modern tendencies in the design and equipment of public parks', JRHS LIV (1929), pp. 333–49; also W. W. Pettigrew, *Municipal Parks* (1937).
42. GC 1869, p. 1305. The quarrel was taken up by Barnes's successor: see GC 1870, p. 7; *JHort* XXI (1871), p. 202.
43. WOOD 1881, p. 2.
44. LATOUCHE 1876, pp. 90–6; LOFTIE 1879, p. 70.
45. John Wills, 'The future of gardening', *JHort* II n.s. (1881), p. 63.
46. BRIGHT 1881, pp. 73–4. See also LOFTIE 1879, pp. 71–2; GC 1901 i 160.
47. EARLE 1897, pp. 23–4; *JHort* LXV n.s. (1912), p. 508.
48. LOFTIE 1879, pp. 73–4; Jekyll, 'Gardens and garden craft', *Edinburgh Review* CLXXXIV (1896), p. 179; CHAMBERLAIN 1892, pp. 42–7; and see JEKYLL 1899, pp. 271–9.
49. BRIGHT 1881, p. 75; LATOUCHE 1876, p. 96. Heckfield: CL XXXI (1898), p. 691.
50. LOFTIE 1879, pp. 73–4; BRIGHT 1881, p. 75.
51. Charles Wade, 'Haphazard Notes' (1979; a National Trust leaflet).
52. JRHS XXVIII (1903–4), p. 141; but see Dean Hole's fear of horticultural democracy in JRHS XX (1896–7), p. 89.
53. J. W. Moorman: *JHort* XXXII n.s. (1896), pp. 249–50, W. W. Pettigrew: GC 1907 i 315. For their respective careers, see *JHort* LVIII n.s. (1909), pp. 418–20, and GC 1947 i 86.
54. GC 1891 ii 695–6. See GC 1869, p. 416, for a yew panel bed at Elvaston that may have served as a model.
55. Gosford House: information from the Earl of Wemyss and March. Broughton Hall: information from Mr H. R. Tempest.
56. Conifer parterre at Canford Manor: *JHort* XXI n.s. (1890), p. 182. Dwarf oak edgings: *JHort* XXXIX n.s. (1899), pp. 265, 290. Dr John Harvey has

drawn my attention to the use of ferns as an edging at Nynehead, Somerset, but this practice has not so far been dated. See 'Combination bedding', *JHort* XLVII n.s. (1903), pp. 355–6.
57. GC 1907 ii 268; *JHort* LV n.s. (1907), p. 154; *GardMag* LVI (1913), p. 821; and see W. F. Rowles, 'Undulation in bedding', *JHort* LXVII n.s. (1913), p. 284.
58. The magazines yield a copious harvest of references to Aldenham between the 1890s and the 1920s; for an overview see Audrey le Lievre, 'An account of the garden of Aldenham House, and of its makers: Henry Hucks Gibbs, Vicary Gibbs and Edwin Beckett', *Garden History* XIV (1986). Goldring's plan for the azalea garden is preserved at Elvetham Park; a similar feature was planted in Ruskin Park.
59. Tubbed plants: James Hudson, 'Plants for terrace gardening', JRHS XXXIII (1908), pp. 369–77. Dry-wall gardening; JEKYLL 1901, pp. 1–9. The Dyffryn trials: *GardMag* LVI (1913), pp. 685, 785, 949, 983; GC 1914 ii 379–81.
60. Alfred Austin, *The Garden that I Love* (1894), *In Veronica's Garden* (1895), *Lamia's Winter Quarters* (1898), *Haunts of Ancient Peace* (1902), and *The Garden that I Love*, second series (1907).
61. H. H. Dombrain, 'The Poet Laureate's garden', GC 1896 ii 295–6.
62. JEKYLL 1899, pp. 266–7.
63. On edgings, see the young Frederick Street, *JHort* XLIII n.s. (1901), p. 510. On colours, see Arthur Proudlock, GC 1907 i 261.
64. *JHort* LIX n.s. (1909), p. 250; see also GC 1907 ii 264, 299.
65. *The Times*, 15 July 1911, p. 6; see *JHort* LXIII (1911), p. 90.
66. *GardMag* LVI (1913), pp. 709, 884; LVIII (1915), p. 550; JEKYLL 1908, pp. 89–105.
67. *GardMag* XLVI (1903), p. 527; *GardMag* LVI (1913), p. 821; see also *JHort* L (1905), p. 204.
68. George R. Kingbourn, 'The maligning of magenta', *Bulletin of the Hardy Plant Society* V (1977), pp. 54–6.
69. See George Paul on rose uses, JRHS XXV (1900–1), pp. 85–90; JEKYLL 1902, p. 71; THOMAS 1977.
70. For the general state of spring gardening, see *JHort* L n.s. (1905), pp. 205–6. A. Dean: 'Winter and spring bedding in flower gardens', JRHS XXI (1897–8), p. 70.
71. A. Dean, ibid., pp. 65–77; W. Wilks, 'A method of winter gardening', JRHS XII (1890), pp. 233–43.
72. GC 1898 ii 156–7.
73. *JHort* LX n.s. (1910), pp. 459–60.
74. WRIGHT 1908, pp. 4–5.
75. *GardMag* LVI (1913), p. 821.

Chapter 9

1. *JHort* XXIV n.s. (1892), pp. 309, 357.
2. For definitions of Dutch gardens, see SEDDING 1891, p. 55, and *JHort* LXI n.s. (1910), p. 405.
3. Lyme Park: THOMAS 1979, p. 166–8. See *JHort* XL n.s. (1900), p. 222, for Italian/Dutch uncertainty at Mentmore.
4. Viscountess Wolseley, *Gardens: their Form and Design* (1919); see also W. F. Rowles, *How to Make and Manage a Garden* (1905), pp. 49–53, 99–102.
5. SEDDING, op. cit.
6. GC 1898 ii 221–3.
7. CURTIS 1904, p. 38.
8. LATOUCHE 1876, p. 89; BRIGHT 1881, pp. 7–8; SEDDING 1891, p. 104.
9. SEDDING 1891, pp. 180–1.
10. Robinson reviewed Sedding in *Garden* XLI (1892), pp. 66–7; see also ROBINSON 1892. For his earlier tolerance, see *Garden* III (1873), p. 451.
11. *GardMag* XXXIV (1891), pp. 434–5; XLVIII (1905), pp. 297–9. See also George Gordon, 'Revival of an old gardening art', *GardMag* XLI (1898), pp. 825–58; CURTIS 1904, p. 36.
12. CURTIS 1904, pp. 33–4.
13. Friar Park: CURTIS 1904, p. 36; *GardMag* XLI (1898), p. 444; CRISP 1910. Headley Court: CL XXXII (1912), pp. 18–25. Mapperton Manor: CL X (1901), pp. 16–20; XXXIV (1913), pp. 490–7. ROBINSON 1892; and see ELLIOTT 1985. Alicia Amherst, 'Victorian gardening', QR CLXXXVIII (1898), p. 63.
14. Art and nature: CURTIS 1904, p. 41, and cf. pp. 77–8; flower gardening: pp. 72–5.
15. BLOMFIELD 1892, p. 12.
16. G. Richards Julian, 'Styles of architecture, and their relation to the art of landscape gardening', GC 1884 ii 682, and 1885 i 140, 203, 263.
17. One of the great Pettigrew dynasty of gardeners: the son of Archibald Pettigrew of Cardiff Castle, and brother of W. W. Pettigrew of the Cardiff parks, whom he replaced in that capacity when W. W. moved on to command the parks of Manchester.
18. I am grateful to Miss M. Carden, Governor of H.M. Youth Custody Centre, Hewell Grange, for providing me with a copy of Andrew Pettigrew's notes on the creation of the garden, printed in *Robert George, Earl of Plymouth 1857–1923* (1932). For Rous Lench, see CLVI (1899), pp. 336–42.
19. I am grateful to Gilly Drummond for information on Rhinefield. Copped Hall: *GardMag* LIX (1916), pp. 3–5. Old Place: *Garden* 1921, pp. 464–6.
20. SEDDING 1891, p. 93.
21. Later Mrs Evelyn Cecil, and then Lady Rockley – a headache for librarians. See STEARN 1977.
22. Newberry: GC 1889 ii 12, 293, 494; 1890 i 74, 197, 258, 417, 482. Reginald Blomfield, *The Formal Garden in England* (1891; third edition, 1907). Alicia Amherst, *History of Gardening in England* (1895; third edition, 1910). Rose Standish Nichols, *English Pleasure Gardens* (1902). Inigo Triggs, *Formal Gardens in England and Scotland* (1902). R. P. Brotherston's articles appeared in *JHort* from 1902 on.
23. SEDDING 1891, p. 87: BLOMFIELD 1892; GC 1895 ii 355–6.
24. Inigo Thomas, 'The garden in relation to the house', *GardMag* XXXIX (1896), pp. 104–5, 118, 135 (the quotation is from p. 105).
25. BLOMFIELD 1892, pp. 89, 135, 142.
26. Ibid., pp. 89–91, 72–4, 151, 217–18.
27. Inigo Thomas, op. cit., p. 118; *Garden* L (1896), p. 482; Alicia Amherst, 'Victorian gardening', QR CLXXXVIII (1898), p. 52.
28. Thomas, op. cit., p. 135.
29. Parnham House guide. I am grateful to Mrs J. Makepeace, Graeme Moore, and David Ottewill for discussing the attribution to Thomas. Markham Nesfield had similarly broken the terrace at Glanusk Park to accommodate existing trees. Thomas's relation to W. B. Thomas, and by marriage to Sir George Sitwell: information from David Ottewill.
30. BLOMFIELD 1892, pp. 16–18, 131–5, 210–22, 230–32. See also FELLOWS 1985.
31. SEDDING 1891, pp. 2–80.
32. *GardMag* XLI (1898), p. 825.
33. GC 1896 ii 788.
34. BLOMFIELD 1892, p. 49.
35. See MAWSON 1900, pp. 67–8.
36. CRISP 1910, pp. 42–72, 88; CRISP 1914, pp. 12–13, 16–17, 35–41.

37. WARWICK 1898, p. 9. See ELLIOTT 1984c.
38. Department of the Environment, Royal Parks Historical Survey: Hampton Court and Bushy Park (1982), I, pp. 70–4. The committee comprised Aston Webb, Ernest Law, Ellen Willmott, F. R. S. Balfour (RHS nominee), William Watson of Kew, and the Colchester nurseryman and landscape gardener Robert Wallace. See also E. V. Boyle, 'Hampton Court in by-gone years', *National Review XXVIII (1897)*, pp. 668–80; and Ernest Law, *The Flower-Lover's Guide to the Gardens of Hampton Court Palace* (1923), and *Hampton Court Gardens: Old and New* (1926).
39. Inigo Thomas, op. cit., p. 105; SCOTT-JAMES 1981.
40. Shakespeare literature: H. N. Ellacombe, *The Plant-lore and Garden-craft of Shakespeare*, 1878 (later editions 1884 and 1896); Leo Grindon, *The Shakespere Flora* (1883); Herbert W. Seager, *Natural History in Shakespeare's Time* (1896); Walter Crane, *Flowers from Shakespeare's Garden* (1906). There was to be a further spurt in the interwar years, with books by Eleanour Sinclair Rohde among others.
41. WARWICK 1898, p. 8. The Pleasaunce: GC 1911 ii 260–1.
42. Brockwell Park: Alicia Amherst (Cecil), *London Parks and Gardens* (1907), pp. 170–2. Battersea Park: GC 1913 ii 141.
43. Ernest Law, *Shakespeare's Garden, Stratford-upon-Avon* (1922).
44. SOUTHEY 1848; GC 1843, p. 400.
45. Baines: *Garden* VII (1875), pp. 156–7; JEKYLL 1900, pp. 236–54; H. P. G. Maule, *GardMag* XLIV (1901), p. 391; MAWSON 1900, p. 201.
46. GC 1908 ii, pp. 146–7, 295.
47. K. N. Sanecki, 'The herb garden', in HARRIS 1979, pp. 123–8.
48. For surveys of the arts-and-crafts movement, see Peter Davey, *Arts and Crafts Architecture* (1980); GRADIDGE 1980 (1980).
49. Voysey, quoted in Duncan Simpson, *C. F. A. Voysey: an Architect of Individuality* (1979), p. 146.
50. Thomas, op. cit., p. 104.
51. M'INTOSH 1853–55, vol. I, pp. 705–13; *Garden* VII (1875), pp. 222–5, 502–3; VIII (1875), p. 371. Fox: *JHort* XXVII (1874), pp. 78–80, 146–8. Barron: GC 1882 ii 77, 180–1.
52. MAWSON 1900, pp. 63–4; also Thomas Mawson, 'The practice of garden design', JRHS XXXIV (1909), pp. 384–93.
53. MAWSON 1900, pp. 22–9, 56–7, 68.
54. Clough Williams-Ellis, *Cottage Building in Cob, Pisé, Chalk and Clay: a Renaissance* (1919). The drawing for Blow's mud cottage is in the RIBA Drawings Collection (cottage for Heale House, Salisbury, 1908).
55. MAWSON 1900: compare an early design like Graythwaite Hall, p. 208, with a more axial plan like Ballimore, p. 189. For Mawson's career see Geoffrey Beard, *Thomas H. Mawson: a Northern Landscape Architect* (1978); David Mawson, 'T. H. Mawson (1861–1933) – landscape architect and town planner', *J. Roy. Soc. Arts* CXXXII (1984), pp. 184–99; and, with a large dose of salt, MAWSON 1927.
56. See Simpson, op. cit., pp. 63–71, and Gradidge, op. cit., pp. 177–83.
57. This view receives its most concentrated expression in Thomas Mawson, 'Garden design – comparative, historical, and ethical', JRHS XXXIV (1909), pp. 361–83.
58. For garden writings by some of these architects, see: E. S. Prior, 'Garden-making', *Studio* XXI (1901), pp. 28–36, 86–95, 176–90; M. H. Baillie Scott, *House and Gardens* (1906). For Weir Schulz, see David Ottewill, 'Robert Weir Schultz (1860–1951): an arts and crafts architect', *Architectural History* XXII (1979), pp. 88–115. For Lorimer, see SAVAGE 1977. For Arnold Mitchell's garden in Harrow, see *Studio* XXVIII (1903), pp. 94–108, and JRHS XXIX (1904–5), pp. 68–76.
59. There is a copious literature on Lutyens. See in particular WEAVER 1913; GRADIDGE 1981; BROWN 1982.
60. Ian C. Laurie, 'Landscape gardeners at Eaton Hall – II', *Garden History* XIII (1985), pp. 143–4.
61. CL XXIV (1908), p. 492.
62. See EARLE 1899, pp. 128–9 on pleached alleys.
63. Ellen E. Frank, 'The domestication of nature: five houses in the Lake District', in KNOEPFLMACHER 1978, pp. 68–92. See James D. Kornwolf, *M. H. Baillie Scott and the Arts and Crafts Movement* (1972), for a somewhat overstated account of his career.
64. Prior, op. cit., p. 28.
65. GC 1900 i 385–6.
66. Inigo Thomas, op. cit., p. 105; MAWSON 1900, pp. 109, 113; SEDDING 1891, pp. 10–11; JEKYLL 1899, pp. 196–9.
67. GRADIDGE 1981, pp. 63–84; Thomas Mawson, *Civic Art* (1907).
68. James Hudson, 'Plants for terrace gardening', JRHS XXXIII (1908), pp. 369–77; 'The gardens by the Lake of Como', JRHS XXXV (1909–10), pp. 204–12.
69. Sledmere: guidebook, 1980. Nashdom: WEAVER 1913, pp. 242–6. Cathays Park: John B. Hilling, *Cardiff and the Valleys* (1973), pp. 145–60.
70. W. P. Tuckermann, *Die Gartenkunst der Italianischen Renaissance-Zeit* (1884); Charles A. Platt, *Italian Gardens* (1894); Vernon Lee, *Limbo* (1897); John Addington Symonds, *Sketches and Studies in Italy and Greece* (1898); Edith Wharton, *Italian Villas and their Gardens* (1904); Charles Latham, *The Gardens of Italy* (1905); Inigo Triggs, *The Art of Garden Design in Italy* (1906); George S. Elgood, *Italian Gardens* (1907); Sir George Sitwell, *An Essay on the Making of Gardens* (1909). See also EARLE 1899, pp. 308–66.
71. Erika Neubauer, 'The garden architecture of Cecil Pinsent, 1884–1964', *J. Gard. Hist.* III (1983), pp. 35–48.
72. *GardMag* L (1907), pp. 135–8.
73. H. Avray Tipping, 'Iford Manor – II', CL LII (1922), pp. 272–7.
74. Joseph Cheal, 'The Old Gardens of Italy', JRHS XXXIV (1909), pp. 446–51.
75. Gavin Astor, *Hever in the Twentieth Century* (1973).
76. GRADIDGE 1981, p. 44; GRADIDGE 1980; ASLET 1982, pp. 127–34; Alastair Service, *Edwardian Architecture* (1977), pp. 170–7.
77. Christopher Hussey, 'Houndsell Place, Sussex', CL CXXIV (1958), pp. 126–9.
78. MACARTNEY 1908. See also H. P. G. Maule, 'The architect and the garden', *GardMag* XLIV (1901), p. 391.
79. Moreton Paddox: GC 1915 i 323; 1916 ii 132; Edward White, 'Garden design', JRHS XXXIX (1913–14), pp. 559–580; Marcus Binney and Anne Hills, *Elysian Gardens* (1979), p. 16.
80. Blomfield: RIBA drawings Collection RAN/C/15; FELLOWS 1985, pp. 67, 131, 169.
81. GC 1898 ii 429–30; Andrew Saint, *Richard Norman Shaw* (1976), pp. 326–31.
82. I have stolen this remark from John Malins.

Bibliography

Contemporary works:
Periodicals

Annals of Horticulture, 1846–50
Birmingham and Midland Gardeners' Magazine, 1852–53
Blackwood's Magazine, 1817–
Builder 1844–1966
Civil Engineer and Architect's Journal, 1837–
Cottage Gardener, 1848–60; continued as *Journal of Horticulture* (abbreviated as *CottGard*)
Country Life, 1897– (abbreviated as CL)
Floral Cabinet, 1837–40
Floral World, 1858–80
Floricultural Cabinet, 1833–59; continued as *Gardener's Weekly Magazine* (abbreviated as FC)
Floricultural Magazine, 1836–42 (abbreviated as FM)
Florist, 1848–61; continued as *Florist and Pomologist*
Florist and Pomologist, continuation of *Florist*; 1862–84 (abbreviated as FP)
Florist's Guide, 1850
Florist's Journal, 1840–48
Garden, 1871–1927
Garden Companion, continuation of *Gardener's Magazine of Botany*; 1852
Gardener, 1867–82
Gardener and Practical Florist, 1843–44
Gardener, Florist and Agriculturist, 1847
Gardener's and Forester's Record, 1833–36
Gardeners' Chronicle, 1841– (abbreviated as GC)
Gardener's Gazette, 1837–44
Gardeners' Magazine, 1826–43 (abbreviated as GM)
Gardener's Magazine, continuation of *Gardener's Weekly Magazine* 1865–1916 (abbreviated as *GardMag*)
Gardener's Magazine of Botany, 1850–51; continued as *Garden Companion* (abbreviated as GMB)
Gardener's Record, 1869–85
Gardener's Weekly Magazine, continuation of *Floricultural Cabinet* 1860–65
Gardening Illustrated, 1879–1956
Gardening World, 1884–1909
Gossip for the Garden, 1856–63
Horticultural Journal, 1833–40 (abbreviated as *HortJ*)
Horticultural Register, 1831–36 (abbreviated as *HortReg*)
Journal of Horticulture, continuation of *The Cottage Gardener*; 1861–1915 (abbreviated as *JHort*)
Journal of the Horticultural Society of London, 1846–55 (abbreviated as JHS)
Journal of the Royal Horticultural Society, 1866– (abbreviated as JRHS)
Ladies' Magazine of Gardening, 1841
Memoirs of the Caledonian Horticultural Society, 1813–29
Midland Florist, 1847–63
Quarterly Review, 1807– (abbreviated as QR)
Paxton's Magazine of Botany, 1834–49 (abbreviated as PMB)
Proceedings of the Royal Horticultural Society, 1859–65
Scottish Gardener, 1852–59
Studio, 1893–
Transactions of the Horticultural Society of London, 1807–1848 (abbreviated as *TransHS*)
United Gardeners' and Land Stewards' Journal, 1845–47 (abbreviated as UGLSJ)

Contemporary sources:
Books

ADAMSON 1851: Robert Adamson, *The Cottage Gardener*
ALISON 1811: Archibald Alison, *Essays on the Nature and Principles of Taste*, 2nd ed.
BARRON 1852: William Barron, *The British Winter Garden*
BARRY 1867: Alfred Barry, *Life and Works of Sir Charles Barry*
BEAN 1908: Walter Jackson Bean, *The Royal Botanic Gardens, Kew*
BEETON 1862: S. O. Beeton, ed., *The Book of Garden Management*
BLOMFIELD 1892: Reginald Blomfield, *The Formal Garden in England*
BOWLES 1914: Edward Augustus Bowles, *My Garden in Spring*
BOYLE 1884: Eleanor Vere Boyle (E.V.B.), *Days and Hours in a Garden*, 2nd ed.
BRIGHT 1879: Henry Arthur Bright, *A Year in a Lancashire Garden*
BRIGHT 1881: Henry Arthur Bright, *The English Flower Garden*
BROOKE 1857: E. Adveno Brooke, *The Gardens of England*
BURBIDGE 1877: Frederick W. Burbidge, *Horticulture*
BURGESS 1854: Henry Burgess, *The Amateur Gardener's Year-Book*

BURRITT 1868: Elihu Burritt, *Walks in the Black Country and its Green Border-land*
CHAMBERLAIN 1892: Edith Chamberlain and Fanny Douglas, *The Gentlewoman's Book of Gardening*
CHEVREUL 1854: Michel-Eugène Chevreul, *The Principles of Harmony and Contrast of Colours*, transl. by Charles Martel
COBBETT 1830: William Cobbett, *Rural Rides*
COLE 1877a; Nathen Cole, *The Royal Parks and Gardens of London*
CONDER 1893: Josiah Conder, *Landscape Gardening in Japan*
CORY 1914: Reginald Cory, *The Horticultural Record*
COUSIN 1848: Victor Cousin, *The Philosophy of the Beautiful*, transl. by Jesse Cato Daniel
CRISP 1910: Frank Crisp, *Friar Park,. Henley-on-Thames. Guide for the Use of Visitors*, 3rd ed.
CRISP 1914: Frank Crisp, *Friar Park, Henley-on-Thames, Guide for the Use of Visitors*, 4th ed.
CURTIS 1904: Charles H. Curtis and W. Gibson, *The Book of Topiary*
DENNIS 1835: John Dennis, *The Landscape Gardener*
DIVERS 1909: W. H. Divers, *Spring Gardening at Belvoir Castle*
EARLE 1897: Maria Theresa Earle, *Pot-pourri from a Surrey Garden*
EARLE 1899: Maria Theresa Earle, *More Pot-pourri from a Surrey Garden*
FARRER 1907: Reginald Farrer, *My Rock-Garden*
FARRER 1909: Reginald Farrer, *In a Yorkshire Garden*
FARRER 1913: Reginald Farrer, *The Rock Garden*
FERRIS 1837: C. F. Ferris, *The Parterre*
FIELD 1817: George Field, *Chromatics*
FLEMING 1864: John Fleming, *Spring and Winter Gardening*
FORBES 1820: Alexander Forbes, *Short Hints on Ornamental Gardening*
FOSTER 1881: Mrs Francis Foster, *On the Art of Gardening.*
FREEMAN-MITFORD 1896: Algernon Bertram Freeman-Mitford, *The Bamboo Garden*
GILPIN 1835: William Sawrey Gilpin, *Practical Hints upon Landscape Gardening*, 2nd ed.
GODFREY 1914: Walter Godfrey, *Gardens in the Making*
HANHAM 1857: Frederick H. Hanham, *A Manual for the Park*
HARVEY 1837: John Harvey, *Guide to Illustrations and Views of Knowle Cottage, Sidmouth, the Elegant Marine Villa Orné of Thos. L. Fish*
HAY 1845: David Ramsay Hay, *The Principles of Beauty in Colouring Systematized*
HIBBERD 1857: Shirley Hibberd, *Rustic Adornments for Homes of Taste*, 2nd ed.
HIBBERD 1870: Shirley Hibberd, *Rustic Adornments for Homes of Taste*, 3rd ed.
HIBBERD 1875: Shirley Hibberd, *The Amateur's Flower Garden*
HOLE 1892: Samuel Reynolds Hole, *The Memories of Dean Hole*
HOPE 1808: Thomas Hope, 'On the Art of Gardening', *Review of Publications of Art*, no ii
HOPE 1881: Frances Jane Hope, *Notes and Thoughts on Gardens and Woodlands*
HUGHES 1866: John Arthur Hughes, *Garden Architecture and Landscape Gardening*
HUNT 1840: Leigh Hunt, *The Seer*
JACKSON 1822: Maria Jackson, *The Florist's Manual*
JEKYLL 1899: Gertrude Jekyll, *Wood and Garden*
JEKYLL 1900: Gertrude Jekyll, *Home and Garden*
JEKYLL 1901: Gertrude Jekyll, *Wall and Water Gardens*
JEKYLL 1902: Gertrude Jekyll and Edward Mawley, *Roses for English Gardens*
JEKYLL 1908: Gertrude Jekyll, *Colour in the Flower Garden*
JEKYLL 1918: Gertrude Jekyll, *Garden Ornament*
JOHNSON 1826: George W. Johnson, *A History of English Gardening*
JOHNSON 1874: Joseph Forsyth Johnson, *The Natural Principles of Landscape Gardening*
JONES 1856: Owen Jones, *The Grammar of Ornament*
KEMP 1850: Edward Kemp, *How to Lay Out a Small Garden*
KEMP 1851: Edward Kemp, *The Parks, Gardens, etc., of London and its Suburbs*
KEMP 1864: Edward Kemp, *How to Lay Out a Garden*, 3rd ed.
KENT 1823: Elizabeth Kent, *Flora Domestica*
KERR 1864: Robert Kerr, *The Gentleman's House*
LATOUCHE 1876: 'John Latouche' (O. J. F. Crawfurd), *Country House Essays*
LINDLEY 1840: John Lindley, *Theory of Horticulture*
LOFTIE 1879: Mrs Loftie, *XLVI Social Twitters*
LOTHIAN 1845: James Lothian, *Practical Hints on the Culture and General Management of Alpine or Rock Plants*
LOUDON 1812: *John Claudius Loudon, Hints on the Formation of Gardens and Pleasure Grounds*
LOUDON 1817: John Claudius Loudon, *Remarks on the Construction of Hothouses*
LOUDON 1822: John Claudius Loudon, *Encyclopaedia of Gardening*, 1st ed.
LOUDON 1824: John Claudius Loudon, *The Green-house Companion*
LOUDON 1830: John Claudius Loudon, *Illustrations of Landscape Gardening and Garden Architecture*, parts I–II (1830–31)
LOUDON 1835: John Claudius Loudon, *Encyclopaedia of Gardening*, 8th ed.
LOUDON 1835–38: John Claudius Loudon, *Arboretum et Fruticetum Britannicum*
LOUDON 1836: John Claudius Loudon, *Encyclopaedia of Cottage, Farm and Villa Architecture*
LOUDON 1838: John Claudius Loudon, *The Suburban Gardener and Villa Companion*
LOUDON 1840a: Jane Wells Loudon, *Practical Instructions in Gardening for Ladies*
LOUDON 1840b: John Claudius

Loudon, *The Derby Arboretum*
LOUDON 1843: John Claudius Loudon, *On the Laying Out, Planting and Managing of Cemeteries*
LOUDON 1845: John Claudius Loudon, *Self-instruction for Young Gardeners*
MACARTNEY 1908: Mervyn Macartney, *English Houses and Gardens in the Seventeenth and Eighteenth Centuries*
M'INTOSH 1838: Charles M'Intosh, *The Flower Garden*
M'INTOSH 1853–55: Charles M'Intosh, *The Book of the Garden*
MCKENZIE 1869: Alexander McKenzie, *The Parks, Open Spaces, and Thoroughfares of London*
MAJOR 1852: Joshua Major, *The Theory and Practice of Landscape Gardening*
MAJOR 1861: Joshua Major and Son, *The Ladies' Assistant in the Formation of their Flower Gardens*
MANGLES 1839: James Mangles, *The Floral Calender*
MARCH 1862: T. C. March, *Flower and Fruit Decoration*
MARTINEAU 1913: Alice Martineau, *The Herbaceous Garden*
MAWSON 1900: Thomas H. Mawson, *The Art and Craft of Garden Making*
MAWSON 1927: Thomas H. Mawson, *The Life and Work of an English Landscape Gardener*
MEYER 1910: F. W. Meyer, *Rock and Water Gardens*
MILNER 1890: Henry Ernest Milner, *The Art and Practice of Landscape Gardening*
MORRIS 1825: Richard Morris, *Essays on Landscape Gardening*
MORRIS 1882: William Morris: *Hopes and Fears for Art*
MURRAY 1863: Andrew Murray, *The Book of the Royal Horticultural Society*
NASH 1839–49: Joseph Nash, *Mansions of England in the Olden Time*
NEWTON 1876: Joseph Newton, *The Landscape Gardener*
NICOL 1810: Walter Nicol, *The Villa Garden Directory*
NIVEN 1838: Ninian Niven, *The Visitor's Companion to the Botanic Garden at Glasnevin*
PAPWORTH 1818: John Buonarotti Papworth, *Rural Residences*
PAPWORTH 1823: John Buonarotti Papworth, *Hints on Ornamental Gardening*
PAUL 1855: William Paul, *The Handbook of Villa Gardening*
PAUL 1892: William Paul, *Contributions to the Literature of Horticulture*
PHILLIPS 1823: Henry Phillips, *Sylva Florifera*
PRICE 1842: *Sir Uvedale Price on the Picturesque: with an essay on the origin of taste . . . by Sir Thomas Dick Lauder*
PUCKLER-MUSKAU 1832: von Pückler-Muskau, *Tour in England, Ireland, and France, in the Years 1828 and 1829*
PULHAM 1877: James Pulham, *Picturesque Ferneries and Rock-garden Scenery*
QUATREMERE 1837: Quatremère de Quincy, *An Essay on the Nature, the End, and the Means of Imitation in the Fine Arts*, transl. by J. C. Kent
REPTON 1840: Humphry Repton, *The Landscape Gardening and Landscape Architecture of the Late Humphry Repton, Esq. . . . a new edition . . . by J. C. Loudon*
RICAUTI 1842: T. J. Ricauti, *Sketches for Rustic Work*
RICHARDSON 1837: Charles James Richardson, *Observations on the Architecture of England during the Reigns of Queen Elizabeth and King James I*
ROBINSON 1868: William Robinson, *Gleanings from French Gardens*
ROBINSON 1869: William Robinson, *The Parks, Promenades, and Gardens of Paris*
ROBINSON 1870a: William Robinson, *Alpine Flowers for English Gardens*
ROBINSON 1870b: William Robinson, *The Wild Garden or, Our Groves and Shrubberies Made Beautiful*
ROBINSON 1871a: William Robinson, *The Subtropical Garden; or, Beauty of Form in the Flower Garden*
ROBINSON 1871b: William Robinson, *Hardy Flowers*
ROBINSON 1883: William Robinson, *The English Flower Garden*
ROBINSON 1892: William Robinson, *Garden Design and Architects' Gardens*
ROBINSON 1894: William Robinson, *The Wild Garden*, 4th ed.
ROE 1845: Freeman Roe, *The Hand Book of Fountains, and a Guide to the Gardens of Versailles*
SCOTT 1836: Sir Walter Scott, *Miscellaneous Prose Works*, vol. XXI (Periodical Criticism, Miscellaneous)
SEDDING 1891: John D. Sedding, *Garden-Craft Old and New*
SITWELL 1909: Sir George Sitwell, *An Essay on the Making of Gardens*
SMEE 1872: Alfred Smee, *My Garden: its Plan and Culture*
SMITH 1852: Charles H. J. Smith, *Parks and Pleasure Grounds*
SOUTHEY 1843: Robert Southey, *The Doctor*, ed. by J. W. Warter
STEUART 1828: Sir Henry Steuart, *The Planter's Guide*
SUTHERLAND 1871: William Sutherland, *Handbook of Hardy Herbaceous and Alpine Flowers*
THOMPSON 1859: Robert Thompson, *The Gardener's Assistant*
THOMPSON 1878: Robert Thompson, *The Gardener's Assistant*, ed. by Thomas Moore
THOMSON 1868: David Thomson, *Handy Book of the Flower Garden*
TRIGGS 1902: Inigo Triggs, *Formal Gardens of England and Scotland*
TURNER 1849: Thomas Hudson Turner, *Observations on the State of Horticulture in England in Early Times*
VEITCH 1906: James Herbert Veitch, *Hortus Veitchii*
WARWICK 1898: Frances Evelyn Greville, Countess of Warwick, *An Old English Garden*
WATSON 1872: Forbes Watson, *Flowers and Gardens*
WEAVER 1913: Lawrence Weaver, *Houses and Gardens by E. L. Lutyens*
WIGHTWICK 1840: George Wightwick, *The Palace of Architecture*

WILKINSON 1858: Gardner Wilkinson, *On Colour and the Necessity for a General Diffusion of Taste among all Classes*
WOOD 1881: Samuel Wood, *The Ladies' Multum-in-Parvo Flower Garden*
WORDSWORTH 1951: William Wordsworth, *A Guide through the District of the Lakes*, ed. by W. M. Merchant
WRIGHT 1908: Walter P. Wright, *The Perfect Garden*
WRIGHT 1912: Walter P. Wright, *The New Gardening*
WYATT 1854: Matthew Digby Wyatt, *Views of the Crystal Palace and Park, Sydenham*

Modern Historical Sources

ALLAN 1982: Mea Allan, *William Robinson, Father of the English Flower Garden*
ALLEN 1969: David Elliston Allen, *The Victorian Fern Craze*
ALLIBONE 1977: Jill Allibone, *Anthony Salvin* (unpublished Ph.D. thesis, Courtauld Institute of Art)
ANTHONY 1973: John Anthony, *Joseph Paxton*
ASLET 1982: Clive Aslet, *The Last Country Houses*
BALLARD 1983: Phillada Ballard, *An Oasis of Delight*
BROWN 1982: Jane Brown, *Gardens of a Golden Afternoon*
CARTER 1982: George Carter, Patrick Goode, and Kedrun Laurie, *Humphry Repton, Landscape Gardener 1752–1818*
CHADWICK 1961: George F. Chadwick, *The Works of Sir Joseph Paxton*
CHADWICK 1966: George F. Chadwick, *The Park and the Town*
CROOK 1981: J. Mordaunt Crook, *William Burges and the High Victorian Dream*
DARLEY 1975: Gillian Darley, *Villages of Vision*
DELLHEIM 1982: Charles Dellheim, *The Face of the Past*
DESMOND 1972: Ray Desmond, 'Who designed the Palm House in Kew Gardens?', *Kew Bulletin*, vol. XXVII
DESMOND 1977: Ray Desmond, 'Victorian gardening magazines', *Garden History*, vol. V no. iii
DIESTELKAMP 1982: Edward Diestelkamp, 'The design and building of the Palm House, Royal Botanic Gardens, Kew', *Journal of Garden History*, vol. II
ELLIOTT 1981a: Brent Elliott, 'Mosaiculture: origins and significance', *Garden History*, vol. IX
ELLIOTT 1981b: Brent Elliott, 'Master of the geometric art', JRHS vol. CVI no. xii
ELLIOTT 1983a: Brent Elliott, 'Victorian Greenhouses and Conservatories', *Period Home*, vol. III no. v
ELLIOTT 1983b: Brent Elliott, 'Changing fashions in the conservatory', *Country Life*, 30 June 1983
ELLIOTT 1984a: Brent Elliott, 'We must have the noble cliff', *Country Life*, 5 January 1984
ELLIOTT 1984b: Brent Elliott, 'When Victorian gardeners ruled', *Country Life*, 30 August 1984
ELLIOTT 1984c: Brent Elliott, 'The Victorian language of flowers', in Roy Vickery, ed., *Plant-Lore Studies*
ELLIOTT 1985: Brent Elliott, 'Some sceptical thoughts about William Robinson', JRHS vol. CX no. v
ELLIOTT 1986a: Brent Elliott, 'The Manchester/Salford parks: two additional notes', *Journal of Garden History*, vol. VI no. ii
ELLIOTT 1986b: Brent Elliott, 'Illuminating the garden', JRHS vol. CXI no. xii
ELLIOTT 1987a: Brent Elliott, 'William and George Paul', *Rose Bulletin* (forthcoming)
ELLIOTT 1987b: Brent Elliott, 'The first table decoration competition', JRHS vol. CXII (forthcoming)
FELLOWS 1985: Richard A. Fellows, *Sir Reginald Blomfield*
FESTING 1983: Sally Festing, 'Cliffs, glades and grotto at Merrow Grange', *Garden History*, vol. XI
FESTING 1984: Sally Festing, '"Pulham has done his work well"', *Garden History*, vol. XIII
FLETCHER 1969: H. R. Fletcher, *The Story of the Royal Horticultural Society*
FRANCIS 1977: A. J. Francis, *The Cement Industry 1796–1914: a History*
GAGE 1969: John Gage, *Colour in Turner*
GIROUARD 1977: Mark Girouard, *Sweetness and Light: The 'Queen Anne' Movement 1860–1900*
GIROUARD 1979: Mark Girouard, *The Victorian Country House* (revised edition)
GLOAG 1970: John Gloag, *Mr. Loudon's England*
GOODHART-RENDEL 1953: H. S. Goodhart-Rendel, *English Architecture since the Regency*
GORER 1975: Richard Gorer, *The Flower Garden in England*
GORER 1978: Richard Gorer, *The Growth of Gardens*
GORER 1979: Richard Gorer and John H. Harvey, 'Early rockeries and alpine plants', *Garden History*, vol. VII no ii
GRADIDGE 1980: Roderick Gradidge, *Dream Houses: the Edwardian Ideal*
GRADIDGE 1981: Roderick Gradidge, *Edwin Lutyens, Architect Laureate*
HARRIS 1979: John Harris, ed., *The Garden*
HAYDEN 1978: Peter Hayden, 'Edward Cooke at Biddulph Grange', *Garden History*, vol. VI no. i
HIPPLE 1957: Walter John Hipple, *The Beautiful, the Sublime, and the Picturesque in Eighteenth-Century British Aesthetic Theory*
HITCHCOCK 1954: Henry-Russell Hitchcock, *Early Victorian Architecture*
HIX 1974: John Hix, *The Glass House*
HODGES 1977: 'A Victorian gardener: Edward Milner', *Garden History*, vol. V no. iii
JACQUES 1983: David Jacques, *Georgian Gardens*

JEKYLL 1934: Francis Jekyll, *Gertrude Jekyll*
KNOEPFLMACHER 1978: U. C. Knoepflmacher and G. B. Tennyson, eds., *Nature and the Victorian Imagination*
LE LIEVRE 1980: Audrey le Lievre, *Miss Willmott of Warley Place*
LEMMON 1962: Kenneth Lemmon, *The Covered Garden*
MACDOUGALL 1980: Elisabeth B. MacDougall, ed., *John Claudius Loudon and the Early Nineteenth Century in Britain*
MALINS 1980a: Edward Malins, 'Indian influences on English houses and gardens at the beginning of the nineteenth century', *Garden History*, vol. VIII no. i
MALINS 1980: Edward Malins and Patrick Bowe, *Irish Gardens and Demesnes from 1830*
MARKHAM 1935: Violet Markham, *Paxton and the Bachelor Duke*
MASSINGHAM 1966: Betty Massingham, *Miss Jekyll: Portrait of a Great Gardener*
MELLER 1975: Hugh Meller, *Blore's Country Houses* (unpublished dissertation, Courtauld Institute of Art)
MEYNELL 1980: Guy Meynell, 'The Royal Botanic Society's Garden, Regent's Park', *London Journal*, vol. VI
NOYES 1968: Russell Noyes, *Wordsworth and the Art of Landscape*
PEVSNER 1972: Nicolaus Pevsner, *Some Architectural Writers of the Nineteenth Century*
SAVAGE 1977: Peter Savage, 'Lorimer and the garden heritage of Scotland', *Garden History*, vol. V no ii
SCOTT-JAMES 1981: Anne Scott-James, *The Cottage Garden*
STEARN 1977: William T. Stearn, 'The Garden History Society's tenth anniversary and some historians of garden history', *Garden History*, vol. V no. i
TAIT 1980: A. A. Tait, *The Landscape Garden in Scotland 1735–1835*
TAYLOR 1951: Geoffrey Taylor, *Some Nineteenth-century Gardeners*
TAYLOR 1952: Geoffrey Taylor, *The Victorian Flower Garden*
THOMAS 1977: Graham Stuart Thomas, 'The influence of Gertrude Jekyll on the use of roses in gardens and garden design', *Garden History* vol. V no i
THOMAS 1979: Graham Stuart Thomas, *Gardens of the National Trust*
TJADEN 1974: W. L. Tjaden, *The History of the Horticultural Club*
TJADEN 1983: W. L. Tjaden, 'The "Gardeners Gazette" 1837–1847 and its Rivals', *Garden History* vol. XI
TOOLEY 1984: M. J. Tooley, ed. *Gertrude Jekyll, Artist, Gardener, Craftswoman*
TURNER 1982: T. H. D. Turner, 'Loudon's stylistic development', *Journal of Garden History*, vol. II
TURNER 1984: T. H. D. Turner, 'John Claudius Loudon and the inception of the public park', *Landscape Design* 140
V & A 1984: Victoria and Albert Museum, *The Discovery of the Lake District*
WATKIN 1968: David Watkin, *Thomas Hope and the Neo-Classical Idea*
WATKIN 1982: David Watkin, *Regency*
WILKES 1980: Lyall Wilkes, *John Dobson: Architect and Landscape Gardener*
WOODBRIDGE 1976: Kenneth Woodbridge, 'The planting of ornamental shrubs at Stourhead: a history, 1746 to 1946', *Garden History*, vol. IV no. i

Index

Abbey, George (1835–?) 182, 196
Abbey Park 171, 201
Abbotsford 67
Abney Park Cemetery 36
Abraham, Robert (1773–1850) 38
Acland, Sir Thomas Dyke (1809–98) 22
Adam, Jean-Louis (*fl.*1820s–1830s) 32
Adam, Robert (1728–1792) 156, 242
Adamson, Robert (*c.*1812–81) 64
Addison, Joseph (1672–1719) 119
Albert, the Prince Consort (1819–61) 77, 119, 140, 143, 166
Albert Memorial 109; *41*
Aldenham House 217
Aldworth 159
Alexandra Gardens *87*
Alexandra Palace 109–10, 174, 179, 200
Alison, Archibald (1757–1839) 8–10
Allen, Grant (1848–99) 184
Alton Towers 37*ff*, 111, 138; *11*
Altrincham, see Stamford Park
Amherst, Alicia (1865–1941) 226
Ammerdown 235, 242
Anderson, James (*c.*1832–99) 132
André, Edouard François (1840–1911) 170–71, 180, 182, 186
Andrews, Benjamin (*fl.*1830s) 47
Appleby, Thomas (*c.*1795–1875) 13, 32, 72, 77, 87, 92, 115–17 *passim*
arboretum 36, 52–4, 72, 91–2, 103, 118, 201
Archer, Thomas (1668–1743) 81
Archerfield 131
Arley Hall 69, 159, 227; *jacket back*
Arnott, Samuel (1852–1930) 189
arts and crafts movement 232–8
Arundel Castle 83
Ascog Hall 186; *74*
Ascott 183, 216, 223
Ashby-de-la-Zouch 179
Ashridge 40, 67
associationism 8–10
Aston Lower Grounds 138
Astor, William Waldorf (1879–1952) 240
Athelhampton 227*f*
Aucaunte (*fl.*1870s–1880s) 186
Audsley, George Ashdown (*fl.*1860s–1910s) 200
Austin, Alfred (1835–1913) 217
Avenham Park 172
avenues 57, 84, 117–18
Ayres, William Port (1815–75) 125*f*

Backhouse, James (1825–90) 177–8
Backhouse, James, and Son 177–8, 187, 189, 190, 196*f*
Bacon, Sir Francis (1561–1626) 67–9 *passim*, 159, 163, 228, 230
Badeslade, Thomas (*c.*1715–50) 241
Bagshot Park 93
Bailey, D. and E. 29, 66
Bailey, Henry (*c.*1804–68) 50
Baillie, William (*fl.*1820s–1830s) 44
Baines, Henry (*c.*1804–68) 58
Baines, Thomas (1823–95) 87, 186, 197, 231
Bainton Rectory 124
Balcarres 145
Ball, Alwyn (*c.*1884–1916) 241
Balmoral Castle 145
Banks, Sir Joseph (1743–1820) 11
Barber, Samuel (d. 1832) 38*f*
Barillet-Deschamps, Jean-Pierre (1824–75) 153
Barncluith 58; *5*
Barnes, James (1806–77) 16, 36, 183, 214
Barnsley, see Locke Park
Baron Hill 163; *II*
Barr and Sugden 94, 153
Barr, Peter (1826–1909) 94, 230
Barron, William (1800–91) 19–20, 32, 35, 79, 83–7, 93–99 *passim*, 103, 115–119 *passim*, 135, 171, 182, 197, 212, 232–3
Barry, Alfred (1826–1910) 76
Barry, Sir Charles (1795–1860) 10, 67*f*, 74–8, 90, 111, 136, 141, 147, 240
Barty, James Strachan (1805–75) 64
Basing Park 136
Bateman, James (1811–97) 102–6, 182, 201, 257 *n.*93
Batsford Park 201

Battersea, Lady, see Flower
Battersea Park 54, 153, 156, 176, 200, 219; *71*
Battle Abbey 58
Battlesden 14
Baxter, William Hart (*c.*1816–90) 111, 257 *n.*24
Bayfordbury 117
Bayham Abbey 58
Bayons Manor 66
Beaconsfield, Earl of, see Disraeli
Beale, Reginald (*c.*1877–1952) 190
Bear Wood 174
Beaton, Donald (1802–63) 10, 14, 18*f*, 56, 58, 64, 71, 77, 89–90, 112, 115, 118, 121, 123–134, 136, 139, 142*f*, 150–153 *passim*, 159, 161, 207*f*, 215
Beaudesert 43, 59, 162
Beaumont, Sir George (1753–1827) 26
bedding 50–1, 87–91, 123–38, 203–5, 208–11, 213, 216–20; see also carpet bedding, massing, sculptural bedding, spring bedding, subtropical bedding
Bedford Lodge 88–9; *36*
Bedgebury 182
Beeton, Samuel (1831–77) 144
Belcher, John (1841–1913) 228
Belgians, King of the, see Leopold I
Bellaggio 238
Belle Vue 52
Belvoir Castle 42, 137, 177–8; *III*
Benson, Edward White (1829–1906) 119
Berkeley, George (1685–1753) 48
Bernard, Thomas (*fl.*1790s) 63
Berry Pomeroy Castle 58
Bessemer, Sir Henry (1813–98) 17, 178
Bethlem Hospital 45
Bicton 35*f*, 214; *10*
Biddulph Grange 102–6, 121–2, 162, 176, 200, 221, 240; *40*
Bilston 57
Birkenhead Park 53–4, 103; *19*
Birmingham, see Cannon Hill Park
Birmingham Botanic Garden 45, 53
Bitton 152
Blenheim Palace 21
Blickling 161-2; *64*
Blomfield, Sir Reginald (1856–1942) 10, 120*f*, 163, 165, 190, 195, 197–8, 223, 226–7, 228, 241*f*
Blore, Edward (1787–1879) 67, 71, 73
Blount, Godfrey (*fl.*1890s) 10
Blow, Detmar Jellings (1867–1939) 233*f*
Boardman, Edward (1833–1910) 197, 232
Bodnant 172, 196
Boleyn, Anne (1507–36) 240
borders, see herbaceous borders
Boscawen, John Townshend (1820–89) 183
Bowes' Manor 42
Bowles, Edward Augustus (1865–1954) 189*ff*, 195, 218
Bowood 14, 32, 77, 118; *IV*
Boyle, Eleanor Vere (1825–1916) 164–5
Brantingham Thorpe 157
Brantwood 183
Bretton Hall 29
Bridge End Gardens 121
Bright, Henry Arthur (1830–84) 150, 157, 161, 214–15
Brighton Aquarium 178
Broadleys 233
Brockwell Park 184, 214, 230
Brooke, E. Adveno (*fl.*1844–64) 83
Broome, Samuel (1806–70) 134*ff*
Brotherston, Robert Pace (1848–1923) 151, 226
Broughton, Lady (*fl.*1820s–1830s) 47
Broughton Castle 231*f*; *95*
Broughton Hall 138*f*, 216*f*
Brown, Lancelot 'Capability' (1715–83) 7, 13, 24, 57, 79, 99, 100, 184, 197*f*, 242
Brunel, Isambard Kingdom (1806–59) 94
Bryanston 241–2
Buccleuch, Duke of, see Scott
Buckfast Abbey 20; *4*
Buckingham Palace 73–74; *26*, *27*
Budding, Edwin Beard (*fl.*1820s–1830s) 16
Buist, Robert (1805–80) 87
Bulstrode Park *73*
Bulwer-Lytton, Sir Edward (1803–73) 68
Burbidge, Frederick William Thomas (1847–1905) 169, 186, 216
Burges, William (1827–81) 167, 200
Burgess, Henry (1806–86) 136
Burn, William (1789–1870) 65, 71
Burnet, Thomas (*c.*1635–1715) 7
Burton, Decimus (1800–81) 66, 72, 107*f*
Bury St Edmunds Botanical Garden 58
Busbridge 57
Buxton Pavilion 173, 179

Caen Wood 93
Caie, John (1811–79) 19, 88–9, 92, 123*f*, 131, 133, 136, 151
Cannell, Henry (1833–1914) 155
Cannon Hill Park *IX*
Canterbury, see Dane John
Cardiff, see Cathays Park
Cardiff Castle 167; *66*
Carlyle, Thomas (1795–1881) 13, 148
Carmontelle, Louis de (1717–1806) 37
carpet bedding 154–8, 166–7, 203–5, 209–11
Cassiobury 40, 47
Castle Ashby 145*ff*, 207, 208–9; *58*
Castle Bromwich 163
Castle Combe 119
Castle Kennedy 59
Cathays Park 179, 238

Cattermole, George (1800–66) 150
Cavendish, William George Spencer, Duke of Devonshire (1790–1858) 14, 64, 80, 110
Caythorpe Court *94*
Cecil, Mrs Evelyn: see Amherst
Cecil, James Brownlow William Gascoyne, Marquis of Salisbury (1791–1868) 68
Cellini, Benvenuto (1500–71) 76
cement 17, 97, 99, 176, 189
cemetery 52; see Abney Park Cemetery
Chamberlain, Edith (*fl.*1890s) 215
Chamberlain, Joseph (1836–1914) 176, 200
Chambers, Sir William (1726–96) 48, 103
Chapel Field 58, 200
Chastleton 58
Chater, William (1802–85) 121
Chatsworth 12, 14, 36, 65–6, 75, 79–83, 87, 91, 94*ff*, 99, 102, 103*f*, 107, 111, 117*f*, 122; *VIII, 7, 32, 38*
Cheal, Joseph (*c.*1848–1935) 179–80, 223, 240
Cheesburn Grange 61
Chelsea Physic Garden 47
Cheney, Robert Henry (*c.*1800–66) 132
Chevreul, Michel-Eugène (1786–1889) 123, 125–6, 150, 205, 208
Chinese garden 103–6, 199–200
Chiswick House 28
Chiswick: see Royal Horticultural Society
Churchtown Botanic Garden 170
Claremont 24, 34, 50, 93
Claridge, George (*fl.*1830s) 17
Clark, Latimer (1822–98) 189
Clarke, Richard Trevor (1813–97) 112
Claude Lorrain (1600–82) 50
Claverton Manor 68
Cliveden 77, 94, 136–7, 154, 155*f*, 240; *Id*
Clumber Park 62; *22*
Cockerell, Charles Robert (1788–1863) 66, 93, 183
Cody, William Frederick, 'Buffalo Bill' (1846–1917) 221
Coke, Sir Edward (1552–1635) 66
Cole, Sir Henry (1808–82) 148
Coleman, William (1827–1908) 118
Coleorton Hall 26–7, 59, 196
Collcutt, Thomas (1840–1924) 236
Colman, Sir Jeremiah (1859–1942) 191
colour 48–51, 87–90, 123–8, 148–52, 180–4, 203–9 *passim*, 217–20
Compton, Charles, Marquis of Northampton (1816–77) 146
Compton Wynyates *90*
Conder, Josiah (*fl.*1880s–1910s) 200
conservatory, see glasshouse
Constable, John (1776–1837) 50
Cooke, Edward William (1811–80) 102–6, 121, 123, 176
Coombe Abbey 112, 144, 146, 209; *85*
Copped Hall 226
Corbett (*fl.*1830s) 95
Cory, Reginald (1871–1934) 217
cottage gardens 63–4, 160, 162, 230, 237
Cousin, Victor (1792–1867) 25, 45
Cowley, Abraham (1618–67) 68
Cowper (Cowper-Temple), William Francis, Baron Mount-Temple (1811–88) 135
Cox, John (1814–86) 48
Cox, William (1822–83) 118
Cragside 195
Cramb, Alexander (1810–77) 18
Crane, Walter (1845–1915) 230
Crawfurd, Oswald John Frederick ('John Latouche') (1834–1909) 214–15, 222
Cremorne Gardens 52, 142
Crewe Hall 139
Crisp, Sir Frank (1843–1919) 189–93 *passim*, 228–9
Crown Point 57
Crystal Palace (Hyde Park) 17, 106–9 *passim*, 127, 148
Crystal Palace (Sydenham) 90, 107-10, 112, 121, 127*f*, 130, 134, 140, 150, 156, 173*f*, 197; *46*
Crystal Palace School of Gardening 173, 196, 224
Crystal Sanatorium 108
Cubitt, Thomas (1788–1855) 77
Culford Hall 135
Culpeper, Nicholas (1616–54) 69
Curtis, Charles Henry (1869–1958) 223–4
Curtis, Samuel (1779–1860) 52
Cutbush, Herbert James (d.1918) 223

D.,J. (Dundas?) 205–7
Dale, Joseph (1815–78) 136
Dalkeith Palace 25, 65
Danby, Francis (1793–1861) 26
Dane John 58
Darwin, Charles Robert (1809–82) 19, 205
Darwin, Erasmus (1731–1802) 43, 125
Daukes, Samuel Whitfield (1811–80) 144
Dawber, Sir Guy (1861–1938) 234
Daylesford Hall 122
Dean, Alexander (1832–1912) 184, 218
Deepdene 74
De L'Isle, Lord, see Sidney
Dennis, John (*fl.*1830s) 62–3
Derby Arboretum 34–5, 52–3, 103, 122, 136
Devey, George (1820–86) 163, 165, 223, 234, 236
Devizes Castle 15, 179
Devonshire, Duke of, see Cavendish
Dezallier d'Argenville, Antoine-Joseph (1680–1765) 71, 139
Dillistone, George (1877–1957) 177

Dickens, Charles (1812–70) 43
Disraeli, Benjamin (1804–81) 164
Dixon, Edmund Saul (1809–93) 12
Dobson, John (1787–1865) 61
Dogmersfield Park 205
Dombrain, Henry Honywood (1818–1905) 160, 217
Donald, James (*fl.*1856–74) 126
Dorchester Public Gardens 196
Douglas, David (1799–1834) 11, 116
Dove Cottage 26–7
Downes, The 164
Downton Castle 66, 139
Doyle, Sir Arthur Conan (1859-1930) 193
Dropmore 33, 44, 51, 88, 93*f*
Drumlanrig Castle, 67; *Ib, 25*
Drummond Castle 62, 67, 77, 111; *VI*
Dryburgh Abbey 58
Dublin, see Phoenix Park
Dudmaston 130
Duncan, James (*fl.*1830s–40s) 136
Durham, Joseph (1814–77) 140
Dutch garden 56, 221–4
Dyce, William (1806–64) 50
Dyffryn 217

Earle, Maria Theresa (1836–1925) 180
Earley, William (*c.*1835–1911) 130
Earl's Court 221
East Park 190
Eastlake, Sir Charles Lock (1793–1865) 125
Eastnor Castle 28, 66, 118
Easton Lodge 240
Eaton Hall 72, 139, 236
Eckford, Henry (1823–1905) 217
Edensor 64
Edgbaston Hall 242
Edinburgh, see Meadows, Princes Street Gardens
Edinburgh Botanical Garden 83
Egerton, Lady Louisa Caroline (*fl.*1860s–70s) 163
Egerton-Warburton, Rowland Eyles (1804–91) 69
Eida, Tass (d.1912) 200
Ellacombe, Henry Nicholson (1822–1916) 152, 230
Elvaston Castle 32, 35, 79, 83–7, 94*f*, 97, 101–105 *passim*, 111, 115, 117*ff*, 122, 135, 200, 210; *34, 35, jacket front*
Elvetham Park 128, 205, 217
enclosure 40, 68–9, 102–6, 122–3, 143, 162–5
Enville Hall 82–3, 108, 130; *VII*
Epping Forest 174, 183
Errington, Robert (1799–1860) 13, 36, 43, 71, 92, 102, 116, 130, 132–3
Escrick Park 58, 179
Essex (*fl.*1830s–40s) 40
Evelyn, John (1620–1706) 68
Eversley, Lord, see Shaw-Lefevre
Ewing, Charles (*fl.*1850s) 17
Ewing, Juliana Horatia (1841–85) 160, 230
Eyles, George (1815–87) 128, 140, 142, 158, 166
Eythrope 195

Fairchild, Thomas (1667–1729) 19
Falkland 68, 124
Fanhams Hall 190, 201
Farnham Castle 58
Farrer, Reginald (1880–1920) 12, 189–92 *passim*, 201, 218
Ferris, C. F. (*fl.*1830s) 71
Field, George (*c.*1777–1854) 206, 259 *n.*96, 266 *n.*12
Fish, David Taylor (1824–1901) 10, 13, 15, 88, 112, 144, 146, 149, 151, 154, 161, 182–4
Fish, Robert (1808–73) 13, 82–3, 88, 111, 131, 142, 151
Fish, Thomas (*fl.*1830s–40s) 42
Flagstaff, The 231
Fleming, George (1809–76) 77, 79, 90–93, 99, 102, 129, 130, 152, 180, 207
Fleming, John (d.1883) 77, 94, 136*ff*, 153–6 *passim*, 208, 218
floral clock 211
Flower, Constance, Lady Battersea (*fl.*1890–1900s) 230
flower garden, see bedding, herbaceous borders
Foley, Lady Emily (d.1900) 138
foliage, see carpet bedding, subtropical bedding
Folly Farm 241
Fonthill Abbey 93
Forbes, Alexander (*fl.*1810s–60s) 58–9
Forrest, Richard (*fl.*1820s–40s) 48
Forsyth, Alexander (*c.*1809–1885) 16, 38*f*, 64, 94, 130, 156
Forsyth, William (1737–1804) 19
Forsyth, William (1772–1835) 55
Fortis Green 71
Fortune, Robert (1812–80) 11, 199, 201
Foster, Mrs John Francis (*fl.*1880s) 164
fountains 80–3 *passim*
Fountains Abbey 180
Fowke, Francis (1823–65) 140–1
Fowler, Archibald (1816–87) 59
Fowler, Charles (1791–1867) 44
Fox, Alfred (1794–1874) 43
Fox, Charles James (1749–1806) 61
Fox, J. Caven (*fl.*1870s) 232
Foxley 27, 57
Freeman-Mitford, Algernon Bertram, Baron Redesdale (1837–1916) 201
Friar Park 190–3 *passim*, 201, 221, 223, 228–9, 232; *77, 80*
Frost, Philip (1804–87) 51, 88, 93*f*

Fyfe, William (d.1912) 219

Gainsborough, Thomas (1727–88) 50
gardenesque 33–6, 113–15, 168
Gardiner, J. A. (*fl.*1897–1907) 229
Garner, Thomas (1839–1906) 224
Garswood 112
Gatton Park 189; *76*
Gauntlett, V. N. (*fl.*1890s–1940s) 202
Gawthorpe Hall 68; *24*
George V (1865–1936) 210
George, Sir Ernest (1839–1922) 234, 241
Gerard, John (1545–1612) 69
Gibson, John (1790–1866) 123
Gibson, John (1815–75) 54, 153–6 *passim*, 178, 219
Gilpin, William Sawrey (1762–1843) 33, 36, 50, 61–2, 118
Ginner, Charles (1878–1952) 220
Glanusk Park 145
glasshouse 17–18, 28–32, 65–6, 107–10, 185–7
Glen Andred 123, 176
Glendinning, Robert (1805–62) 13, 36, 84, 87, 90, 92, 95, 97, 101–2, 111, 116, 118*f*, 251 *n*.74
Glendurgan 43; *14*
Glenny, George (*c*.1793–1874) 12, 16
Glossop, see Howard Park
gnomes 192–3
Godfrey, Walter (1881–1961) 165, 189
Godwin, A. (*fl*.1830s) 82
Godwin, Edward William (1833–86) 200
Goethe, Johann Wolfgang von (1749–1832) 123, 125, 126
Goldring, William (1854–1919) 173, 196, 199, 207, 217, 265 *n*.43
Goldsmith, Oliver (1728–74) 22
Gordon, George (1841–1914) 66, 228
Gore, Spencer Frederick (1878–1914) 220
Gorrie, David (1822–56) 56, 58, 99–101, 159
Gosford House 216
Gothic revival 66, 67–8, 108–9
grafting 32
Grange, The (Northington) 30
Grange, The (Wallington) 123
gravels 71–2, 138–42 *passim*, 166, 169, 209, 216
Gravesend Terrace Garden 53
Gravetye Manor 169
Gray, James (1810–83) 108
Great Tew 64
Gregory, Gregory (1786–1854) 64
Greville, Frances Evelyn, Countess of Warwick (1861–1938) 229*f*
Grey, Frederick (1805–78) 50
Grey Walls 235
Grieve, Peter (1812–95) 135
Grimston Park 77
Gunnersbury Park 201

Haddon Hall 226
Hagley Hall 24
ha-ha 61
Halifax, see People's Park
Hall Barn 21
Halton House 197, 209–10, 216; *86*
Hampstead Heath 93–4, 183, 214
Hampton Court 121, 126, 226, 229–30; *61*
Hardwick Hall 139, 163, 227
Hardwicke House *44*
Harewood House 77
Harland, Henry (*fl*.1870s) 185*f*
Harlaxton 64, 65, 68, 71
Harpham, T. B. (*fl*.1870s–90s) 185, 190
Harpur, W. (*fl*.1890s–1900s) 238
Harpur-Crewe, Henry (1830–83) 160
Harrington, Earl of, see Stanhope
Harrison, Joseph (d.*c*.1855) 12
Hartley, James (*fl*.1840s) 17
Hartley, Thomas (*fl*.1880s–90s) 200
Hartsholme Hall 112
Hartweg, Carl Theodor (1812–71) 11, 116
Hatfield House 68*f*, 121, 227
Hatton 170–1
Haussmann, Georges Eugène, Baron (1809–91) 170
Hawkins, Benjamin Waterhouse (*fl*.1830s–1850s) 105, 121
Hay, David Ramsay (1798-1866) 88, 123, 206
Hayward, P. S. (*fl*.1900s–1910s) 202
Headington Hill Hall 111; *45*
Headley, A. (d.1899) 149
Headley Court 223
Heckfield Place 13, 136, 203–5, 215, 218; *52, 83*
hedges, 85–6, 119–20, 143, 162–4
Hegel, Georg Wilhelm Friedrich (1770–1831) 10
Hendon Rectory, 28; *6*
herb gardens 231–2
herbaceous borders 69, 132–4, 159–60, 206–8
Herbert, Catherine, Countess of Pembroke (1783–1856) 75
Herbert, William (1778–1847) 19
Herrick, Robert (1591–1674) 159
Hesketh Park 171
Heslington Hall 120–1
Hestercombe 235–6
Hever Castle 240
Hewell Grange 224; *91, 92*
Hibberd, James Shirley (1825–90) 10, 13, 18*f*, 44, 46, 112–14 *passim*, 123, 130*f*, 134, 142–3, 148, 150–4 *passim*, 159, 162, 166, 178, 203
Hidcote 183, 223
Highbury 176

Highclere 50, 93
Highnam Court 99
Hill, Thomas ('Didymus Mountaine') (*fl.*1540s–70s) 69, 228, 230
Hinchingbrooke 201; *82*
Hoar Cross 162
Hoddesdon Hall 97, 99
Hodge (*fl.*1920s) 215–16
Hogarth, William (1697–1764) 44
Hogg, Adam (*fl.*1880s) 179
Hogg, Robert (1818–97) 13
Holkham Hall 139; *54*
Holland, Henry (1745–1806) 57
Holland House 201
Holme Lacy 57
Hooker, Sir Joseph Dalton (1817–1911) 52, 195
Hoole House 47*f*, 97; *17*
Hope, Alexander James Beresford (1820–87) 142
Hope, Frances Jane (d.1880) 150, 153, 203
Hope, Thomas (1769–1831) 60, 74
Hornblower, Lewis (fl. 1860s–70s) 170
Horticultural Society of London: see Royal Horticultural Society
Hough Hole House 122
Houndsell Place 241
Howard, Elizabeth, Duchess of Rutland (1780–1825) 42
Howard Park 173
Howick Grange 50
Howlett, H. (*fl.*1850s) 41
Hudson, James (1846–1932) 201, 217, 238
Hughes, John Arthur (*fl.* 1850s–60s) 112, 117, 128, 138, 144, 147
Hull 195; see also East Park, Pearson Park
Hull Botanic Garden 195; *78*
Humphreys, Henry Noel (1810–79) 32, 42, 56, 111*f*, 119, 130, 167, 179–80
Hunt, Leigh (1784–1859) 28, 51
Huntercombe Manor 164; *65*
Huxley, Thomas Henry (1825–95) 10
Hyde Park 14, 52, 74, 107, 134–5, 168, 209

Iford Manor 221, 240; *99*
Impney Hall 168–9, 173, 196
Ingram, William (1820–94) 137, 177–8, 208
Inverary Castle 89
Inverewe 182
Ipswich Arboretum 54
Isham, Sir Charles (*fl.*1840s–90s) 97, 192–3, 200
Isola Bella 76–7, 238
Italian garden 56–7, 74–8, 141–3, 221–2, 238–40
Ivy House 200
Iwerne Minster 173, 196

Jackman, Arthur George (1866–1926) 197
Jackson, Maria Elizabeth (*fl.*1790s–1820s) 44, 61
James, John (d.1746) 71, 121, 138
Japanese garden 199–202
Jeckyll, Thomas (1827–81) 200
Jeffrey, Francis, Lord (1773–1850) 8–9
Jekyll, Gertrude (1843–1932) 205, 206–9, *216ff, 231f, 234–7 passim*
Jesmond Dene 214
Johnson, George William (1802–86) 12, 55–6, 159
Johnson, Joseph Forsyth (*fl.*1870s–1900s) 49, 182*f*
Jones, Inigo (1573–1652) 66
Jones, Owen (1809–74) 127*f*, 148, 206, 208
Jones, T. (*fl.*1880s–90s) 205
Julian, G. Richards (*fl.*1880s) 224, 226

Kelmscott Manor 163*f*
Kelway and Son 160
Kemp, Edward (1817–91) 53, 66, 99–105, 112, 114, 120–3 *passim*, 134, 139, 171–2, 178, 180
Kempe, Charles Eamer (1834–1907) 226
Kennedy, George (*fl.*1820s–50s) 62, 77
Kennedy, Lewis (1789–*c.*1840) 60, 62
Kensington: see Royal Horticultural Society
Kensington Gardens 35
Kent, Elizabeth (*fl.*1820s) 28
Kent, J. C. (*fl.*1830s) 24
Kent, William (1684–1748) 56, 197*f*
Kenwood, see Caen Wood
Kerr, Robert (1823–1904) 174
Kew, Royal Botanic Gardens 11, 52, 72–3, 110, 118, 124*ff*, 130, 133*f*, 155–6, 166, 190, 242; *29, 60*; Palm House 65–6, 72, 107*f*, 185; Temperate House 108
Kiddington Hall 43; *3*
Killerton 22
King, Thomas (1835–1902) 15, 179
Kingsley, Charles (1819–75) 152
Kingston, Robert Creaser (1818–95) 157
Kinmel Hall 145
Kip, Johannes (*c.*1652–1722) 165, 168, 241
Kirkstall Abbey 179–80
Knebworth 68, 232, 236
Knight, Richard Payne (1750–1824) 23–4, 57, 61, 66*f*, 139
Knole 57
Knowle Cottage 42
Knowles, Philip O. (*fl.*1890s–1900s) 190
Knyff, Leonard (1650–1721) 241
Knypersley Hall 102

Lamport Hall 97, 192–3, 196, 200; *79*
landscape garden 7–8, 21–3, 56, 62–3, 110–18, 166–74, 180–4, 196–9, 233–4, 241–2
Langley, Batty (1696–1751) 43
Lascelles, W. H. (d.1885) 108
'Latouche, John': see Crawfurd, O. J. F.

Lauder, Sir Thomas Dick (1784–1848) 9–10, 22, 25, 27, 62, 67, 94
Law, Ernest (1854–1930) 230
Lawley, Sir Robert, Lord Wenlock (1768–1834) 58
lawn 16, 168, 242
Lawrence, Sir James John Trevor (1831–1913) 11
Lawson, William (*fl.*1570s–1610s) 69, 228, 230
Laxton, Henry 40, 43
Lee, Charles (1808–1881) 182
Lee, Vernon: see Paget, Violet
Leicester Abbey 58; see also Abbey Park
Leighton Hall 122
Le Nôtre, Andre (1613–1700) 19, 59
Leopold I (1790–1865) 24
Le Rouge, Georges Louis (*fl.*1770s–80s) 46
Letton Hall *81*
Levens Hall 58–9, 68, 210, 223; *20*
Leveson-Gower, Anne, Duchess of Sutherland, Countess of Cromartie (1829–88) 162
Leveson-Gower, George Granville, Duke of Sutherland (1786–1861) 21
Lews Castle *23*
Lincoln Arboretum 172
Lindley, John (1799–1865) 12*ff*, 18, 57, 69, 99–101, 118, 125–6, 142, 163, 166, 199
Lindsay, Jeanne Eudoxie, Lady Lindsay (*c.*1830–97) 145
Linton Park 77, 127–8, 132, 167
Liverpool Botanic Garden 11
Liverpool, see Princes Park, Sefton Park, Stanley Park
Llewellyn, John Dillwyn (*c.*1810–82) 30–2, 186
Lloyd, Nathaniel (1867–1933) 223
Lobb, William (1809–64) 116
Lochleven 58
Locke, John (1632–1704) 8, 48
Locke Park 171; *69*
Lockinge 176, 219
Loddiges, Conrad, and Sons 11, 36, 53
Loddiges, George (1784–1846) 18, 36
Loftie, Martha Jane (*fl.*1860s–90s) 184, 214–16
London, parks 54; see also Battersea Park, Brockwell Park, Hyde Park, Kennington Park, Kensington Gardens, Peckham Rye Park, Regent's Park, Ruskin Park, St James's Park, Victoria Embankment, Victoria Park
Longleat 194
Lorimer, Sir Robert (1864–1929) 234
Lothian, James (*fl.*1840s) 47
Lothian, Lady, see Talbot
Loudon, Jane Wells (1807–58) 21, 41–2, 156, 159
Loudon, John Claudius (1783–1843) 12–13, 15, 17, 21–59 *passim*, 63–4, 66*f*, 71, 74*f*, 79, 81, 84, 86*f*, 93, 99, 101*f*, 108, 112, 114, 118, 130, 138, 159, 166, 169, 178, 180, 198
Lowe, Edward Joseph (1825–1900) 153
Luckhurst, Edward (*c.*1840–1906) 95, 176, 201, 210
Lutyens, Sir Edwin Landseer (1869–1944) 233–8 *passim*, 241*f*
Lyme Park 222

Macaulay, Thomas Babington (1800–59) 63
Macartney, Sir Mervyn (1853–1932) 241
McEwen, George (d.1858) 83, 130
Macfarlane, Walter, and Company 17, 108
McHattie, John W. (*c.*1859–1923) 211
M'Intosh, Charles (1794–1864) 10, 12, 16, 24–5, 34, 45, 48, 56, 76, 114, 166, 224
Mackenzie, Alexander (*c.*1829–93) 168–70, 174, 264 *n.*114
Mackenzie, Sir George Steuart (1780–1848) 28, 93, 108
Mackenzie, Peter (*fl.*1840s–50s) 96
Maclise, Daniel (1806–70) 159
Madresfield Court 117–18, 176
Main, James (*c.*1775–1846) 28
Major, Joshua (*c.*1787–1866) 10, 22, 44, 50, 54, 63, 81*f*, 94, 96*f*, 99–102, 134, 166, 170, 180, 212, 213
Mallows, Charles E. (1864–1915) 234
Manchester, parks 54, 134; see also Philips Park, Queens Park
Mangles, James (1786–1867) 47, 50, 76–7, 88–9
Mangles, Robert (d.1860) 51
Manners, Lord John, Duke of Rutland (1818–1906) 134–5
Mapperton Manor 223
Marble Hill 21
March, T.C. (d.1898) 127
Marnock, Robert (1800–89) 12, 29, 35*f*, 40, 56, 61, 65, 138, 168–70 *passim*, 173–4, 178, 196, 201, 263 *n.*95.
Marochetti, Carlo (1805–1867) 123
Marot, Daniel (1661–1752) 86
Marsh Court 233
Marshall, Simeon (*c.*1836–1910) 196–7, 222
Marshall, William (1745–1818) 7, 43
Martin, John (1789–1854) 26, 117
Masey, Philip (*fl.*1830s) 43
Mason (*fl.*1870s) 203
Mason, George (1735–1806) 7
massing 87–8, 151–2; see also bedding
Masters, Maxwell Tylden (1833–1907) 12
Masters, William (1796–1874) 58, 77
Maule, Hugh Patrick Guarin (1873–1940) 231

Mawson, Thomas Hayton (1861–1933) 10, 199, 231–8 *passim*
Maxwell, James Clerk (1831–79) 150, 205–6
Meader, James (*fl.*1770s–1780s) 48
Meadows, The 52
Meldon Park 61
Mellerstain 242; *100*
Mellor, James (*c.* 1797–1891) 122
Melrose Abbey 58
Mentmore 77
Merrow Grange 187
Meston, Joseph Fyfe (*c.*1827–91) 168*f*, 196
Meyer, F. W. (d.1906) 189, 216
Mickle, Adam (*fl.*1750s–1809) 40
Middleton, Ann, Lady (d.1867) 90, 215
Miles, George Francis (1852–91) 161
Millbank Prison 17
Miller, William (1828–1909) 146, 209, 216
Miller Park 172
Milner, Edward (d.1884) 110, 112, 170, 172–4, 176, 178, 196
Milner, George (1829–1914) 164
Milner, Henry Ernest (*c.*1845–1906) 172–3, 196, 198*f*, 221
Milton, John (1608–74) 159
Minley Manor 216–17
Minton, Herbert (1793–1858) 17, 141
Mitchell, Arnold Bidlake (1863–1944) 234
mixing 51, 87–8, 132–4, 151
Molesworth, Sir William (1810–55) 95
Mongredien, Augustus (*c.*1806–88) 153
Monk Coniston Hall 28
Montacute 68, 226, 228
Montreal Park 50
Moore, Albert (1841–93) 150
Moore, Thomas (1821–87) 153, 156
Moorman, J. W. (1843–?) 216
Moreton Paddox 241
Morris, Richard (*fl.*1820s–30s) 49, 55
Morris, William (1834–96) 163*f*, 232
'Mountaine, Didymus': see Hill, Thomas
Mulready, William (1786–1863) 50
Munstead 206–7
Munstead Wood 235
Murchison, Sir Roderick Impey (1792–1871) 176
Murray, Andrew (1812–78) 87, 144, 148–9, 162
Myddelton House 189

Nash, John (1752–1835) 54, 59, 74
Nash, Joseph (1809–78) 68–9
Nashdom 238
Nesfield, Markham (*c.*1842–74) 135, 144–5, 152, 170, 180, 182, 261 *n.*183
Nesfield, William Andrews (1793–1881) 38, 71–4, 76*f*, 107, 112, 118, 129, 135, 138–47, 158, 161, 166, 168, 197, 209, 216–17, 236, 242, 255 *n.*81
Nesfield, William Eden (1835–88) 144–5, 164
Newberry, Percy Edward (1869–1949) 226
Newcastle, see Jesmond Dene
New Place 230
Newstead Abbey 159, 201, 226
New Tarbet 162
Newton, Ernest (1856–1922) 234
Newton, Sir Isaac (1642–1727) 123, 125
Newton, Joseph (*fl.*1860s–1870s) 143, 147, 168, 170–1, 179, 182
Nicol, Walter (d.1811) 50
Nietzsche, Friedrich (1844–1900) 10
Niven, James Craig (1828–81) 137, 195
Noble, John (d.1890) 157
'North, Christopher': see Wilson, John
North Runcton Hall 71
Northampton, Marquis of, see Compton
Norwich, see Chapel Field
Nottingham Arboretum 52–3
Nuneham Courtenay 22, 50

Oakworth House 186–7; *75*
Old Place 226
Old Warden 43, 64, 185; *15*
old-fashioned garden 162–5, 230–1, 234–7
Oliver, Samuel Pasfield (1838–1907) 179
Olmsted, Frederick Law (1822–1903) 54
Ongley, Robert, Lord (1803–77) 43
Orchard, The *96*
Ormson, Henry (1816–77) 108
Osborne 77
Osmaston Hall 176
Ostwald, Carl Wilhelm (1883–1943) 126
Oulton Park 36
Owlpen Manor 120
Oxburgh Hall 71
Oxford Botanic Garden 111, 116

Packwood House 120–1, 227
Page, William Bridgewater (1790–1871) 61
Paget, Violet (1856–1935) 240
Painshill 48
Papworth, John Buonarotti (1775–1847) 59–60
Paracelsus, Theophrastus Bombastus von Hohenheim (*c.*1490–1541) 221
Parc Monceau 37, 153
Paris, see Parc Monceau
Park Place 154, 157
Parkinson, John (1567–1650) 69
Parkinson Society 230
parks, public 52–4, 121–2, 134–5, 170–2, 211–14
Parnham House 228; *93*
Parry, Thomas Gambier (1816–1888) 99
Parsons, Alfred William (1847–1920) 194
parterre, embroidered 71–2, 138–40, 145–7, 166, 216

Pas, Crispin de (d.1670) 222, 229
Paul, George (1841–1921) 182–3
Paul, William (1822–1905) 111, 116, 182–3
Paxton, Sir Joseph (1803–65) 12, 14, 16*f*, 29, 36, 52–4, 64, 77, 79–83, 93, 99, 102, 104, 107–8, 110, 112, 124, 134, 158, 171–2, 197, 216
Peach, Charles Pierrepont (*c*.1829–86) 151*f*, 178, 189
Peak, Edward A. (1833–1902) 190
Pearson, Frank Loughborough (1864–1947) 240
Pearson Park 210
Peckham Rye Park 230
Pembroke, Lady, see Herbert
Pencarrow 95; *39*
Penllergare 30, 32, 186
Pennethorne, Sir James (1801–71) 54, 74
Penshurst Place 165, 227
People's Park 83, 110; *33*
Perry, Matthew (1794–1858) 199
Peto, Harold Ainsworth (1854–1933) 240
Pettigrew, Andrew (*c*.1830–1903) 167
Pettigrew, Andrew A. (*fl*.1890s–1920s) 224
Pettigrew, William Wallace (*c*.1867–1947) 213, 216
Petworth House 157
Phelips, Ellen (1816–1911) 68
Philips Park, 213; *88*
Phillips, Henry (1779–1840) 59
Phoenix Park 50–51
picturesque 23–6, 99–102, 110–15 *passim*, 153, 180, 185
Pince, Robert Taylor (*c*.1804–71) 258 *n*.29, 264 *n*.130
pinetum 103, 115–18
Pinsent, Cecil (1884–1964) 240
Pitt, William (1759–1806) 59
Plantation, The (Leighton Buzzard) 35
Plantation, The (Norwich) 179
Pleasaunce, The 230
Plymouth, Earl of, see Windsor-Clive
Poles Park 111, 185; *43*
Pollock, Sir Frederick (1845–1937) 183
Pontey, William (*fl*.1830s–60s) 54
Pope, Alexander (1688–1744) 43, 47, 119
Powerscourt 77
Pre-Raphaelite Brotherhood 50, 150, 164
Preston, see Avenham Park, Miller Park
Price, Sir Uvedale (1747–1829) 7–10, 22, 23–7 *passim*, 33, 46–7, 50, 57, 60–1, 63, 99, 101, 113–14
Pridham (*fl*.1840s–50s) 68
Princes Park 52, 203
Princes Street Gardens 211
Prior, Edward Schroeder (1852–1932) 234, 237
Pückler-Muskau, Hermann, Prince (1785–1871) 34, 52
Pugin, Augustus Welby Northmore (1812–52) 38, 65, 68, 109, 232
Pulham, James (d.1838) 97
Pulham, James (*c*.1820–98) 17, 97, 99, 176, 178, 185, 187, 189
Pulham, James Robert (1873–1957) 189
Purkinje, Jan Evangelista (1787–1869) 124
Putteridge Bury 131; *50*

Quatremère de Quincy, Antoine Chrysostome (1755–1849) 24–5, 32
Queens Park 100–1
Quilter, H. G. (1824–93) 138

Radclyffe, Dick (*fl*.1870s) 185
Rangemore Hall 172, 173; *70*
Ransome, J. R. and A. 16
Raphael (1483–1520) 150
Red House 164
Redleaf 48, 102; *9*
Regent's Park 35, 52, 135, 145, 147, 190, 218; see also Royal Botanic Society
Reinagle, Ramsay Richard (1775–1862) 36, 47
Renishaw 208
Repton, Humphry (1752–1818) 10, 21, 23–6, 40, 43, 46, 49–50, 55–7 *passim*, 59, 61, 67, 99, 112, 115
Repton, John Adey (1775–1860) 64
revivalism 55–78, 100, 159–65, 221–42; see also Dutch garden, Gothic revival, Italian garden, old-fashioned garden, rococo revival, Tudor revival
Reynolds, Sir Joshua (1723–92) 50
Rhianva 77, 111
Rhinefield House 224, 226
Ricardo, Halsey (1854–1928) 234
Ricauti, T. J. (*fl*.1840s) 41
Richardson, Charles James (1806–71) 68
Rivernook *97*
Rivers, Thomas (1798–1877) 17
roads, approach 22, 112
Robinson, Peter Frederick (1776–1858) 64
Robinson, William (1838–1935) 10, 12*f*, 94, 111, 145, 152–6 *passim*, 160–1, 166, 169*f*, 176, 177–8, 180, 184, 186, 189*f*, 192, 194–5, 197, 203, 206, 223, 227
Robson, Edward Robert (1835–1917) 122
Robson, John (d.1886) 13, 18, 95, 127–8, 132, 153, 195, 200
Rochester Castle 179–80
rock garden 46–8, 94–9, 102–6 *passim*, 123, 176–9, 187–92
Rockhills 110
Rockley, Lady, see Amherst
rockworks in glasshouses 185–7
rococo revival 42–6
Roe, Freeman (*fl*.1840s) 47, 110
Rohde, Eleanour Sinclair (1881–1950) 232

Rolle, Louisa Barbara, Baroness (1796–1885) 16, 214
Rollisson, William (*c.*1765–1842) 19
Rollisson, William (*c.*1802–75) 45
Romaine-Walker, William Henry (1854–1940) 224, 226
Roos, Alexander (*fl.*1840s) 68, 139
Rose, John (*c.*1621–77) 13
Ross Priory 43
Rossetti, Dante Gabriel (1828–82) 163
Rothamsted 19
Rougham Hall 182–3
Rous Lench Court 224
Rousdon 168
Rowles, William Francis (*fl.*1900s–1910s) 199
Royal Botanic Society 88; garden (Regent's Park) 29, 40, 88, 135, 140, 145, 152, 168; *12*
Royal Horticultural Society (formerly Horticultural Society of London) 11*ff*, 84, 140, 153, 166, 182, 185; gardens: Chiswick 14, 66, 79, 126; Kensington 121, 140–3, 147, 148, 163, 166, 211, 227, 232; 55; Wisley 189
Rubens, Sir Peter Paul (1577–1640) 128, 150
ruins 57–8, 178–80
Ruskin, John (1819–1900) 22, 64, 123, 139, 149, 151, 183, 232*f*
Ruskin Park 214, 230
rusticwork 40–42, 46, 232
Rutger, Thomas (*fl.*1820s–1850s) 38, 110
Rutland, Duchess of, see Howard
Rutland, Duke of, see Manners
Rydal Mount 26–7

St Anne's Hill 61
St Cloud 80
St James's Park 73
St Osyth's Priory 41
Salford parks 54
Salisbury, Marquis of, see Cecil
Saltaire 64
Salvin, Anthony (1799–1881) 65*f*, 71, 144, 166
Sandringham 147, 167, 176
Saul, Michael (1817–92) 67
Scarisbrick Hall 68
Schulz, Robert Weir (1861–1951) 234
Scotney Castle 71
Scott, Mackay Hugh Baillie (1865–1945) 215, 234, 237
Scott, Sir George Gilbert (1811–78) 119
Scott, John (*c.*1807–86) 131
Scott, Sir Walter (1771–1832) 10, 67, 178
Scott, Walter Francis, Duke of Buccleuch (1806–84) 25
sculptural bedding 209–11
Sedding, John Dando (1838–91) 10, 164, 195, 198–9, 204, 222–3, 226, 237
Sefton Park 168, 170, 180, 182; *68*
Selfe-Leonard, H. (d.1902) 196
Sennowe Hall 117
Sexby, John James (*fl.*1870s–1910s) 214, 230
Sezincote 46
Shakespeare, William (1564–1616) 159, 163, 230–1
Shanks, Alexander, and Son 16
Shaw, John (*c.*1812–1890) 170, 212
Shaw, Richard Norman (1831–1912) 144, 164, 234, 241*f*
Shaw-Lefevre, Charles, Lord Eversley (1794–1888) 215
Sheffield Botanic Garden 12
Sherwood, William (*fl.*1890s) 209, 216
Shrewsbury, Earls of, see Talbot
Shrubland Park 13, 77–8, 89*f*, 111, 121, 130, 227; *XI, 31*
Sidney, Philip, Lord De L'Isle (1828–98) 165
Siebeck, Rudolph (*fl.*1850s–60s) 170–1
Sitwell, Sir George Reresby (1860–1943) 9, 10, 199, 240
Sledmere 238
Smee, Alfred (1818–77) 123
Smirke, Sir Robert (1781–1867) 17, 28
Smirke, Sydney (1798–1877) 140
Smith, Charles H. J. (*fl.*1820s–1850s) 50, 99–101, 117*f*, 138, 180
Smith, Worthington George (1835–1917) 178–9
Snowshill 215–16
Somerleyton Hall 72, 83, 121
Southey, Robert (1774–1843) 63, 69, 231
Southgate Lodge 21
Southport, see Churchtown Botanic Garden, Hesketh Park
Speechly, William (*c.*1733–1819) 13
Spencer, John (1809–81) 14, 32, 118
Spenser, Edmund (*c.*1552–99) 159
spring bedding 136–8, 218
Stamford Park 170, 212
Stancliffe Hall 176; *72*
standards 32
Stanhope, Charles, Earl of Harrington (1780–1851) 84–7
Stanley Park 122, 171–2
Steuart, Sir Henry (1759–1836) 19, 43
Stevens, Zadok (*c.*1833–86) 14–15, 150
Stoke Edith 138
Stoke Rochford 71
Stowe 43
Strathfieldsaye 211
Strawberry Hill 21, 24
Strutt, Joseph (1765–1844) 52
subtropical bedding 92, 152–8; see also carpet bedding

Sudeley Castle 119; *48*
Surrey Zoological Garden 48
Sutherland, Dukes of, see Leveson-Gower
Swinford Old Manor 217
Swinton Park 40
Sydnope Hall 176
Sykes, Godfrey (1825–65) 140
Syon Park 44, 48, 71, 83

Talbot, Charles, Earl of Shrewsbury (1753–1827) 37–8
Talbot, Constance Harriet, Lady Lothian (1836–1901) 161
Talbot, John, Earl of Shrewsbury (1791–1852) 38
Tasso, Torquato (1544–95) 147
Tate, Sir Henry (1819–99) 178
Taylor, Tom (1817–80) 64
Taylor, Warrington (*c.*1837–70) 168
Taylor, William (*fl.*1850s–1910s) 194
Tegg, James (1832–1902) 174
Tempest, Sir Charles (1794–1865) 138
Temple Bar 179
Temple Gardens 136
Temple, Mungo (1834–1902) 168
Tennyson, Alfred, Lord (1809–92) 159, 164
terraces 61–3, 66–9, 74–8, 110–11, 168–9, 174, 197–8, 225–8
Teulon, Samuel Saunders (1812–73) 128
Thackeray, William Makepeace (1811–63) 164, 241
Theobalds Park 179
Thomas, Francis Inigo (1866–1950) 197, 226*ff*, 231*f*, 237
Thomas, William Broderick (1811–?1898) 147, 166*f*, 176, 178, 227, 261 *n.*188
Thompson, Robert (1798–1869) 94, 114
Thomson, David (1823–1909) 131
Thomson, George (*c.*1824–1901) 156–7
Thoresby Hall 166
Thornbridge Hall 196–7, 222
Tingrith House 32
Tipping, H. Avray (1856–1933) 229, 236
topiary 58–9, 69, 72–3, 85–7, 118–21, 162–3, 210, 222–4
transcendentalism 24–6, 79–102 *passim*
transplanting 19–20, 84
Trentham 15, 75–7, 79, 90–4, 101*f*, 122, 130, 138, 150, 152, 164, 180, 240; *X*, *37*
Trevor, Henry (1819–97) 179
Triggs, H. Inigo (1876–1923) 226, 240
Trinder, George (*fl.*1880s–90s) 205
Tuckermann, W. P. (*fl.*1880s) 238
Tudor revival 66–70, 224–30
Tuileries 80
Tully Castle 200–1
Turner, Joseph Mallard William (1775–1851) 50, 127
Turner, Richard (*c.*1798–1881) 66, 107*f*
Turner, Thomas Hudson (1815–52) 68

Underscar 123

Vauxhall Gardens 52
Veitch, Sir Harry James (1840–1924) 176
Veitch, James (1815–69) 37
Veitch, James, and Sons 116
Veitch, John Gould (1839–70) 201
Veitch, Robert Toswill (1823–85) 189, 197, 216, 223
Versailles 28, 74, 80, 110, 168, 228
Vertegans, Richard H. (*fl.*1870s) 171, 212
Victoria, Queen (1819–1901) 73
Victoria Embankment 168
Victoria Park 156
Villa Albani 141
Villa Borghese 240
Villa Carlotta 238
Villa d'Este 77
Vinters 68
Viollet-le-Duc, Eugène Emmanuel (1814–79) 66
Virginia Water 57; *21*
Voysey, Charles Francis Annesley (1857–1941) 233

Wade, Charles (1883–1956) 215–16
Wahliss, Ernest (*fl.*1900s) 193
Waldershare Park 52
Walker, Frederick (1840–75) 164
Walmer Castle 59
Walter, John (1818–94) 174
Ward, Nathaniel Bagshaw (1791–1868) 18, 32, 123
Wardian case 18
Wardie Lodge 153
Ware, Samuel (1781–1860) 28
Warley Place 186, 190
Warwick, Countess of, see Greville
Warwick Castle 169, 196
Watcombe Park 94
Waterer, John, Sons and Crisp 190
Watson, Forbes (1840–69) 150*ff*
Weaver, Sir Lawrence (1876–1930) 234, 238
Webb, Sir Aston (1849–1930) 196
Webb, Philip Speakman (1831–1915) 164
Wedgwood, John (1766–1844) 11
Weeks, James, and Company 18
Welbeck Abbey 13, 46, 118
Wellesley, Arthur, Duke of Wellington (1769–1852) 95
Wellesley, Henry, Duke of Wellington (1846–1900) 211
Wellington, Dukes of, see Wellesley
Wellington College *47*
Wells, William (1768–1847) 48, 102
Welton Place 28, 112; *42*
Wenlock, Lord, see Lawley

West London Gardeners' Association 88
West Park, Wolverhampton 212
Westbury Court 241
Westmacott, Sir Richard (1775–1856) 75
Westonbirt 118
Weymouth, see Alexandra Gardens
Wharton, Edith (1862–1937) 240
Whim, The 118
Whistler, James Abbott McNeill (1834–1903) 150
White, Edward (*c.*1873–1952) 241
White, John P. (*fl.*1900s–1920s) 238
White Knights 21
Whitmore Lodge 32, 51
Wightwick, George (1802–72) 105
wild gardening 93–4, 194–6
Wildsmith, William (*c.*1838–90) 136, 156, 203–5, 215, 217–18
Wilkinson, Sir John Gardner (1797–1875) 126–7, 130, 206, 208
Williams, Sir John Hay (*fl.*1840s–1860s) 77, 111
Willmott, Ellen Ann (1858–1934) 186, 190
Willows, The *XII*
Wills, John (1832–95) 109, 185, 214–15
Wilson, John ('Christopher North') (1785–1854) 13, 68
Wilton House 74–5, 224; *30*
Windsor, Royal Lodge 57
Windsor-Clive, Robert George, Earl of Plymouth (1857–1923) 224
winter garden 26, 135–6, 139, 218; see also glasshouse
Wisley, see Royal Horticultural Society
Witley Court 144, 147, 164; *56*
Woburn Abbey 40, 64
Wollaton Hall 77
Wolseley, Frances Garnett, Viscountess (1872–1936) 222
Wolverhampton, see West Park
Wood, Samuel (*fl.*1870s–90s) 214
Woodside 235; *98*
Woolverstone Park *8*
Wordsworth, Mary (1770–1859) 38–9
Wordsworth, William (1770–1850) 10, 26–8, 38–9, 54, 59, 136, 164, 178
Worsley Hall 71; *28*
Wortley Hall 12
Wray Castle 27–8
Wright, Walter Page (1864–1940) 10, 201, 219–20
Wroxton Abbey 57
Wyatt, Benjamin Dean (1775–*c.*1855) 42
Wyatt, James (1746–1813) 66, 74–5, 85, 242
Wyatt, Sir Matthew Digby (1820–1877) 77, 145–6
Wyatville, Sir Jeffrey (1766–1840) 80

Yates, Richard Vaughan (1785–1856) 52
Yeatton Peverey 196
York Minster 58, 179
York Museum 58